The AUERBACH Annual
1979
Best Computer Papers

The AUERBACH Annual 1979 Best Computer Papers

Isaac L. Auerbach, Editor

President
AUERBACH Corporation for Science and Technology
AUERBACH Publishers Inc.
Isaac L. Auerbach Inc. Consultants

NORTH HOLLAND
New York • Oxford

Elsevier North Holland, Inc.
52 Vanderbilt Avenue
New York, New York 10017

Distributors outside the U.S. and Canada:

Thomond Books
(A Division of Elsevier/North-Holland Scientific Publishers, Ltd.)
P.O. Box 85
Limerick, Ireland

ISBN: 0-444-00350-9
ISSN: 0092-6507

Desk Editor Philip Schafer
Design Edmée Froment
Art Assistant José García
Production Manager Joanne Jay
Compositor Typographic Services, Inc.
Printer Haddon Craftsmen

Printed in the United States of America

Contents

Preface

The accelerated growth rate within the computer field has lead to such a plethora of scientific and technical papers that it is nearly impossible to keep up with the literature. It is the intent of this book to identify some of the significant contributions to the information processing field that have been made during the year.

Committees of some of the leading professional societies in the field have submitted papers that have been selected or honored. Other papers, in my judgment or that of my colleagues, have been selected because of their substantive value.

These papers should provide the reader with a selected list of noteworthy contributions from the literature.

Any one of these papers may contain the seed of an idea that will assist you or your organization to better understand some of the developments in information technology or to identify an application that may meet your needs.

I want to acknowledge my indebtedness and appreciation to all of the organizations that have assisted me in making this book possible.

Isaac L. Auerbach

List of Contributors

VICTOR R. BASILI, *University of Maryland*
Structured Programming

BOBBY R. BROWN, *University of Iowa*
The Whens and Hows of Computer Based Instructional Simulation

A. K. BURSTON, *University of Manchester*
A Design Language for Asynchronous Logic

C. I. C. CAMPBELL, *University of Cambridge*
On Making Graphic Arts Quality Output by Computer

E. G. COFFMAN, JR., *Pennsylvania State University*
An Application of Bin-packing to Multiprocessor Scheduling

R. F. DEUTSCHER, *University of Saskatchewan*
Key-to-address Transformation Techniques

B. DROR, *Israel Aircraft Industries, Ltd.*
Development and Application of Computer Aided Design Technology At Israel Aircraft Industries

ROBERT S. ELLINGER, *University of Iowa*
The Whens and Hows of Computer Based Instructional Simulation

EDWARD A. FEIGENBAUM, *Stanford University*
The Art of Artificial Intelligence—Themes and Case Studies of Knowledge Engineering

M. R. GAREY, *Bell Laboratories*
An Application of Bin-packing to Multiprocessor Scheduling

GEORGE GLASER, *Centigram Corporation*
The EFT Revolution: Did Someone Call It Off or Did It Happen When I Wasn't Looking?

J. HARRADINE, *University of Cambridge*
On Making Graphic Arts Quality Output by Computer

MALCOLM J. HEIMENDINGER, *Cities Service Company*
The Emerging Philosophy of Data Processing Management

D. S. JOHNSON, *Bell Laboratories*
An Application of Bin-packing to Multiprocessor Scheduling

HILARY KAHN, *University of Manchester*
A Design Language for Asynchronous Logic

D. J. KINNIMENT, *University of Manchester*
A Design Language for Asynchronous Logic

H. G. MACKENZIE, *Commonwealth Scientific and Industrial Research Organization*
The Implementation of a Database Management System

CLEVE MOLER, *University of New Mexico*
Nineteen Dubious Ways to Compute the Exponential of a Matrix

MICHAEL J. POWERS, *Illinois State University*
A Management Information System for Academic Administrators

J. L. SMITH, *Commonwealth Scientific and Industrial Research Organization*
The Implementation of a Database Management System

P. G. SORENSON, *University of Saskatchewan*
Key-to-address Transformation Techniques

J. P. TREMBLAY, *University of Saskatchewan*
Key-to-address Transformation Techniques

REIN TURN, *California State University*
Crytography as a Control Feature

CHARLES VAN LOAN, *Cornell University*
Nineteen Dubious Ways to Compute the Exponential of a Matrix

N. E. WISEMAN, *University of Cambridge*
On Making Graphic Arts Quality Output by Computer

The AUERBACH Annual
1979
Best Computer Papers

PART I

AMERICAN FEDERATION OF INFORMATION PROCESSING SOCIETIES

Won the Best Paper Award
at the National Computing Conference
1978

"The Art of Artificial Intelligence—Themes and
Case Studies of Knowledge Engineering"
Edward A. Feigenbaum

The American Federation of Information Processing Societies is a national federation of professional societies established in 1961 to represent the member societies on an international level and for the advancement and diffusion of knowledge of the information processing sciences. It sponsors the annual National Computer Conference and acts as national spokesman for the information processing community in matters dealing with, or affected by, computing, data processing, and related sciences. It represents the United States in the International Federation for Information Processing (IFIP) and in a variety of international information processing activities.

The AFIPS Press publishes proceedings of annual conferences and many other publications of interest to both its members and to the public and is the distributor of IFIP publications in the United States.

AFIPS headquarters address is 210 Summit Avenue, Montvale, New Jersey 07645.

The Art of Artificial Intelligence—Themes and Case Studies of Knowledge Engineering

Edward A. Feigenbaum
Stanford University
Stanford, California

INTRODUCTION—AN EXAMPLE

This paper will examine emerging themes of knowledge engineering, illustrate them with case studies drawn from the work of the Stanford Heuristic Programming Project, and discuss general issues of knowledge engineering art and practice.

Let me begin with an example new to our workbench: a system called PUFF, the early fruit of a collaboration between our project and a group at the Pacific Medical Center (PMC) in San Francisco.*

A physician refers a patient to PMC's pulmonary function testing lab for diagnosis of possible pulmonary function disorder. For one of the tests, the patient inhales and exhales a few times in a tube connected to an instrument/computer combination. The instrument acquires data on flow rates and volumes, the so-called flow-volume loop of the patient's lungs and airways. The computer measures certain parameters of the curve and presents them to the diagnostician (physician or PUFF) for interpretation. The diagnosis is made along these lines: normal or diseased; restricted lung disease or obstructive airways disease or a combination of both; the severity; the likely disease type(s) (e.g., emphysema, bronchitis, etc.); and other factors important for diagnosis.

PUFF is given not only the measured data but also certain items of informa-

* Dr. J. Osborn, Dr. R. Fallat, John Kunz, and Diane McClung.

EDITOR'S NOTE: *Reprinted from Volume 47 of the AFIPS National Computer Conference Proceedings, 1978, by permission of the publisher, American Society of Information Processing Societies, and the author.*

tion from the patient record, e.g., sex, age, number of pack-years of cigarette smoking. The task of the PUFF system is to infer a diagnosis and print it out in English in the normal medical summary form of the interpretation expected by the referring physician.

Everything PUFF knows about pulmonary function diagnosis is contained in (currently) 55 rules of the IF. . . THEN. . . form. No textbook of medicine currently records these rules. They constitute the partly-public, partly-private knowledge of an expert pulmonary physiologist at PMC, and were extracted and polished by project engineers working intensively with the expert over a period of time. Here is an example of a PUFF rule (the unexplained acronyms refer to various data measurements):

RULE 31

IF:
1. The severity of obstructive airways disease of the patient is greater than or equal to mild, and
2. The degree of diffusion defect of the patient is greater than or equal to mild, and
3. The tlc (body box) observed/predicted of the patient is greater than or equal to 110 and
4. The observed-predicted difference in rv/tlc of the patient is greater than or equal to 10

THEN:
1. There is strongly suggestive evidence (.9) that the subtype of obstructive airways disease is emphysema, and
2. It is definite (1.0) that "OAD, Diffusion Defect, elevated TLC, and elevated RV together indicate emphysema." is one of the findings.

One hundred cases, carefully chosen to span the variety of disease states with sufficient exemplary information for each, were used to extract the 55 rules. As the knowledge emerged, it was represented in rule form, added to the system and tested by running additional cases. The expert was sometimes surprised, sometimes frustrated, by the occasional gaps and inconsistencies in the knowledge, and the incorrect diagnoses that were logical consequences of the existing rule set. The interplay between knowledge engineer and expert gradually expanded the set of rules to remove most of these problems.

As cumulation of techniques in the art demands and allows, a new tool was not invented when an old one would do. The knowledge engineers pulled out of their toolkit a version of the MYCIN system (to be discussed later), with the rules about infectious diseases removed, and used it as the inference engine for the PUFF diagnoses. Thus PUFF, like MYCIN, is a relatively simple backward-chaining inference system. It seeks a valid line-of-reasoning based on its rules and rooted in the instrument and patient data. With a little more work at fitting some existing tools together, PUFF will be able to explain this line-of-reasoning, just as MYCIN does.

As it is, PUFF only prints out the final interpretation, of which the following is an example:

PATIENT DATA:
The degree of dyspnea: MODERATELY-SEVERE
The severity of coughing: MILD
Sputum production MODERATELY-SEVERE
The number of pack-years of smoking: 48
referral diagnosis: BRONCHITIS
IVC/IVC-predicted: 80
RV/RV-predicted: 191
FVC/FVC-predicted: 87
TLC(body box)observed/predicted: 127
Predicted FEV1/FVC: 83
TLC(DLCO)observed/predicted: 83
FEV1/FVC ratio: 50
RV/TLC observed-predicted: 21
MMF/MMF-predicted: 19
the DLCO/DLCO-predicted: 48
The slope (F50_obs-F25_obs)/FVC_obs: 19

DEGREE OF OBSTRUCTIVE AIRWAYS DISEASE:

OAD degree by SLOPE: (MODERATELY-SEVERE 700)
OAD degree by MMF: (SEVERE 900)
OAD degree by FEV1: (MODERATELY-SEVERE 1/700)
FINAL OAD DEGREE: (MODERATELY SEVERE 910) (SEVERE 900)
No conflict. Final degree:
(MODERATELY-SEVERE 910)

INTERPRETATION:

Obstruction is indicated by curvature of the flow-volume loop.
Forced Vital Capacity is normal and peak flow rates are reduced, suggesting airway obstruction.
Flow rate from 25–75 of expired volume is reduced, indicating severe airway obstruction.
OAD, Diffusion Defect, elevated TLC, and elevated RV together indicate emphysema.
OAD, Diffusion Defect, and elevated RV indicate emphysema.
Change in expired flow rates following bronchodilation shows that there is reversibility of airway obstruction.

The presence of a productive cough is an indication that the OAD is of the bronchitic type.
Elevated lung volumes indicate overinflation.
Air trapping is indicated by the elevated difference between observed and predicted RV/TLC ratios.

Improvement in airway resistance indicates some reversibility of airway.
Airway obstruction is consistent with the patient's smoking history.
The airway obstruction accounts for the patient's dyspnea.
Although bronchodilators were not useful in this one case, prolonged use may prove to be beneficial to the patient.
The reduced diffusion capacity indicates airway obstruction of the mixed bronchitic and emphysematous types.
Low diffusing capacity indicates loss of alveolar capillary surface.
Obstructive Airways Disease of mixed types

One hundred and fifty cases not studied during the knowledge acquisition process were used for a test and validation of the rule set. PUFF inferred a diagnosis for each. PUFF-produced and expert-produced interpretations were coded for statistical analysis to discover the degree of agreement. Over various types of disease states, and for two conditions of match between human and computer diagnoses (''same degree of severity'' and ''within one degree of severity''), agreement ranged between approximately 90 percent and 100 percent.

The PUFF story is just beginning and will be told perhaps at a later NCC. The surprising punchline to my synopsis is that the current state of the PUFF system as described above was achieved in less than 50 hours of interaction with the expert and less than 10 man-weeks of effort by the knowledge engineers. We have learned much in the past decade of the art of engineering knowledge-based intelligent agents!

In the remainder of this essay, I would like to discuss the route that one research group, the Stanford Heuristic Programming Project, has taken, illustrating progress with case studies, and discussing themes of the work.

ARTIFICIAL INTELLIGENCE AND KNOWLEDGE ENGINEERING

The dichotomy that was used to classify the collected papers in the volume *Computers and Thought* still characterizes well the motivations and research efforts of the AI community. First, there are some who work toward the construction of intelligent artifacts, or seek to uncover principles, methods, and techniques useful in such construction. Second, there are those who view artificial intelligence as (to use Newell's phrase) ''theoretical psychology,'' seeking explicit and valid information processing models of human thought.

For purposes of this essay, I wish to focus on the motivations of the first group, these days by far the larger of the two. I label these motivations "the intelligent agent viewpoint" and here is my understanding of that viewpoint:

> The potential uses of computers by people to accomplish tasks can be 'one-dimensionalized' into a spectrum representing the nature of instruction that must be given the computer to do its job. Call it the WHAT-to-HOW spectrum. At one extreme of the spectrum, the user supplies his intelligence to instruct the machine with precision exactly HOW to do his job, step-by-step. Progress in Computer Science can be seen as steps away from the extreme 'HOW' point on the spectrum: the familiar panoply of assembly languages, subroutine libraries, compilers, extensible languages, etc. At the other extreme of the spectrum is the user with his real problem (WHAT he wishes the computer, as his instrument, to do for him). He aspires to communicate WHAT he wants done in a language that is comfortable to him (perhaps English); via communication modes that are convenient for him (including perhaps, speech or pictures); with some generality, some vagueness, imprecision, even error; without having to lay out in detail all necessary subgoals for adequate performance—with reasonable assurance that he is addressing an intelligent agent that is using knowledge of his world to understand his intent, to fill in his vagueness, to make specific his abstractions, to correct his errors, to discover appropriate subgoals, and ultimately to translate WHAT he really wants done into processing steps that define HOW it shall be done by a real computer. The research activity aimed at creating computer programs that act as intelligent agents near the WHAT end of the WHAT-to-HOW spectrum can be viewed as the long-range goal of AI research. (Feigenbaum, 1974.)

Our young science is still more art than science. Art: "the principles or methods governing any craft or branch of learning." Art: "skilled workmanship, execution, or agency." These the dictionary teaches us. Knuth tells us that the endeavor of computer programming is an art, in just these ways. The art of constructing intelligent agents is both part of and an extension of the programming art. It is the art of building complex computer programs that represent and reason with knowledge of the world. Our art therefore lives in symbiosis with the other worldly arts, whose practitioners—experts of their art—hold the knowledge we need to construct intelligent agents. In most "crafts or branches of learning" what we call "expertise" is the essence of the art. And for the domains of knowledge that we touch with our art, it is the "rules of expertise" or the rules of "good judgment" of the expert practitioners of that domain that we seek to transfer to our programs.

Lessons of the Past

Two insights from previous work are pertinent to this essay.

The first concerns the quest for generality and power of the inference engine used in the performance of intelligent acts (what Minsky and Papert [see Goldstein and Papert, 1977] have labeled "the power strategy"). We must hypothesize from our experience to date that the problem solving power exhibited in an intelligent agent's performance is primarily a consequence of the specialist's knowledge employed by the agent, and only very secondarily related to the generality and power of the inference method employed. Our agents must be knowledge-rich, even if they are methods-poor. In 1970, reporting the first major summary-of-results of the DENDRAL program (to be discussed later), we addressed this issue as follows:

> . . . general problem-solvers are too weak to be used as the basis for building high-performance systems. The behavior of the best general problem-solvers we know, human problem-solvers, is observed to be weak and shallow, except in the areas in which the human problem-solver is a specialist. And it is observed that the transfer of expertise between specialty areas is slight. A chess master is unlikely to be an expert algebraist or an expert mass spectrum analyst, etc. In this view, the expert is the specialist, with a specialist's knowledge of his area and a specialist's methods and heuristics. (Feigenbaum, Buchanan, and Lederberg, 1971, p. 187.)

Subsequent evidence from our laboratory and all others has only confirmed this belief.

AI researchers have dramatically shifted their view on generality and power in the past decade. In 1967, the canonical question about the DENDRAL program was: "It sounds like good chemistry, but what does it have to do with AI?" In 1977, Goldstein and Papert wrote of a paradigm shift in AI:

> Today there has been a shift in paradigm. The fundamental problem of understanding intelligence is not the identification of a few powerful techniques, but rather the question of how to represent large amounts of knowledge in a fashion that permits their effective use and interaction. (Goldstein and Papert, 1977.)

The second insight from past work concerns the nature of the knowledge that an expert brings to the performance of a task. Experience has shown us that this knowledge is largely heuristic knowledge, experiential, uncertain—mostly "good guesses" and "good practice," in lieu of facts and rigor. Experience has also taught us that much of this knowledge is private to the expert, not because he is unwilling to share publicly how he performs, but because he is unable. He knows more than he is aware of knowing. (Why else is the Ph.D. or the Internship a guild-like apprenticeship to a presumed "master of the craft?" What the masters really know is not written in the textbooks.) But we have learned also that this private knowledge can be uncovered by the careful, painstaking analysis of a second party, or sometimes by the expert himself, operating in the context of a large number of highly specific performance problems. Finally, we have learned that expertise is multifaceted, that the expert brings to bear many and varied sources of knowledge in performance. The approach to capturing his expertise must proceed on many fronts simultaneously.

The Knowledge Engineer

The knowledge engineer is that second party just discussed. She works intensively with an expert to acquire domain-specific knowledge and organize it for use by a program. Simultaneously she is matching the tools of the AI workbench to the task at hand—program organizations, methods of symbolic inference, techniques for the structuring of symbolic information, and the like. If the tool fits, or nearly fits, she uses it. If not, necessity mothers AI invention, and a new tool is created. She builds the early versions of the intelligent agent, guided always by her intent that the program eventually achieve expert levels of performance in the task. She refines or reconceptualizes the system as the increasing amount of acquired knowledge causes the AI tool to "break" or slow down intolerably. She also refines the human interface to the intelligent agent with several aims: to make the system appear "comfortable" to the human user in his linguistic transactions with it; to make the system's inference processes understandable to the user; and to make the assistance controllable by the user when, in the context of a real problem, he has an insight that previously was not elicited and therefore not incorporated.

In the next section, I wish to explore (in summary form) some case studies of the knowledge engineer's art.

CASES FROM THE KNOWLEDGE ENGINEER'S WORKSHOP

I will draw material for this section from the work of my group at Stanford. Much exciting work in knowledge engineering is going on elsewhere. Since my intent is not to survey literature but to illustrate themes, at the risk of appearing parochial I have used as case studies the work I know best.

My collaborators (Professors Lederberg and Buchanan) and I began a series of projects, initially the development of the DENDRAL program, in 1965. We had dual motives: first, to study scientific problem solving and discovery, particularly the processes scientists do use or should use in inferring hypotheses and theories from empirical evidence; and second, to conduct this study in such a way that our experimental programs would one day be of use to working scientists, providing intelligent assistance on important and difficult problems. By 1970, we and our co-workers had gained enough experience that we felt comfortable in laying out a program of research encompassing work on theory formation, knowledge utilization, knowledge acquisition, explanation, and knowledge engineering techniques. Although there were some surprises along the way, the general lines of the research are proceeding as envisioned.

THEMES

As a road map to these case studies, it is useful to keep in mind certain major themes:

Generation-and-test. Omnipresent in our experiments is the "classical" generation-and-test framework that has been the hallmark of AI programs for two decades. This is not a consequence of a doctrinaire attitude on our part about heuristic search, but rather of the usefulness and sufficiency of the concept.

Situation⇒action rules. We have chosen to represent the knowledge of experts in this form. Making no doctrinaire claims for the universal applicability of this representation, we nonetheless point to the demonstrated utility of the rule-based representation. From this representation flow rather directly many of the characteristics of our programs: for example, ease of modification of the knowledge, ease of explanation. The essence of our approach is that a rule must capture a "chunk" of domain knowledge that is meaningful, in and of itself, to the domain specialist. Thus our rules bear only a historical relationship to the production rules used by Newell and Simon (1972) which we view as "machine-language programming" of a recognize ⇒ act machine.

The domain-specific knowledge. It plays a critical role in organizing and constraining search. The theme is that in the knowledge is the power. The interesting action arises from the knowledge base, not the inference engine. We use knowledge in rule form (discussed above), in the form of inferentially rich models based on theory, and in the form of tableaus of symbolic data and relationships (i.e., frame-like structures). System processes are made to conform to natural and convenient representations of the domain-specific knowledge.

Flexibility to modify the knowledge base. If the so-called "grain size" of the knowledge representation is chosen properly (i.e., small enough to be comprehensible but large enough to be meaningful to the domain specialist), then the rule-based approach allows great flexibility for adding, removing, or changing knowledge in the system.

Line-of-reasoning. A central organizing principle in the design of knowledge-based intelligent agents is the maintenance of a line-of-reasoning that is comprehensible to the domain specialist. This principle is, of course, not a logical necessity, but seems to us to be an engineering principle of major importance.

Multiple sources of knowledge. The formation and maintenance (support) of the line-of-reasoning usually require the integration of many disparate sources of knowledge. The representational and inferential problems in achieving a smooth and effective integration are formidable engineering problems.

Explanation. The ability to explain the line-of-reasoning in a language convenient to the user is necessary for application and for system development (e.g., for debugging and for extending the knowledge base). Once again, this is an engineering principle, but very important. What constitutes "an explanation" is not a simple concept, and considerable thought needs to be given, in each case, to the structuring of explanations.

CASE STUDIES

In this section I will try to illustrate these themes with various case studies.

DENDRAL: Inferring chemical structures

Historical note

Begun in 1965, this collaborative project with the Stanford Mass Spectrometry Laboratory has become one of the longest-lived continuous efforts in the history of AI (a fact that in no small way has contributed to its success). The basic framework of generation-and-test and rule-based representation has proved rugged and extendable. For us the DENDRAL system has been a fountain of ideas, many of which have found their way, highly metamorphosed, into our other projects. For example, our long-standing commitment to rule-based representations arose out of our (successful) attempt to head off the imminent ossification of DENDRAL caused by the rapid accumulation of new knowledge in the system around 1967.

Task

To enumerate plausible structures (atom-bond graphs) for organic molecules, given two kinds of information: analytic instrument data from a mass spectrometer and a nuclear magnetic resonance spectrometer; and user-supplied constraints on the answers, derived from any other source of knowledge (instrumental or contextual) available to the user.

Representations

Chemical structures are represented as node-link graphs of atoms (nodes) and bonds (links). Constraints on search are represented as subgraphs (atomic configurations) to be denied or preferred. The empirical theory of mass spectrometry is represented by a set of rules of the general form:

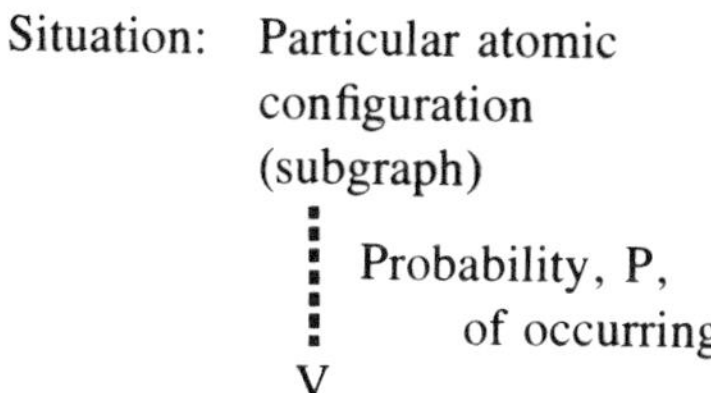

Action: Fragmentation of the particular configuration (breaking links)

Rules of this form are natural and expressive to mass spectrometrists.

Sketch of method

DENDRAL's inference procedure is a heuristic search that takes place in three stages, without feedback: generate–test–plan.

"Generate" (a program called CONGEN) is a generation process for plausible structures. Its foundation is a combinatorial algorithm (with mathematically proven properties of completeness and nonredundant generation) that can produce all the topologically legal candidate structures. Constraints supplied by the user or by the "plan" process prune and steer the generation to produce the plausible set (i.e., those satisfying the constraints) and not the enormous legal set.

"Test" refines the evaluation of plausibility, discarding less worthy candidates and rank-ordering the remainder for examination by the user. "Test" first produces a "predicted" set of instrument data for each plausible candidate, using the rules described. It then evaluates the worth of each candidate by comparing its predicted data with the actual input data. The evaluation is based on heuristic criteria of goodness-of-fit. Thus, "test" selects the "best" explanations of the data.

"Plan" produces direct (i.e., not chained) inference about likely substructure in the molecule from patterns in the data that are indicative of the presence of the substructure. (Patterns in the data trigger the left-hand sides of substructure rules). Though composed of many atoms whose interconnections are given, the substructure can be manipulated as atom-like by "generate." Aggregating many units entering into a combinatorial process into fewer higher-level units reduces the size of the combinatorial search space. "Plan" sets up the search space so as to be relevant to the input data. "Generate" is the inference tactician; "Plan" is the inference strategist. There is a separate "plan" package for each type of instrument data, but each package passes substructures (subgraphs) to "generate." Thus, there is a uniform interface between "plan" and "generate." User-supplied constraints enter this interface, directly or from user-assist packages, in the form of substructures.

Sources of knowledge

The various sources of knowledge used by the DENDRAL system are: Valences (legal connections of atoms); stable and unstable configurations of atoms; rules for mass spectrometry frgamentations; rules for NMR shifts; experts' rules for planning and evaluation; user-supplied constraints (contextual).

Results

DENDRAL's structure elucidation abilities are, paradoxically, both very general and very narrow. In general, DENDRAL handles all molecules, cyclic and treelike. In pure structure elucidation under constraints (without instrument data), CONGEN is unrivaled by human performance. In structure elucidation with instrument data, DENDRAL's performance rivals expert human performance only for a small number of molecular families for which the program has been given specialist's knowledge, namely, the families of interest to our chemist collaborators. I will spare this computer science audience the list of names of these families. Within these areas of knowledge-intensive specialization, DENDRAL's performance is usually not only much faster but also more accurate than expert human performance.

The statement just made summarizes thousands of runs of DENDRAL on problems of interest to our experts, their colleagues, and their students. The results obtained, along with the knowledge that had to be given to DENDRAL to obtain them, are published in major journals of chemistry. To date, 25 papers have been published there, under a series title "Applications of Artificial Intelligence for Chemical Inference: ⟨specific subject⟩" (see for example, the Buchanan, Smith et al., 1976, reference).

The DENDRAL system is in everyday use by Stanford chemists, their collaborators at other universities and collaborating or otherwise interested chemists in industry. Users outside Stanford access the system over commercial computer/communications network. The problems they are solving are often difficult and novel. The British government is currently supporting work at Edinburgh aimed at transferring DENDRAL to industrial user communities in the UK.

Discussion

Representation and extensibility. The representation chosen for the molecules, constraints, and rules of instrument data interpretation is sufficiently close to that used by chemists in thinking about structure elucidation that the knowledge base has been extended smoothly and easily, mostly by chemists themselves in recent years. Only one major reprogramming effort took place in the last nine years—when a new generator was created to deal with cyclic structures.

Representation and the integration of multiple sources of knowledge. The generally difficult problem of integrating various sources of knowledge has been made easy in DENDRAL by careful engineering of the representations of objects, constraints, and rules. We insisted on a common language of compatibility of the representations with each other and with the inference processes: the language of molecular structure expressed as graphs. This leads to a straightforward procedure for adding a new source of knowledge, say, for example, the knowledge associated with a new type of instrument data. The procedure is this: write rules that describe the effect of the physical processes of the instrument on molecules using the situation⇒action form with molecular graphs on both sides; any special inference process using these rules must pass its results to the generator only (!) in the common graph language.

It is today widely believed in AI that the use of many diverse sources of knowledge in problem solving and data interpretation has a strong effect on quality of performance. How strong is, of course, domain-dependent, but the impact of bringing just one additional source of knowledge to bear on a problem can be startling. In one difficult (but not unusually difficult) mass spectrum analysis problem,* the program using its mass spectrometry knowledge alone would have generated an impossibly large set of plausible candidates (over 1.25 million!). Our engineering response to this was to add another source of data and knowledge, proton NMR. The addition on a simple interpretive theory of this NMR data, from which the program could infer a few additional constraints, reduced the set of plausible candidates to one, the right structure! This was not an isolated result but showed up dozens of times in subsequent analyses.

DENDRAL and data. DENDRAL's robust models (topological, chemical, instrumental) permit a strategy of finding solutions by generating hypothetical "correct answers" and choosing among these with critical tests. This strategy is opposite to that of piecing together the implications of each data point to form a hypothesis. We call DENDRAL's strategy largely model-driven, and the other data-driven. The consequence of having enough knowledge to do model-driven analysis is a large reduction in the amount of data that must be examined since data is being used mostly for verification of possible answers. In a typical DENDRAL mass spectrum analysis, usually no more than about 25 data points out of a typical total of 250 points are processed. This important point about data reduction and focus-of-attention has been discussed before by Gregory (1968) and by the vision and speech research groups, but is not widely understood.

Conclusion. DENDRAL was an early herald of AI's shift to the knowledge-based paradigm. It demonstrated the point of the primacy of domain-specific knowledge in achieving expert levels of performance. Its development brought to the surface important problems of knowledge representation, acquisition, and use. It showed that, by and large, the AI tools of the first decade were sufficient to cope with the demands of a complex scientific problem-solving task, or were readily extended to handle unforeseen difficulties. It demonstrated that AI's conceptual and programming tools were capable of producing programs of applications interest, albeit in narrow specialties. Such a demonstration of competence and sufficiency was important for the credibility of the AI field at a critical juncture in its history.

---

* The analysis of an acyclic amine with formula $C_{20}H_{45}N$.

META-DENDRAL: inferring rules of mass spectrometry

Historical note

The META-DENDRAL program is a case study in automatic acquisition of domain knowledge. It arose out of our DENDRAL work for two reasons: first, a decision that with DENDRAL we had a sufficiently firm foundation on which to pursue our long-standing interest in processes of scientific theory formation; second, by a recognition that the acquisition of domain knowledge was the bottleneck problem in the building of applications-oriented intelligent agents.

Task

META-DENDRAL's job is to infer rules of fragmentation of molecules in a mass spectrometer for possible later use by the DENDRAL performance program. The inference is to be made from actual spectra recorded from known molecular structures. The output of the system is the set of fragmentation rules discovered, summary of the evidence supporting each rule, and a summary of contraindicating evidence. User-supplied constraints can also be input to force the form of rules along desired lines.

Representations

The rules are, of course, of the same form as used by DENDRAL that was described earlier.

Sketch of method

META-DENDRAL, like DENDRAL, uses the generation-and-test framework. The process is organized in three stages: reinterpret the data and summarize evidence (INTSUM); generate plausible candidates for rules (RULEGEN); test and refine the set of plausible rules (RULEMOD).

INTSUM: gives every data point in every spectrum an interpretation as a possible (highly specific) fragmentation. It then summarizes statistically the "weight of evidence" for fragmentations and for atomic configurations that cause these fragmentations. Thus, the job of INTSUM is to translate data to DENDRAL subgraphs and bond-breaks, and to summarize the evidence accordingly.

RULEGEN: conducts a heuristic search of the space of all rules that are legal under the DENDRAL rule syntax and the user-supplied constraints. It searches for plausible rules, i.e., those for which positive evidence exists. A search path is pruned when there is no evidence for rules of the class just generated. The search tree begins with the (single) most general rule (loosely put, "anything" fragments from "anything") and proceeds level-by-level toward more detailed specifications of the "anything." The heuristic stopping criterion measures whether a rule being generated has become too specific, in particular whether it is applicable to too few molecules of the input set. Similarly there is a criterion for deciding whether an emerging rule is too general. Thus, the output of RULEGEN is a set of candidate rules for which there is positive evidence.

RULEMOD: tests the candidate rule set using more complex criteria, including the presence of negative evidence. It removes redundancies in the candidate rule set; merges rules that are supported by the same evidence; tries further specialization of candidates to remove negative evidence; and tries further generalization that preserves positive evidence.

Results

META-DENDRAL produces rule sets that rival in quality those produced by our collaborating experts. In some tests, META-DENDRAL re-created rule sets that we had previously acquired from our experts during the DENDRAL project. In a more stringent test involving members of a family of complex ringed molecules for which the mass spectral theory had not been completely worked out by chemists, META-DENDRAL discovered rule sets for each subfamily. The rules were judged by experts to be excellent and a paper describing them was recently published in a major chemical journal (Buchanan, Smith et al., 1976).

In a test of the generality of the approach, a version of the META-DENDRAL program is currently being applied to the discovery of rules for the analysis of nuclear magnetic resonance data.

MYCIN and TEIRESIAS: Medical diagnosis

Historical note

MYCIN originated in the Ph.D. thesis of E. Shortliffe (now Shortliffe, M.D. as well), in collaboration with the Infectious Disease group at the Stanford Medical School (Shortliffe, 1976). TEIRESIAS, the Ph.D. thesis work of R. Davis, arose from issues and problems indicated by the MYCIN project but generalized by Davis beyond the bounds of medical diagnosis applications (Davis, 1976). Other MYCIN-related theses are in progress.

Tasks

The MYCIN performance task is diagnosis of blood infections and meningitis infections and the recommendation of drug treatment. MYCIN conducts a consultation (in English) with a physician-user about a patient case, constructing lines-of-reasoning leading to the diagnosis and treatment plan.

The TEIRESIAS knowledge acquisition task can be described as follows:

In the context of a particular consultation, confront the expert with a diagnosis with which he does not agree. Lead him systematically back through the line-of-reasoning that produced the diagnosis to the point at which he indicates the analysis went awry. Interact with the expert to modify offending rules or to acquire new rules. Rerun the consultation to test the solution and gain the expert's concurrence.

Representations:

MYCIN's rules are of the form:

IF ⟨conjunctive clauses⟩ THEN ⟨implication⟩

Here is an example of a MYCIN rule for blood infections.

RULE 85

IF:

1. The site of the culture is blood, and
2. The gram stain of the organism is gramneg, and
3. The morphology of the organism is rod, and
4. The patient is a compromised host

THEN:

There is suggestive evidence (.6) that the identity of the organism is pseudomonas-aeruginosa

TEIRESIAS allows the representation of MYCIN-like rules governing the use of other rules, i.e., rule-based strategies. An example follows.

METARULE 2

IF:

1. The patient is a compromised host, and
2. There are rules which mention in their premise pseudomonas
3. There are rules which mention in their premise klebsiellas.

THEN:

There is suggestive evidence (.4) that the former should be done before the latter.

Sketch of method

MYCIN employs a generation-and-test procedure of a familiar sort. The generation of steps in the line-of-reasoning is accomplished by backward chaining of the rules. An IF-side clause is either immediately true or false (as determined by patient or test data entered by the physician in the consultation); or is to be decided by subgoaling. Thus, "test" is interleaved with "generation" and serves to prune out incorrect lines-of-reasoning.

Each rule supplied by an expert has associated with it a "degree of certainty" representing the expert's confidence in the validity of the rule (a number from 1 to 10). MYCIN uses a particular ad hoc but simple model of inexact reasoning to cumulate the degrees of certainty of the rules used in an inference chain (Shortliffe and Buchanan, 1975).

It follows that there may be a number of "somewhat true" lines-of-reasoning—some indicating one diagnosis, some indicating another. All (above a threshold) are used by the system as sources of knowledge indicating plausible lines-of-reasoning.

TEIRESIAS' rule acquisition process is based on a record of MYCIN's search. Rule acquisition is guided by a set of rule models that dictate the form and indicate the likely content of new rules. Rule models are not given in advance, but are inferred from the knowledge base of existing rules.

Language of interaction

The language used looks like it might be English but is actually the dialect "Doctor-ese" used by practicing members of the health field. Reasonably simple language processing methods suffice. When ambiguities of interpretation are encountered, they are fed back to the user for decisions about meaning.

Example diagnosis and treatment plan

The following is an example of a diagnosis reported by MYCIN to one of its users following a consultation. An example consultation will not be shown, but one can be found in Shortliffe's book (Shortliffe, 1976).

> My therapy recommendations will be designed to treat for organisms that are either very likely or, although less likely, would have a significant effect on therapy selection if they were present. It is important to cover for the following probable infection(s) and associated organism(s):
>
> INFECTION-1 is CYSTITIS
> ⟨Item 1⟩ PSEUDOMONAS-CEPACIA [ORGANISM-5]
> ⟨Item 2⟩ CITROBACTER-DIVERSUS [ORGANISM-4]
> ⟨Item 3⟩ E. COLI [ORGANISM-3]
>
> INFECTION-2 is UPPER-RESPIRATORY INFECTION
> ⟨Item 4⟩ LISTERIA [ORGANISM-2]
>
> INFECTION-3 is BACTEREMIA
> ⟨Item 5⟩ ENTEROCOCCUS [ORGANISM-1]
>
> [REC-1] My preferred therapy recommendation is as follows:

In order to cover for items ⟨1 2 3 4 5⟩: Give the following in combination:
1. KANAMYCIN
Dose: 750 mg (7.5 mg/kg) q12h IM (or IV) for 28 days
Comments: Modify dose in renal failure
2. PENICILLIN
Dose: 2,500,000 units (25000 units/kg) q4h IV for 28 days

Results

No clinical evaluation of MYCIN is currently being done. In a prelinimary evaluation, done outside of the clinical setting, a panel of expert judges was asked to rate MYCIN's performance along a number of dimensions (e.g., infecting organism identification, organism significance). In 90 percent of the cases submitted to the judges, a majority of the judges said that the program's decisions were the same as or as good as the decisions they would have made.

Explanation

MYCIN can expose its line of reasoning by offering explanations of various kinds. "Why" and "How" questions can be asked by the user during the consultation. "Why" is the user's way of inquiring, "Why do you want to know that?" "How" is his way of asking, "How did you conclude that. . . ?" In a postconsultation, he can similarly inquire about how the diagnostic conclusions were reached, and inquire about the reasons why certain other conclusions were ruled out. Examples of the MYCIN-TEIRESIAS explanation capabilities follow:

MYCIN: Is the patient's illness with ORGANISM-1 a hospital-acquired infection?
USER: WHY
TEIRESIAS: (i.e., WHY is it important to determine whether or not the infection with ORGANISM-1 was acquired while the patient was hospitalized?)

[1.0] This will aid in determining the category of ORGANISM-1.

It has already been established that

[1.1] the gram stain of ORGANISM-1 is gramneg, and
[1.2] the morphology of ORGANISM-1 is rod, and
[1.3] the aerobicity of ORGANISM-1 is facultative

Therefore, if

[1.4] the infection with ORGANISM-1 was not acquired while the patient was hospitalized then

there is strongly suggestive evidence (.8) that the category of ORGANISM-1 is enterobacteriaceae

Also: there is weakly suggestive evidence (.1) that the identity of

ORGANISM-1 is pseudomonas-aeruginosa [RULE 37]
USER: HOW 1.3
TEIRESIAS: [i.e., HOW was it established that the aerobicity of ORGANISM-1 is facultative?]

The following were used:

[3.1] RULE 27 indicated there is strongly suggestive evidence (.8) that the aerobicity of ORGANISM-1 is facultative
[3.2] RULE 27 indicated there is weakly suggestive evidence (.2) that the aerobicity of ORGANISM-1 is anaerobic

Since this gave a cumulative CF of (.8) for facultative, and (.2) for anaerobic, it has been established that the aerobicity of ORGANISM-1 is facultative.
USER: WHY DIDN'T YOU CONSIDER STREPTOCOCCUS AS A POSSIBILITY FOR ORGANISM-1?
TEIRESIAS: The following rule could have been used to determine that the identity of ORGANISM-1 was streptococcus: RULE 33

But clause 2 (''the morphology of the organism is coccus'') was already known to be false for ORGANISM-1, so the rule was never tried.

Discussion

A few short comments aimed at knowledge engineering are in order.

English is the language most natural and comfortable for our experts and users, and was therefore the language chosen for interactive consultation, explanation, and external representation of the rules (the internal format is INTERLISP). This situation is not peculiar to doctors; in most areas of application of intelligent agents I believe that English (i.e., natural language) will be the language of choice. Programming an English language processor and front-end to such systems is not a scary enterprise because:

a. the domain is specialized, so that possible interpretations are constrained.
b. specialist-talk is replete with standard jargon and stereotyped ways of expressing knowledge and queries—just right for text templates, simple grammars and other simple processing schemes.
c. the ambiguity of interpretation resulting from simple schemes can be dealt with easily by feeding back interpretations for confirmation. If this is done with a pleasant ''I didn't quite understand you. . .'' tone, it is not irritating to the user.

English may be exactly the wrong language for representation and interaction in some domains. It would be awkward, to say the least, to represent DENDRAL's chemical structures and knowledge of mass spectrometry in English, or to interact about these with a user.

Simple explanation schemes have been a part of the AI scene for a number of years and are not hard to implement. Really good models of what explanation is as a transaction between user and agent, with programs to implement these models, will be the subject (I predict) of much future research in AI.

Without the explanation capability, I assert, user acceptance of MYCIN would have been nil, and there would have been a greatly diminished effectiveness and contribution of our experts.

MYCIN was the first of our programs that forced us to deal with what we had always understood: that experts' knowledge is uncertain and that our inference engines had to be made to reason with this uncertainty. It is less important that the inexact reasoning scheme be formal, rigorous, and uniform than it is for the scheme to be natural to and easily understandable by the experts and users.

All of these points can be summarized by saying that MYCIN and its TEIRESIAS adjunct are experiments in the design of a see-through system, whose representations and processes are almost transparently clear to the domain specialist. "Almost" here is equivalent to "with a few minutes of introductory description." The various pieces of MYCIN—the backward chaining, the English transactions, the explanations, etc.—are each simple in concept and realization. But there are great virtues to simplicity in system design; and viewed as a total intelligent agent system, MYCIN/TEIRESIAS is one of the best engineered.

SU/X: signal understanding

Historical note

SU/X is a system design that was tested in an application whose details are classified. Because of this, the ensuing discussion will appear considerably less concrete and tangible than the preceding case studies. This system design was done by H. P. Nii and me, and was strongly influenced by the CMU Hearsay II system design (Lesser and Erman, 1977).

Task

SU/X's task is the formation and continual updating, over long periods of time, of hypotheses about the identity, location, and velocity of objects in a physical space. The output desired is a display of the "current best hypotheses" with full explanation of the support for each. There are two types of input data: the primary signal (to be understood); and auxiliary symbolic data (to supply context for the understanding). The primary signals are spectra, represented as descriptions of the spectral lines. The various spectra cover the physical space with some spatial overlap.

Representations

The rules given by the expert about objects, their behavior, and the interpretation of signal data from them are all represented in the situation ⇒ action form. The "situations" constitute invoking conditions and the "actions" are processes that modify the current hypotheses, post unresolved issues, recompute evaluations, etc. The expert's knowledge of how to do analysis in the task is also represented in rule form. These strategy rules replace the normal executive program.

The situation-hypothesis is represented as a node-link graph, treelike in that it has distinct "levels," each representing a degree of abstraction (or aggregation) that is natural to the expert in his understanding of the domain. A node represents an hypothesis; a link to that node represents support for that hypothesis (as in HEARSAY II, "support from above" or "support from below"). "Lower" levels are concerned with the specifics of the signal data. "Higher" levels represent symbolic abstractions.

Sketch of method

The situation-hypothesis is formed incrementally. As the situation unfolds over time, the triggering of rules modifies or discards existing hypotheses, adds new ones, or changes support values. The situation-hypothesis is a common work-space ("blackboard," in HEARSAY jargon) for all the rules.

In general, the incremental steps toward a more complete and refined situation-hypothesis can be viewed as a sequence of local generate-and-test activities. Some of the rules are plausible move generators, generating either nodes or links. Other rules are evaluators, testing and modifying node descriptions.

In typical operation, new data is submitted for processing (say, N time-units of new data). This initiates a flurry of rule-triggerings and consequently rule-actions (called "events"). Some events are direct consequences of data; other events arise in a cascade-like fashion from the triggering of rules. Auxiliary symbolic data also cause events, usually affecting the higher levels of the hypothesis. As a consequence, support-from-above for the lower level processes is made available; and expectations of possible lower level events can be formed. Eventually all the relevant rules have their say and the system becomes quiescent, thereby triggering the input of new data to reenergizee the inference activity.

The system uses the simplifying strategy of maintaining only one "best" situation-hypothesis at any moment, modifying it incrementally as required by the changing data. This approach is made feasible by several characteristics of the domain. First, there is the strong continuity over time of objects and their behaviors (specifically, they do not change radically over time, or behave radically differently over short periods). Second, a single problem (identity, location and velocity of a particular set of objects) persists over numerous data gathering periods. (Compare this to speech understanding in which each sentence is spoken just once, and each presents a new and different problem.) Finally, the system's hypothesis is typically "almost right," in part because it gets numerous opportunities to refine the solution (i.e., the numerous data gathering periods), and in part because the availability of many knowledge sources tends to over-determine the solution. As a result of all of these, the current best hypothesis changes only slowly with time, and hence keeping only the current best is a feasible approach.

Of interest are the time-based events. These rule-like expressions, created by certain rules, trigger upon the passage of specified amounts of time. They implement various "wait-and-see" strategies of analysis that are useful in the domain.

Results

In the test application, using signal data generated by a simulation program because real data was not available, the program achieved expert levels of performance over a span of test problems. Some problems were difficult because there was very little primary signal to support inference. Others were difficult because too much signal induced a plethora of alternatives with much ambiguity.

A modified SU/X design is currently being used as the basis for an application to the interpretation of x-ray crystallographic data, the CRYSALIS program mentioned later.

Discussion

The role of the auxiliary symbolic sources of data is of critical importance. They supply a symbolic model of the existing situation that is used to generate expectations of events to be observed in the data stream. This allows flow of inferences from higher levels of abstraction to lower. Such a process, so familiar to AI researchers, apparently is almost unrecognized among signal processing engineers. In the application task, the expectation-driven analysis is essential in controlling the combinatorial processing explosion at the lower levels, exactly the explosion that forces the traditional signal processing engineers to seek out the largest possible number-cruncher for their work.

The design of appropriate explanations for the user takes an interesting twist in SU/X. The situation-hypothesis unfolds piecemeal over time, but the "appropriate" explanation for the user is one that focuses on individual objects over time. Thus the appropriate explanation must be synthesized from a history of all the events that led up to the current hypothesis. Contrast this with the MYCIN-TEIRESIAS reporting of rule invocations in the constructions of a reasoning chain.

Since its knowledge base and its auxiliary symbolic data give it a model-of-the-situation that strongly constrains interpretation of the primary data stream, SU/X is relatively unperturbed by erroneous or missing data. These data conditions merely cause fluctuations in the credibility of individual hypotheses and/or the creation of the "wait-and-see" events. SU/X can be (but has not yet been) used to control sensors. Since its rules specify what types and values of evidence are necessary to establish support, and since it is constantly processing a complete hypothesis structure, it can request "critical readings" from the sensors. In general, this allows an efficient use of limited sensor bandwidth and data acquisition processing capability.

Other case studies

Space does not allow more than just a brief sketch of other interesting projects that have been completed or are in progress.

AM: mathematical discovery

AM is a knowledge-based system that conjectures interesting concepts in elementary mathematics. It is a discoverer of interesting theorems to prove, not a theorem proving program. It was conceived and executed by D. Lenat for his Ph.D. thesis, and is reported by him in these proceedings.

AM's knowledge is basically of two types: rules that suggest possibly interesting new concepts from previously conjectured concepts; and rules that evaluate the mathematical "interestingness" of a conjecture. These rules attempt to capture the expertise of the professional mathematician at the task of mathematical discovery. Though Lenat is not a professional mathematician, he was able successfully to serve as his own expert in the building of this program.

AM conducts a heuristic search through the space of concepts creatable from its rules. Its basic framework is generation-and-test. The generation is plausible move generation, as indicated by the rules for formation of new concepts. The test is the evaluation of "interestingness." Of particular note is the method of test-by-example that lends the flavor of scientific hypothesis testing to the enterprise of mathematical discovery.

Initialized with concepts of elementary set theory, it conjectured concepts in elementary number theory, such as "add," "multiply" (by four distinct paths!), "primes," the unique factorization theorem, and a concept similar to primes but previously not much studied called "maximally divisible numbers."

MOLGEN: planning experiments in molecular genetics

MOLGEN, a collaboration with the Stanford Genetics Department, is work in progress. MOLGEN's task is to provide intelligent advice to a molecular geneticist on the planning of experiments involving the manipulation of DNA. The geneticist has various kinds of laboratory techniques available for changing DNA material (cuts, joins, insertions, deletions, and so on); techniques for determining the biological consequences of the changes; various instruments for measuring effects; various chemical methods for inducing, facilitating, or inhibiting changes; and many other tools.

Some MOLGEN programs under development will offer planning assistance in organizing and sequencing such tools to accomplish an experimental goal. Other MOLGEN programs will check user-provided experiment plans for feasibility; and its knowledge base will be a repository for the rapidly expanding knowledge of this specialty, available by interrogation.

In MOLGEN the problem of integration of many diverse sources of knowledge is central since the essence of the experiment planning process is the successful merging of biological, genetic, chemical, topological, and instrument knowledge. In MOLGEN the problem of representing processes is also brought into focus since the expert's knowledge of experimental strategies—protoplans—must also be represented and put to use.

One MOLGEN program (Stefik, 1978) solves a type of analysis problem that is often difficult for laboratory scientists to solve. DNA structures can be fragmented by chemicals called restriction enzymes. These enzymes cleave DNA at specific recognition sites. The fragmentation may be complete or partial. One or more enzymes may be used. The fragmented segments of the DNA are collected and sorted out by segment length using a technique called gel electrophoresis. The analytical problem is similar to that faced by DENDRAL: given an observed fragmentation pattern, hypothesize the best structural explanation of the data. More precisely the problem is to map the enzyme recognition sites of a DNA structure from complete or partial "fragmentations."

The program uses the model-driven approach that is similar to DENDRAL's and is discussed earlier. The method is generate-and-test. A generator is initiated that is capable of generating all the site-segment maps in an exhaustive, irredundant fashion. Various pruning rules are used to remove whole classes of conceivable candidates in light of the data. Some of the pruning rules are empirical and judgmental. Others are formal and mathematically based.

The program solves simple problems of this type of analysis better than laboratory scientists. The harder problems, however, yield only to the broader biological knowledge known by the scientists and not yet available to the program's reasoning processes. In a recent test case, a problem whose solution space contained approximately 150,000,000 site-fragment "maps" was solved in 27 seconds of PDP-10 time using the INTERLISP programming system.

Interestingly, the computer scientist's formal understanding of the nature of the problem, his formal representation of the knowledge used for pruning out inappropriate candidates, and the computational power available to him enable him to suggest a few new experiment designs to his geneticist collaborators that were not previously in their repertoire.

CRYSALIS: inferring protein structure from electron density maps

CRYSALIS, too, is work in progress. Its task is to hypothesize the structure of a protein from a map of electron density that is derived from x-ray crystallographic data. The map is three-dimensional, and the contour information is crude and highly ambiguous. Interpretation is guided and supported by auxiliary information, of which the amino acid sequence of the protein's backbone is the most important. Density map interpretation is a protein chemist's art. As always, capturing this art in heuristic rules and putting it to use with an inference engine is the project's goal.

The inference engine for CRYSALIS is a modification of the SU/X system design described above. The hypothesis formation process must deal with many levels of possibly useful aggregation and abstraction. For example, the map itself can be viewed as consisting of "peaks," or "peaks and valleys," or "skeleton." The protein model has "atoms," "amide planes," "amino acid sidechains," and even massive substructures such as "helices." Protein molecules are so complex that a systematic generation-and-test strategy like DENDRAL's is not feasible. Incremental piecing together of the hypothesis using region-growing methods is necessary.

The CRYSALIS design (alias SU/P) is described in a recent paper by Nii and Feigenbaum (1977).

SUMMARY OF CASE STUDIES

Some of the themes presented earlier need no recapitulation, but I wish to revisit three here: generation-and-test; situation ⇒ action rules; and explanations.

Generation-and-test

Aircraft come in a wide variety of sizes, shapes, and functional designs and they are applied in very many ways. But almost all that fly do so because of the unifying physical principle of lift by airflow; the others are described by exception. If there is such a unifying principle for intelligent programs and human intelligence it is generation-and-test. No wonder that this has been so thoroughly studied in AI research!

In the case studies, generation is manifested in a variety of forms and processing schemes. There are legal move generators defined formally by a generating algorithm (DENDRAL's graph generating algorithm); or by a logical rule of inference (MYCIN's backward chaining). When legal move generation is not possible or not efficient, there are plausible move generators (as in SU/X and AM.) Sometimes generation is interleaved with testing (as in MYCIN, SU/X, and AM). In one case, all generation precedes testing (DENDRAL). One case (META-DENDRAL) is mixed, with some testing taking place during generation, some after.

Test also shows great variety. There are simple tests (MYCIN: "Is the organism aerobic?"; SU/X: "Has a spectral line appeared at position P?") Some tests are complex heuristic evaluations (AM: "Is the new concept 'interesting'?"; MOLGEN: "Will the reaction actually take place?") Sometimes a complex test can involve feedback to modify the object being tested (as in META-DENDRAL).

The evidence from our case studies supports the assertion by Newell and Simon that generation-and-test is a law of our science (Newell and Simon, 1976).

Situation⇛action rules

Situation⇛action rules are used to represent experts' knowledge in all of the case studies. Always the situation part indicates the specific conditions under which the rule is relevant. The action part can be simple (MYCIN: conclude presence of particular organism; DENDRAL: conclude break of particular bond). Or it can be quite complex (MOLGEN: an experiential procedure). The overriding consideration in making design choices is that the rule form chosen be able to represent clearly and directly what the expert wishes to express about the domain. As illustrated, this may necessitate a wide variation in rule syntax and semantics.

From a study of all the projects, a regularity emerges. A salient feature of the situation⇛action rule technique for representing experts' knowledge is the modularity of the knowledge base, with the concomitant flexibility to add or change the knowledge easily as the experts' understanding of the domain changes. Here too one must be pragmatic, not doctrinaire. A technique such as this cannot represent modularity of knowledge if that modularity does not exist in the domain. The virtue of this technique is that it serves as a framework for discovering what modularity exists in the domain. Discovery may feed back to cause reformulation of the knowledge toward greater modularity.

Finally, our case studies have shown that strategy knowledge can be captured in rule form. In TEIRESIAS, the metarules capture knowledge of how to deploy domain knowledge; in SU/X, the strategy rules represent the experts' knowledge of "how to analyze" in the domain.

Explanation

Most of the programs, and all of the more recent ones, make available an explanation capability for the user, be he end-user or system developer. Our focus on end-users in applications domains has forced attention to human engineering issues, in particular making the need for the explanation capability imperative.

The intelligent-agent viewpoint seems to us to demand that the agent be able to explain its activity; else the question arises of who is in control of the agent's activity. The issue is not academic or philosophical. It is an engineering issue that has arisen in medical and military applications of intelligent agents, and will govern future acceptance of AI work in applications areas. And on the philosophical level one might even argue that there is a moral imperative to provide accurate explanations to end-users whose intuitions about our systems are almost nil.

Finally, the explanation capability is needed as part of the concerted attack on the knowledge acquisition problem. Explanation of the reasoning process is central to the interactive transfer of expertise to the knowledge base, and it is our most powerful tool for the debugging of the knowledge base.

ACKNOWLEDGMENT

The work reported herein has received long-term support from the Defense Advanced Research Projects Agency (DAHC 15-73-C-0435). The National Institutes of Health (5R24-RR00612, RR-00785) has supported DENDRAL, META-DENDRAL, and the SUMEX-AIM computer facility on which we compute. The National Science Foundation (MCS 76-11649, DCR 74-23461) has supported research on CRYSALIS and MOLGEN. The Bureau of Health Sciences Research and Evaluation (HS-10544) has supported research on MYCIN. I am grateful to these agencies for their continuing support of our work.

I wish to express my deep admiration and thanks to the faculty, staff and students of the Heuristic Programming Project, and to our collaborators in the various worldly arts, for the creativity and dedication that has made our work exciting and fruitful.

REFERENCES

General

Feigenbaum, E. A., "Artificial Intelligence Research: What is it? What has it achieved? Where is it going?," invited paper, Symposium on Artificial Intelligence, Canberra, Australia, 1974.

Feigenbaum, E. A. and J. Feldman, Computers and Thought, New York: McGraw-Hill, 1963.

Goldstein, I. and S. Papert, "Artificial Intelligence, Language, and the Study of Knowledge," Cognitive Science, Vol. 1, No. 1, 1977.

Gregory, R., "On How So Little Information Controls so Much Behavior," Bionics Research Report No. 1, Machine Intelligence Department, University of Edinburgh, 1968.

Lesser, V. R. and L. D. Erman, "A Retrospective View of the HEARSAY-II Architecture," Proceedings of the Fifth International Artificial Intelligence-1977 Vol. 1, Cambridge, Massachusetts: Massachusetts Institute of Technology, August 22–25, 1977.

Newell, A. and H. A. Simon, Human Problem Solving, Prentice-Hall, 1972.

Newell, A. and H. A. Simon, "Computer Science as Empirical Inquiry: Symbols and Search," Com ACM, 19, 3, March 1976.

DENDRAL and META-DENDRAL

Feigenbaum, E. A., B. G. Buchanan, and J. Lederberg, "On Generality and Problem

Solving: a Case Study Using the DENDRAL Program," Machine Intelligence 6, Edinburgh University Press, 1971.

Buchanan, B. G., A. M. Duffield, and A. V. Robertson, "An Application of Artificial Intelligence to the Interpretation of Mass Spectra," Mass Spectrometry Techniques and Applications, G. W. A. Milne, ed., John Wiley & Sons, Inc., p. 121, 1971.

Michie, D. and B. G. Buchanan, "Current Status of the Heuristic DENDRAL Program for Applying Artificial Intelligence to the Interpretation of Mass Spectra," Computers for Spectroscopy, R. A. G. Carrington, ed., London: Adam Hilger, 1974.

Buchanan, B. G., "Scientific Theory Formation by Computer," Nato Advanced Study Institutes Series, Series E: Applied Science, 14:515, Noordhoff-Leyden, 1976.

Buchanan, B. G., D. H. Smith, W. C. White, R. J. Gritter, E. A. Feigenbaum, J. Lederberg, and C. Djerassi, "Applications of Artificial Intelligence for Chemical Inference XXII. Automatic Rule Formation in Mass Spectrometry by Means of the Meta-DENDRAL Program," Journal of the ACS, 98:6168, 1976.

MYCIN

Shortliffe, E. Computer-based Medical Consultations: MYCIN, New York: Elsevier, 1976.

Davis, R., B. G. Buchanan, and E. H. Shortliffe, "Production Rules as a Representation for a Knowledge-Based Consultation Program," Artificial Intelligence, 8, 1, February 1977.

Shortliffe, E. H. and B. G. Buchanan, "A Model of Inexact Reasoning in Medicine," Mathematical Biosciences, 23:351, 1975.

TEIRESIAS

Davis, R., "Applications of Meta Level Knowledge to the Construction, Maintenance and Use of Large Knowledge Bases," Memo HPP-76-7, Stanford Computer Science Department, Stanford, California, 1976.

Davis, R., "Interactive Transfer of Expertise I: Acquisition of New Inference Rules," Proceedings of the Fifth International Joint Conference on Artificial Intelligence-1977, Cambridge, Massachusetts: Massachusetts Institute of Technology, August 22–25, 1977.

Davis, R. and B. G. Buchanan, "Meta-Level Knowledge: Overview and Applications," Proceedings of the Fifth International Joint Conference on Artificial Intelligence-1977, Cambridge, Massachusetts: Massachusetts Institute of Technology, August 22–25, 1977.

SU/X

Nii, H. P. and E. A. Feigenbaum, "Rule Based Understanding of Signals," Proceedings of the Conference on Pattern-Directed Inference Systems, 1978 (forthcoming), also Memo HPP-77-7, Stanford Computer Science Department, Stanford, California, 1977.

AM

Lenat, D., "AM: An Artificial Intelligence Approach to Discovery in Mathematics as Heuristic Search," Memo HPP-76-8, Stanford Computer Science Department, Stanford, California, 1976.

MOLGEN

Martin, N., P. Friedland, J. King, and M. Stefik, ''Knowledge Base Management for Experiment Planning in Molecular Genetics,'' Proceedings of the Fifth International Joint Conference on Artificial Intelligence-1977, Cambridge, Massachusetts: Massachusetts Institute of Technology, August 22–25, 1977.

Stefik, M., ''Inferring DNA Structures from Segmentation Data,'' Artificial Intelligence, 1978 (in press).

CRYSALIS

Engelmore, R. and H. P. Nii, ''A Knowledge-Based System for the Interpretation of Protein X-Ray Crystallographic Data,'' Memo HPP-77-2, Department of Computer Science, Stanford, California, 1977.

PART II

BRITISH COMPUTER SOCIETY

Papers selected by the British Computer Society.

"On Making Graphic Arts Quality Output by Computer"
N.E. Wiseman, C.I.C. Campbell, and J. Harradine

"A Design Language for Asynchronous Logic"
A.K. Burston, D.J. Kinniment, and Hilary Kahn

The British Computer Society was formed in 1957 to:

further the development and use of computational machinery and the techniques related thereto

facilitate the exchange of information and views and to inform public opinion on the subject

hold conferences and meetings for the reading of papers and delivery of lectures

publish information for the benefit of members

organize and conduct examinations for members and others in subjects requiring a knowledge of or otherwise in any way concerning the development and use of computational machinery and the techniques related thereto, and in any allied subjects.

BCS is a member of the International Federation for Information Processing (IFIP). The Society has two major publications: *The Computer Journal*, and the weekly *Computing*.

BCS address is 29 Portland Place, London, W1N 4HU, England.

On Making Graphic Arts Quality Output by Computer

N. E. Wiseman, C. I. C. Campbell, and J. Harradine

Computer Laboratory, University of Cambridge, Corn Exchange Street, Cambridge CB2 3QG

The design and production of high-quality page images falls within the competence of the printing/publishing profession and tends to be regarded as specialized and difficult by those outside it. Modern developments in computer driven output devices, (COM machines, film setters and precision plotters) makes available the facilities for production of such images much more widely and it seems inevitable that they will influence greatly, if not determine, the future of printing. There is, however, much to learn. Printing is a craft industry with variable, but often highly aesthetic, technical standards which are difficult to measure and dispense to newcomers. The use of new technology may relieve the craft of some previous limitations, but may also impose new ones for which different standards have to be devised.

This paper presents some of the basic techniques which are being developed for the use of the Laser Scan HRD-1 display plotter in the production of high-quality images and some of the problems encountered which are connected with the subjective assessment of such images.

INTRODUCTION

The moves in the printing industry from the long established letterpress methods towards lithography are accompanied by many changes in composition practice. The principal reason for change is that film images, the companion of lithographic printing methods, are much less easy to prepare and modify manu-

---

EDITOR'S NOTE: *From THE COMPUTER JOURNAL, Vol. 21 No. 1, pp. 2–6, February 1978. Reprinted by permission of the publisher, British Computer Society.*

ally than lead castings. The traditional manual methods are usually replaced or augmented using specialized machinery developed by printing engineers and driven by computers. Generally speaking, however, the new technology follows the pattern of the old and the function of a modern film setter is closely comparable with that of a type casting machine, so while the manual operations may undergo radical change or even vanish, there is little change at the more fundamental level of making things to print. In particular the view persists that a page is assembled from a smallish number of rigidly stylized components (the letters and marks) and a few less disciplined components (the illustrations). The two categories are processed on paths unrelated to each other throughout the composition process and are assembled together at the last possible moment—just prior to plate making. Most available filmsetters are therefore designed solely to deliver text and, even though the repertoire of sorts and sizes may be large, only some of the pages required to make a typical book can be made without subsequent hand work being needed. Direct production of microfiche as a publishing medium is restrained by such limitations of technique. Are the limitations necessary? We think not. There are now becoming available a few interesting machines which are able to make arbitrary images of graphics art quality and which can produce line diagrams and halftones as readily as text. An example is the Laser Scan HRD-1 Display Plotter which has a resolution of at least 3500 × 5000 and an accuracy commensurate with this. It writes by deflecting a laser beam under computer control over diazo film of microfiche size (10 cm × 15 cm). Figure 1 shows a collage of the sort of work it produces. For the purpose of this paper we can consider that the laser beam is off or on and that the deflection system can move it to any position on a rectangular grid of 10,000 × 15,000 points, giving a 10-micron spacing on each coordinate direction (the machine actually has greater addressibility and flexibility than this). We discuss below the techniques we have used to produce the different effects required for high quality images and the means by which complete pages may be designed and drawn.

GENERAL

Drawing images with a line as fine as that of the HRD-1 requires that practically every feature is treated as an area of many addressible locations and that the beam visits them all to fill in the area. Even a straight line feature in a diagram must be drawn as many parallel strokes of the beam to make it reach the desired thickness (a single stroke is only clearly visible under considerable magnification). Suppose a straight line of thickness t is required between two points P1 and P2. One approach would be to envisage a rectangle centered on the line P1–P2 of width t and then to zigzag the beam inside the rectangle to fill it in. Two possible arrangements are shown in Figure 2(a) and (b). Method (a) requires that more line segments be drawn and hence more changes in the direction of drawing—this may be a disadvantage if the drawing system has a

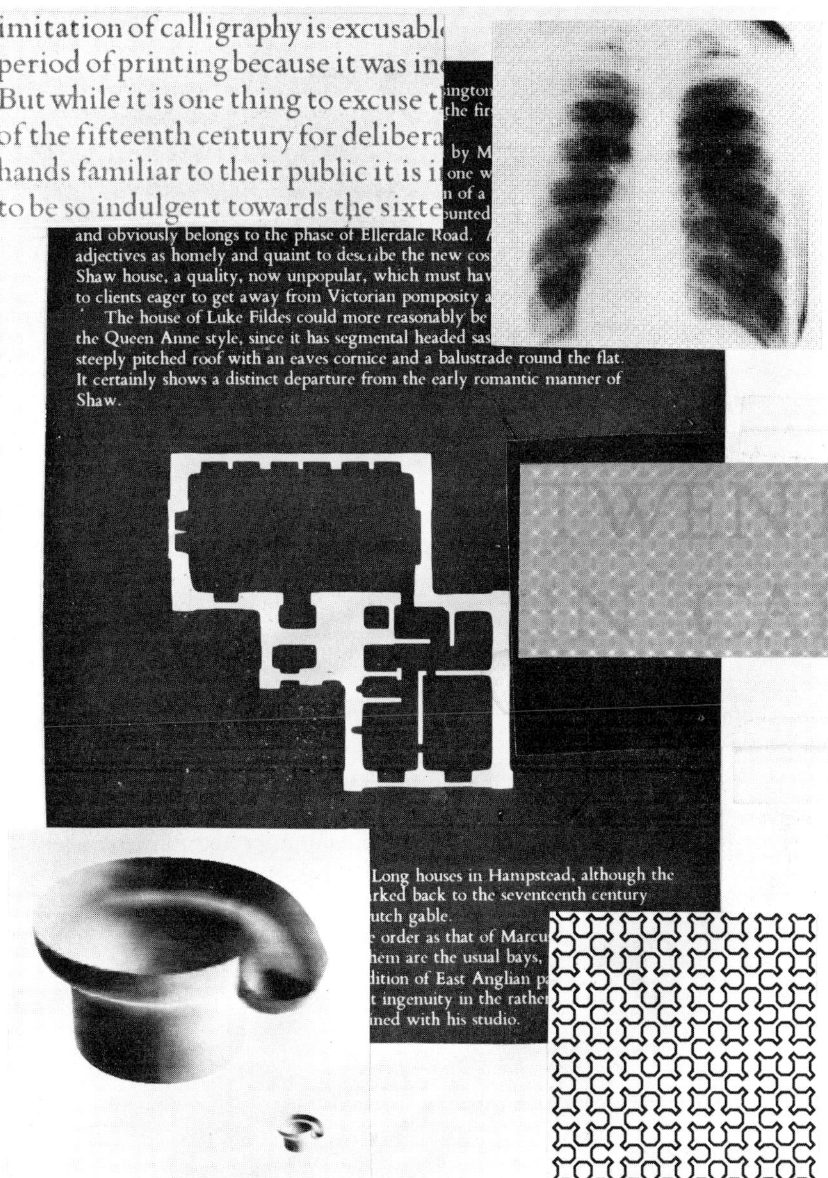

imitation of calligraphy is excusabl
period of printing because it was in
But while it is one thing to excuse t
of the fifteenth century for delibera
hands familiar to their public it is i
to be so indulgent towards the sixte
and obviously belongs to the phase of Ellerdale Road.
adjectives as homely and quaint to describe the new cos
Shaw house, a quality, now unpopular, which must hav
to clients eager to get away from Victorian pomposity a
The house of Luke Fildes could more reasonably be
the Queen Anne style, since it has segmental headed sas
steeply pitched roof with an eaves cornice and a balustrade round the flat.
It certainly shows a distinct departure from the early romantic manner of
Shaw.
Long houses in Hampstead, although the
rked back to the seventeenth century
utch gable.
order as that of Marcu
hem are the usual bays,
dition of East Anglian p
t ingenuity in the rathe
ined with his studio.

Figure 1 Collage.

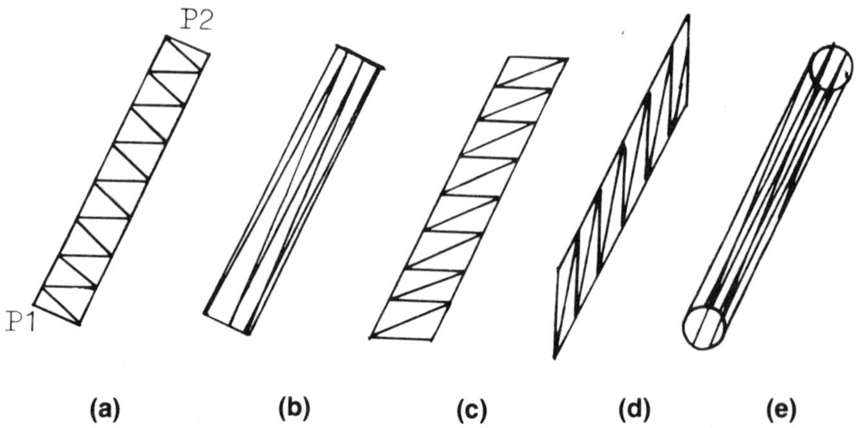

Figure 2 Methods for line drawing.

high inertia for it will increase the time it takes to fill in the rectangle. (The HRD-1 has a very low inertia.) On the other hand, the reinforcement of image density where the direction changes, caused by the overlap of adjacent strokes, may give a crisper edge to the finished line. Similar methods, shown in Figure 2(*c*) and (*d*) may be preferred when joining line segments together since they butt together easily. A trivial change allows trapezoidal areas rather than parallelograms to be drawn and the next section describes the way in which they have been used to produce contoured densely filled areas. A final suggestion for drawing line segments is shown in Figure 2(*e*) in which a succession of points is joined on circles of diameter t centered at P1 and P2, alternately. A convenience of this method is that chains of lines at different orientations are smoothly blended into one another without further computation (see Figure 3).

The production of gray scale images requires a method for achieving contrast control which is reasonably linear and stable. If the image is to be utilised for printing by ink transfer it must use a gray scale simulated by the gradation

Figure 3 Smooth blending of line chain.

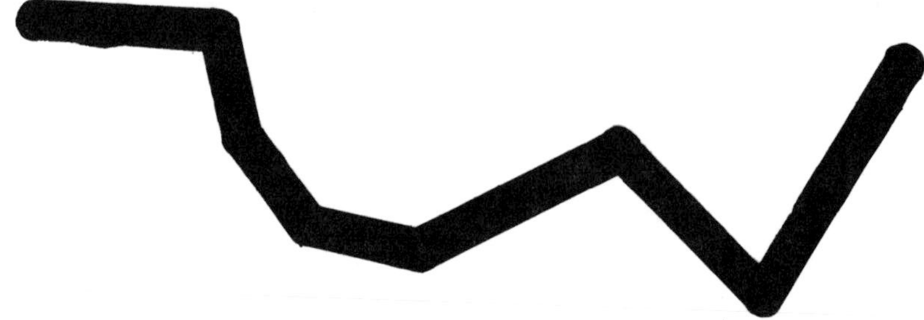

TABLE 1.

Pixel Side in	Number of Points	Allocated as Follows	Resulting Grey Levels
1	1	0,1	2
2	4	0,1,2,4	4
3	9	0,1,2,4,9	5
4	16	0,1,2,4,8,16	6
5	25	0,1,2,4,7,12,25	6
6	36	0,1,2,4,8,17,36	7
7	49	0,1,2,5,11,24,49	7
8	64	0,1,2,4,8,16,32,64	8

of line density. This exchanges spatial resolution for brightness and in conventional printing methods is done by an optical screening process with a grating of regular pattern through which the image is copied. For computer drawn images the screening effect can be calculated before output and is, of course, not limited by any manufacturing difficulties with optical screens.

We consider the image to be held in a computer in digital form as an array of picture elements, known as pixels, and on outputting each pixel its area is filled in proportion to its desired intensity. Suppose a pixel is represented as a square cell of $n \times n$ resolvable points. By filling in x points, an apparent intensity in the range $0 \leq x/n^2 \leq 1$ can be attained. The eye perceives intensity on a logarithmic, rather than a linear, scale and the number of distinguishable values varies with n roughly in the manner shown in Table 1. Although the gray level of each pixel is fixed by the proportion of points lit in it, the fine structure is affected by which actual points are selected. Figure 4 shows some examples for the 8×8 pixel for gray level 6, (32 points lit).

The choice of format would be based on a compromise between drawing difficulty and uniformity and is more important for low resolution images (few pixels) where pixel structure is more noticeable. Although, of course, the infor-

Figure 4 Pixel patterns.

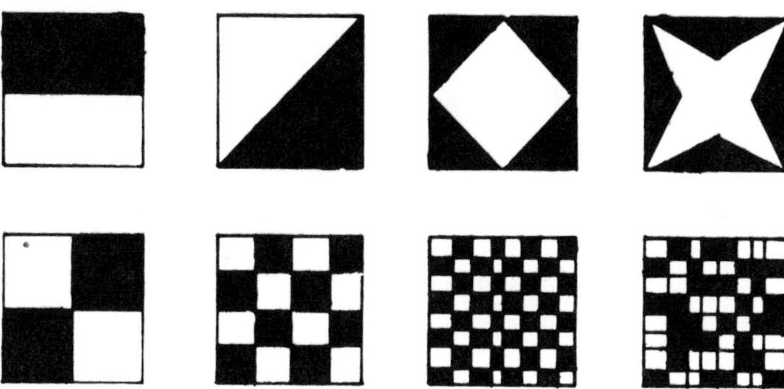

mation content of the image is not affected by this texture the subjective impression of "quality" is strongly dependent on it. Across the entire process of computation, generation and reproduction, a spatial resolution limitation persists which will impose restrictions on the quality which can be achieved. These limitations are least understood in the reproduction processes but mechanical precision, paper characteristics and surface tension effects in ink transference have a dominant effect. Rendering each pixel with a finer and finer texture will ultimately be defeated by one of these factors. With the improved control of texture provided by computer generation of images it becomes of much greater interest to understand the reproduction process in detail, and it may well be that such a better understanding would permit the present printing machines to achieve better results.

The image, drawn as a succession of pixels, can be assembled in any convenient order, but some form of area coding may be preferred to minimize the storage requirements. A simple form of coding, known as run length coding, is applicable when the image is drawn as a modulated raster covering an area enclosing the image. Each scan line in the raster is stored as a succession of integer pairs R–B where R gives the number of contiguous pixels following in the scan direction at brightness B. Except in highly detailed images where most values of R are very small, run length coding may be expected to reduce storage requirements by a useful factor—10 being typical in many applications. Even so a high resolution image may require a million bits or more of storage and occupy the laser scan display for half an hour. However, the flexibility of the technique and the development potential of the machine persuade us that these figures are acceptable. Much more compact codings for the picture data are possible and several are described in the literature but of course the drawing time is determined by hardware performance and we can't do much about that. Possibly something can be done, and to explain it a bit more detail about the deflection system used in the HRD-1 is needed. The deflection of the laser beam is done in two cascaded stages, one covering a large angle at relatively low speed and the other a small angle at much higher speed. The combination is used to decouple the mechanical inertia of the first from the total beam movement—after a large move the minor deflection system corrects positional errors of the main deflection system and allows drawing to continue while these errors decay. We could use this deflection system in a different way, for drawing halftones. For reasonably sized pixels the minor deflection system is able to cover the required angles with no movement of the main deflectors at all and the proposed method for writing halftones is thus to move the main deflectors so that the beam is in the center of the next pixel, write the pixel with the minor deflector and then move on to the next. This should make possible a drawing speed ten times faster than that presently achieved.

The component parts for a high quality page generating program can be assembled using the techniques described above. A particular implementation is described in the next section.

TEXT GENERATION

Most printing alphabets have richly detailed character forms and it is tempting to try to simplify them when arranging to draw them by computer from internally stored descriptions. Much care is needed. The detailing should not be seen as decoration whose main purpose is to satisfy some aesthetic need of the type designer. The long tradition of printing has taken account of many subjective factors which influence such things as legibility and reading speed under the sort of distortion and degradation introduced by the reproduction process. The measurement and assessment of these factors is, however, quite vague and readability itself is not well understood. It did not seem to us wise to couple any significant change in form with a switch of technology and therefore we have adopted faces closely similar to well known metal types. There is a sense in which we have taken certain liberties with the design of a format but we have had expert advice and guidance and believe that the traditions are being properly upheld and honored. We will return to this point later.

Every character is drawn as a succession of trapezoidal elements made after the fashion of Figure 2(*c*) and (*d*). With this method, the beam does not waste time scanning over the unlit parts of the character, as it would if a modulated raster were adopted. Each trapezium is defined by a 5-tuple (X, Y, A1, A2, DIR) where X, Y gives the relative beam movement (i.e., P2–P1 in Figure 2), A1 and A2 are the starting and finishing amplitudes and DIR selects a horizontal or vertical orientation (as In Figure 2(*c*) and (*d*) respectively). A character definition will comprise from 4 to 50 or more trapezia according to complexity and Figure 5 shows a few large scale characters drawn with different stroke spacing from the same stored definitions.

Changing the stroke spacing makes it possible to exchange drawing speed with image quality to produce proof and finishing modes, shadow characters, and special effects. For any given effect, the stroke spacing is normally held constant to produce a uniform density, and the strokes are generated from the stored definition as they are needed by the display. Changing the scale at which characters are drawn will alter the amount of detail which can be seen and the program does not attempt to draw trapezia which are small compared with the stroke spacing. This effect is clearly visible in the serifs of corresponding characters in Figure 5. It is an example of the manner in which drawing time of a picture can be saved by omitting unnecessary detail.

A font of 100 character definitions comprises some 2000 trapezia descriptions. Various features recur in different characters and the definitions for them are stored once only. The top serif on the lower case *i* and *h* (Figure 5) is an example. Each character definition thus comprises a mixture of trapezia descriptions, beam movement commands and references to other definitions. The code for each character indexes a table giving its width (amount of beam movement horizontally) and the start of its definition in the font. The prime data for a font is held as a character file, allowing easy editing and transportation, but

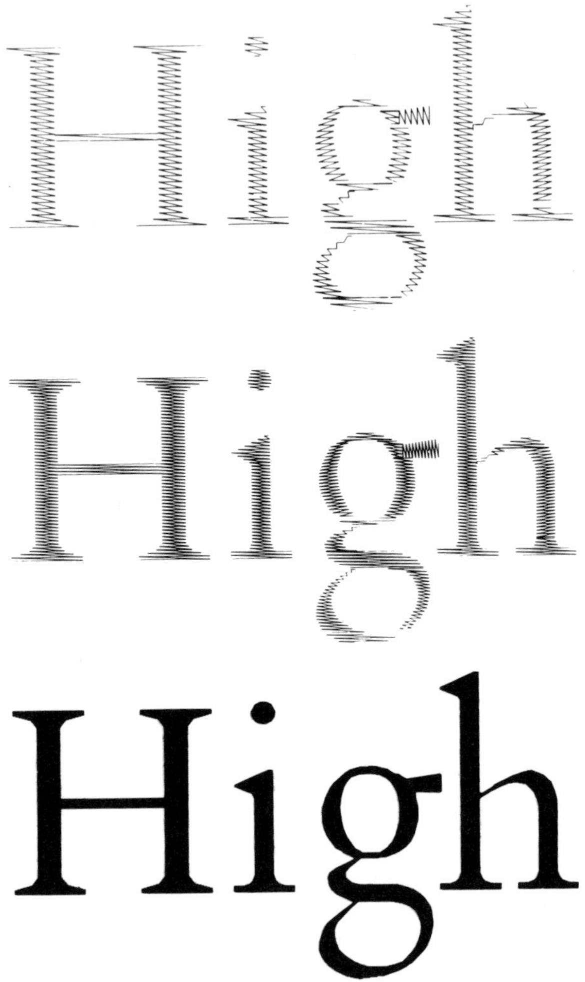

Figure 5 Changing stroke spacing.

when in use it is converted to a compact in-core representation which can be interpreted rapidly by the program displaying a text. The character form is produced either by a program using the output of a picture scanner, or by hand generation, and can be edited by another program which gives immediate feedback on a CRT display of the effect of each change on the graphical form it represents. This editor has been found useful in identifying the factors which influence the subjective quality of letter forms and some research into centering and spacing characters has had startling results which will be reported elsewhere. Here it is claimed simply that such a facility is required to put a digitized graphic arts quality font in good order.

LINE DIAGRAMS

The production of simple line features, such as rules, can be done using few special "characters" in an augmented, or alternative, font. The control program mentioned above, has the facility for sizing, positioning and repeating characters and for selecting arbitrary fonts, and nothing new is therefore needed to make simple line diagrams, displayed mathematical expressions, and tables.

When this is not satisfactory, for example when a smooth curve is being drawn, a simple facility allows the font descriptions to be bypassed and the source data to contain drawing commands embedded in the text. This is also the means by which the font can be augmented temporarily with special characters wanted for one use only. Figure 6 shows part of a diagram made using this method. The boxes and other symbols are part of a special font, the ellipses and interconnecting lines are embedded commands and the text characters are from the standard font.

HALFTONE ILLUSTRATIONS

Many experiments were carried out to determine the factors which influence texture and reproducibility. Referring again to Figure 4, we found that varying the number of dots per pixel was preferable to varying the size of a single dot, the examples 1, 5, 6, 7 being ranked in order of improving quality. A comparison of the results given by a constant and regular arrangement of dots (7) with a variable and random one for the same size of dot and pixel (8) was made, with

Figure 6 A line diagram.

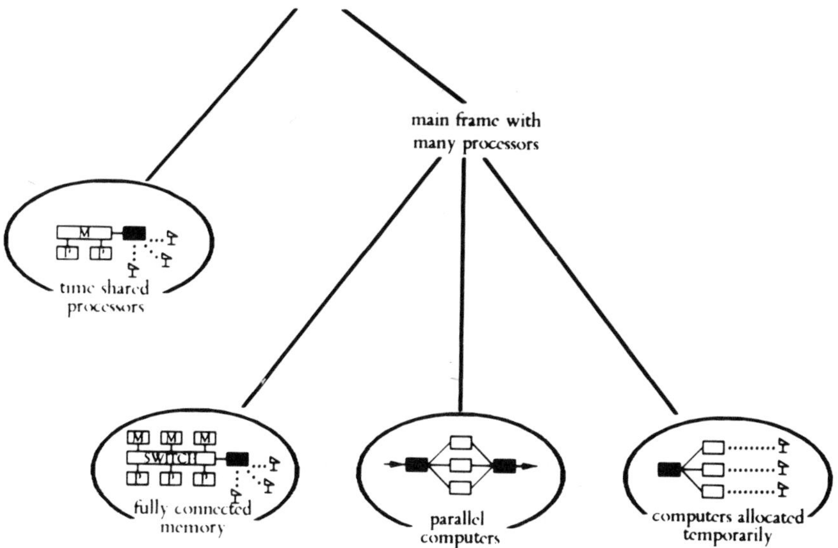

unexpected results. It was supposed that the random arrangement, varying the sites occupied by dots from pixel to pixel would make the pixel rhythm less noticeable and hence would be preferred. However, an objectionable increase in graininess occurred as the enlargment of a test piece shows in Figure 7. This graininess arises because of the increase in low spatial frequencies which the randomizing causes—while pixels have a constant arrangement of dots, there is a low frequency cut off at the pixel spacing over a uniformly gray area and it is this which is lost.

Having decided that the pixel format should be constant for a given gray value, the drawing of a halftone resembles closely the drawing of a text using an alphabet of pixels. The control program is therefore designed to receive a run-coded gray scale picture and treat it similarly to a straightforward text. The run length parameter is used as a command to repeat the brightness parameter the required number of times and the brightness parameter is treated as a character from a special font of pixels. Thus a 32 gray level picture requires a font carrying 32 pixel definitions. (The example shown in Figure 7 has only 8.)

GENERAL ORGANIZATION

The output facilities described above allow any desired graphic effect to be achieved on the Laser Scan output fiche. The production of full page images using a mixture of the various techniques was a prime objective and this paper concludes with a brief discussion of the work we are doing in composing such images and preparing them for output. This work is at an early stage of development and only some rather general comments will be made here.

Very few computer composition systems have been built with the ability to make full pages, even when illustrations are omitted completely. One system which can is described in Wiseman (1973). It achieves good composition standards by permitting a certain amount of interaction between compositor and program using a CRT display with keyboard and trackball for the man–computer interface. The positioning of headings and folios, footnotes and displayed matter is done automatically by the program, with reference to a job description document for matters of design and style. It is when a style rule cannot be obeyed that interaction with the compositor is valuable, and the normal action is that the program shows the page on which some problem has arisen, explains the problem and waits for help. The help is given by editing some typographical commands into the page on display to represent the compositor's decision, after which automatic processing resumes. This method of working has proved very successful and we have adopted it, with various improvements, in the system described here.

The passage of some document from an early sketch, through various draft stages, to a finished form ought, we believe, to be supported by the computer and our system differs markedly from that needed for a printing house by catering for all these phases. The intention is that authors should be able to con-

Figure 7 Screened halftone.

trol the whole process, right up to the final form for printing. Since, in general, authors will not understand the printers' craft in depth, the system is supposed to contribute a minimal acceptable standard in the form of a default style and design (which can, of course, be overridden by anyone who knows what he wants and how to get it).

We allow any document held as a text file in the computer to be sent to the paginator, whether or not this has been anticipated by the introduction of typographical commands into the text to control its format. An initial dialogue with the user prepares the program to size the pages, add heads and folios and starts in a specified font with certain typographical details set (measure, indention, bodysize, leading, letter spacing and so on). The text may be set line for line right, left or center aligned or justified to the measure according to simple rules.

The result of the paginator is a further text file containing embedded typographical commands, ready to be sent to the Laser Scan control program. Two important points should be made regarding this approach.:

1. The paginated material is quite easy to read as a text document and simple text edits can be made to it to change the words or the style before it is written to microfiche. Thus one is never prevented from amending some defect or curiosity of style made by the paginator.

2. The paginated material, even after manually incorporated changes, can be reprocessed by the same program, which will attempt to preserve its format according to some criterion of minimum change. For this purpose it is proposed that rules should have tolerances and be ranked in order of importance. The program then tries to absorb each change by adjusting the tolerances in the given order and only if this fails does it ask for help. This function may be carried out at a CRT terminal as in the system mentioned earlier.

The material processed by the paginator can include text, line diagrams and halftone illustrations. As remarked in the opening section of this paper, this allows the generation of page images with no attendant handwork. It also simplifies the paginator and makes possible the building of better pages. This is because the diagrams will be scaled to within a tolerance of the designer's wish and, during pagination and the absorbtion of any subsequent amendments, this tolerance is available to the program as a parameter unique to this method of working.

CONCLUSIONS

The techniques described are applicable to COM machines, some plotters and filmsetters and are simple to implement. We believe that as more computers have peripherals capable of making graphic arts quality output the publishing and printing of technical material may change radically, and that authors may regain control of the composition of their work. Many activities, related to, but not contained within, this sphere may also profit from the increase in flexibility: reports and memoranda, even business letter writing. A typewriter has always been a poor substitute for the pen.

ACKNOWLEDGMENTS

The system described in Wiseman (1973) was commissioned by Cambridge University Press and is in production use there. Early work on its development was carried out by Annette Howarth, Patrick O'Callaghan, Dick Wakefield, and Peter Wallis, with one of the authors (N. E. Wiseman). A trial version of the Paginator is being built by Thuria Khunji and the containment of change is being studied by Alison Pringle. Advice on typographical matters has been sought from the staff of CUP, and David Kindersley has given much of his time and expert eye to help us with letter forms. Research in collaboration with him is going on over letter spacing and readability.

REFERENCES

Berg, N. E., A full-page real-time composition system: The Designer and User reaction, presented at PIRA Conference on Developments in Data Capture and Photocomposition, London, 1977.

Klensh, R. J., D. Meyerhofer, and J. J. Walsh, Electronically Generated Half-tone

Pictures, Technical Association for Graphic Arts, Proceedings, pp. 302–320, 1970.

Laser Scan Ltd, The HRD-1 Display Plotter Technical Manual, Cambridge Science Park, Milton Road, Cambridge CB4 4BH.

Wiseman, N. E., A Computer Graphics System Written in BCPL, IRIA-AFCET Colloques, *Journees Graphique*, pp. 77–85, 1973.

A Design Language for Asynchronous Logic

A. K. Burston, D. J. Kinniment, and Hilary Kahn

Department of Computer Science, University of Manchester, Manchester, M13 9PL

This paper discusses the restrictions and problems of conventional design systems for digital hardware. From this is derived a set of requirements for an improved design system. Using these requirements, a discussion of existing design systems and the known requirements of designers of large systems, a set of criteria for a design system for large, fast, parallel, asynchronous hardware is produced. Most of the paper involves a description of the ADL design language, which is then viewed in terms of the original criteria. An example of the use of the ADL is included as an Appendix.

1 INTRODUCTION

The design medium used for digital hardware in the past has generally been the logic diagram supplemented by English narrative and flowcharts. These last two tend to be incomplete and ambiguous; the first tends to be too detailed and hence confusing. Because of this, communication of a design to others (e.g., designers, commissioning and maintenance engineers) is difficult. A particular problem arises if a designer leaves and his successor must pick up the threads, as the documentation is unlikely to be in step with any existing hardware.

Communication problems are not restricted to interdesigner communication but extend to the designer/machine interface when software design aids (such as simulation) are used. There is a clear requirement for a formal design medium,

EDITOR'S NOTE: *From THE COMPUTER JOURNAL, Vol. 21, No. 4, pp. 347–354, November 1978. Reprinted by permission of the publisher, British Computer Society.*

which defines the intended operation of a piece of hardware in a form comprehensible by both designer and machine.

Design at the gate level is time consuming and involves the designer in repetitious, detailed work which obscures the real problems which must be solved. Design at a higher level should therefore be considered if certain criteria are met, namely,

1. That the high level design may be readily translated to the level of the physical building blocks, normally gate level.
2. That the resulting logic created be efficient in time and volume when compared with that designed at a lower (gate) level.
3. Preferably the translation should be automatic, i.e., by machine. This is related to criterion four.
4. The high level design should be machine interpretable.

Both the communication and design level problems yield to a common solution: a hardware design language, translatable by machine to a gate level design. Even with a design language the problem of keeping the documentation synchronized with the real hardware exists. This may be solved by keeping the two levels of design in computer files and allowing access to the design via programs which will prevent changes in the logic not being reflected in the high level design, or vice versa.

The optimal solution to the data storage problem is probably the use of a data base system and the design language to be presented in this paper is intended for use with a formal data base which contains the design files.

1.1 Formal design methods

A number of high-level design systems already exist. These cover a variety of different levels of design and are aimed at a variety of architecture, or even none at all. The aim of the current work is to provide a formal design aid for large, fast, asynchronous, parallel systems (e.g., ICL 2900, MU5, etc.). This paper is not intended to be a survey of design languages and methods and hence only a limited number of references will be given. The first (*Computer*) is a source of a large number of others in this field.

A number of languages exist for the description of machines at a very high level (e.g., PMS, ISP, SFD-ALGOL), but these have limited use for actual implementation as the translation to logic leaves too much to the translation system to guarantee efficient logic. Other languages are aimed at synchronous or serial systems (e.g., APL, CDL, DDL) and have limited use in highly parallel systems.

Two approaches that are both suited to parallel systems use a pictorial representation; these are the LOGOS system and Petri nets. The primary disadvantage of graphical methods is that in current graphic hardware only a small part of a design may be displayed at once. The LOGOS system suffers also from problems in that a system is represented by two pictures between which extensive cross references must be made. These represent the control and data structures; this does, however, represent a useful division. Petri nets mainly suffer from the problem that it is difficult to follow the flow of control within a net.

Few, if any, existing design systems completely satisfy the requirements for a parallel, asynchronous logic design aid. This paper describes a hardware design language that attempts to overcome some of the problems. The language is called A Design Language (ADL) and was originally specified by Giumale (1975) and later extensively revised (Burston, 1975); the current version is ADL2.1. The language was designed with the following objectives in mind:

1. It must deal effectively with parallelism.
2. It must allow modular design.
3. It must provide good design documentation.
4. It must translate to efficient, fast logic.
5. It must allow the designer to maintain control over the gate level logic generated.

The remainder of the paper describes this language.

2 AN INTRODUCTION TO ADL

ADL is a language with a modular input, in that ''blocks'' in the language may be declared separately and combined later (cf. FORTRAN subroutines). An ADL ''program'' is therefore a block definition. Within the definition are references to constituent ''blocks'' which have been, or will be, declared elsewhere. These in turn are defined as blocks with further constituents. The input is therefore hierarchical. When all the descriptions have been entered to the data base, a program can generate actual logic for a block. This logic may then be simulated or, via another suite of programs, converted to hardware specifications (e.g., printed circuit board layouts).

At the lowest level of the hierarchy will appear such blocks as a ''register.'' At this stage the design language becomes cumbersome as, for units of this type, efficiency of the designed logic is more important. Design at the gate level becomes both practical and necessary. These low level blocks could be dealt with in one of two ways:

1. By providing, in the language, a set of primitives such as ''register'' and restricting the user to these (a common solution).
2. By providing a system by which the user may input (to the data base) blocks that have been designed in logic terms. This also has the advantage that special devices may be included as and when needed. The main advantage of the first method, the removal from the average designer of the need to design his primitives, is solved in this case by the additional provision of a predefined but extendable library of common primitives, such as the ''register'' exemplified.

The second system has been adopted in ADL. A designer therefore has access to two types of block to use as subblocks:

1. Those designed in ADL, called simply "subblocks."
2. Those designed outside ADL, called "basic subblocks."

Both types are available in the block only in terms of their interface. The interface for a block and hence a subblock is defined in terms of data "ports" and control "signals."

Control within a block is made up of control "paths" of which there may be several; these may operate in serial or parallel and may branch into other paths. Systems exist for synchronizing the flow of control in parallel paths. A single path is divided into alternate sections of "tasks" and control "sequences." A task is a set of concurrent events in the control that occur when the task is "activated" and continue until the task is "deactivated." Activation is caused by control passing to the task from a preceding control sequence. Deactivation is caused by the occurrence of a combination of control signals for which the task "waits." When the task is deactivated control passes to the following control sequence.

An active task may cause the temporary interconnection of two (or more) ports and the setting and resetting of control signals.

The control sequence between tasks may be empty or may contain statements to cause the branching of the control path (unconditionally or conditionally according to the state of some data), the terminating of a path and the setting and resetting of control signals.

The control sequences are assumed to allow control to flow at infinite speed (in practice, the delay is set by the speed of the logic used). Tasks are assumed to hold their state for finite intervals.

Example 1 A typical section of control.

```
T1: 'SET' a;                    (1)
    'FLOW' p ← q;               (2)
    'WAIT FOR' b;               (3)
    'IF' x = y 'THEN' → T3;(4)
T2:                             (5)
```

Task number one ("T1") covers lines 1, 2 and 3; line 4 is a control sequence and line 5 is the start of T2.

Assuming T1 is active, signal a is set (a may be a control signal out of the current block, into a subblock or local to the block). Simultaneously the ports p and q are interconnected (p may be a data output of the current block or the input of a subblock, q is the converse.).

This situation persists until control signal b is activated (b may be an input of the current block or an output of a subblock or local to the block).

When this occurs (normally as a response to the setting of a) the task is deactivated, the flow disconnected and control passes to the control sequence of line 4. Signal b is automatically reset; a is not.

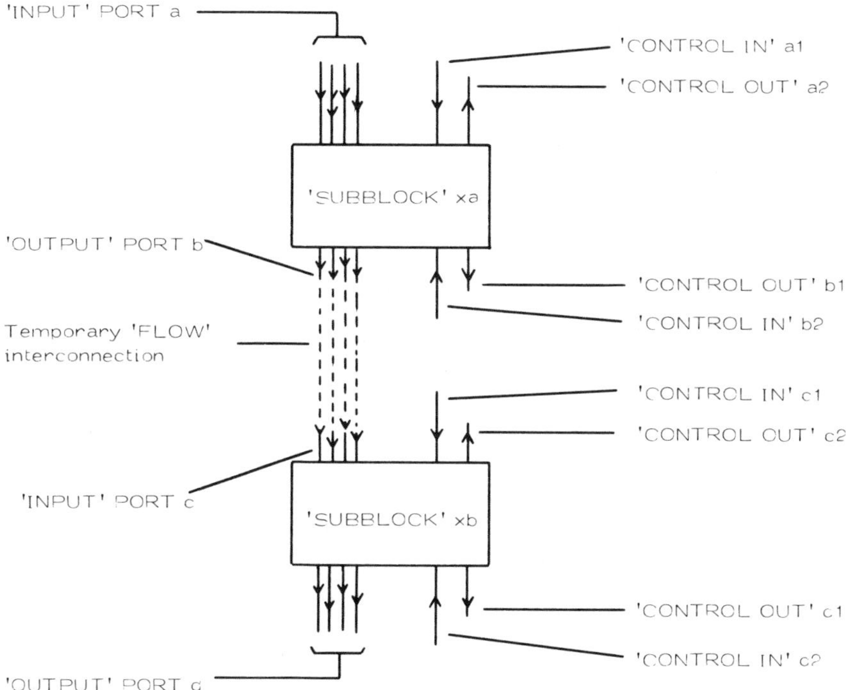

FIGURE 1 Subblock model for example 2.

Line 4 is an IF statement. This makes the decision that if the data on ports *x* and *y* is the same the path continues with T3 being activated, otherwise T2.

Example 2 Data transfer between two subblocks

T1:	'SET' *b*2;	(acknowledge data taken from *xa*)
	'WAIT FOR' *b*1;	(wait for new data from *xa*)
T2:	'FLOW' $c \leftarrow b$;	(connect ports)
	'SET' *c*1;	(set 'data available' signal)
	'WAIT FOR' *c*2;	(wait for 'data taken' signal)

Figure 1 shows the structure relating the two subblocks.

3 A DESCRIPTION OF ADL

3.1 The block structure

ADL has a hierarchical block structure; for each block is defined its interface, the interfaces of the blocks used within it and a description of the control and data structures linking these interfaces.

The interface of a block is defined by the block heading, e.g.,

'BLOCK' A ['INPUT' AIN1[0:31],AIN2[− 31:0]/

```
        AIN2R/AIN2A/
      'OUTPUT' AOUT1[0:63]
      'CONTROL IN' ACIN1,ACIN2
      'CONTROL OUT' ACOUT1,ACOUT2];
```

This statement defines two input ports to the block, one output port, three control inputs and three control outputs. Two of these control signals (AIN2R & AIN2A) are defined to be specifically related to the control of data flow via port AIN2. They form an acknowledge/request pair. This type of control organization is called a "handshake" system. Many other signalling systems may be used based on the setting of control signals and waiting for responses.

Following the block heading are the subblock definitions, e.g.,

```
'SUBBLOCK' SUBTYPE1—
    B ['INPUT' BIN1[0:15] 'OUTPUT'BOUT1[0:15]
      'CONTROLIN'BCIN1'CONTROLOUT'BCOUT1],
    C ['INPUT'CIN1[16:31]'OUTPUT'COUT1[ − 15:0]
      'CONTROLIN'CCINI'CONTROLOUT'CCOUT1];
'BASIC SUBBLOCK' SUBTYPE2—
    D ['INPUT'DIN1[0:31]/DIN1R/DIN1A/,DIN2[0:15]/
      DIN2R//
      'OUTPUT'DOUT1[0:15]//DOUT1A/,DOUT2[0:15]
      'CONTROLIN'DCIN1,DCIN2'CONTROL OUT'
      DCOUT1];
```

The first statement defines two subblocks of the same type. SUBTYPE1 will appear (or will have appeared) in a block heading elsewhere. Note that the port bounds vary between the two occurrences of SUBTYPE1 but the width does not. The second statement defines one occurrence of SUBTYPE2. This will be (or will have been) defined outside ADL.

3.2 Local control signals

In addition to control signals that form part of the interface of a block it is useful to have control signals wholly within a block to allow communication between separate sections of control. These are called local control signals and are defined in a LOCAL CONTROL statement; e.g.,

```
'LOCAL CONTROL'LC1,LC2,LC3;
```

Control signals have an associated flag which is set when the control signal is set; this flag can be examined by the control of the block and used to govern the timing of the block. The flag can be reset implicitly or explicitly.

Note: The example declarations above are consistent with the remainder of the examples in this section. The examples are not however intended to be consistent with each other.

3.3 Fixed structures

Within a block certain data paths will be invariant with time and it is preferable that these should not use the FLOW mechanism which will cause logic to be added to control the flow of data in the data path, but be declared statically. This may be done using the CONNECTION statement, e.g.,

'CONNECTION' BIN1 ← COUT1;

This implies a permanent connection and hence port BIN1 may not be used in a FLOW statement. In addition to merely connecting two ports it is possible to interpose some combinational logic network or form combinations of ports and sections of ports, e.g.,

'CONNECTION' BIN1*DIN2 ← COUT1*DOUT1 & AIN;

The operator "*" implies a concatenation of the bits of the port with those of another and the operator "&" implies a bit by bit logical "and" of two ports or "multiports."

Single wires of a port or a contiguous group of wires (called a "slice") may be referenced by subscripting a port name (e.g., BIN1[1] or COUT1[– 12: – 4]). Other operators are the binary "or," "equivalence," "not equivalence," and "equals" (already encountered in example 1, this yields a single bit result from two multibit operands), the unary "not," "and," "or" and "equivalence" (the last three yielding a single bit result). Brackets may be used to override precedence. Constant information may be included as a bit pattern, defined as a binary/hexadecimal constant, e.g.,

101@A0 which represents the bit string 10110100000

The fixed interconnection system may be extended to control signals if the interaction of two interfaces is simple, e.g.,

'CONNECTION' 'CONTROL' BCIN1 ← CCOUT1;

i.e., each time that CCOUT1 is set (inside C) BCIN1 is set (the flag in B is set). Expressions may not appear and control and data may not be connected. A pipeline connection may be defined between ports with acknowledge and request signals by a CONNECTION statement, e.g.,

'CONNECTION' 'ALL' DIN1 ← AIN

This is equivalent to:

'CONNECTION DIN1 ← AIN2,
'CONTROL' DIN1R ← AIN2A,
'CONTROL' AIN2R ← DIN1A;

3.4 The Initial State

When a digital system is initially "powered up," a predefined state must be set into all the storage elements within it to ensure correct operation. This is normally achieved by a general reset signal. An ADL block requires that all control signal flags and tasks be initialized by the general reset signal. All tasks and control flags are set into the inactive state except those excluded by an INITIALIZE or INITIALIZE CONTROL statement, which are set as active, e.g.,

```
'INITIALIZE' T1,T2,T3;
'INITIALIZE CONTROL' ACIN1,LC1;
```

3.5 Control Section

After the declarations of static structures for the block is a description of the dynamic data and control structures in the "control section." This is delimited by BEGIN and END statements, e.g.,

```
'BEGIN';     'END';
```

Two subsections may appear at the head of the control section. The MACRO section defines any commonly occurring control paths (see 3.12). The DECISION section defines any isolated control sequences that may appear (see 3.9).

3.6 Tasks

A task is delimited by the task label and a timing statement of which the WAIT FOR statement is the most common, e.g.,

```
T45: statements
     'WAIT FOR' LC1;
```

The WAIT FOR statement has the effect of suspending the control within the task until the flag associated with the named control signal becomes active at which time the task is deactivated and the control sequence after the task executed. The flag for the control signal is automatically reset.

If two or more concurrent actions are initiated by the task the correct conditions for termination may require two or more responses; this may be represented by the AND operator, e.g.,

```
'WAIT FOR' BCOUT1 & BCOUT2;
```

Both flags are reset. Another possible termination condition may be to wait for a response from one or two or more sources which are mutually exclusive; the OR operator achieves this, e.g.,

```
'WAIT FOR' LC1 + LC2;
```

No other operators are meaningful in control expressions but combinations of "+" and "&" may be used.

3.7 Data flows

Within a task a data flow is specified using a FLOW statement, e.g.,

'FLOW' BIN1 ← COUT1;

This causes a temporary interconnection of the ports, normally a control signal into block B will be set to inform it that data is available. A single port may be "flowed" from many sources at different times. The FLOW statement may have all the options concerning expressions used in a CONNECTION statement. Control signals may not be used.

3.8 Control Signal Setting and Resetting

Setting of a control signal is accomplished with the SET statement, e.g.,

'SET' LC1, ACOUT1, CCIN1;

This may appear within a task, in which case the control signal is set when the task is activated, or in a control sequence, in which case the control signal is set when control passes through that statement.

Resetting of control signals is normally done implicitly by using the WAIT FOR statement but may be done explicitly by using the RESET statement, e.g.,

'RESET' LC1, ACIN1, CCOUT1;

This may appear anywhere that a SET statement may appear.

3.9 Control Transfer in a Parallel Environment

Control paths must be able to vary their courses or split into more than one path, both conditionally and unconditionally. This is achieved by sequencing statements. The simplest of these is the GO TO (→) statement, e.g.,

→ T1;
→ (T2,T3);

The first form specifies that the control path is to continue with the activation of task 1. The second form indicates that tasks 2 and 3 are to be activated simultaneously. The section after the arrow is called a destination. The next sequencing statement is the IF statement which allows a simple conditional control transfer, e.g.,

'IF' COUT1 = @8000 'THEN'→ (T4,T5);

Any data expression yielding a single bit result may be used.

A second form of conditional sequencing instruction is a general switch called the DECODE statement, e.g.,

'DECODE' BOUT1[1:3] → [T1,(T2,T3),T4];

Control will be transferred to all destinations for which the corresponding bit of the port slice is at a logical one. If they are all zero this has the effect of a NO GO statement (see below).

Finally, it is possible to terminate the execution of a control path by use of the NO GO statement, which indicates no further statements are to be obeyed in that path, e.g.,

*;

A "*" may also appear as a destination in any of the preceding statements and indicates a null control transfer. The first three of the preceding statements may operate in one of two modes, serial or parallel. In parallel mode, not only is the current statement evaluated but the next one as well, irrespective of any conditions. In serial mode, the statement itself is evaluated first and *then* the next one, conditionally. Switching between the two modes is done using the parallel marker (//) and serial marker (#). Serial is selected by default at the head of a control sequence, e.g.,

```
T1: statements
      'WAIT FOR' condition;
      'IF' condition 'THEN' → T3;
      → T4;
T2:
```

In this case either task 3 or task 4 follows task 1.

```
T1: statements
      'WAIT FOR' condition;
      'IF' condition 'THEN' → T3;
//      → T4;
T2:
```

In this case tasks 2 and 4 will be activated after task one irrespective of the condition; task 3 will only be activated if the condition is satisfied.

In order to provide a facility for multilevel decision making and to allow the sharing of identical control sequences, a facility called a DECISION is implemented. These are declared at the head of the control section in a decision section delimited by DECISION and END DECISION statements, e.g.,

'DECISION'; 'END DECISION';

They consist of a decision label followed by a control sequence, e.g.,

D1: control sequence

A decision label may replace a task label in any destination.

3.10 Priority Selection

In a parallel system two or more control paths in the same block or different blocks may request the action of another control path by setting a control signal. Assuming only one request can be handled at one time a decision must be made between them. This may be done in the requested control path in ADL by means of the PRIORITY WAIT/PRIORITY BLOCK mechanism. This is divided into two parts; firstly, a special type of subblock is declared called a priority block, e.g.,

```
'PRIORITY BLOCK' PTYPE1—
    E [4'INPUT' EIN1 1:3],
    F [4'INPUT' FIN1 1:3];
```

This defines two priority blocks of type PTYPE1 which are capable of deciding between four conflicting requests. This is used in a PRIORITY WAIT statement which replaces the WAIT FOR statement after a task, e.g.,

```
T1: 'PRIORITY WAIT' E—
    P1: 'WHEN' LC1 'THEN' → T2,
    P2: 'WHEN' LC2 'THEN' → T3,
    P3: 'WHEN' LC3 'THEN' → T4,
    P4: 'WHEN' ACIN1 'THEN' → T5;
```

The effect is as follows: assuming task 1 is active when one (or more) of the named control signals occurs, the states of all four control signals are statiscised and presented to four input terminals of the priority block along with a special "start decision" signal. After a delay a 'decision made' signal will be set by the priority block and *one* of the four output wires will be active corresponding to one of the active control signals. This will cause control to pass to *one* of tasks 2 to 5. The selected control signal will be reset. A priority decision has been made. The port EIN1 may have data presented to it while the task is active and this may change the relative priorities dynamically.

All the options for destinations may be used. Control signal expressions can replace simple control signals.

3.11 The Mutual Exclusion Problem

The mutual exclusion problem is one well known in parallel programming theory as well as in logic design theory. The problem is one of sharing a common resource among two or more parallel control paths such that both do not have simultaneous access. In programming the conventional solution involves the use of a semaphore. In ADL a hardware equivalent is provided. This involves the use of a different form of the priority wait statement.

As before, a priority block must be declared, e.g.,

```
'CONTROLLED PRIORITY BLOCK' PTYPE2—
G[2];
```

and two, or more, priority waits using the same block, e.g.,

T1: 'PRIORITY WAIT' G—
P1: 'WHEN LC1' 'THEN' → T3;
T2: 'PRIORITY WAIT' G—
P2: 'WHEN' LC2 'THEN' → T4;

The PRIORITY WAIT statements will be situated at the head of the sections of control path concerned with accessing the shared resource. This is called the "critical section" of the path. The effect is as follows: assume both tasks 1 and 2 are active; when either LC1 or LC2 are set then a priority decision is made, as before, and *one* is selected. The control continues with task 3 or 4. The other path is suspended. The priority block is now "locked" (i.e., no further paths will be allowed to pass through it). When the active path has finished its critical section it unlocks the priority block by using the release statement, e.g.,

'RELEASE' G;

This may appear in a control sequence. After the execution of the release a new priority decision will be made on any outstanding requests.

A task may exist purely to gain control of the mutual resource, in which case a simplified form of the PRIORITY WAIT is allowed, e.g.,

T1: 'PRIORITY WAIT' G—
P1: → T3;

In this case the priority block is accessed as soon as the task is activated.

3.12 Miscellaneous Statements

Commonly recurring sections of control may be defined as MACROs and a MACRO CALL statement may replace the control section. Control signals may be passed as parameters to a MACRO. They form a purely textual facility and will not be discussed further here.

Comments may be included in the text and a mechanism exists for saving these to appear in automatically produced documentation, e.g.,

! a comment;

Compiler directives may be included and are preceded by a $; these are implementation dependent.

4 CONCLUSIONS

ADL is intended to be part of a complete computer aided computer design system encompassing programs for logic design, simulation, placement, tracking and documentation, all centered around a common data base.

In the ADL part of the system it is hoped to have programs to simulate ADL at a high level and to generate block and flow diagrams of the system being designed automatically from the ADL description.

So far, a translator has been written which checks the correctness of an ADL block definition and generates a detailed internal model of the block. This internal form is suitable for use by a logic generating program, a drawing program and a simulator. Work is well advanced on the translation to logic.

In the introduction five design objectives were stated for a design language and ADL may now be considered in the light of these:

1. Parallelism: the mechanism of multiple parallel control paths allows any number of actions to take place simultaneously. In addition events within a task or control sequence may take place concurrently.
2. Modularity: the hierarchical form of ADL (blocks within blocks) leads to a natural modular design.
3. Documentation: an ADL program in itself provides a clear and complete description of a design at a readily understood level. Additional documentation programs in the form of an automatic flowcharting and block diagram package will provide a comprehensive documentation facility.

4 & 5. Efficiency and control: each construct in ADL has a simple equivalent in logic. For example: the ADL control is based on a system of asynchronous control in which individual tasks are represented by discrete memory cells, the active ones containing a logic "1." Other implementations (e.g., microprogramming) are not however precluded. Because of this simple one-to-one correspondence the designer has control over the final logic.

   In addition, the logic corresponding to various control constructs is essentially simple and fast. These lead to fast and efficient logic if the design language can express algorithms simply, which experience seems to indicate that it can.

An example of the use of the language is given in Appendix 2. This shows a multiplier based on one used in the MU5 computer (Ibbett, 1972; Addyman, 1969). A similar design, although more detailed, has been translated by hand to logic and timing estimates made. These estimates show an increase in the time taken that resulted mainly from the replacement of the original delay line control by one based on one flip-flop per task. Though the original delay line control had the advantage of speed, interlocks between parallel paths cannot always be provided and subsequent system modifications have unpredictable effects. In view of this and the dependence of delay line control on "fine tuning" for speed it can be concluded that the use of ADL itself does not lead to a slower piece of hardware and the change of control has positive advantages.

No additional logic was generated in the data paths but the amount of logic in the control paths increased considerably. However, as these are parts of integrated circuits rather than discrete delay lines the package count and cost is, at most, fractionally increased.

This may be weighed against a total design effort, including debugging, of one man-day.

APPENDIX 1 Flowchart Symbols

Each ADL control structure has an equivalent flowchart symbol. This allows a pictorial representation of the control. It should be noted that, as ADL allows parallelism, so the flowchart has branching flowlines to represent this. Figure 2 is the set of symbols used.

APPENDIX 2 An Example of ADL

The example derived from a 16-bit multiple algorithm used in a development of the MU5 index arithmetic unit. The multiplier always keeps the result at the correct significance so that multiplication by small numbers (common in index arithmetic) is not delayed by normalization.

The algorithm used consists of decoding three bits of the multiplier and depending on these adding 1,2,0− 2, −1 times the multiplicand to the running total. The multiplier is

FIGURE 2 ADL flowchart symbols.

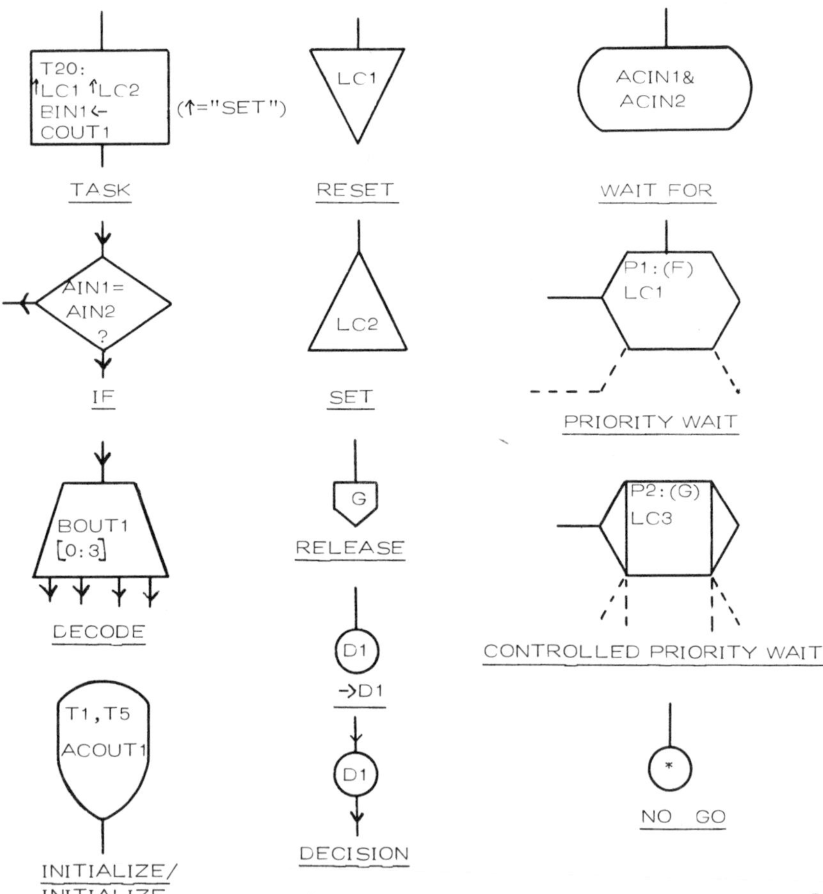

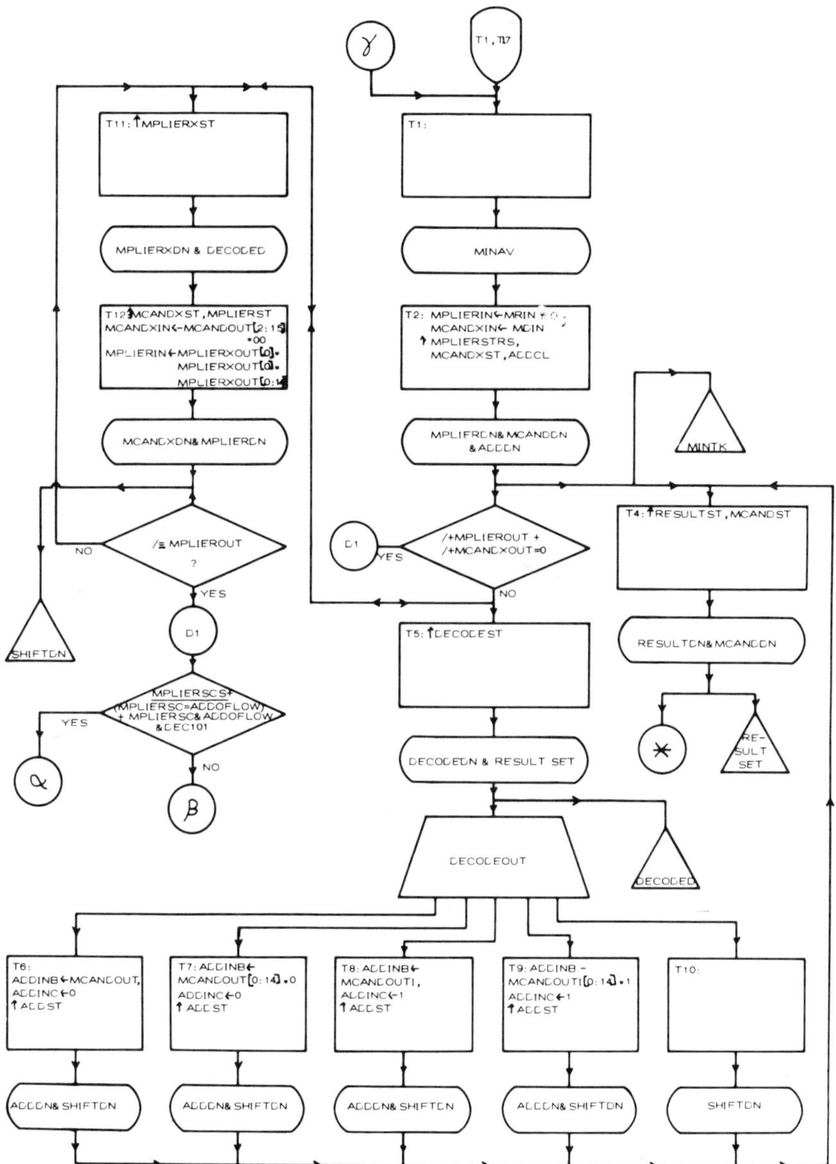

FIGURE 3(a) Flowchart for multiplier.

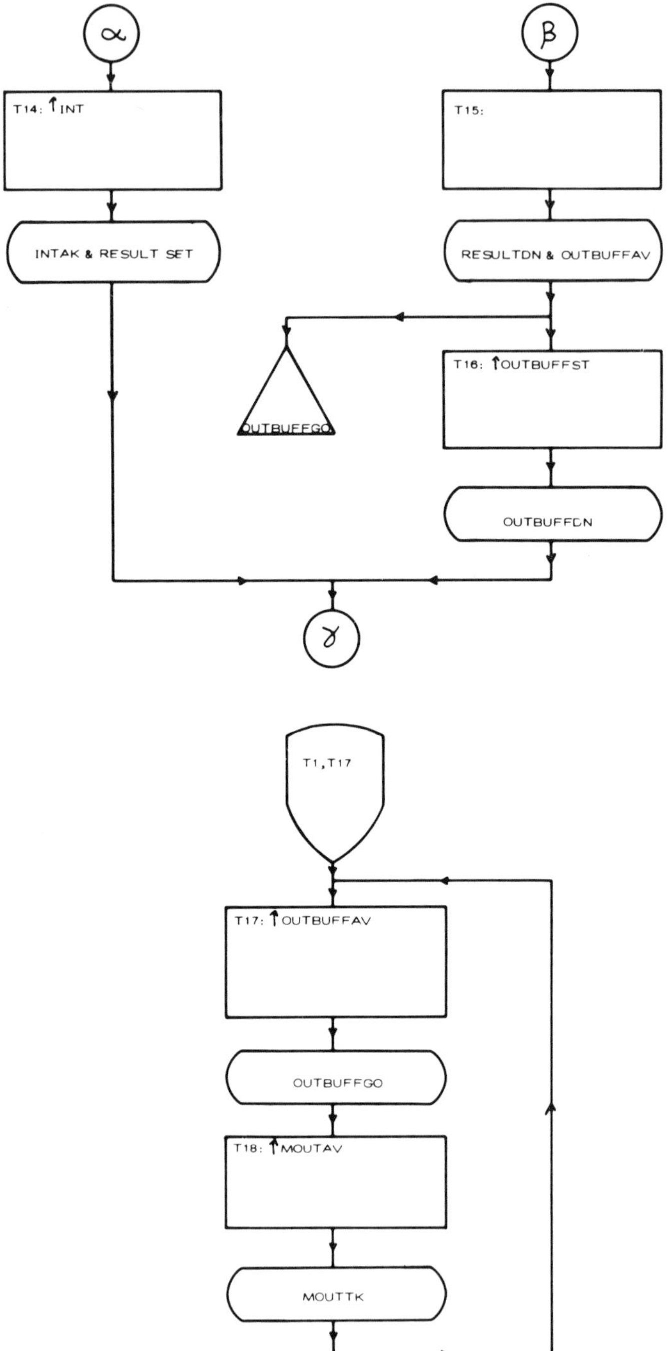

FIGURE 3(b) Flowchart for multiplier—continued.

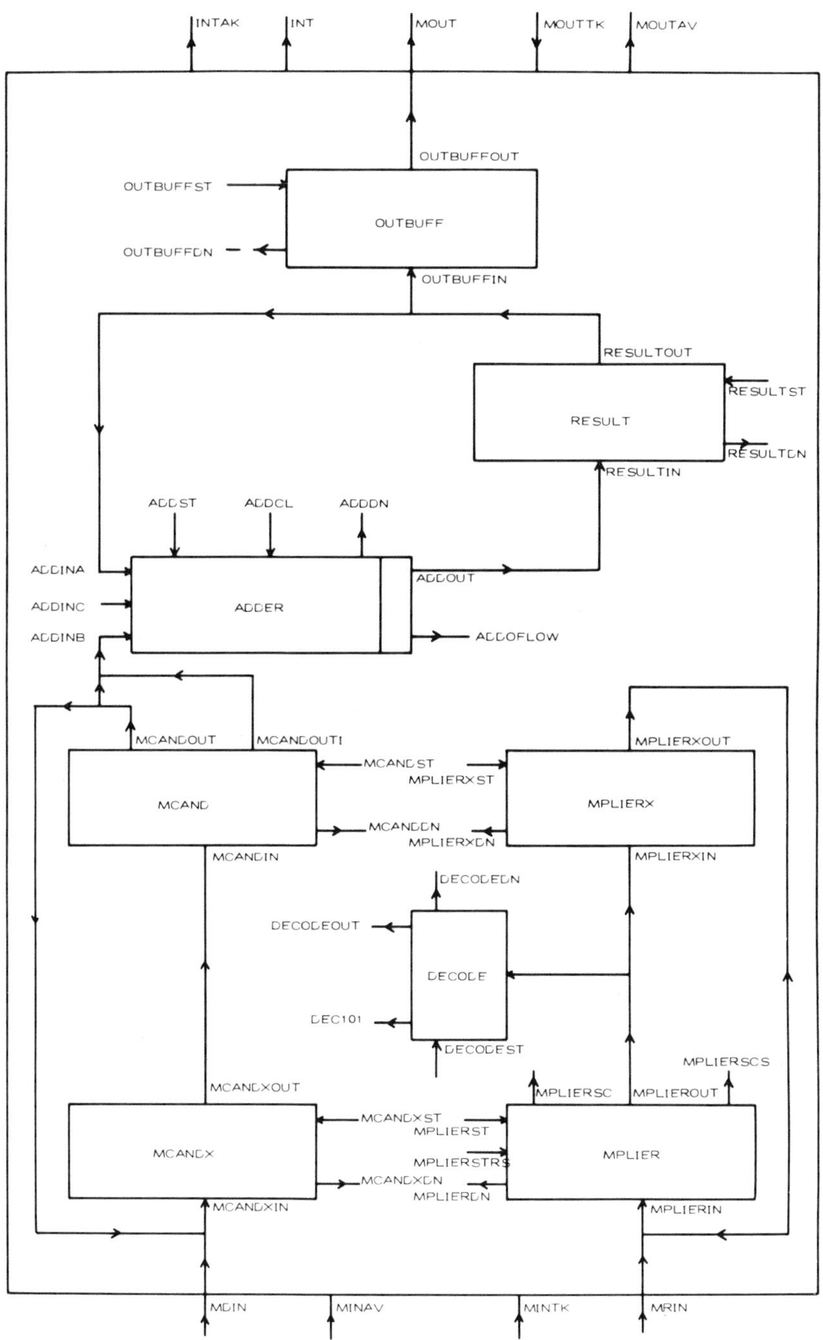

FIGURE 4 Block diagram for multiplier.

then shifted left two binary places and the multiplicand right two and the operation repeated. This continues until there are no significant digits in the multiplier.

The unit is a buffered pipeline device. Data is transferred into two registers MPLIER and MCAND and then the data input is placed in a register, OUTBUFF and completion signalled. A new multiplication may commence immediately. This will not run to completion until the data from OUTBUFF has been accepted by the outer block.

Registers MPLIER and MPLIERX form a shifter for the multiplier and MCAND and MCANDX for the multiplicand. ADDER is a 16-bit adder with built-in buffer register for the result. RESULT is a register holding the running total.

Adding −1, −2, 0, 1, 2 times the multiplicand is achieved by adding the multiplicand (+) or its inverse (−) shifted one (*2) or zero times (*1). A carry is forced into the adder for negative addends. No add cycle occurs for a zero add.

The control is in two sections, the one starting with task 1 performs the multiplication, the one starting at task 17 performs the transfer data to the output. These head parallel paths.

Overflow for this algorithm is defined to have occurred if, when the multiply is complete, any of the following conditions holds:

1. There was a shift overflow on the multiplier and a further shift occurred.
2. There was a shift overflow on the multiplier on the last shift and the last decoded triple was "101" and the adder overflowed.
3. There was a shift overflow on the multiplier on the last shift and the adder did not overflow, or vice versa.

The details of the overflow conditions are not important to the understanding of the algorithm. Special flag outputs are included in some subblocks to indicate the conditions for testing overflow. Decision 1 tests if overflow occurred and if so an interrupt signal is set instead of the output available signal. The multiplier is held up until this is acknowledged. Details of the multiplier are shown in the flowchart (Figure 3), block diagram (Figure 4) and program listing.

```
'BLOCK'    MULT ['INPUT' MRIN[0:15],MDIN[0:15]
                 'OUTPUT' MOUT[0:15]/MOUTAV/MOUTTK/
                 'CONTROL IN' MINAV,INTAK
                 'CONTROL OUT' MINTK, INT     ];

           !DEFINITION OF BLOCK INTERFACE;
           !(MRIN) MULTIPLIER INPUT;
           !(MDIN)MULTIPLICAND INPUT;
           !(MOUT) MULTIPLIER OUTPUT;
           !(MOUTAV) MULTIPLIER OUTPUT AVAILABLE;
           !(MOUTTK) MULTIPLIER OUTPUT TAKEN;
           !(MINAV) INPUT AVAILABLE;
           !(MINTK) INPUT TAKEN;
           !(INT) OVERFLOW INTERRUPT;
           !(INTAK) INTERRUPT ACCEPTED;


'SUBBLOCK'  ADD16 -
         ADDER ['INPUT' ADDINA[0:15],ADDINB[0:15],ADDINC
```

```
              'OUTPUT' ADDOUT[0:15],ADDOFLOW
              'CONTROL IN' ADDST,ADDCL
              'CONTROL OUT' ADDDN ];

        !(ADDINA) INPUT TO ADDER;
        !(ADDINB) INPUT TO ADDER;
        !(ADDINC) CARRY INPUT TO ADDER;
        !(ADDOUT) OUTPUT FROM ADDER;
        !(ADDST) START ADDER;
        !(ADDCL) RESET ADDER OUTPUT TO ZERO AND CLEAR
                 OVERFLOW FLAG;
        !(ADDOFLOW) ADDER OVERFLOW FLAG;
        !(ADDDN) ADDER FINISHED OPERATION, OUTPUT AVAILABLE;


'BASIC SUBBLOCK'  DECMULT -
         DECODE['INPUT' DECODEIN[1:3]
              'OUTPUT' DECODEOUT[1:5],DEC101
              'CONTROL IN' DECODEST
              'CONTROL OUT' DECODEDN ];
        ! DECODER TO SELECT MULTIPLE OF MULTIPLICAND
          TO ADD;
        !(DECODEIN) DECODER INPUT;
        !(DECODEOUT) MULTIPLES OF MULTIPLICAND;
        !(DEC101) LAST TRIPLE WAS '101' FLAG;
        !(DECODEST) START DECODE;
        !(DECODEDN) DECODE DONE;



'BASIC SUBBLOCK' REG17 -
         MPLIER['INPUT' MPLIERIN[0:16]
              'OUTPUT' MPLIEROUT[0:16],MPLIERSC,MPLIERSCS
              'CONTROL IN' MPLIERST,MPLIERSTRS
              'CONTROL OUT' MPLIERDN  ];

        !17 BIT MULTIPLIER REGISTER;
        !(MPLIERIN) DATA INPUT;
        !(MPLIEROUT) DATA OUT;
        !(MPLIERSC) SET IF NEW DATA LOADED IN REGISTER IS
                    OF DIFFERENT SIGN TO OLD DATA;
        !(MPLIERSCS) SET IF MPLIERSC IS SET AND FURTHER
                     LOAD OCCURS;
        !(MPLIERST) STROBE REGISTER;
        !(MPLIERSTRS) CLEAR FLAGS;
        !(MPLIERDN) OPERATION COMPLETE;


'BASIC SUBBLOCK' REG16I -
          MCAND['INPUT' MCANDIN[0:15]
              'OUTPUT' MCANDOUT[0:15],MCANDOUTI[0:15]
              'CONTROL IN' MCANDST
              'CONTROL OUT' MCANDDN ];
```

```
          ! 16 BIT REGISTER WITH INVERSE OUTPUT;
          !(MCAND) HOLDS MULTIPLICAND;
          !(MCANDIN) DATA IN;
          !(MCANDOUT) DATA OUT;
          !(MCANDOUTI) INVERSE DATA OUT;
          !(MCANDST) STROBE REGISTER;
          !(MCANDDN) REGISTER LOADED;


'BASIC SUBBLOCK' REG16 -
        MPLIERX['INPUT' MPLIERXIN[0:15] 'OUTPUT' MPLIERXOUT[0:15]
                'CONTROL IN' MPLIERXST 'CONTROL OUT' MPLIERXDN  ],
        MCANDX ['INPUT' MCANDXIN [0:15]  'OUTPUT' MCANDXOUT[0:15]
                'CONTROL IN' MCANDXST  'CONTROL OUT' MCANDXDN   ],
        RESULT ['INPUT' RESULTIN[0:15]  'OUTPUT' RESULTOUT[0:15]
                'CONTROL IN' RESULTST  'CONTROL OUT' RESULTDN   ],
        OUTBUFF['INPUT' OUTBUFFIN[0:15] 'OUTPUT' OUTBUFFOUT[0:15]
                'CONTROL IN' OUTBUFFST 'CONTROL OUT' OUTBUFFDN  ];

          !16 BIT REGISTER;
          !(MPLIERX) TEMPORARY MULTIPLIER STORAGE FOR SHIFTING;
          !(MCANDX) TEMPORARY MULTIPLICAND STORAGE FOR SHIFTING;
          !(RESULT) RUNNING TOTAL REGISTER;
          !(OUTBUFF) OUTPUT BUFFER;


'LOCAL CONTROL'  OUTBUFFAV,OUTBUFFGO,RESULTSET,SHIFTDN,DECODED ;

'CONNECTION'
          DECODEIN <-  MPLIEROUT[14:16],
          MPLIERXIN<-  MPLIEROUT[0:15 ],
          MCANDIN  <-  MCANDXOUT,
          RESULTIN <-  ADDOUT,
          OUTBUFFIN<-  RESULTOUT,
          MOUT     <-  OUTBUFFOUT,
          ADDINA   <-  RESULTOUT;
          !(1) PERMANENT DATA CONNECTION;


'INITIALIZE' T1,T17;
          ! TASKS INITIALLY ACTIVE ON 'POWER UP';


'BEGIN';


'DECISIONS' ;
       D1: ! TEST TO SEE IF OVERFLOW OCCURRED;
           'IF' MPLIERSCS  + 'NOT' (MPLIERSC = ADDOFLOW) +
           MPLIERSC &ADDOFLOW & DEC101 'THEN'  ->  T14;
           -> T15;
'END DECISIONS' ;

       T1: 'WAIT FOR' MINAV;
```

```
       !ANY DATA TO PROCESS?;

   T2: ! COPY DATA FROM INPUTS TO REGISTERS AND RESET
       ALL FLAGS;
       'FLOW'  MPLIERIN <- MRIN * 0 ;
       'FLOW'  MCANDXIN <- MDIN ;
       'SET'   MPLIERSTRS,MCANDXST,ADDCL;
       'WAIT FOR' MPLIERDN&MCANDDN&ADDDN;
       'SET' MINTK;
//     -> T4;
 #     'IF' /+MPLIEROUT + /+ MCANDXOUT = 0 'THEN' -> D1;
       !IF EITHER OPERAND IS ZERO THEN EXIT;
       -> (T11,T5);

   T4: 'SET' RESULTST,MCANDST;
       !COPY ADDER OUTPUT TO RESULT REGISTER AND
        COMPLETE SECOND HALF OF MULTIPLICAND SHIFT;
       'WAIT FOR' RESULTDN&MCANDDN;
       'SET' RESULTSET;
       ! SET LOCAL CONTROL TO INDICATE COMPLETION;
       *;
       !TERMINATE CONTROL PATH;

   T5: 'SET' DECODEST;
       !START DECODING OF TRIPLE;
       'WAIT FOR' DECODEDN & RESULT SET;
       !WAIT FOR DECODING DONE AND THE RESULT TO
        BE IN THE CORRECT REGISTER;
       'SET' DECODED;
       'DECODE' DECODEOUT -> [T6,T7,T8,T9,T10];
       !SELECT MULTIPLE OF MULTIPLICAND TO ADD;

   T6: 'FLOW'    ADDINB <- MCANDOUT,
                 ADDINC <- 0;
       'SET' ADDST;
       !ADD 1 TIMES MULTIPLICAND TO RUNNING TOTAL;
       'WAIT FOR' ADDDN & SHIFTDN;
       -> T4;

   T7: 'FLOW'    ADDINB <- MCANDOUT[0:14] * 0,
                 ADDINC <- 0;
       'SET' ADDST;
       !ADD 2 TIMES MULTIPLICAND;
       'WAIT FOR' ADDDN & SHIFTDN;
       -> T4;

   T8: 'FLOW'    ADDINB <- MCANDOUTI,
                 ADDINC <- 1;
       'SET' ADDST;
       !ADD -1 TIMES MULTIPLICAND;
       'WAIT FOR' ADDDN & SHIFTDN;
       -> T4;

   T9: 'FLOW'    ADDINB <- MCANDOUTI[0:14]*1,
```

```
               ADDINC <- 1;
         'SET' ADDST;
         !ADD -2 TIMES MULTIPLICAND;
         'WAIT FOR' ADDDN & SHIFTDN;
         -> T4;

    T10: ! ADD 0 TIMES MULTIPLICAND;
         'WAIT FOR' SHIFTDN;
         -> T4;

    T11: 'SET' MPLIERXST;
         !HALF SHIFT MULTIPLIER;
         'WAIT FOR' MPLIERXDN  & DECODED;
         !WAIT FOR DECODING DONE TO COMPLETE SHIFT;

    T12: 'FLOW' MCANDXIN <-  MCANDOUT[2:15] *00,
                MPLIERIN <-  MPLIERXOUT[0] * MPLIERXOUT[0] *
                             MPLIERXOUT[0:14];
         'SET'  MCANDXST,MPLIERST;
         !FINISH MULTIPLIER SHIFT AND HALF SHIFT MULTIPLICAND;
         'WAIT FOR' MCANDXDN & MPLIERDN;
         'SET' SHIFTDN;
         'IF'  /'EQV' MPLIEROUT  ->  D1;
         !IF NO SIGNIFICANT BITS IN MULTIPLIER EXIT;
         -> (T5,T11);

    T14: 'SET' INT;
         !SET INTERRUPT - OVERFLOW;
         'WAIT FOR' INTAK  & RESULTSET;
         !WAIT FOR ACKNOWLEDGE AND LAST ADD CYCLE DONE;
         -> T1;

    T15: !WAIT FOR RESULT TO APPEAR IN CORRECT REGISTER;
         'WAIT FOR' RESULTSET & OUTBUFFAV ;

    T16: 'SET' OUTBUFFST;
         !LOAD DATA TO OUTPUT BUFFER;
         'WAIT FOR' OUTBUFFDN ;
         'SET' OUTBUFFGO;
         ! START THE OUTPUT CYCLE;
          -> T1;

    T17: 'SET' OUTBUFFAV;
         ! THE OUTPUT BUFFER IS FREE;
         'WAIT FOR' OUTBUFFGO;
         !WAIT UNTIL THE OUTPUT CYCLE IS STARTED;

    T18: 'SET' MOUTAV;
         !INDICATE THAT THE DATA IS AVAILABLE;
         'WAIT FOR' MOUTTK;
          ->  T17;

'END';
```

REFERENCES

Addyman, A. M., Some Aspects of the Design of a B-Arithmetic Unit, M.Sc. Thesis, University of Manchester, 1969.

Burston, A. K., The Development of a Computer Logic Design Language, M.Sc. Thesis, University of Manchester. Computer, December 1974.

Giumale, C., Languages for the Description and Design of Logic, Ph.D. Thesis, University of Manchester, 1975.

Ibbett, R. N., The MU5 Instruction Pipeline, The Computer Journal, Vol. 15, No. 1, 1972.

PART III

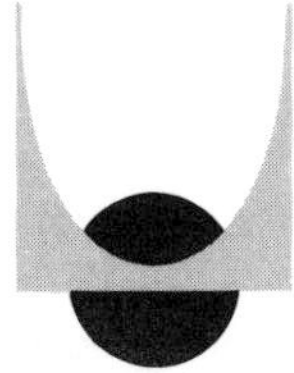

THIRD JERUSALEM CONFERENCE ON INFORMATION TECHNOLOGY

Two papers selected
by the Information Processing Association of Israel
as the best presented during JCIT-3.

"Development and Application of Computer Aided Design Technology at Israel Aircraft Industries"
B. Dror

"The EFT Revolution:
Did Someone Call It Off or Did It Happen
When I Wasn't Looking?"
George Glaser

The Information Processing Association of Israel organized the Third Jerusalem Conference on Information Technology, held in Jerusalem in August 1978.

The purpose of JCIT-3 was to provide a meeting place for experts to exchange views on the role of computers in the transfer of technology from larger to smaller, from developed to developing countries; and to exchange views on the state-of-the-art.

The conference was sponsored by IFIP, AFCET, BCS and CIPS, in cooperation with ACM.

IPA can be contacted at P.O. Box 13009, Jerusalem, Israel.

Development and Application of Computer Aided Design Technology at Israel Aircraft Industries

B. Dror

Engineering Division
Israel Aircraft Industries, Ltd.
Ben-Gurion Airport, Israel

A synopsis of Computer Aided technology currently being developed at Israel Aircraft Industries is presented. The iterative aeronautical design process from concept through detail design is studied, and the impact of CAD technology on it is discussed. A technical overview of CAD software systems already developed and employed at IAI is presented, and initial experiences are analyzed. IAI views the application of CAD technology to engineering design, analysis and manufacture as a necessary modern tool which can produce substantial savings in flight-vehicle design cycle time and cost, while increasing product quality.

INTRODUCTION

Basic Concepts

A little over three years ago, Engineering Division embarked upon an ambitious program of developing and introducing Computer Aided Design technology into all phases of the flight-vehicle design process, where considered feasible and cost-effective. Computer Aided Design at IAI is defined as the synergistic use of computers in the design and manufacturing process, featuring direct conversational communication between computer and engineer, typified by the use of interactive graphic displays in conjunction with computerized data bases.

Four distinct phases of the flight-vehicle design/manufacturing process may be distinguished:

1. Preliminary Design—in which phase various geometric design

EDITOR'S NOTE: *Reprinted from the Proceedings of JCIT-3 by permission of the publisher, North-Holland Publishing Company, Amsterdam.*

configurations are evaluated, and the one which best meets specified performance requirements is selected.

2. Primary Structure and System Design—in which phase primary structure and systems which best meet functional, strength and weight requirements are designed.
3. Detail Structure and System Design—in which phase detail design of structure and systems is carried out and production drawings are produced.
4. Manufacture—in which phase all flight-vehicle components are manufactured and assembled.

Since true design synthesis is not as yet a viable technology, the entire flight-vehicle design process, regardless of phase or system to be designed, is typified by numerous intra- and interdisciplinary iterative cycles involving the following steps:

Specification of system performance requirements.

Establishment of design criteria.

Creation of an initial design based on experience, ingenuity, and other empirical factors.

Creation of a mathematical (or test) model of the system.

Analysis (or test) of the system.

Evaluation of results.

System modification, if required, and additional iteration.

Over the past twenty years, the digital computer has become the major, if not the sole, medium with which engineers could carry out extensive analyses and parameter studies of their designs. However, by its very nature, the computer understands and deals only with digits, whereas the designer/engineer produces his thoughts and concepts in terms of pictures and geometry. Thus, in the past, interfacing between man's creative ability and that of the computer to crunch numbers necessitated the creation of discretized mathematical models, which could be described to the computer only via massive quantities of numeric input, reflecting system geometry and properties. Following the numerical analysis by the computer, the results too were received in massive digital form, which necessitated yet further reduction into evaluation-worthy form. Application of this process in a noninteractive computer environment further aggravated the situation.

This iterative process, being by its very nature time-consuming, error-prone, and overly frustrating, introduces extensive time lags and bottlenecks into the design/manufacturing process, which greatly increase product cost and preclude the possibility of optimum system design. Moreover, the digital computer has not been utilized in the past at its full potential in the storage, handling and transfer of engineering design and analysis data among diverse technologies. Conventional methods of interdisciplinary data handling constitute an additional source of error, delay and frustration in the design process.

Consequently, it was realized by Engineering Division management, that many of these problems could be alleviated, and design cycle time shortened, with the introduction of CAD technology into the design process at IAI. This would entail acquisition of the capabilities defined by the three basic CAD technology components, namely,

Direct interactive communication between engineer and computer—which provides the conversational environment for synergistic design and evaluation.

Interactive computer graphics—which bridges the language gap between man and machine by providing for pictorial and geometric conversation with the computer.

Computerized central data bases—which provide for the on-line storage, handling and transfer of reliable and up-to-date engineering data among all disciplines.

Historical Sketch

The CAD concept has been in development in world industry for over the past fifteen years and has proved to be a powerful technique for a broad range of engineering and manufacturing applications.

CAD was first introduced in the U.S. aerospace industry in the early 1960s with the advent of the refreshed graphics display terminal and other computer controlled graphics and manufacturing systems. The Lockheed-Georgia Company, which was the first airframe manufacturer to fully realize the potential of CAD, invested heavily in producing many noteworthy CAD software packages.[1-4]

Shortly afterwards, development of CAD technology spread to other aerospace companies and was applied to all phases of flight-vehicle design. Thus, in the preliminary design phase, modularly constructed and interfaced systems were developed for accelerated optimization of flight-vehicle aerodynamic configuations.[5-24] In the primary structure design phase, similarly constructed systems were developed, emphasizing automated interface between diverse disciplines and analysis modules.[25-36] In the detail design and manufacture phases, interactive graphics were emphasized in creating CAD technology geared towards simplifying the engineering/manufacturing interface.[37-48]

With the increased level of CAD development throughout the U.S. aerospace industry and the resulting duplication of effort, NASA has recently decided to finance the development of a major comprehensive CAD system which would address itself to all phases of flight-vehicle design.[49-52] The NASA system, named IPAD (Integrated Programs for Aerospace-vehicle Design), is expected to be released to U.S. industry in the early 1980s, following a ten-year development program expected to cost nearly $10 million.

In a similar move, the U.S. Air Force has recently embarked upon a major new initiative in the field of aerospace manufacturing, namely the ICAM program (Integrated Computer Aided Manufacturing). Thus far, $76 million in DOD funds have already been earmarked for this project through FY1982.[53] Possible interface between IPAD and ICAM is also being studied, with the goal of affording the U.S. aerospace industry a comprehensive "cradle-to-grave" CAD/CAM capability for design and production of flight vehicles.

CAD Development Considerations

In 1974, Engineering Division at IAI conducted a feasibility study, with the purpose of examining whether integrated CAD technology should at all be introduced, and, if so, then in which design phases and disciplines, and whether such technology should be purchased or developed in-house.[54] Some of the conclusions reached were:

1. Apart from the conventional benefits experienced by most industries employing CAD technology, IAI could realize additional benefits, namely,
   Being a young aerospace industry, IAI could offset its relative lack of design experience by more efficiently evaluating a wider range of design alternatives utilizing CAD technology.
   Since IAI is not bogged down by historic inertia involving methodology, its relatively young designers and engineers are prone to accept the use of modern computer-augmented technology.
   IAI would not in essence be vanguarding CAD. It is a field-tested and viable technology in many industries throughout the U.S. and Europe; thus IAI development risks would be minimized.
2. Aside from the fact that only one of the CAD systems referenced above was commercially available at the time, most were specifically tailored to the work processes and hardware environment of the developers, and none represented a cost-effective solution to IAI requirements.
3. Most of the referenced systems were developed to operate in conjunction with first generation interactive graphic equipment, the cost-effectiveness of which is considered to be less than acceptable in the present day CAD environment. Associated CAD software was cumbersome and system-dependent. The vast resources poured into the development of these systems and their application in a production environment make it highly difficult for these developing companies to update their systems to comply with the much higher levels of cost-effectiveness made possible with present CAD hardware and software technology.
4. If IAI initiates an in-house CAD development program, it is anticipated that both developmental and operational costs would be much lower than those experienced in the U.S. This would occur as a result of (a) lower labor costs, and (b) IAI not having any inertia in the CAD field. Thus, a fresh start could be made using low-cost present-day hardware in conjunction with high-level software languages.

It was thus recommended that IAI proceed with a broad program of CAD development and application, following the basic guidelines specified below:

1. Establish an "across-the-board" CAD capability in all phases of flight-vehicle design, emphasizing:
   Widespread utilization of interactive graphics technology in conjuction with on-line data bases.
   Computerized engineering/manufacture interface.
   Computerized interdisciplinary and intermodular design/analysis interface.
2. Evolutionary development philosophy—based on immediate application to existing projects of completed subsystems as they are evolved, with high-payoff low-risk items being developed and applied first.
3. Build cost-effective CAD systems based on hardware and software modularity, expandability, and flexibility of incorporating and assimilating acquired software packages.

In accordance with the above recommendations a CAD Technology Project Office was formed and development commenced. The following sections contain brief descriptions of the major CAD systems in use and under development in the Engineering Division of IAI. A schematic overview of the CAD software and hardware environment is depicted in Figure 1, and the system acronyms are identified in Table 1.

TABLE 1. CAD Software Systems at IAI

PRELIMINARY DESIGN PHASE	
CACTUS	— Computer Aided Configuration Tradeoff Utility System.
GEODEF	— Interactive system for flight-vehicle surface GEOmetry DEFinition.
GEOBASE	— Interactive interrogation and manipulation of flight-vehicle GEOmetry data BASE.
ADIDAS	— Aerodynamic Data Integration, Display and Analysis System.
ASRIDAS	— Aircraft Store Release Integration, Display and Analysis System.
PRIMARY STRUCTURE AND SYSTEMS DESIGN PHASE	
ISSAS	— Interactive Structural String and Analysis System.
FLUSYS	— Computer aided design of FLUidic SYStems.
CAESAR1	— Computer Aided Electrical System Analysis and Reporting (macro-design).
DETAIL DESIGN PHASE	
NIKI	— Two dimensional interactive system for design, drafting and NC machining of airframe structures.
DOG	— (Design Oriented Graphics) Three dimensional interactive system for design, drafting and machining of aircraft structural components.
CAESAR2	— Computer Aided Electrical System Analysis and Reporting (detail design).
MANUFACTURING PHASE	
CAM	— Computer Aided Manufacturing system.

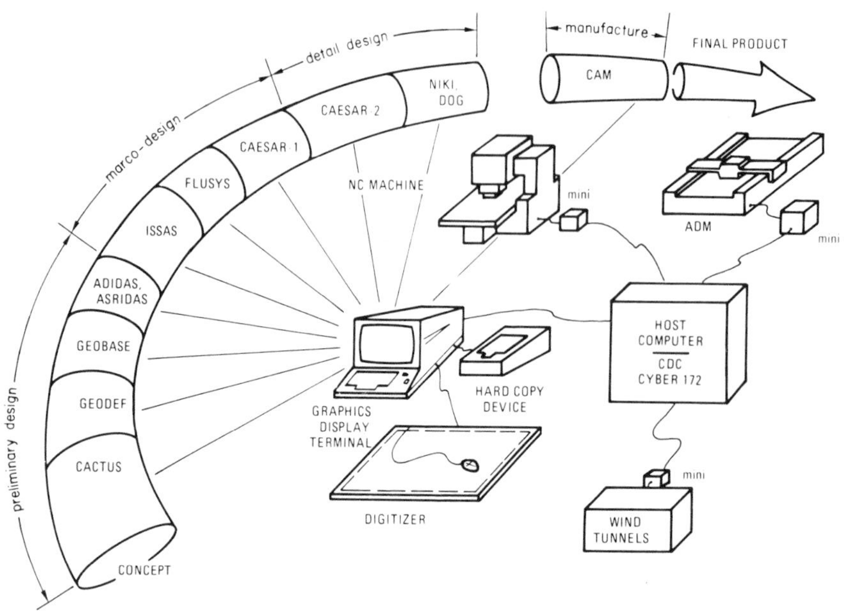

FIGURE 1 Schematic overview of CAD hardware/software environment at IAI's Engineering Division.

PRELIMINARY DESIGN

The CACTUS System

CACTUS (Computer Aided Configuration Tradeoff Utility System) is a modular CAD system which interfaces those disciplines involved in the flight-vehicle configuration evaluation process. Developmental work on this project has only recently begun, and the system has thus far undergone basic definition and initial structuring.

The main principles underlying the development philosophy of the CACTUS system are (a) its modularity and flexibility—which will allow the system to grow, mature and extend its capabilities continuously over the next two decades, and (b) the use of graphic display terminals, which provide the most natural and effective mode of communication between the engineer and the computer.

A schematic diagram of the CACTUS system construction is shown in figure 2. The analytical modules will be based upon existing batch mode programs modified to fit into the CACTUS time-shared environment, and to interface with interactive graphic pre- and postprocesses. The program control executive system will afford the engineer at the graphics terminal the possibility of (a) supplying any system module with data either directly in alphanumeric or

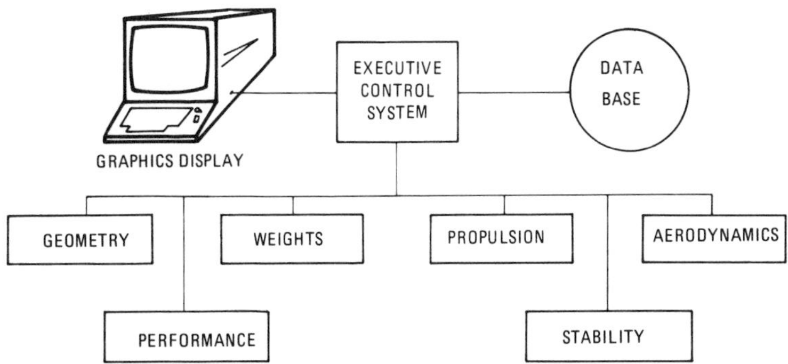

FIGURE 2 CACTUS modular construction.

graphic form, or by retrieval from the system data base, and (b) executing one or more of the modules in any technically feasible sequence he may choose.

The CACTUS system will be similar in construction to other modular CAD systems which have already been developed at IAI (e.g., ISSAS); thus, a large portion of existing executive system routines could be transplanted into the system.

The GEODEF System

GEODEF is an interactive system for flight-vehicle surface *GEO*metry *DEF*inition, either by polynomial section methods or by creation of a continuous mesh of discrete surface patches.

In the polynomial section method,[55] a number of select design cross sections of the aircraft, or body to be considered, are mathematically defined and connected via longitudinal control curves. Each cross section is defined as a continuous pricewise string of 2D mathematical functions, which are conveniently controlled by enforcing slope compatibility at their interface points. The longitudinal control curves are similarly constructed to coincide with specified points, slopes, and other geometric constraints. The select cross sections and control curves provide the basis for subsequent generation of a continuous set of parallel cross section curves, which together constitute the definition of the entire surface. An example of the KFIR aircraft inlet defined in this fashion is shown in Figure 3.

In the Coons patch method of surface definition,[55 56] space curves are established in such a way as to create a spatial gridwork of four-sided surfaces, which define the total shape of the body. The designer defines four points through which he desires to fit a surface, and specifies the two edge tangents at each point. The surface mesh thus derived may be faired, and its continuity assured, via use of control functions which are applied by the designer in the required directions, and which pass through the patch nodes points (Figure 4).

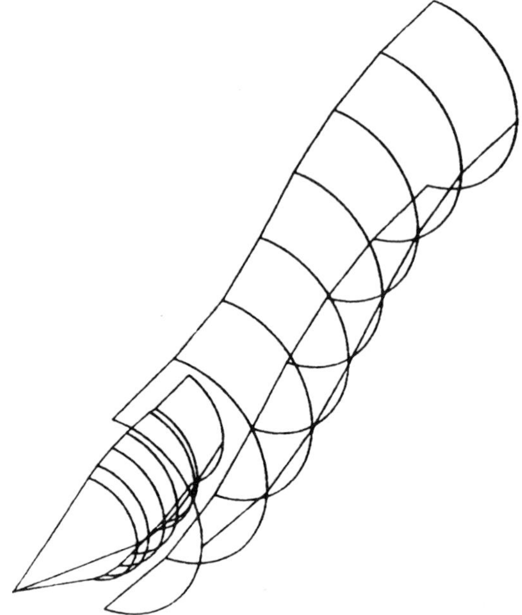

FIGURE 3 Geometric definition of KFIR aircraft inlet duct.

FIGURE 4 Typical surface defined by Coons patches.

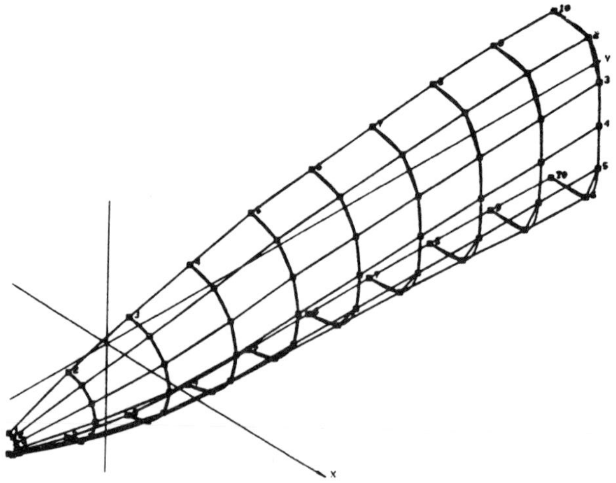

GEODEF is operated in an interactive fashion via graphic display terminals. Its basic features include:

Creation of required section cuts.

Display of desired 3-D views.

Change of control curve boundary conditions.

Area rule computations for a given geometry.

Calculation of points on control curves.

Visual operations; e.g., zoom, rotate, etc.

Generation of files used to produce full scale drawings of the aircraft geometry.

GEODEF has been operational at IAI for the past two years, during which time it has exhibited high effectiveness. Designers with no previous experience in surface definition succeeded in mastering the system with relative ease. The surface definitions are also used to produce cutter tool path files for NC manufacturing of aircraft wind-tunnel models and full scale components.

The GEOBASE System

GEOBASE is a software system for interrogation and handling of a computerized flight-vehicle GEOmetry data BASE.[55] The various surfaces which comprise the vehicle geometry are interrelated within the computer via a set of transformation matrices and are fused to form a complete data base of the aircraft geometry common to all engineering disciplines.

The system, which is interactively operated via graphic display terminals, allows the user to

define the local working coordinate system which may be one of the fixed subassembly systems or one which is arbitrarily defined by the user;

define a list of the assemblies which he would like to interrogate; e.g., if several assemblies are defined by the user, then a requested cutting plane would produce intersections with all selected subassemblies;

define a cutting plane in various manners;

extract coordinate information from any desired surface;

find the intersection point of a line and a surface;

find the intersection curve of two surfaces;

execute recurrent extraction operations; e.g., create a set of parallel sections at a given interval, etc.;

rotate selected portions of an assembly about an arbitrary space axis;

general offset surfaces;

execute various graphic functions; e.g., zoom, rotate, etc.

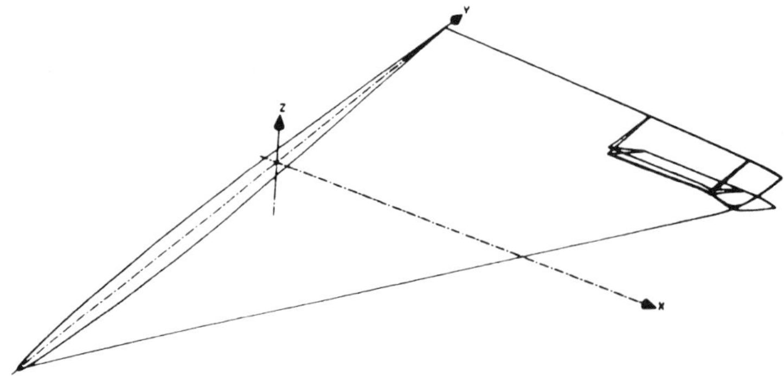

FIGURE 5 KFIR aircraft wing and rotated elevon.

All of the geometric information described above may be extracted from the data base via direct command of any FORTRAN program operating in the Engineering Division environment. Surface data resident in the data base may also be directly transformed into cutter tool paths for 3-axis NC machining of the required surfaces. Figure 5 shows a projection of KFIR aircraft wing depicting rotation of the outboard elevon. Figure 6 depicts an isometric view of the ARAVA aircraft basic surface loft lines.

The GEOBASE system provides for centralized management and control of

FIGURE 6 ARAVA basic surface loft lines in GEOBASE. (symmetric)

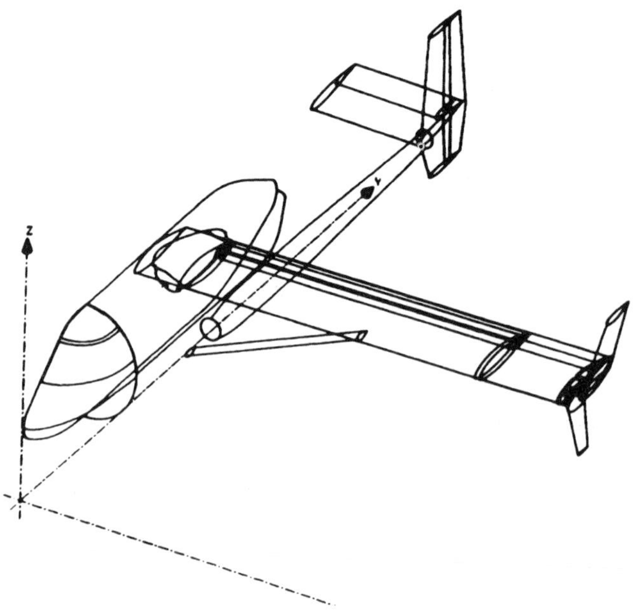

aircraft configuration geometry during all phases of the design and manufacturing process. It also serves as the sole source of updated geometric data, which may be conveniently interrogated by any user in an interactive mode and interfaced with other software systems. GEOBASE ascertains uniformity of geometric data used by all engineering disciplines, provides for close-tolerance manufacturing as defined by the design office, and results in much shorter data dissemination time, while appreciably reducing error sources. The system has been in wide operational use at IAI for the past two years, and has proven to be a most convenient and cost-effective interdisciplinary tool.

The ADIDAS System

The Aerodynamic Data Integration, Display and Analysis System (ADIDAS) is a highly interactive computerized system capable of manipulating large quantities of wind tunnel test data through the use of low-cost graphic display terminals.[57] The system affords the analyst a tool with which he may store large quantities of wind tunnel data in a computerized data bank. The data may at any time be easily retrieved, displayed, compared, cross-plotted and otherwise manipulated in an interactive fashion.

The system consists of two main modules—the data base management module and the analysis module. The data base management module[58] interfaces all data formats which originate at various wind tunnel facilities, and protects the resulting data base from unintentional modifications or deletions. The data base itself resides on a disk pack which may rapidly be mounted and interrogated on-line. The analysis module allows the analyst to interactively retrieve and display data from many tests, either simultaneously or one at a time. The system offers three main analysis options:

Local derivative calculation, effected by interactively moving and rotating a reference line to any position on a curve which best fits the chosen data range according to the user's judgment. Associated with this option are the following capabilities: (a) Zoom a chosen range of graphical data, (b) delete test data points from the display, and (c) add data points by interpolation.

Calculate and display differences between ordinates of two curves at the abscissa values of either.

Display ordinates of given curves at abscissa values graphically specified on the display (cross plotting).

At any stage of the interactive session, the analyst may obtain on-line hard copies of displayed data, and on completing the analysis he can automatically produce a final summary report via an off-line drum plotter. The advantages of the ADIDAS system are its flexibility and the rapidity with which the analyst may reduce and evaluate wind tunnal data from many different tests. The system has been operational at IAI for the past two years, and it has shown a consistent 10:1 savings over previously used conventional data reduction methods.

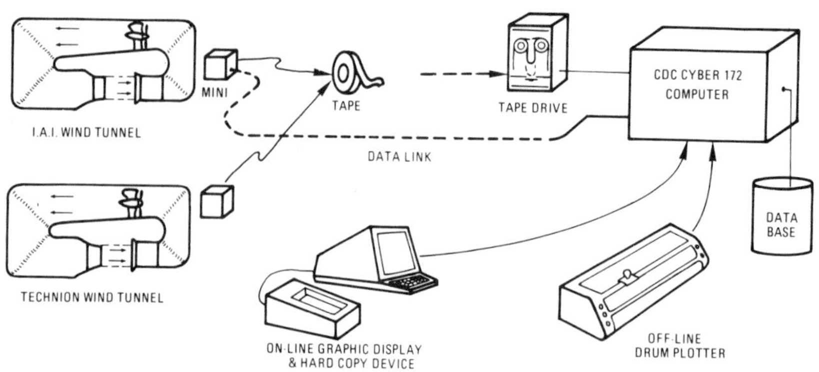

FIGURE 7 ADIDAS hardware environment.

A similar data reduction system, ASRIDAS[59] (Aircraft Store Release Integration, Display and Analysis System), has also been developed. ASRIDAS is used to analyze visually aircraft store release and trajectory data from both test and analysis results.

Figure 7 shows a schematic of the ADIDAS hardware environment, and Figure 8 depicts an ASRIDAS display of store separation from a wing.

PRIMARY STRUCTURE AND SYSTEMS DESIGN

The ISSAS System

The Interactive Structural Sizing and Analysis System (ISSAS) is a modular and highly flexible CAD system for preliminary sizing and design of flight vehicle structures.[60–63] The system is based on the use of analytic program modules which can be interactively interfaced and sequence-controlled via use of low-cost graphic terminals. The ISSAS system consists of six analytic modules and six major ICG (Interactive Computer Graphic) modules, as depicted in figure 9.

FIGURE 8 ASRIDAS display of aircraft store release and separation.

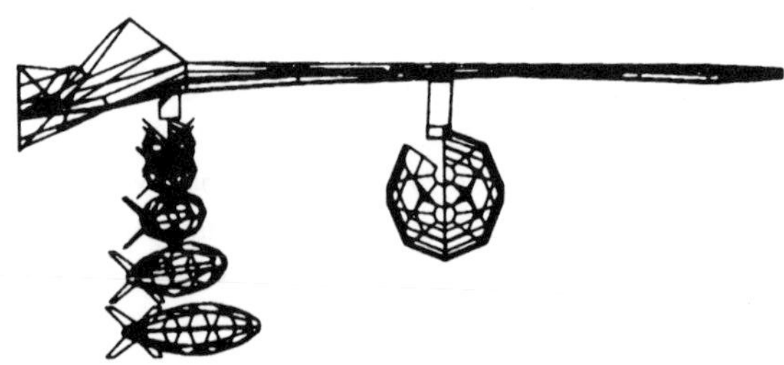

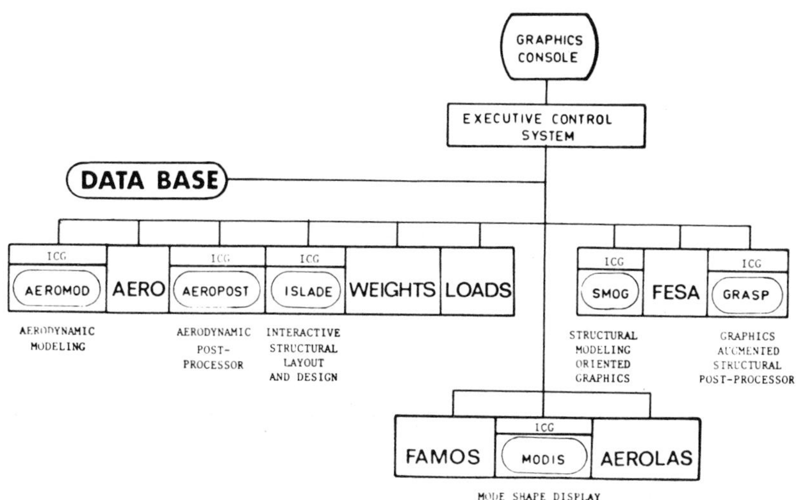

FIGURE 9 ISSAS modular construction.

The analytical modules are:

AERO: aerodynamic analysis module.

WEIGHTS: mass properties analysis module

LOADS: integrated loads analysis module.

FESA: finite element structural analysis and automated design module.

FAMOS: frequencies and mode shapes module.

AEROLAS: aeroelastic analysis module.

The interactive graphic modules are:

AEROMOD (AEROdynamic MODeling module): provides for automated/ICG generation and visual checkout of 3-D geometric discretization data required for aerodynamic analyses.

AEROPOST (AEROdynamic POST-processing module): provides for 3-D interactive visualization of aerodynamic loads, pressures and flow parameters.

ISLADE (Interactive Structural Layout And DEsign module): provides for ICG layout, design and modification of primary lifting surface and fuselage structures.

SMOG (Structural Modeling Oriented Graphics module): provides for automated/ICG generation, visual checkout and modification of 3-D structural analysis finite element models.

GRASP (GRaphics Augumented Structural Postprocessing module): provides ICG visualization of structural strength response parameters.

MODIS (MOde shape DISplay module): provides ICG visualization of vibration mode shapes.

The system is structured so that an engineer working at the graphics console can input data from the central data base and execute one or more of the analytic or ICG modules in any technically feasible sequence. The engineer may at any time discontinue the process and restart it later at the previous termination point. A typical procedure for interactive sizing and analysis of an aircraft lifting surface structure using ISSAS is depicted in Figure 10 and described below.

The GEOBASE data base containing an external aircraft surface definition is first interrogated in the process of creating a mathematical model for aerodynamic load computation. An ICG/automated mesh generation and checkout module[61] is employed, with which grid meshes may be generated by combined use of interactive and automated methods. Geometric panel data is produced in a format directly usable by the aerodynamic analysis module, which computes the unit aerodynamic loads on these panels.

The designer then makes use of the ICG structural design module,[62] which offers him the capability of interactively introducing an internal structural arrangement layout and specifying gages and material properties for the initial structure. The master geometry data base again provides the basic data for this module.

Next, the designer links with the ICG/automated finite element modeling module,[62] with which he may generate the mathematical model required for a finite element structural analysis. Grid and element meshes may be rapidly generated by selective or combined use of interactive and automated methods. All model data thus generated may be visually checked and corrected, after which they are filed in the master ISSAS data base.

Once the structural model is completed, the Mass Properties module is called and the structural weight is combined with other weights and lumped at the relevant structrual degrees of freedom for subsequent input into the loads and/or dynamic analysis modules. The general loads module may then be accessed and inertia loads computed and integrated with the previously computed aerodynamic loads to produce the various design load vectors distributed at the structural degrees of freedom.

The next major step in the iterative process involves accessing the finite element structural analysis module, which may be employed either as a "one-shot" analysis tool, or as the basic module in the automated resizing process of the structure. Two automated optimization modules are presently available:[63] fully stressed design and displacement-limited design. The dominant resizing step is usually determined by the first fully stressed design cycle. These results may be displayed, and based on them the engineer may either introduce modifications or allow the fully stressed design routine to continue, with the option of being able to display the results after each resizing. If displacement

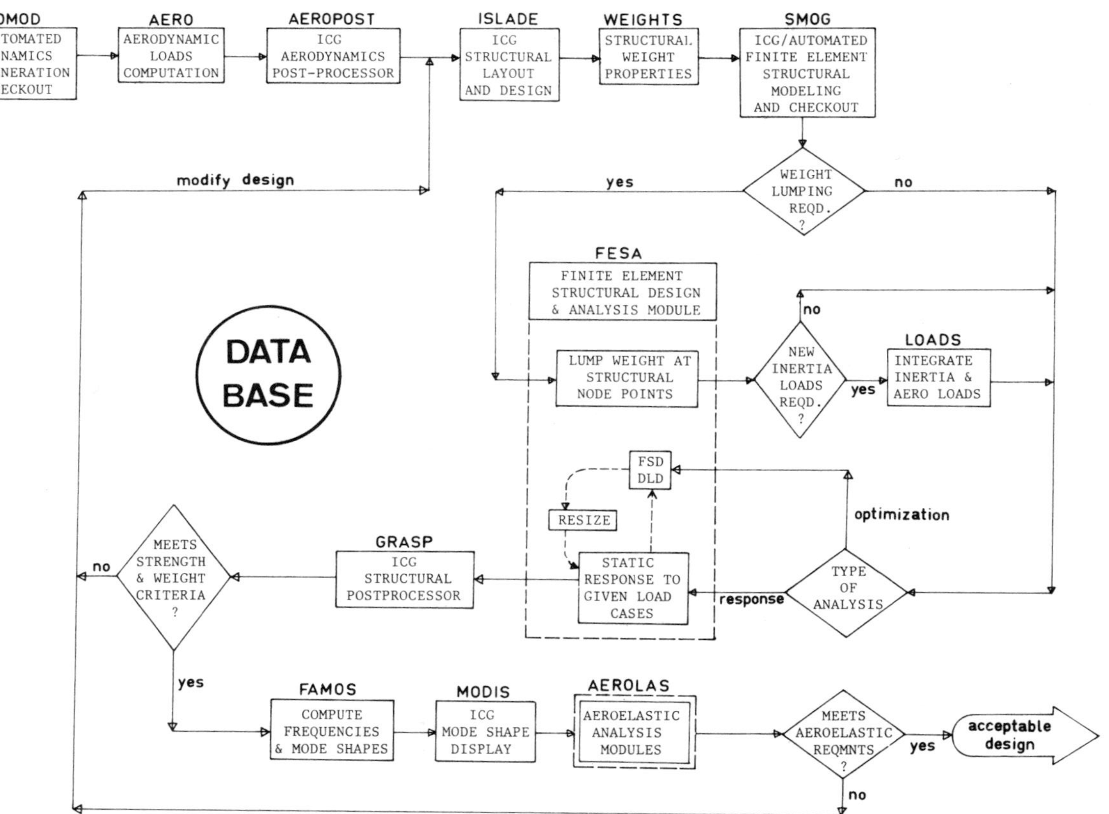

FIGURE 10 Typical ISSAS sequence flow for design of lifting surface structure.

constraints are also placed on the structure and the engineer finds that they are being violated, he may reroute the process via application of the displacement-limited design routine that will reduce the critical displacements by increasing the structure's stiffness. In this way the advantages of both automated optimization and interactive modifications are combined to efficiently produce the required structural design.

Once the structure has been resized, the ICG structural postprocessor module is called. The engineer may interactively select various graphical outputs of structural analysis results for viewing on the display screen. These include deflected shapes, stress plots and contours, bending moments, shear diagrams, etc. The engineer can also obtain an on-line hard copy of the picture he is viewing, or he may request a larger, more detailed off-line plot. Figure 11 depicts a zoomed view of the KFIR aircraft wing and elevon deformation under a given load.

After studying the results and evaluating them relative to the design criteria, the engineer may decide on certain structural modifications to be made; either a resizing of selected element gages and properties, or a rearrangement of the internal structural layout. Both types of modifications are effected by reemployment of the ICG structural design module and selective repetition of the entire process.

Once an acceptable design has been achieved relative to the strength criteria, the dynamic and aeroelastic criteria are to be satisfied as well. The stiffness

FIGURE 11 Zoomed view of KFIR wing deformation.

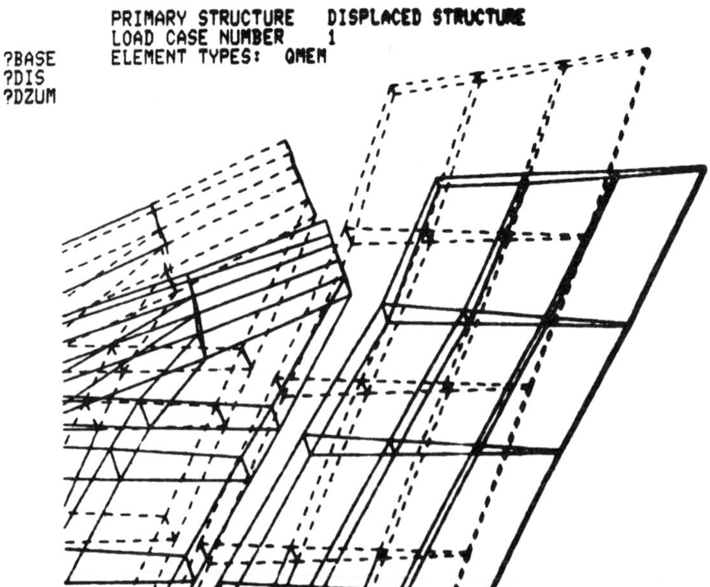

and mass matrices derived earlier in the process may be extracted from the data base, processed and used in the vibrations module to obtain the natural frequencies and mode shapes in terms of the dynamic degrees of freedom. Selected frequencies and shapes may then be processed and employed in an aeroelastic analysis module. If the dynamic criteria are not met, the engineer may again introduce structural modifications using the ICG structural design module. The entire process is thus recycled until a totally acceptable design is achieved.

The ISSAS system was developed with the goal of creating a flexible and efficient tool which could appreciably accelerate the conventional macrodesign process of aircraft structures. This has been achieved by the development of ICG/automated routines which interface standard off-the-shelf analytic modules, slightly modified to comply with the basic philosophies of modularity, data base management, interactivity, and graphic I/O. Initial experience with ISSAS has shown substantial savings in structural design and analysis cycle time.

The FLUSYS Package

FLUSYS is a software package for the computer aided design of FLUidic SYStems. The package is composed of three basic sub-systems, namely those dealing with:

Computer aided design of aircraft hydraulic systems.

Computer aided design of aircraft environmental control systems.

Computer aided design of aircraft fuel systems.

The first two systems are built around analytic modules which are interfaced with graphic pre- and post-processors. These systems permit interactive modeling, and modification of the respective networks and components, and data reduction following the network analysis.

The fuel system design package deals with the interactive graphic examination of the effect of various flight conditions on fuel attitude and flow in the tanks of the network.

DETAIL DESIGN

The NIKI System

NIKI is a two-dimensional interactive graphics system for design, drafting and NC manufacture of sheet metal aircraft structural components and their associated forming tools.[64]

The NIKI system enables the definition, storage, interconnection and manipulation of geometric and textual entities which make up the part definition. The system operates in conjunction with GEOBASE and an internal data base, which is dynamically updated during the on-line design process. A programmed function keyboard overlay is used in conjunction with the system's prompting routines for basic function selection.

Some of the basic functions available are:

Lines, circles, arcs, splines, etc.

Flat pattern development (including bend angle notation and display).

Joggles, fillets, mirror images, etc.

Positioning of standard repetitive symbols (rivets, bolts, etc.).

Creation and positioning of repetitive group entities (cutouts, etc.).

Entering and positioning textual notations and callouts.

Operational software permits entry, deletion, erasure, grouping, extraction and display of the entities in the data base.

Automatic housekeeping functions see to the proper and efficient storage of data, including automatic compaction.

Once the visually iterative design process is completed and the component is in its final form, it may be retrieved from the data base and postprocessed to produce a high-quality drawing on an automatic drafting machine. The same digital definition may also be retrieved and operated on interactively to produce the required cutter tool path for subsequent manufacture of the part on an NC machine, either through creation of a tape or directly via an inter-computer data link.

Whereas conventional methods of sheet metal component design and manufacture necessitate release of precise full-scale manual drawings, the NIKI system represents a tool which greatly decreases the time span required to manufacture a part, while increasing its level of precision. It also delivers as an invaluable byproduct a digital definition of the structural component which can be further used as input to various analysis programs.

The NIKI system has been operational at IAI during the past two years and has proven to be a most convenient and cost-effective design tool. Figures 12 and 13 depict typical sheet metal aircraft components designed with NIKI.

The DOG System

The natural sequel to NIKI is the DOG system (Design Oriented Graphics), which is presently under development.[55] The new system will provide the designer with the capability of creating 3-D definitions of structural and mechanical parts, store them in an easily accessible data base, apply various analyses to them, and at the end of the part design process generate data which can be used by production personnel to manufacture them accurately and cost-effectively.

DOG is a highly modular system. It consists of a main executive program and a set of functional subsystems which perform the various commands and operations made available to the designer.

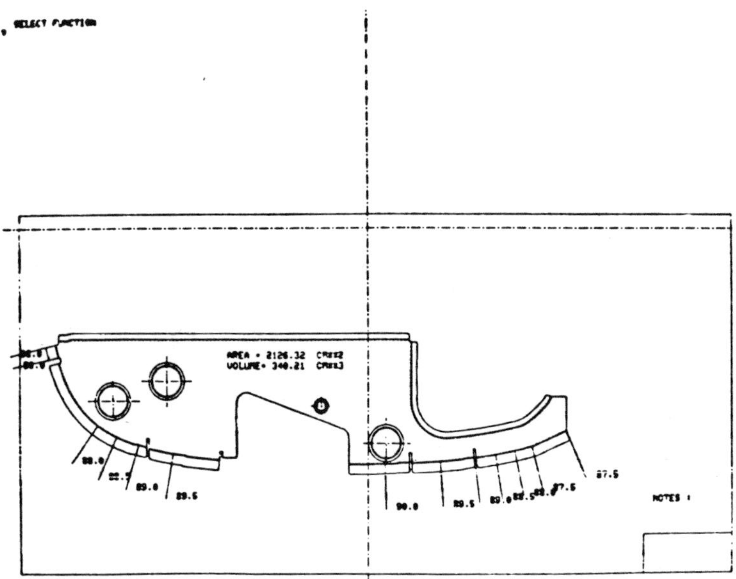

FIGURE 12 Typical sheet metal aircraft component designed with the NIKI system.

FIGURE 13 Zoomed view of sheet metal frame designed with the NIKI system.

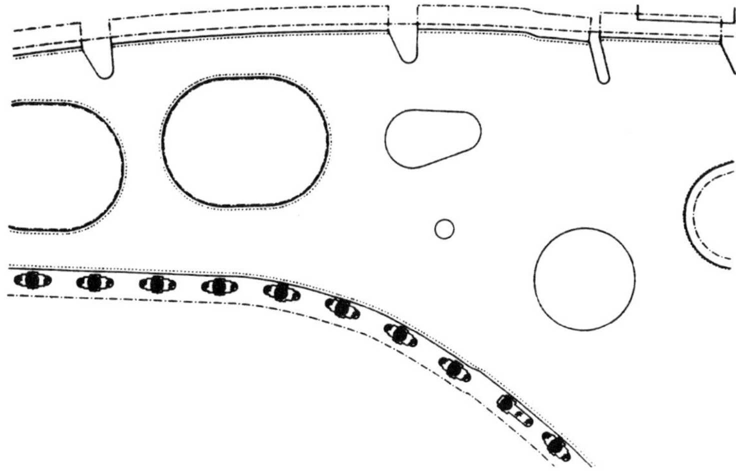

Fully utilizing the system's capability of efficiently handling complex 3-D geometric data, the DOG functional specifications include almost all standard engineering design functions, some of these being:

Structural and mechanical part definition, including section and mass properties.

3-D kinematics of mechanical systems.

Preparation of engineering production drawings of defined parts, both undimensioned and dimensioned.

Generation of data for NC machining (APT Source), on either paper or magnetic tape, or Direct NC.

Surface definition—external surfaces and ducts.

Preparation of assembly drawings and tools.

Preparation of mathematical models for disciplinary analyses.

It is believed that implementation of the DOG system in the CAD environment at IAI will represent a leap forward in CAD/CAM technology which will drastically reduce the time lags and bottlenecks so commonly experienced in the engineering-manufacture interface.

The CAESAR System

CAESAR (Computer Aided Electrical System Analysis and Reporting) is an interactive graphics system for the design, analysis and production of flight-vehicle circuitry.[65] The system is built up of several independent modules which may be interactively interfaced with an on-line data base. The data base is set up during the first stage of the design process, in which the basic circuit layout is reduced to a wiring diagram.

The basic software units of the system are:

A module which enables the engineer to interactively lay out and draft his circuits as wiring diagrams and, at the same time, set up the data base which contains all the information required for subsequent operations.

A module which extracts the relevant information from the data base to create lists of parts and wire bundles for production purposes.

A module which translates the information in the data base to drive an X-Y plotter for hardcopy drawings.

A module which analyzes circuit logic and system behavior.

A module which checks for EMI (electromagnetic incompatibility) phenomena.

Most of the above modules are currently operational. Preliminary cost-effectiveness studies indicate that full implementation of the system will produce much greater design efficiency relative to conventional methods, in addition to significant savings in time, effort and cost.

Figure 14 depicts a schematic of the CAESAR system, and Figure 15 shows a typcial CAESAR-drawn circuit.

HARDWARE ENVIRONMENT

Until recently, IAI Engineering Division had been employing an XDS Sigma-7 computer operating under the CP-V time-sharing system. In 1976 all Computer Aided Design and analysis software was converted to the Division's new CDC Cyber 172 mainframe operating under the NOS 1.2 time-sharing system. This computer is presently supporting simultaneously a total of 60 alpha-numeric and 30 DVST (Direct View Storage Tube) graphic display terminals. Peripheral I/O equipment consists of the standard devices, including a drum plotter, direct links to a high resolution matrix plotter and large Gerber ADM (automatic drafting machine). Additional links to minicomputers driving various engineering facilities, such as the wind tunnels and NC machines, also exist or are being planned. The DVST graphic display terminals used are Tektronix 4014 (19″) models operating from remote locations over voice-grade 2400 baud communication lines. On-line hard copy units are used with most of the terminals and large digital tablets serve as input devices where applicable.

IAI has been operating DVSTs for a number of years and much experience has been gathered about their effective utilization. It has, in fact, been IAI's experience that most picture editing operations, including "pick" and "track" functions, may be effectively carried out with a DVST by clever use of the cursor in conjunction with appropriate software. However, one of the known disadvantages of the DVST is that the nonrefreshable nature of the display requires that the picture be repainted each time an item is deleted or modified. At a communication rate of 2400 bauds (dictated by the hardware configuration) in an 80-user time-shared environment, this has proven to be a somewhat frustrating procedure in cases where busy pictures are to be edited.

In attempting to alleviate these difficulties, a study was undertaken which revealed that utilization of 4014 displays, operated at their capacity rate of 9600 bauds in conjunction with limited local processing capability, would represent a satisfactory and cost-effective solution to most of IAI's interactive graphics needs.

In the light of this study, Engineering Divison initiated development of microprocessor-based technology for enhancing distributed system communications and providing limited local processing capability with the DVSTs. Some of these developments are:

A microprocessor card which slips into a Tektronix 4014 slot and provides a limited amount of refresh capability using the existing write-through mode.[66] Various other utility programs, which reside in the CDC, have been written

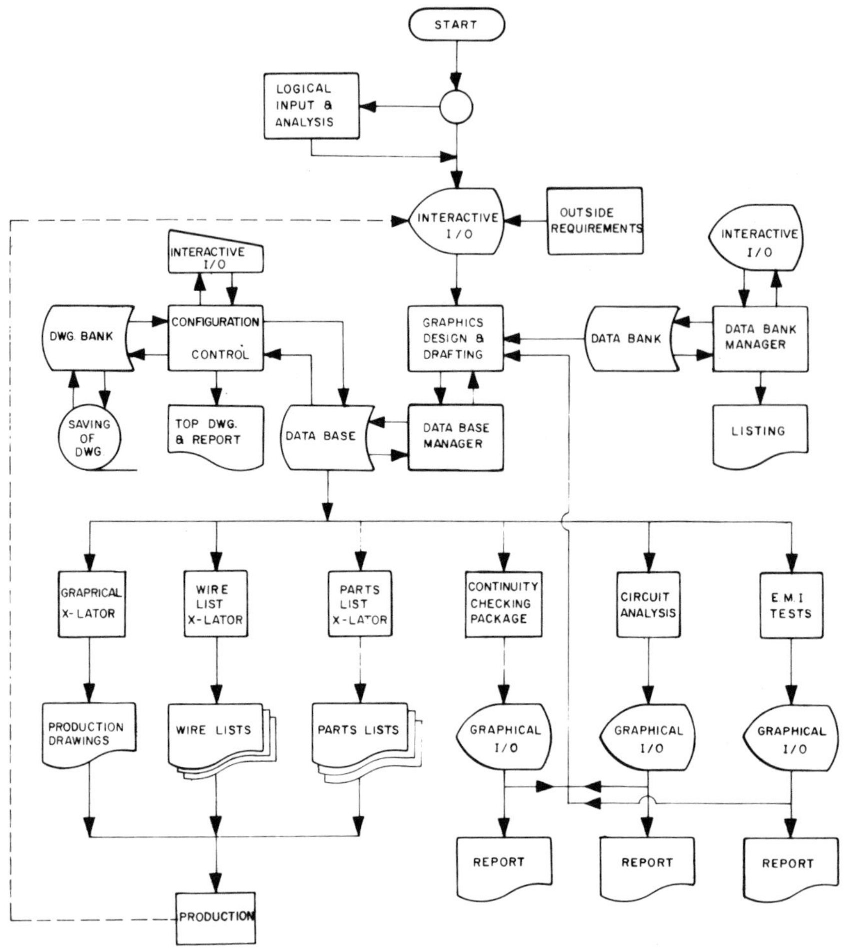

FIGURE 14 Schematic of CAESAR system.

for this microprocessor, and these may be loaded into the local CP for application as required.

A 32K FORTRAN-programmable microcomputer which front-ends each Tektronix terminal and provides local computer power at 9600 bauds for highly interactive picture construction and editing operations.

A diskette-based microprocessor for cost effective and reliable data communication between the mainframe and remote process-control minicomputers.

IAI has also evaluated in detail various refreshed display systems; however, these were found to fall short of Engineering Division environment cost-effectiveness requirements.

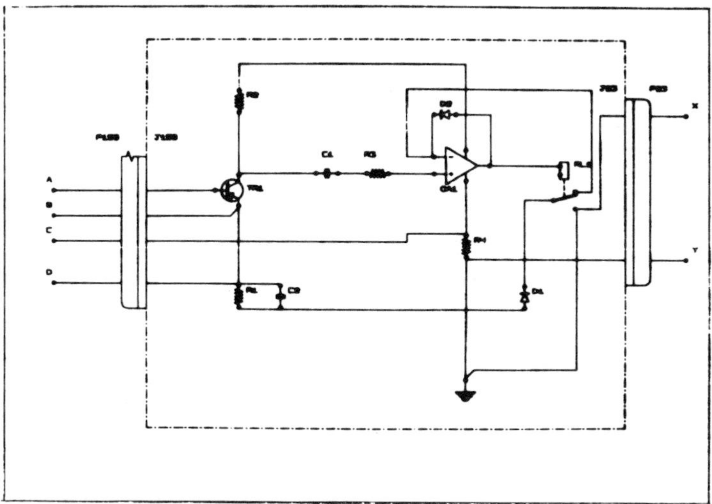

FIGURE 15 Typcial electrical circuit drawn with CAESAR.

CONCLUDING REMARKS

An overview of Computer Aided Design technology development and application at Israel Aircraft Industries was presented. The CAD software and hardware environment was described, and the underlying philosophy of development was delineated. Initial experiences at IAI have already shown that application of CAD technology in the flight-vehicle design/manufacture process can produce substantial savings in design cycle time and cost, while increasing product quality.

REFERENCES

1. Prince, M.D., "Man-Computer Graphics for Computer Aided Design," Proc. IEEE, Vol. 54, No. 12, pp. 1689–1708, December 1966.
2. Chasen, S.H. and R.N. Seitz, "On-line Systems and Man-Computer Graphics," Astro. Aero., pp. 48–55, April 1967.
3. Sayer, R.B., "Computer Aided Aircraft Structural Design," AIAA Paper 68–326, April 1968.
4. Boyles, R.Q., "Aircraft Design Augmented by a Man-Computer Graphics System," J. Aircraft, Vol. 5, No. 5, pp. 486–497, 1968.
5. Vernon, L.A., G.H. Ball, E.A. Wadsworth, and W.J. Moran, "Computerized Aircraft Synthesis," J. Aircraft, Vol. 4, No. 5, pp. 402–408, September–October 1967.
6. Gebman, J.R., "Computer Aided Advanced Design and Performance of Airborne Vehicles," Rand Corporation Report P-4313, March 1970.
7. Baals, D.D., A.W. Robins and R.V. Harris, "Aerodynamic Design Integration of Supersonic Aircraft," J. Aircraft, Vol. 7, No. 5, pp. 385–394, September 1970.

8. Ladner, F.K. and A.J. Roch, ''A Summary of the Design Synthesis Process,'' SAWE Paper No. 907, May 1972.
9. Ridenour, R.W., ''Configuration Analysis as Applied to Aerospace Vehicle Design Synthesis,'' SAWE Paper No. 911, May 1972.
10. Peyton, R.S., ''An Aerodynamics Model Applicable to the Synthesis of Conventional Airplanes,'' AIAA Paper 72–793, August 1972.
11. Wallace, R.S., ''A Computerized System for the Preliminary Design of Commercial Airplanes,'' AIAA Paper 72–793, August 1972.
12. Ardema, M.D., and Williams, L.J., ''Automated Synthesis of Transonic Transports,'' AIAA Paper 72–794, August 1972.
13. Reed, T.F. and M.P. Karll, ''BALSIZ—Interactive Graphics Program for Aircraft Sizing and Balance,'' General Dynamics, Convair Doc. No. GDCA ERR-1736, December 1972.
14. Taylor, R.J. and E.R. Cobb, ''The CAMS Preliminary Missile Design Automation Program,'' ACM/IEEE 10th Design Automation Workshop, Portland, pp. 233–239, June 1973.
15. Straub, W.L., ''Managerial Implications of Computerized Aircraft Design Synthesis,'' AIAA Paper 73–799, August 1973.
16. O'Connor, W.M., ''Evaluation of Advanced Air Vehicle Designs in the USAF,'' SAE Paper No. 730945, October 1973.
17. Ward, R.D. and E.G. Koeller, ''Computer Graphics Speeds and Simplifies Design Development,'' Automotive Engineering, Vol. 81, No. 11, pp. 27–35, November 1973.
18. Rau, T.R. and J.P. Decker, ''ODIN—Optimal Design Integration System for Synthesis of Aerospace Vehicles,'' AIAA Paper 74–72, January 1974.
19. Crookes, W.A., P.J. Cooper, and E. Webb, ''CAPS—A Computer-Based Aid to Aircraft Project Studies,'' Computer Aided Design, Vol. 6, No. 2, pp. 82–92, April 1974.
20. Glatt, C.R., R.W. Abel, G.N. Hirsch, and G.E. Alford, ''Computer Graphics Application in the Engineering Design Integration System,'' NASA SP-390, Computer Graphics in Engineering, pp. 257–286, October 1975.
21. Wennagel, G.J., H.H. Loshigian, and J.D. Rosenbaum, ''RAVES—Rapid Aerospace Vehicle Evaluation System,'' ASME 1975 Winter Annual Meeting, Houston, Texas, November 1975.
22. LaFavor, S.A. and A.E. Doelling, ''Some Implications of Interactive Computer Application to Aircraft Development,'' McDonnell-Douglas Document No. MCAIR 75-010, December 1975.
23. Galloway, T.L. and M.R. Smith, ''General Aviation Design Synthesis Utilizing Interactive Computer Graphics,'' SAE Paper No. 760476, April 1976.
24. Hitch, H.P.Y., ''Computer Aided Aircraft Project Design,'' *Aeronautical J.*, pp. 51–62, February 1977.
25. Wennagel, G.J., P.W. Mason, and J.D. Rosenbaum, ''IDEAS—Integrated Design and Analysis System,'' SAE Paper No. 680728, October 1968.
26. Giles, G.L., C.L. Blackburn, and S.C. Dixon, ''Automated Procedures for Sizing Aerospace Vehicle Structures,'' J. Aircraft, Vol. 9, No. 12, pp. 812–819, December 1972.
27. Ascani, L. and G. Hayase, ''An Integrated Approach to Structural Weight Estimation,'' SAE Paper No. 730936, October 1973.
28. Giles, G.L., ''Computer Aided Design of Aircraft Structures,'' Ph.D. Dissertation, University of Virginia, July 1974.

29. Fulton, R.E. and H.G. McComb, "Automated Design of Aerospace Structures," ASME J. Eng. Ind., pp. 217–225, February 1974.
30. Dreisbach, R.L., "ATLAS—An Integrated Structural Analysis and Design System (User's Manual)," Boeing Company, Document No. D6-25400-0003TN, January 1975.
31. Batdorf, W.J., J.F. Holliday, and J.L. Peed, "A Graphic Program for Aircraft Design—GPAD System," AIAA Paper 75–136, January 1975.
32. Lopatka, R., "Engineering Computer Graphics in Engineering, pp. 475–493, October 1975.
33. Miller, R.E. Jr., "Structures Technology and the Impact of Computers," ASME 1975 Winter Annual Meeting, Houston, Texas, November 1975.
34. Ascani, L., "The Role of Integrated Computer Systems in Preliminary Design," ASME 1975 Winter Annual Meeting, Houston, Texas, November 1975.
35. Rainey, J.A., "Detailed Requirements Document for the Integrated Structural Analysis System—ISAS," NASA-CR-147550, February 1976.
36. Sakata, I.F., G.W. Davis, J.C. Robinson, and E.C. Yates, "Design Study of Structural Concepts for an Arrow-Wing Supersonic Cruise Aircraft," J. Aircraft, Vol. 13, No. 11, pp. 880–888, November 1976.
37. Anonymous, "CADAM"—Computer Augmented Design and Manufacturing System," Lockheed-California Company Sales Brochure, 1973.
38. Walter, H., "Computer Aided Design in the Aircraft Industry," Computer Aided Design, Proc. IFIP Conf. on C.A.D., Eindhoven, Holland, October 1972, North Holland, pp. 355–378, 1973.
39. English, C.H., "Computer Aided Design Drafting (CADD)—Engineering and Manufacturing Tool," J. Aircraft, Vol. 10, No. 12, pp. 747–751, December 1973.
40. Dyson, L.H., "Computer Aids to Aircraft Design Draughting," IEEE Publication No. 111, International Conference on C.A.D., pp. 206–211, April 1974.
41. Feder, A., "Test Results on Computer Graphics Productivity for Aircraft Design and Fabrication," AIAA Paper 75-967, August 1975. (Also J. Aircraft, Vol. 14, No. 1, pp. 77–84, January 1977.
42. Klomp, C.W. and R.A. Gern, "The Concept of an Interactive Graphic Design System (IGDS) with Distributed Computing," AIAA Paper 75-966, August 1975.
43. Coles, W.A., "Use of Graphics in the Design Office at The Military Aircraft Division of British Aircraft Corporation," NASA SP-390, Computer Graphics in Engineering, pp. 203–231, October 1975.
44. Flygare, R.M., "Distributed CAD/CAM with Database Management Common to Both Engineering and Manufacturing," SME Paper MS76-738, 1976.
45. Aughton, P., "A Computer System for Design and Manufacture of Aircraft Components," Proceedings, CAD-76, 2nd International Conference on Computers in Engineering and Building Design, London, pp. 145–149 March 1976.
46. Boyer, C.H., "Lockheed Links Design and Manufacturing," *Industrial Engineering,* Vol. 9, No. 1, pp. 14–21, January 1977.
47. Hanratty, P.J., "AD-2000—A System Built Today to Grow for Tomorrow," Paper presented to Institute of Manufacturing Engineers in the United Kingdom, 1977.
48. Profant, J.E. and A. Feder, "Cost-effectiveness of Two and Three Dimensional Computer Aided Design Systems," Paper presented at ORSA/TIMS Meeting, San Francisco, California, May 1977.
49. Fulton, R.E., J. Sobieszczanski, and E.J. Landrum, "An Integrated Computer System for Preliminary Design of Advanced Aircraft," AIAA Paper 72–796, August 1972.

50. Fulton, R.E., et al., "Application of Computer Aided Aircraft Design in a Multidisciplinary Environment," J. Aircraft, Vol. 11, No. 7, pp. 369–370, July 1974.
51. Miller, R.E., Jr., et al., "Feasibility Study of an Integrated Program for Aerospace Vehicle Design (IPAD)," ACM/IEEE 11th Design Automation Workshop, Denver, Col., pp. 335–346, June 1974.
52. Miller, R.E., Jr. et al., "Cost-effectiveness of Integrated Analysis/Design System (IPAD)—An Executive Summary," AIAA Paper 74-960, August 1974.
53. Winsosky, D., "ICAM—The Air Force's Integrated Computer Aided Manufacturing Program," *Astronautics and Aeronautics*, pp. 52–59, February 1977.
54. Dror, B., "Computer Aided Design Feasibility Study," IAI Report No. 4830/8280, September 1974.
55. Aryeh, F., "Two and Three Dimensional Systems for Computer Aided Geometric Design of Aircraft Surfaces and Components," Collection of Papers, 19th Annual Israel Conference on Aviation and Astronautics, Tel-Aviv, pp. 339–363, March 1977.
56. Coons, S.A., "Surfaces for Computer Aided Design of Space Forms," MIT, Project MAC, Report MAC-TR-41, 1967.
57. Yaakov, B., E. Nissan, and B. Dror, "A Computerized Interactive Graphics System to Store, Display and Analyze Wind Tunnel Test Data," Collection of Papers, 18th Annual Israel Conference on Aviation and Astronautics, Tel-Aviv, pp. 34–48, May 1976.
58. Yaakov, B., "ADIBASE" On-line Data Base System for Wind Tunnel Test Data (User's Manual)," IAI Report No. 4890/14535, December 1977.
59. Yaakov, B., "ASRIDAS—Aircraft Store Release Integration Display and Analysis System (User's Manual)," IAI Report No. 4890/15044, October 1977.
60. Bendavid, D., E. Somekh, et al., "Computer Graphics in Sizing and Analysis of Aircraft Structures," Computers and Graphics, Vol. 2, No. 2, pp. 81–89, 1976.
61. Emil. S., Y. Haim, B. Yaakov, and B. Dror, "Interactive Computer Graphics System for Aerodynamic Loads Analysis," Paper presented at 10th Israel Conference on Mechanical Engineering, Beer-Sheva, pp. 96–97, June 1976.
62. Dror, B., S. Emil, J. Burns, and H. Kalman, "Interactive Design and Optimization of Flight-Vehicle Lifting Surface Structures," Computers and Structures, Vol. 8, No. 3, June 1978. (Also Collection of Papers, 19th Annual Israel Conference on Aviation and Astronautics, Tel-Aviv, pp. 312–338, March 1977.)
63. Emil, S. and B. Dror, "An Automated Procedure for Optimization of Aircraft Structures using a Fully Stressed Design Approach," Collection of Papers, 18th Annual Israel Conference on Aviation and Astronautics, Tel-Aviv, pp. 49–74, May 1976.
64. Aryeh, F., D. Jacob, and K. Eliezer, "Two-Dimensional Interactive Graphics System for Design, Drafting and Manufacture of Airframe Components," Paper presented at 10th Israel Conference on Mechanical Engineering, Beer-Sheva, June 1976.
65. Dror, B., S. Isaac, and W. Eric, "Computer Aided Design of Aircraft Electrical Systems," Computers and Graphics, Vol. 3, No. 1, 1978.
66. Basil, M., "A Microprocessor-based Refreshing Buffer for Storage Tube Graphics Terminals," Computers and Graphics, Vol. 2, No. 4, pp. 205–208, 1977.

The EFT Revolution: Did Someone Call It Off or Did It Happen When I Wasn't Looking

George Glaser

Centigram Corporation
Sunnyvale, California, U.S.A.

Today's payments media and practices are products of an historical evolution that continues to progress in response to economic incentives, as public and private providers of these services seek to improve transaction efficiency and to provide additional services and convenience to consumers. Tomorrow's consumers will continue to use cash and checks, but for many types of payments they will undoubtedly turn to electronic payment services as EFT's efficiency and convenience increase.

The Final Report of the
National Electronic Fund Transfers Commission

A reasonable person might well ask whether the Electronic Funds Transfer (EFT) revolution had been called off, or whether it had taken place when he wasn't looking.

If indeed the EFT revolution was called off, how does one explain the fact that there are approximately 6400 automated teller machines and cash dispensers, and over 20,000 EFT transaction terminals, and approximately 250,000 point-of-sale terminals installed in the U.S. today; or that a major U.S. bank recently reported that traffic through its credit authorization message switch increased by more than 100% during the final months of 1977 over traffic during the same period in the previous year; or that over 2 million interchange credit card sales drafts were cleared recently in a single night; or that on an average day, more than $40 million in interchange transactions are processed —transactions that originate on only one of the several bank credit cards now in use in the United States and in 30 or so other countries. By any standards, such numbers offer impressive testimony to substantial activity on a broad front.

If, on the other hand, there has been an EFT revolution, it certainly was a quiet one. To date, EFT services have been greeted with less than universal enthusiasm by the general public. The automated deposit of payroll checks and other credits to individual accounts has hardly been a big winner. Bill paying by telephone, presumably an attractive service to consumers, has similarly come out of the blocks in a slow crawl; fewer than 100 financial institutions now offer such a service, although IBM's recently announced software package is expected to stimulate the introduction of additional service offerings.

Debit cards, which in their basic form, allow the cardholder to draw directly on his deposited funds in payment of a transaction, would seem to be an appealing service for consumers who have an aversion to the use of credit. Yet, as of early 1978, only 50 banks offered debit cards usable nationwide to their customers; transaction volumes were of the order of only $50 million per year—very small when compared to total bank credit card volume of approximately $50 billion.

These figures, while not trivial, hardly qualify as the hallmarks of a revolution—notwithstanding the knee-jerk protestations of those who have used the word "revolution" to characterize a phenomenon they wish to use as a whipping boy in arguing for or against social change.

Yet it is very clear that an enormous amount of effort—and funds—have been expended on what has come to be called Electronic Funds Transfer. And it also is clear that EFT has become a national problem—or opportunity—that has attracted fans, skeptics and critics in large numbers.

Let me digress at this point to state that my remarks thus far—and those that follow—are based largely on EFT in the U.S. I concede that limitation —without apologizing for it—so that those of you from other countries can put into perspective the conclusions I come to later. My U.S. focus grows out of the fact that that is where my experience lies; it should not imply that the only EFT developments worth noting are taking place in the U.S. On the contrary, the SWIFT project in Western Europe is an ambitious undertaking by any measure; and the GIRO system with which many of you outside the U.S. are very familiar is being eyed as a model of the kind of funds transfer system the U.S. should adopt.

Having thus declared myself, I'd now like to return to the subject as seen through U.S. eyes and hope that all of you—whatever nation you represent—will find nourishment in what follows.

The National Commission on Electronic Fund Transfers (NEFTC), created by the U.S. Congress to "(C)onduct a thorough study and investigation and recommend appropriate administrative action and legislation necessary in connection with the possible development of public or private electronic funds transfer systems . . . ," described today's payments media and practices as "products of an historical evolution."[1] The Commission went on to point out that tomorrow's consumers will continue to use cash and checks, but that electronic payment services would offer than an alternative. That doesn't sound very revolutionary to me nor did it, apparently, to the Commission.

Whether you conclude that evolution or revolution accurately characterizes

EFT, you might nonetheless share the concern that thoughtful observers have expressed about the social changes that might result from technological innovations in EFT. One such observer, Professor James B. Rule of the State University of New York at Stony Brook in a paper titled "Value choices in Electronic Funds Transfer Policy,"[2] stated that ". . . value questions are authentic and inescapable in Electronic Funds Transfer policy." He went on to point out that ". . . not all social goods or values involved—including convenience, efficiency, privacy and personal autonomy—can simultaneously be maximized." Professor Rule's concerns, and the conclusion he draws from his study of the subject, seem both pertinent and reasonable. They certainly are thought provoking.

Does the use of modern technology to accelerate the historical evolution referred to by the Commission alter the character of the changes that unquestionably are taking place? Professor Rule thinks so, likening the differences between EFT processes and their pre-EFT counterparts to those that distinguish transcontinental communications from the man-on-horseback Pony Express system used to deliver mail in frontier days. The analogy is certainly colorful, but is it apt?

Regardless of which characterization of EFT you prefer, it's clear that the payments mechanism is changing at a rapid rate and on a broad front. Yet it would be hard to argue that the rate is any more rapid, or the front more broad, than those that characterize other arenas impacted by technology throughout the world—including energy, communications and health care. Each of these has, indeed, seen significant social, political and economic impact. Change has that effect; and rapid change on a broad front always is disruptive, whether triggered by technology or by a despotic government. Resistance to change—or, at the very least, apprehension about the effects of change—is to be expected even though change per se is neither intrinsically good nor evil.

Anyone hoping to form a balanced—and hopefully enlightened—point of view on EFT is faced with a torrent of newspaper clippings, reports, and speeches, in which literally hundreds of institutions and individuals have addressed the subject, each from a particular—often parochial—perspective. Some express views that are statesmanlike; others are narrow and self-serving. Still others are plaintive or outraged; and some are just plain tedious and boring. In the aggregate, the verbiage is overwhelming.

To cut through the morass of pro and con, perhaps it would be useful to assess the feasibility of Electronic Funds Transfer as a proposed project? May I suggest the following four questions:

1. Technical feasibility—can the system be built to achieve the desired performance objectives?
2. Operational feasibility—is the system needed and wanted by those it is intended to serve? Will they use it effectively?
3. Economic feasibility—can the system be built, operated and maintained at an affordable cost? Will users be willing to pay for its services?

4. Legislative feasibility—do the laws imposed by the existing governmental and social structures allow the system to function effectively?

Before launching into an analysis of EFT under these four headings, I would like to argue that there is no such thing as a single Electronic Funds Transfer system in the sense of a monolithic collection of terminals, message switches and processors. Instead, the "system" is a heterogeneous aggregation of many systems. Some of these will be local in scope, others national; some will be owned and operated by independent business organizations, some by regulated financial institutions, and still others by governmental agencies; some will provide attractive services at attractive prices, others will perform poorly and, mercifully, will soon die (unless kept alive by fiat or taxation).

It is this very heterogeneity which, I believe, guarantees the ultimate success of those EFT services that deserve to succeed and the ultimate failure of those that do not. It is true that heterogeneity causes enormous difficulties for technocrats and bureaucrats alike—both of whom, in their own way, aspire to the power that comes with unfettered control over such an important national resource. But I am thankful that those difficulties exist, for the dispersion of control over anything as important as the payments mechanism is key to my peace of mind.

Returning to the subject of feasibility, and to the first of four headings under which the feasibility of EFT will be examined, one finds an abundance of useful technology that should allow almost any EFT service yet proposed to be implemented without great difficulty. This rather trite observation should surprise no one, given the wide variety of EFT services relying heavily on advanced computer and communications technology that already are operational.

Technological abundance aside, the NEFTC pointed out in its final report that "Uncertainties in regulations; standards, and other factors have tended to retard EFT technological advances." The Commission concluded, however, that "It is premature, at this point, to establish federally mandated standards for EFT systems and related terminals."

Other observers feel even more strongly: Mr. Dee Hock, President of VISA U.S.A. Inc., commented in a recent speech that "Standardization throughout the value exchange system is impossible. It is the most expensive, least effective way to utilize electronics. It is far more effective to utilize technology and standards uniquely suitable to the primary task of each element of the value system, and (to) reformat data as it moves between those nonstandard elements."[3]

Few, if any, EFT standards exist now in the U.S., although a number of well-qualified individuals are working to develop them. The American National Standards Institute (ANSI) has formed Working Groups on security and on telecommunications, among others. X9A.3 is wrestling with such subjects as the "Management and Use of Personal Identification Numbers"; X9A.2 recently circulated an Interchange Message Specification document to its members for comments. Yet despite the fact that serious practitioners in the field are trying to develop standards, I suspect that the Commission is correct in calling standard setting "premature" and that Mr. Hock also is correct in stating that "Standardization *throughout* the . . . system is impossible." (Emphasis added).

In short, one would have to conclude that with the exceptions just mentioned, the technical feasibility of EFT systems is good and getting better.

Operational feasibility should be examined next. Operational feasibility, you will recall, asks whether the system will be used effectively by those for whom it is designed. Another way of putting the question is to ask whether the system will accomplish its objectives in the broad sense, i.e., does it not only meet its technical design objectives but also function well from the *user's* point of view?

Operational feasibility is always related to complexity, one aspect of which is the number and variety of participants involved in the design, operation and use of a system. By any measure, the number and variety of participants in EFT is bewilderingly complex. In its first phase report on EFT to the National Science Foundation, Arthur D. Little, Inc., identified the following as "participants who might feel direct impacts:

> All types of banking and other financial institutions, a large fraction of all retailing organizations, many service organizations, most general businesses (and specifically the providers of equipment and technical services in the areas affected), a large number of governmental agencies, many legal, consumer, labor, and similar organizations and most importantly, the individual.[4]

That's quite a gaggle of folks; it's hard to imagine getting them all in uniform and onto the playing field at one time. It's even harder to imagine that any single system (or small number of large integrated systems) could ever be designed to satisfy more than a few of them.

Consider the individual, properly identified above as most important, in his role as consumer of EFT services. The nice thing about being a consumer is that you've got a lot of people trying to protect you (whether you want to be protected or not) from things you didn't even know were problems. Seldom do those who offer themselves as champions and protectors of the consumer's rights point out that the consumer pays handsomely for such protection, usually through taxation or the high service fees that fund the protectors.

The Commission pointed out that consumers are reluctant to accept certain EFT concepts. They went on to state that while "Some consumer concerns may result from a lack of experience with these new ideas, . . . others are well founded." It also concluded, accurately I think, that it is "difficult to provide adequate consumer protection (without) unduly interfer(ing) with the competitive market place, which the Commission recognized as the best means for protecting consumers by providing them with the greatest choice among payment alternatives at the lowest cost." Personally, I was pleased to see this blow struck for Free Enterprise, but it will be interesting to see how future legislation interprets the phrase "greatest choice among payment alternatives at the lowest cost.'' I'm not at all optimistic that legislators can resist the urge to create a hopelessly entangled skein of burdensome—and oft-times counterproductive—regulations.

The Commission also concluded that present legal safeguards for the privacy of financial transaction information are not adequate to deal with the threats to that privacy arising from EFT; it then went on to identify five specific ways in which EFT might propose threats to individual privacy. Perhaps one of its most important conclusions was that ''EFT calls for much stricter controls than now apply to Government access to an individual's financial record.''

Individual privacy, as you well know, presents extraodinary complex problems and evokes particularly strong—and often strident—reactions from its defenders. Few argue against the concept of individual privacy per se but debate has been raging for years over the extent to which it can be protected—and the means for doing so—in light of conflicting demands by law enforcement and governmental authorities who need access to detailed (and often sensitive) information about individuals; example, the administration of welfare payments. Without a doubt, EFT has exacerbated the arguments. Professor Rule, in the paper mentioned above, concluded that it will be a contentious matter to know where to draw the line between individual and institutional perogatives and concluded that ''. . . no policy can claim to protect all . . . values equally.''

To sum up, the operational feasibility of EFT systems is far from assured. I suspect that it declines to the vanishing point for large monolithic, highly-integrated systems. But even when setting objectives for and designing smaller, less ambitious systems, operational feasibility cannot be taken for granted. These, too, will fail unless compromises can be reached that will protect the interests of all the participants, including especially those of the consumer.

The third dimension of feasibility is economic. If life were more simple, determination of economic feasibility would be relatively straightforward: One would estimate the revenues that might be generated by a new service, subtract the cost of providing that service, and decide whether the net result warranted the investment of the funds required to put the service in operation. Unfortunately, life isn't that simple and the economics of real systems are unclear, at best. Many proposed EFT systems will provide services that have never before been offered to the public; as a result, transaction volumes can only be guessed at. Pricing also is a problem and for the same reason; one can only guess how much the consumer will pay for a service he has never before been offered. This makes the projection of revenues a hazardous undertaking, since neither the transaction volumes nor the unit prices can be confidently estimated.

The Commission recognized the importance of understanding EFT costs and benefits; as its final report describes, it went to some length to collect such data for analysis. One of its less-than-sensational conclusions was that ''Many of the expected or alleged benefits of EFT are of a nature that defies quantitative measurement.'' Frustrating, but true.

Costs are almost as troublesome to estimate as revenues. Fortunately, the industry has amassed a base of relevant experience in the cost of designing and installing computer-based systems. Nonetheless, certain costs have been routinely underestimated by EFT pioneers (with embarassing results) just as they were by those who installed non-EFT computer-based systems. For example, the costs of promoting new concepts and services, maintaining systems once they are operational, and servicing large numbers of customers drawn from the general public can be painfully high, and there is no reason to believe that the lessons of the past have yet been learned by those building EFT systems today.

The Commission also concluded that ". . . over time and with sufficient consumer acceptance and transaction volume, the cost of EFT transactions probably will be lower than those of alternative paper-based systems." One senses a certain lack of conviction in that assessment, although the Commission did go on to observe that larger systems generally have lower costs and, hence, the ability to charge lower prices than smaller ones. As a case in point, VISA U.S.A. has experienced such dramatic increases in transaction volumes that it has reduced the fee it charges its members for switching credit authorization from 30 cents per transaction to 7.5 cents; even more recently, it reduced the fee for clearing an interchange sales draft from 2.5 cents per draft to 1 cent per draft.

When all is said and done, the economics are generally unknown and, in some cases, practially unknowable. Most would agree that indeed there are certain economies of scale but, since there is so much uncertainty about transaction volumes, it remains difficult to estimate costs with any precision. The Commission found, for example, that there was ". . . no useful data for estimating the limits of scale economies in POS applications."

One can only conclude, therefore, that the economic feasibility of EFT systems is tenuous. Intuitively, it would seem obvious that electronic systems that process large quantities of transactions could do so at a lower cost than nonelectronic systems. No doubt, this principle has been fundamental to the justification of many of the systems that currently exist or that now are on the drawing board. But at the same time, the lack of crisp and convincing economic justification is probably the single most important factor underlying the slow—even tentative—progress to date.

The final element of feasibility is legislative. There once was a time when legislative matters were hardly of concern to designers of computer-based systems; that is no longer the case in the United States. For financial systems (or others that handle quantities of personal data), legislation (or the threat/promise of legislation) becomes a critically important consideration.

In the U.S., legal issues seems to fall under four headings:

Those related to branch banking (affecting only commercial banks at the moment)

Those that deal with privacy considerations

Those dealing with such matters as the responsibilities of the parties in a variety of day-to-day commercial transactions (for example, cashing a check); these are closely related to ambiguities that arise in applying the Uniform Commercial Code to EFT transactions

Those issues (related to antitrust and fair-trade laws) dealing with who must share what EFT systems and equipment, and the degree to which a competitive environment will be mandated.

Certain aspects of the law in each of these four areas are now being appealed in courts at all levels; others are awaiting review by the United States Supreme Court.

In another recent speech—this one to the American Bankers Association—Mr. Hock of VISA reported on a VISA study recently of expected legislation, its sponsors, proponents and opponents. According to Hock, several things were apparent:

> First: There are powerful interests on nearly every side of every issue, with little prospect of agreement or reconciliation of interests.
>
> Second: Many areas are of great attraction to bureaucrats, whether on congressional staffs or in government agencies; for bureaucrats spawn on the regulation of minutiae, and the financial industry has much minutiae.
>
> Third: There are many emotional issues such as privacy and interest on demand deposits, the adverse ramifications of which a politican need not understand, nor explain, in order to generate public support.
>
> Fourth: There is much complex economic and technical information necessary to an understanding of why such legislation will be adverse to the public. It is boring, if not incomprehensible, to the public and to most legislators.
>
> Fifth: The nature of the matters to be legislated heavily favor the so-called consumerists and the bureaucrats, and will be extremely difficult for the industry to resist.
>
> The stage is set for two or three years of classical political struggle affecting the very heart of our business, as well as the entire financial industry. It will be fought by special interests, and won by those best organized and best able to manipulate public opinion.

I share Mr. Hock's obvious distaste for politically inspired legislation and his apprehension that we are likely to see a great deal of it.

To sum up, it appears that the legislative feasibility of EFT is much in question and likely to get worse. It's entirely posible that progress in EFT within the U.S. will be slowed dramatically—if not crippled altogether—by the legislative onslaught that appears to be developing.

To review the four feasibility elements: The technical feasibility of EFT looks good and should get even better; the operational feasibility is far from assured at this time but I expect it to improve, albeit slowly; the economic feasibility is largely unknown but the odds are that it will improve as technology improves and consumer acceptance broadens; the legislative feasibility is questionable and likely to get worse.

I conclude from the above that the EFT revolution was not called off, nor has it already happened. Instead, we're in the midst of it. It's just a more quiet revolution than we had been led to expect. The battles being fought are not as dramatic as some had anticipated, and they produce no clear winners—only the wounded and worn. There seems little basis for hysteria, yet ample opportunities for rhetoric by legislators, businessmen and consumerists alike.

The EFT scene—already exciting—is likely to remain so. Yet in spite of the clamor, confusion and controversy, I'm confident that EFT will lead to useful innovations in financial services—and to genuine improvements in those already in place—that should benefit all of us.

PART IV

CANADIAN INFORMATION PROCESSING SOCIETY

Paper selected by CIPS
as the best paper submitted during 1978

"Key-to-address Transformation Techniques"
P.G. Sorenson, J.P. Tremblay, and R.F. Deutscher

The Canadian Information Processing Society (CIPS) was formed in 1958, shortly after a national conference, and is concerned with the advancement of the electronic computer and all its applications.

CIPS holds meetings and conferences, collaborates with educational institutions and other groups, provides educational programs for the membership, serves as an information exchange between members and similar associations and is a national source of information and representation. CIPS is a member of the International Federation for Information Processing (IFIP) and hosted the IFIP Congress 77 in Toronto.

The Society's publications include the bimonthly *CIPS REVIEW* and the *INFOR Journal*, published jointly by CIPS and the Canadian Operational Research Society.

The address of CIPS is 212 King Street West, Suite 214, Toronto, Ontario M5H 1K5, Canada.

Key-to-address Transformation Techniques

P.G. Sorenson, J.P. Tremblay, and R.F. Deutscher

Department of Computational Science, University of Saskatchewan, Saskatoon

A number of key-to-address transformations are surveyed with particular emphasis given to distribution-dependent hashing methods. The open addressing, separate chaining, coalesced chaining, and rehashing collision resolution techniques are discussed. A comparison of the different key-to-address transformation techniques is presented. The application of these techniques is considered and the notion of an order-preserving transformation is introduced.

On examine un nombre de transformations des procédés allant des valeurs-clé aux valeurs réelles en insistant surtout sur les méthodes de distribution et de compilation enclenchée. Font l'objet de discussions: les techniques d'opérations libre, d'enchaînement séparé, d'enchaînement imbriqué et les techniques des opérations resultant des compliations osculatrices. On fait une comparaison entre les differentes techniques d'opération. On analyse la mise en pratique des techniques et la notion d'une transformation respectant une marche à suivre.

1 INTRODUCTION

The purpose of this paper is to provide a survey of a number of key-to-address transformation techniques that have been proposed and experimented with in the literature. A number of survey or survey-like papers have been written on this subject before and included among them are papers by Peterson,[1] Buchholz,[2] Morris,[3] Lum, Yuen, and Dodd,[4] Maurer and Lewis,[5] and Severance and Duhne.[6] In addition, Knuth's book entitled *Sorting and Searching*[7]

EDITOR'S NOTE: *From INFOR, Vol. 16, No. 1, February 1978. Reprinted by permission of the publisher, Canadian Information Processing Society.*

presents a detailed examination of many of the techniques described in this paper—in fact, many of the results that will be cited are attributed to analytical and empirical studies completed by Knuth. This paper differs from the others in the following respects.

1. The descriptions of the various techniques are from a practitioner's viewpoint with detailed algorithms given for some of the more complex methods.
2. The results from a number of previous studies are summarized in such a way as to identify which techniques should be applied under what conditions.
3. Distribution-dependent functions are characterized, compared with distribution-independent functions, and their behavior under various conditions is identified.
4. The notion of an order-preserving transformation is introduced and a discussion of how such a transformation can be implemented is included.

The paper begins by defining a number of important concepts related to key-to-address transformations. The next section presents a number of distribution-independent and distribution-dependent hashing functions. Collision resolution techniques are outlined in the fourth section. The fifth section summarizes many of the results of previous experiments in hashing techniques and the final section describes how hashing algorithms can be applied in a number of application areas.

The reader should be warned that in Sections 3–5 the term file is interpreted to mean external file (i.e., a file stored on an auxiliary memory device). However, many of the techniques described in these sections can be succcessfully applied to tables (i.e., internal files). In the final section, we clearly identify which techniques are most applicable to tables and which are most applicable to external files.

2 CONCEPTS AND NOTATION

A *record* is a collection of information items about a particular entity. It is convenient to divide each record into elements called fields. A *field* is some unit of meaningful information. If a number of entities exist which are related to one another, then the set of records corresponding to those entities is a *file*. The field used to identify uniquely a record in a file is a *key*.

In this paper we assume that a file will be stored on a direct access storage device (DASD). A DASD provides the capability of storing data in addressable areas on its recording surface. One of the most commonly used DASDs is a disk device with movable read/write heads.

Important organizational and timing characteristics of disk devices can be presented without digressing to an extensive physical description. The storage area of a disk device is divided into consecutively numbered buckets. As a general rule, a *bucket* is a uniquely addressable block of storage containing one or more records, and these buckets may correspond to physical tracks or sectors. The number of record locations contained in a bucket is called the *bucket capacity*. Because the disk device being considered has movable read/write heads, only a certain number of buckets can be accessed while the heads are in a fixed position. The storage area to or from which data can be transferred without movement of the read/write heads is termed a *seek area*. Such areas are arranged consecutively in disk storage. A *seek* is a movement of the heads to locate a seek area.

The performance of a disk device is measured in terms of its *access time*. This is the time that elapses between the initiation of a computer command to access a bucket and that bucket becoming available for use. Access time is the sum of several delays such as *seek time, rotational delay,* and the *data transfer rate*. The most significant delay is seek time, and when accessing data in disk storage it is therefore desirable to minimize the average number of seeks required.

Throughout this paper, we are concerned with only one type of file organization; namely, direct file organization. *Direct organization* of a file permits rapid random processing of records. In a direct file, the key of each record is used to determine the bucket in which that record should be stored.

In constructing and maintaining a direct file, we are concerned with the problem of storing or accessing records which possess given keys or identifiers. These keys are elements in the set K of possible keys which is called the *key space*. The records in the file are identified by a subset $S = \{x_1, x_2, \ldots, x_n\}$ of n distinct keys from K. The key space K is assumed to be a set of consecutive integers. If the keys are alphabetic or alphanumeric, their computer representation is still numeric, and they may also be converted to a more convenient numeric representation as discussed by Buchholz [2] and Lum et al.[4]

The records are stored in a number of storage locations specified by the set of addresses or *address space* $A = \{c + 1, c + 2, \ldots, c + m\}$ (for a constant memory location c). Each bucket has b record locations so that it is possible to have mb records in the storage area defined by A. A measure of space utilization in a direct file is the *load factor,* which is defined as the ratio of number of records to the number of record locations. In this case the load factor is $n/(mb)$.

If it is possible to have the number of keys in K equal to the number of record locations specified by A and still maintain a high load factor (efficient space utilization), then a transformation can be defined which assigns to each bucket of A exactly b keys (and thus b records) from K. This is termed *direct addressing* of a direct file and is only used when most of the keys from K are included in the subset S which identifies existing records.

In most situations, however, S is only a small subset of K and direct addressing would result in ridiculously low utilization of direct access storage. *In-*

direct addressing must be implemented in such cases. For indirect addressing, an algorithm consisting of two components determines where a record should be located. The first component is a *hashing function* (or hashing method, or hashing transformation) which is defined as a mapping $H : K \rightarrow A$ from the key space to the address space. Given a key x identifying a record, $H(x)$ is the address of the bucket where that record should be stored, if possible. Unfortunately, more than b keys may be mapped to the same bucket, so a second component called a *collision resolution technique* must be included in the algorithm to resolve the subsequent conflicts or collisions by searching for empty record locations for the overflow records. The indirect addressing algorithm must be used both for storing new records and locating existing records. Therefore, it is required that the algorithm map a key to the same bucket, and, if necessary, probe the same overflow storage locations, every time it is invoked.

In this paper a performance measure is required to compare different hashing functions and the measure most widely adopted is the *average length of search* (ALOS). For a set of records in a direct file, it is the average number of accesses to the storage device required to retrieve a record.

Many transformations have been proposed for use as hashing functions with indirect addressing. A criterion which a transformation should attempt to meet is the uniform distribution of keys over the elements of the address space. It is virtually impossible to obtain a perfectly uniform distribution of keys over buckets, so one is generally faced with the problem of finding a hashing function which yields the most uniform distribution.

In the following sections, the address space is considered to be $\{1,2, \ldots , m\}$, so that certain discussions and formulas can be simplified. Note that if $H(x)$ gives addresses in this address space, then $H(x) + c$ can be used to address the address space $\{c + 1, c + 2, \ldots , c + m\}$.

3 HASHING FUNCTIONS

Several hashing functions are discussed in this section. These functions fall into two classes: distribution-independent and distribution-dependent functions. A distribution-independent hashing function does not use the distribution of the keys of a file in computing the position of a record. A distribution-dependent hashing function, on the other hand, is obtained by examining the subset of keys corresponding to known records.

3.1 Distribution-independent Functions

Most of the popular distribution-independent hashing functions are briefly described here. These include the division, midsquare, folding, radix transformation, algebraic coding, and multiplicative hashing methods. Before describing a number of hashing functions, the key space K is investigated more closely.

Each element of K contains a value which is numeric, alphabetic, or alphanumeric. The hashing functions to be discussed transform keys to addresses through the use of arithmetic or logical operations. Such transformations can still be applied to alphabetic or alphanumeric keys, if the internal numeric representation of those keys is accessible. As an alternative, Lum, Yuen, and Dodd[4] suggest encoding $A, B, \ldots, Z$ as decimal numbers 11, 12, ... , 36. For example, KNUTH and HZS630 are encoded as 2124313018 and 183629060300, respectively. The uniqueness of alphabetic keys is preserved by this encoding. The key space is assumed to be composed of integral values, since it is always possible to convert keys to integers.

In certain instances the numeric representation of a key is too large to be stored in one computer word. Consequently, if multiple precision operations are not available, then the keys must be compressed. Certain hashing functions which are described in the following paragraphs involve the use of key compression techniques. Frequently, one hashing function is used to map keys to an intermediate space and then a second hashing function is used to map the values in that space to the address space.

A well-known and widely accepted distribution-independent hashing function is the *division method* which is defined as

$$H(x) = x \bmod m + 1$$

for divisor m. It has been used since the early days of direct access storage devices and is mentioned by Dumey.[8]

When the division method maps keys to addresses, it preserves, to a certain extent, the uniformity that exists in a key set. Clusters of keys are mapped to unique addresses. For example, keys 1000, 1001, ... , 1013, and 1014 are mapped to addresses 21, 22, ... , 34, and 35, if the divisor for the division method is 49. This preservation of uniformity is a disadvantage, however, if two or more clusters of keys are mapped to the same addresses. For example, if another cluster of keys is 1985, 1986, 1987, 1988, ... , 1998, 1999, and 2000, then these keys are mapped to addresses 26, 27, 28, 29, ... , 40, and 41 by divisor 49 and there are several collisions with keys from the cluster starting at 1000. The reason for this behavior is that keys in these two clusters are congruent modulo 49.

More generally, the division method with divisor m can perform poorly in cases where many keys are congruent modulo d, and m is not relatively prime to d . Such behavior occurs in the preceding example where $m = d = 49$. As another example, consider the case where all the keys in a file are congruent modulo 5 and the divisor is 75. In this case the keys are mapped to only 15 different buckets. Because it is uncommon for a number of keys to be congruent modulo m where m is a large prime number, Buchholz[2] suggests using a prime divisor. Lum et al.,[4] however, have found that odd divisors without factors less than 20 are also satisfactory. In particular, assuming that the address space is $\{1, 2, \ldots, m\}$, divisors which are even numbers are to be avoided since even and odd keys are mapped to odd and even addresses, respectively. This behavior is a problem in a file whose keys are predominantly even or predominantly odd.

In the *midsquare hashing method*, an address is obtained by first multiplying a key by itself and then truncating bits or digits at both ends of the product until the remaining number of bits or digits is equal to the desired address length. The same positions must be used for all products. The midsquare method has been criticized by Buchholz[2] but Lum et al.[4] found that it gave good results when applied to some key sets.

The *folding hashing method* partitions a key into a number of parts, each of which have the same length as the required address, with the possible exception of the last part. These parts are then added together, with the final carry ignored, to form an address. If the keys are in binary form, then the exclusive-or operation can replace addition. Folding is a useful hashing method for compressing multiword keys so that other hashing functions can be used.

The *radix transformation hashing method* attempts to produce a random distribution of keys over addresses of the address space. It was originally proposed by Lin. In this method, the radix q (q is usually 2 or 10) representation of a key is considered to be a number expressed in radix p, where p is greater than q and p and q are relatively prime. This radix p number is then converted to its radix q equivalent and an address is formed by choosing the right-most digits or bits or by applying the division method.

Another hashing method called *algebraic coding* is a cluster-separating hashing function based on algebraic coding theory. This method was developed by Schay and Raver[10] in conjunction with Hanan and Palermo.[11] An r-bit key $(k_1k_2 \ldots k_r)_2$ is considered as a polynomial

$$K(x) \times \sum_{i=1}^{r} k_i x^{i-1}.$$

If an address in the range 0 to $m = 2^t - 1$ is required, then a polynomial

$$P(x) \times x^t + \sum_{i=1}^{t} p_i x^{i-1}.$$

is used to divide $K(x)$. The remainder

$$K(x) \bmod P(x) \times \sum_{i=1}^{t} - \; h_i x^{i-1},$$

which is obtained using modulo 2 polynomial arithmetic, gives the address $(h_1h_2 \ldots h_t)_2$. Algebraic coding was originally proposed for implementation in hardware rather than in software.

Another method, the *multiplicative hashing function*, has been found to be quite useful by Knott[12] and Knuth.[7] For a nonnegative integral key x, the function is $H(x) + \lfloor m(\,cx \bmod 1)\rfloor + 1$, where $0 < c < 1$, $cx \bmod 1$ is the fractional part of cx, and $\lfloor\;\rfloor$ denotes the greatest integer less than or equal to its contents (i.e., the floor function). This hashing function can give good results if the constant c is properly chosen. This choice, however, may be difficult to make.

Knott,[12] Lum et al.,[4] London,[13] Knuth,[7] and Buchholz[2] present studies of these hashing functions which have been described briefly. Although some of these methods often give a uniform distribution of keys over addresses, it is still necessary to experiment with hashing functions as applied to specific key sets. We shall elaborate on some of these results in Section 5.

We now turn to a discussion of distribution-dependent hashing functions.

3.2 Distribution-dependent Functions

Five distribution-dependent functions are discussed in this section. All functions except the first are discussed in detail. Knott[12,14] has published discussions of such distribution-dependent functions and characterizes them as follows.

For $S \subseteq K$ it is required to find a hashing function H which maps the elements of S to the address space $\{1,2, \ldots , m\}$ uniformly. The required function can be obtained from the discrete cumulative distribution function $F_Z(x) = P(Z \leq x)$, where Z denotes a random variable that assumes values of keys in S. If S contains n distinct keys, then the random variable $F_Z(Z)$ is such that $P(F_Z(Z) \leq k/n) = k/n$ for $0 \leq k \leq n$. It follows that $F_Z(Z)$ and $mF_Z(Z)$ have a discrete uniform distribution on $\{(1/n), \ldots , [(n - 1)/n]\ 1\}$, and $\{(m/n), (2m/n), \ldots , m\}$, respectively. Therefore $\lceil mF_Z(Z) \rceil$, where $\lceil\ \rceil$ denotes the least integer greater than or equal to its contents (i.e., the ceiling function), is approximately uniform on $\{1, 2, \ldots , m\}$. This is particularly the case when $m \leq n$. Consequently, the distribution-dependent hashing function H for a given key x is defined by $H(x) = \lceil mF_Z(x) \rceil$.

Since in many cases F_Z is not known, it must be approximated. The distribution-dependent hashing functions studied in this paper (except the digit analysis method) vary only in the approach used to estimate F_Z. One or more scannings of the subset of keys corresponding to the known records must be performed before these functions can be defined. Since frequent insertions into and deletions from the file may change this subset drastically, periodic redefinition of the hashing function and reorganization of the direct file may be required.

Four such estimations of F_Z are now described, using algorithms and mathematical notation. It should be emphasized, however, that the first method to be discussed does not involve the computation of an estimate to F_Z.

Digit analysis is a hashing transformation which is, in a sense, distribution dependent. Digits or bits of the original key are selected and then shifted in order to form addresses. As an example, a key 123456789 would be transformed to an address 7654 if digits in positions 4 through 7 were selected and their order reversed. For a given key set, the same positions of the key and the same rearrangement pattern must be used consistently. The key positions to be used in forming an address are selected on the basis of an analysis which is performed on a sample of the key set.

A *piece-wise linear function* is a second distribution-dependent hashing function that can be used to approximate F_Z. Isaac and Singleton[15] first suggested this method. A formulation of the necessary function was presented by

Kronmal and Tarter.[16] The key space consists of integers in the interval (a,d). This interval is divided into j equal subintervals of length L, i.e., $L = (d - a)/j$. The interval location of a given key x is given by the formula

$$i = 1 + \lfloor (x - a)/L \rfloor .$$

The j intervals can be described as:

$$I_i = \begin{cases} (a, a + L) & i = 1 \\ \lfloor a + (i - 1) L, a + iL \rfloor . & 2 \leqslant i \leqslant j \end{cases}$$

Let N_i be defined as the number of keys from S contained in the interval I_i, and G_i be the corresponding number of keys less than $a + iL$. Therefore, N_i and G_i are the frequency and cumulative frequency respectively of the interval I_i. Using N_i and G_i, the equation

$$P_i(x) = (G_i + ((x - a)/L - i)N_i)/n$$

gives a linear approximation of the cumulative frequency distribution function F_Z for x in the interval I_i. The required hashing function for a key x on interval I_i is, therefore, $H_i(x) = \lceil mP_i(x) \rceil$, $1 \leqslant i \leqslant j$ for an address space of size m.

The following algorithm illustrates how the piece-wise linear function for indirect addressing is calculated.

Algorithm Piece Wise (piece-wise linear parameter calculation). *Given j, a, d, m, and n as previously defined and a key set* $\{x_1, x_2, \ldots, x_n\}$, *it is required to calculate interval length L and the frequencies and cumulative frequencies* N_i *and* G_i, $1 \leqslant i \leqslant j$, *for the piece-wise linear function.*

Table 1

N	G
10	10
16	26
30	56
6	62
18	80
26	106
40	146
32	178
24	202
18	220

1. [*Initialize array N to zero*]
   Repeat for $i = 1, 2, \ldots, j$:
   Set $N_i \leftarrow 0$.
2. [*Determine interval length and interval frequencies*]
   Set $L \leftarrow (d - a)/j$.

Repeat for $k = 1, 2, \ldots, n$:
Set $i \leftarrow 1 + \lfloor (x_k - a)/L \rfloor$ and $N_i \leftarrow N_i + 1$.
3. [*Calculate interval cumulative frequencies*]
Set $G_1 \leftarrow N_1$.
Repeat for $i = 2, 3, \ldots, j$:
Set $G_i \leftarrow G_{i-1} + N_i$.
Exit.

This simple algorithm requires only one scan of the key set in order to determine the N and G vectors. From the given parameters, the following assignment statements can be used to calculate an address H from a key x in the interval (a,d).

Set $i \leftarrow 1 + \lfloor (x - a)/\rfloor$L.
If $G_i \neq$ T 0,
then Set $H(x) \leftarrow \lceil m(G_i + ((x - a) L - i)N_i)/n \rceil$;
otherwise Set $H(x) \leftarrow 1$.

Note that if G_i is zero, then the hash value returned for a key in a dynamic key set (i.e., a key set involving the addition of a record with a key that was not in the original key set) must be 1 to avoid returning a value outside the address space. This should rarely happen but, unfortunately, must be checked for explicitly.

As an example of this method, consider the case where $a = 0$, $d = 1000$, $j = 10$, $n = 220$, and the vectors N and G are given in Table 1. Then $L = (1000 - 0)/10 = 100$. For a key value $x = 410$, with $m = 250$,

$$i = 1 + \lfloor (410 - 0)/100 \rfloor = 5$$

and

$$H(x) = \lceil 250(80 + ((410 - 0)/100 - 5)18))/\ 220 \rceil = 73.$$

Another estimate of F_Z has been devised by Deutscher et al.[17, 18] It involves the use of multiple frequency distributions. In this method an initial piece-wise linear estimate of the frequency distribution of the subset S of the key space is used to map that subset into an equivalent key space instead of the address space. This tends to spread out clusters of keys and condense sparsely populated intervals. The total effect is that the distribution of keys in the key space becomes more uniform. The piece-wise linear estimate of the distribution of the transformed keys is found and may be used in conjunction with the first piece-wise linear function to form a hashing function. Alternatively, a number of iterations may be performed until the hashing function obtained is judged to be good. The criterion used for determining the number of iterations is to stop iterating when the average length of search does not decrease by more than an insignificant amount (say .02) from one iteration to the next. A key from the original key set S is used to generate an address by being transformed through a number of key sets. A different piece-wise linear estimate is used for each transformation.

This hashing method is designated as the *multiple frequency distribution function* and can be described by using variables similar to those given in the description of the piece-wise linear function.

Algorithm Multiple Frequency (multiple frequency address calculation). *Assume that n keys in the subset S have been transformed into a second key set, then to a third key set, and so on up to a $(q + 1)$st key set. This requires q transformations using piecewise linear functions for each transformation. All key sets are in the interval (a, d), and the length of all subintervals is L. Let N_{ik} be the number of keys in interval I_i of the kth key set, and let G_{ik} be the number of keys less than $a + iL$ in the same key set k. It is required to calculate H, the value of the function $H(x)$ for a key x from the initial key set, using q frequency distribution mappings.*

1. [*Initialize auxiliary variable*]
   Set $y \leftarrow x$.
2. [*Transform through key sets*]
   Repeat for $k = 1, 2, \ldots, q$:
   Set $i \leftarrow 1 + \lfloor (y - a)/L \rfloor$ and
   $F \leftarrow (G_{ik} + ((y - a)/L - i)\, N_{ik})\, /n$.
   If $k < q$,
   then set $y \leftarrow \lfloor (d - a)\, F + a \rfloor$.
3. [*Calculate an address*]
   If $F \neq 0$ then Set $H \leftarrow \lceil mF \rceil$; otherwise Set $H \leftarrow 1$.
   Exit.

Observe that in the algorithm an explicit test is again made for the situation in which a new record is being inserted at the beginning of the file (i.e,. when $F = 0$).

The determination of the number of transformations, q, requires an algorithm for calculating the ALOS. Two such algorithms using open addressing and chaining as collision resolution techniques are given in Section 4. N_{ik} and G_{ik} for $1 \leq i \leq j$ and $k = 1$ are calculated using Algorithm Piece Wise. The ALOS is determined for the set of keys under consideration. Following this, the piece-wise linear function is used to map the keys to a second key set and N_{ik} and G_{ik} for $k = 2$ are calculated. The ALOS using the two piece-wise linear functions is determined, and if it does not decrease by more than .02 from the first ALOS, then the multiple frequency function is complete and q is 2. If the ALOS increases in comparison to the first ALOS, then only the first piece-wise linear estimate should be used in forming the function, so q is 1.

In tests performed by Deutscher[19] the process of using previous piece-wise linear functions to determine another set of N_{ik} and G_{ik} elements is continued until ALOS does not decrease by more than .02 or until $q = 5$. If i distributions are formed in the construction of this function, then $i + 1$ scans of the keys in a key set are required. If each successive distribution decreases the ALOS, then q is equal to i. If the final distribution increases ALOS, however, then q is equal to $i - 1$. Thus, either $q + 1$ or $q + 2$ scans of the key set are necessary.

Deutscher et al.[17] devised another function for estimating the frequency distribution of a key set. This function is also based on a piece-wise linear estimate. The key space is initially divided into an arbitrary number of equally sized intervals. The storage of a subset S of keys is then simulated. If the ALOS of an interval is greater than a predetrmined ALOS, then this interval is further subdivided, so that a better estimate of the frequency distribution can be obtained for that interval. This interval-splitting process is performed in an iterative manner so that subintervals may also be split. The hashing function thus obtained is denoted as the *piece-wise linear function with interval splitting*. This process requires the use of a data structure that can be represented by an array. An example of the interval-splitting process and its representation is given in Figure 1.

FIGURE 1. Representation of a data structure for the piece-wise linear function with interval splitting.

KEY-TO-ADDRESS TRANSFORMATION TECHNIQUES

	i	N	G
interval length = (d-a)/10	1	3	3
	2	5	8
	3	7	-11
	4	2	17
	5	0	17
	6	1	18
	7	2	20
	8	3	23
	9	11	-13
	10	10	-15
half-interval length = (d-a)/20	11	3	11
	12	4	15
	13	6	-17
	14	5	-19
	15	3	37
	16	7	-21
quarter-interval length = (d-a)/40	17	1	24
	18	5	-23
	19	4	33
	20	1	34
	21	3	40
	22	4	-25
eighth-interval length = (d-a)/80	23	3	27
	24	2	29
	25	2	42
	26	2	44

The range of the key space (a, d) in Figure 1 is initially divided into ten intervals of length $(d - a)/10$. N_i denotes the frequency of the ith interval. If this interval has not been split, then G_i has a value which represents cumulative frequency for that interval. If G_i contains a negative value, however, then the absolute value of G_i gives the location of the first of two consecutive pairs of array elements $N_{|Gi|}$ and $G_{|Gi|}$, and $N_{|Gi|+1}$ and $G_{|Gi|+1}$. These elements correspond to the half-intervals of interval i. Each half-interval has a length of $(d - a)/20$. The values $N_{|Gi|}$ and $N_{|Gi|\ 1}$ denote the frequencies of the first and second half-intervals of interval i, respectively. Let k be either $|G_i|$ or $|G_i| + 1$. A nonnegative value for G_k indicates that it represents the cumulative frequency of the corresponding half-interval. For negative G_k, $|G_k|$ indicates the location of the first of two consecutive pairs of array elements which give information for the two quarter-intervals of the corresponding half-interval. This process is continued to obtain eighth-intervals and so on.

Consider interval 9 with $N_9 = 11$ and $G_9 = -13$. A negative value for G_9 indicates that this interval is split, so $|G_9| = 13$ references N_{13}, G_{13}, N_{14}, and G_{14}. These entries contain information on the half-intervals of interval 9. N_{13} is 6 and since $G_{13} = -17$ the first half-interval is also split. N_{17}, G_{17}, N_{18}, and G_{18} correspond to its quarter-intervals. The first quarter-interval, having one key in it, is not split. The second quarter-interval, however, is split, as indicated by $G_{18} = -23$. N_{23}, G_{23}, N_{24}, and G_{24} give the frequencies and cumulative frequencies for the eighth-intervals of the second quarter-interval. The eighth-intervals are not split, as indicated by $G_{23} = 27$ and $G_{24} = 29$. Consequently, the splitting process for the first half-interval of interval 9 terminates at this point. By repeating this splitting process for other intervals, the splitting of the original key set can be observed.

The algorithm which follows calculates a hashing function based on the piece-wise linear function with interval splitting. It is assumed that intervals may be split to no less than $(1/2)^{p-1}$ of their initial size. Consequently, if $p = 1$, then the algorithm computes the piece-wise linear function.

Algorithm Interval Splitting. *Given L, a, m, n, and p as previously defined and arrays N and G whose content is exemplified by figure 1, it is required to calculate an address H in {1, 2, ... , m} from the key x.*

1. [*Calculate initail interval number*]
   Set $r \leftarrow i \leftarrow 1 + \lfloor (x - a)/L \rfloor$.
2. [*Calculate interval number and array index if interval or subinterval is split*]
   Repeat for $k = 1, 2, \ldots, p - 1$ while $G_i < 0$:
   Set $r \leftarrow 1 + \lfloor (x - a)/(L/2^k) \rfloor$ and $i \leftarrow -G_i - (r \bmod 2) + 1$.
3. [*Calculate address*]
   If $G_i = 0$ then Set $H \leftarrow \lceil m\,(G_i + ((x - a)/\,(L/2^{k-1}) - r)\,N_i)/n \rceil$; otherwise Set $H \leftarrow 1$.
   Exit.

In step 2, note that the computed value for r is such that $1 \leqslant r \leqslant 2^k j$. This value of r is used in the address calculation of step 3, and is also used to adjust $-G_i$ in step 2. If r is odd, then $-G_i$ is unchanged, but if it is even, then $-G_i$ is incremented by 1. This calculation determines i, the index to the array elements corresponding to the required half-interval. In step 2, note that k is incremented before it is compared with $p - 1$ and G_i is tested.

An algorithm for constructing the N and G arrays has a slow execution time. It requires that the key set be scanned $2p - 1$ times.

A final technique which estimates F_Z makes use of Fourier series and is due to Tarter and Kronmal.[20,21] The hashing function is termed the *Fourier hashing function* here. Let

$$x = \frac{1}{n} \sum_{1 \leqslant i \leqslant n} x_i \tag{1}$$

for the n elements of the subset S of the key space defined by (a, d). Also let

$$c_i = \frac{2}{(d-a)n} \sum_{1 \leqslant j \leqslant n} \cos\left[i\, \pi(x_j - a) / (d-a)\right], \qquad 1 \leqslant i \leqslant t$$

$$s_i = \frac{2}{(d-a)n} \sum_{1 \leqslant j \leqslant n} \sin\left[i\, \pi(x_j - a) / (d-a)\right], \qquad 1 \leqslant i \leqslant t \tag{2}$$

where t is the greatest integer such that

$$\frac{1}{4}(d-a)^2(c_t^2 + s_t^2) > 2 \bigg/ \left(\frac{m-1}{m-n}\, n + 1\right) \tag{3}$$

holds. Then the Fourier estimate to F_Z is

$$F_{nt}(x) = \frac{1}{2} + \frac{x - \bar{x}}{2(d-a)} + \frac{d-a}{2\pi} \sum_{1 \leqslant i \leqslant t} \frac{1}{i}\left(c_i \sin\left[i\,\pi\,\frac{x-a}{d-a}\right] - s_i \cos\left[i\,\pi\,\frac{x-a}{d-a}\right]\right) \tag{4}$$

and the Fourier hashing function is

$$H(x) = \lceil mF_{nt}(x) \rceil. \tag{5}$$

To reduce the number of arithmetic operations required in calculating an address from a key x with the Fourier hashing function, we use the following algorithm.

Algorithm Fourier (Fourier hashing function address calculation). *Given a, m, n, c_i, and s_i from Equation (2), and t from Equation (3), this algorithm calculates address H in $\{1, 2, \ldots, m\}$ from the key x according to Equations (4) and (5).*

1. [*Initialize*]
   Set DIFF $\leftarrow d - a$ and $z \leftarrow \pi(x - a)/\text{DIFF}$.
2. [*Iterate*]
   Set SUM $\leftarrow$ 0.
   Repeat for $i = 1, 2, \ldots, t$:
     Set SUM $\leftarrow$ SUM + $(c_i \sin[iz] - s_i \cos[iz])/i$.
3. [*Calculate address*]
   Set $H \leftarrow \lceil m(.5 + (x - \bar{x})/(2^* \text{DIFF}) + (\text{DIFF}/2\pi) * \text{SUM}) \rceil$ and exit.

Calculation of the Fourier coefficients using the Equations (2) is very inefficient as the key set must be scanned t times, and for each key scanned, the sin and cos functions must be evaluated. If t is large, then calculation of F_{nt} using Algorithm FOURIER is also time-consuming. The determination of t using Inequality (3) is possible only when $m > n$. Tarter and Kronmal formulated this stopping condition for a bucket capacity of one. For larger bucket capacities, m is generally less than n.

A comparison of the last four distribution-dependent hashing functions and the division method as to the space and number of operations required is given in Section 5. This application of these distribution-dependent functions to searching and sorting is discussed in Section 6.

4 COLLISION RESOLUTION TECHNIQUES

As pointed out in Section 3, a hashing function often maps a number of keys to the same address. If the number of colliding records mapped to a particular address becomes greater than the capacity of the bucket for that address, then some of the colliding records must be stored and accessed at other storage locations, as determined by a collision resolution technique. There are basically four such techniques, namely, *open addressing, separate chaining, coalesced chaining, and rehashing*. In this section, we describe these collision resolution techniques, present algorithms which illustrate how each type of collision resolution can be implemented, and discuss the performance of each technique based on a probabilistic model.

4.1 Open Addressing

Open addressing is a collision resolution technique first described by Peterson.[1] In open addressing, if a key x of a record to be inserted is mapped to a bucket d, and this bucket has already reached its bucket capacity b, then other buckets in the file are scanned until a free record location is found. The overflow record is then inserted in the free location. It should be observed that a free record location may contain a record which was previously marked deleted. In such instances the key of the "deleted" record, say K_i, is set to a special negative value called MARK, which is not equal to the value of any key.

Buckets are scanned according to a sequence which can be defined in many ways. The simplest technique for handling collisions is to use the following sequence:

$$d,\ d + 1,\ \ldots,\ m - 1,\ m,\ 1,\ 2,\ \ldots,\ d - 1.$$

A free record location is always found if at least one is available; otherwise, the search halts after scanning m buckets. To retrieve a record, the same sequence of buckets is scanned until the record is located, or until an empty (never used) location is found. In the latter case, the required record is not in the file and the search fails. This method of collision resolution is called *linear probing* or *progressive overflow*.

The following algorithm inserts a record into a file using open addressing with the sequence $d,\ d + 1,\ \ldots,\ m - 1,\ m,\ 1,\ 2,\ \ldots,\ d - 1$. The file contains m buckets each with a capacity of b records. The jth record in the ith bucket B_i is referred to as B_{ij}. The key K_{ij} is the field of B_{ij} containing the record's key, and it is assumed that if B_{ij} has never been an active record, then K_{ij} has a negative value. While the use of a negative key is by no means a standard method of representing an unused record location, the algorithm to follow can be easily modified to work regardless of what method is adopted.

Algorithm OPENLP. *Given a record R identified by key x, it is required to insert R into the file. The hashing function H is used to calculate an initial address.*

1. [*Apply hashing function*] Set $i \leftarrow d \leftarrow H(x)$.
2. [*Scan for available storage*]
   Repeat for $j = 1, 2, \ldots, b$:
   If $K_{ij} < 0$, then set $B_{ij} \leftarrow R$ and exit.
3. [*Increment and test bucket index*]
   Set $i \leftarrow i + 1$.
   If $i > m$, then set $i \leftarrow 1$.
   If $i = d$, then exit unsuccessfully; otherwise, go to step 2.

In step 1 of algorithm OPENLP, an initial address is calculated using a hashing function as discussed in Section 3. A bucket is scanned in step 2 and if one or more record locations are available, the record is stored in the first location encountered and the algorithm terminates successfully. Otherwise, i is incremented and reset to 1, if necessary, in step 3. If i has become equal to d, its initial value, then no record locations are available and the algorithm terminates unsuccessfully.

A similar algorithm is used to retrieve a record and can be obtained from algorithm OPENLP by replacing step 2 with the following:

2. [*Scan for record with key x*]
   Repeat for $j = 1, 2, \ldots, b$:
   If $x = K_{ij}$, then set $R \leftarrow B_{ij}$ and exit; otherwise, if $K_{ij} < 0$ and $K_{ij} \neq$ MARK, then exit unsuccessfully.

TABLE 2. ***E*****[ALOS] for Open Addressing in a Successful Search**

Bucket capacity b	**Load factor,** α .10	.20	.30	.40	.50	.60	.70	.80	.90	.95
1	1.0556	1.1250	1.2143	1.3333	1.5000	1.7500	2.167	3.000	5.500	10.5
5	1.0000	1.0007	1.0039	1.0124	1.0307	1.0661	1.136	1.289	1.777	2.7
20	1.0000	1.0000	1.0000	1.0000	1.0003	1.0020	1.010	1.036	1.144	1.4

Notice that one storage access is required each time that step 2 of algorithm OPENLP is executed for either an insertion or a retrieval. If all n records in a file are stored or retrieved, then the number of times that step 2 is executed divided by n is the ALOS.

A probabilistic model for analysing collision resolution techniques has been developed by Knuth.[7] From this model he is able to derive formula for the expected average length of a successful search (E[ALOS]). The model assumes that each key has probability of $1/m$ of being mapped to each of the m buckets in the file. Given this assumption, there are m^n ways of mapping keys to the address space. Knuth shows that the expected average length of search for open addressing is dependent upon α, the load factor where $\alpha = n/(mb)$, and the bucket capacity b in the following manner.
For $b = 1$,

$$E[\text{ALOS}] = -\frac{1}{2} \quad 1 + \frac{1}{1-\alpha} \tag{6}$$

Using

$$R(\alpha, b) \frac{b}{b+1} + \frac{b^2\alpha}{(b+1)(b-2)} + \frac{b^3\alpha^2}{(b+1)(b+2)(b+3)} + \cdots \tag{7}$$

$$t_b(\alpha) = \frac{e^{-b\alpha} b^b a^b}{b!} (1 - (1 - \alpha) R(\alpha, b)), \tag{8}$$

the formula for E[ALOS] for any bucket capacity is

$$E[\text{ALOS}] = 1 + t_b(\alpha) + t_{2b}(\alpha) = t_{3b}(\alpha) + \cdots \tag{9}$$

Table 2 gives E[ALOS] as calculated, using Approximations (6) and (9) with a number of different load factors and bucket capacities. This table presents a subset of the values presented in a table in Knuth[7]. E[ALOS] increases with increasing load factor since a greater number of collisions is probable as more records are being stored in the file.

Note that Equations (6)–(9) and Table 1 are results for the average number of accesses in a successful search using linear probing. Knuth[7] also discusses and provides results using linear probing in an unsuccessful search.

It should be evident from the results given that a larger bucket capacity is useful in reducing the probability of collisions occurring and thus for reducing

E[ALOS]. However, Buchholz[2] warns that larger buckets provide an advantage in search time only if the access time to the successive records within a bucket is much shorter than the access time to the bucket itself. Note that E[ALOS] indicates only the number of bucket accesses and not the time of the accesses. It takes a greater time to search a bucket as its capacity increases. In addition, the bucket capacity is directly related to the amount of main memory buffer space that is required to hold a bucket. Therefore a limit must be imposed on bucket capacity.

A simple variation of algorithm OPENLP is obtained by changing step 3 to the following.

3. [*Increment and test bucket index*]
Set $i \leftarrow i + c$.
If $i > m$, then set $i \leftarrow i - m$.
If $i = d$, then exit unsuccessfully; otherwise, go to step 2.

The constant increment c must be chosen so that it is relatively prime to m, and thus guarantees that all buckets are scanned if necessary. This variation of open addressing does not change E[ALOS] for algorithm OPENLP, but Knuth[7] states that c can be chosen to minimize latency delays between consecutive accesses in a rotational form of auxiliary memory (e.g., magnetic disk or drum).

4.2 Separate Chaining

Chaining can be used in a variety of ways to handle overflow records; however, we shall present only two of the more popular methods. The first method, called *separate chaining*, involves the chaining of overflow records in a special overflow area which is separate from the *prime area* (i.e., the area into which records are initially hashed). When chaining into a separate overflow area, a pointer must be maintained in each primary bucket and a pointer must accompany each record in the overflow area. We denote the pointer in bucket B_i as PTR_i. If there are no overflow records for a bucket, then PTR_i has the special pointer value NULL; otherwise it points to the first record in a list of records in the overflow area.

An overflow record location consists of two major parts: OR, which contains an overflow record, and LINK, which contains the address of the next node in the list of overflow records for a given primary location. KEY is the key of the record contained in OR. If the overflow record is at location P in storage, then these records' parts are referenced by OR (P), KEY (P), and LINK (P). If a record at location Q follows a record at location P in an overflow list, then the value of LINK (P) is the address Q. If the record at location P is the last record in the linked list of records, then LINK (P) has the special value NULL designating the end of the list.

A description of an algorithm for chaining into a separate overflow area is now given.

Algorithm CHAINSL. *Given a record R with a key x, it is required to insert R into the file B. If an overflow results, then R is stored in a record location in a separate overflow area. The hashing function H is used to calculate the initial primary address.*

1. [*Apply hashing function*] Set $i \leftarrow H(x)$
2. [*Scan the primary bucket location*]
   Repeat for $j = 1, 2, \ldots, b$:
   If $K_{ij} < 0$, then set $B_{ij} \leftarrow R$ and exit.
3. [*Put R in overflow storage*]
   Obtain a free overflow record location from a list of available locations and assign its address to P.
   Set OR $(P) \leftarrow R$, LINK$(P) \leftarrow PTR_i$, $PTR_i \leftarrow P$, and exit.

In step 2, the record is placed in the bucket it is "hashed" to if a record location is available. Otherwise, an overflow location is obtained, its address is assigned to P, record R is placed in the location, and pointers LINK (P) and PTR_i are altered so that the new record location is the first in the overflow chain.

An algorithm for retrieving a record from a file when using chaining into a separate overflow area is achieved by replacing steps 2 and 3 in algorithm CHAINSL by the following two steps.

2. [*Search the bucket indicate d*]
   Repeat for $j = 1, 2, \ldots, b$:
   If $x = K_{ij}$, then set $R \leftarrow B_{ij}$ and exit; otherwise, if $K_{ij} < 0$ and $K_{ij} \neq$ MARK, then exit unsuccessfully.
   Set $P \leftarrow PTR_i$.
3. [*Search the overflow chain*]
   If P = NULL, then exit unsuccessfully.
   If Key $(P) = x$, then set $R \leftarrow$ OR(P) and exit; otherwise, set $P \neq$ LINK(P) and repeat this step.

For chaining, the length of search is 1 for records stored in primary buckets and is $1 + k$ for an overflow record, where k is the record's position in the overflow list.

Knuth[7] has derived formulae for the expected average length of search (i.e., E[ALOS] with chaining, using a probabilistic model similar to that used for the open addressing case. For a bucket capacity of one and a load factor α,

$$E[\text{ALOS}] \simeq + \tfrac{1}{2}\alpha. \tag{10}$$

Using Equations (7) and (8) given earlier, the approximation for any bucket capacity is

$$E[\text{ALOS}] \simeq 1 + (1 - \tfrac{1}{2}b(1 - \alpha))t_b(\alpha)$$

$$+ \frac{e^{-b\alpha}b^b\alpha^b}{2b!} R(\alpha, b) + \text{Order of } (1/m). \tag{11}$$

Table 3 gives E[ALOS] as calculated using Approximations (10) and (11).

When comparing E[ALOS] for open addressing and chaining as given in Tables 2 and 3, we can make the following observations. It is possible for E[ALOS] to be less with open addressing than with chaining for bucket capacities greater than 1. The reason for this is that for chaining, overflow records generally are stored individually and not in buckets. In one disk access at most one overflow record can be retrieved regardless of bucket capacity. With open addressing, overflow records are stored in buckets, and therefore one or more may be retrieved in one access to disk storage. If E[ALOS] is less with open addressing than with chaining for a certain b and α, then the difference is usually very small. On the other hand, for high load factors and small bucket capacities, E[ALOS] is much less for chaining than for open addressing. It must be considered, however, that open addressing is a simpler collision resolution technique to implement. Chaining with separate lists requires the use of pointers and additional storage for overflow records. Because chaining uses overflow storage, it is not fair to compare open addressing and chaining for the same load factor. For chaining, the load factor is actually lower than indicated by using the formula $\alpha = n/(mb)$.

Olson[22] demonstrates how to estimate space utilization for a direct file using chaining with separate lists. His estimates of the main file and overflow storage utilizations are based on a random distribution of keys over addresses, the same assumption made in Knuth's model. Olson also investigates space utilization in the case of insertion and deletion activity, and finds that the overflow storage requirements do not stabilize until the number of additions to overflow storage is equal to the number of deletions from it. He assumes that if a record is deleted from a bucket of the main storage area, then no relocation of overflow records takes place.

A variation of separate chaining, which involves a self-organization concept, can be used to reduce access times, especially when a large number of record retrievals are required in a file. By retaining access statistics on data records, it

TABLE 3. E[ALOS] for Chaining with Separate Lists

Bucket capacity b	Load factor, α									
	.10	.20	.30	.40	.50	.60	.70	.80	.90	.95
1	1.0500	1.1000	1.1500	1.2000	1.2500	1.3000	1.350	1.400	1.450	1.5
5	1.0000	1.0008	1.0046	1.0151	1.0358	1.0699	1.119	1.186	1.286	1.3
20	1.0000	1.0000	1.0000	1.0000	1.0005	1.0038	1.018	1.059	1.150	1.2

becomes possible to move often accessed records towards the front of a chain of colliding records and thereby reduce the overall ALOS. Heising[23] first noted the effects of such a strategy.

4.3 Chaining with Coalescing Lists

A second overflow handling technique involving chaining is referred to as coalesced chaining by Knuth[7] and by Severance and Duhne.[6] With this method, a colliding record is placed in an open prime area location. The record is linked together with other records with the same hash value in a list starting at the prime bucket to which the record was initially mapped. Therefore, when a record is retrieved, a search commences through a chain of prime area buckets until the required record or an empty record location is found. Note that a record may now be mapped to a location which contains only overflow records. Because there is only one pointer field, say PTR_i, for each bucket, say B_i, it is necessary to traverse a linked list of buckets beginning with PTR_i until the desired record is found. In such instances, therefore, it is necessary that more than one overflow list be coalesced (i.e., in a chain of buckets, keys which are mapped to different addresses can be found.)

An algorithm for coalesced chaining follows.

Algorithm CHAINCOL. *Given a record R with a key x and a record location s which indicates where a search for an open location begins, it is required to insert R into the file B with m buckets. If an overflow results, then R is stored at the first open location in the last bucket of the overflow list for that record. If no such location is found then the record is placed in the first bucket with an open location which precedes bucket s + 1 in the file. Buckets s + 1 through m are assumed to be completely filled.*

1. [*Apply hashing function*] Set $i \leftarrow H(x)$.
2. [*Find end of list*]
   Repeat while $PTR_i \neq$ NULL: set $i \leftarrow PTR_i$.
3. [*Find an open location in the list if available*]
   Repeat for $j = 1, 2, \ldots, b$:
      If $K_{ij} < 0$, then set $B_{ij} \leftarrow R$, and exit.
4. [*Find a bucket with an open location*]
   Set $q \leftarrow i$. (q is a temporary index)
   Repeat for $i = s, s - 1, \ldots, 1$:
      Repeat for $j = 1, 2, \ldots, b$:
         If $K_{ij} < 0$,
         then set $B_{ij} \leftarrow R$, $PTR_q \leftarrow i$, $s \leftarrow i$, and exit.
5. [*Emit error*]
   Print "file overflow" and exit.

Algorithm CHAINCOL does not insert a record in a location marked deleted.

For extremely volatile files, an improvement in performance is achieved if this change was made to the algorithm. Another variation of the algorithm involves keeping a linked list of buckets with locations that are open or marked deleted. When a new bucket is required (i.e. , step 4), then it can be located immediately instead of searching buckets s to 1.

To retrieve a record R with a key of x using coalesced chaining, we replace steps 2 through 5 in algorithm CHAINCOL by the following. (Note that TRAVERSING is used as a logical variable.)

2. [*Initialization for traversal*] Set TRAVERSING←true.
3. [*Traverse through coalesced chain*]
   Repeat steps 4 and 5 while TRAVERSING:
4. [*Examine the individual record locations for bucket i*]
   Repeat for $j = 1, 2, \ldots, b$:
     If $K_{ij} =$, then set $R \leftarrow B_{ij}$ and exit;
     otherwise, if $K_{ij} < 0$ and $K_{ij} \neq$ MARK, then exit unsuccessfully.
5. [*Check pointer field for bucket i*]
   If PTR_i = NULL, then set TRAVERSING← false;
   otherwise, set $i \leftarrow PTR_i$.
6. [*Finished*] Exit unsuccessfully.

An analysis by Knuth[7] establishes a formula for the expected number of probes in a random successful search as

$$E[\text{ALOS}] \simeq 1 + \tfrac{1}{8}\alpha(e^2a - 1 - 2\alpha) + \alpha/4.$$

This assumes a bucket capacity of one. No such analysis has been formulated for bucket capacities greater than 1. Table 4 gives E[ALOS] with different load factors for a bucket capacity of 1. Note that the ALOS values for small load factors (i.e., .10 to .70) are less than those for separate chaining. These values should be identical with or slightly larger than the comparable values for separate chaining. The discrepancies are due to the approximations introduced in the derivations of the closed-form formulas for both methods. In general, the ALOS values for coalesced chaining fall between those for separate chaining and open addressing. Results are not supplied for load factors greater than one, since an analysis of this case has not been completed and remains an open and difficult problem.

It should be obvious that coalesced chaining can be viewed as a hybrid of the open addressing and separate chaining techniques and, as such, it assumes many of the advantages and disadvantages of each technique. The main advantage with the coalesced chaining method is that all records are kept in the prime area and, if algorithm CHAINCOL is modified so as to search for an open location as close as possible to the home bucket, then the potential seek time overhead (i.e., the amount of time to position the read/write heads over the desired track) is reduced when compared to chaining into a separate overflow

TABLE 4. E[ALOS] **for Coalesced Chaining in a Successful Search**

Bucket capacity of 1	Load factor, α									
	.10	.20	.30	.40	.50	.60	.70	.80	.90	.95
	1.0253	1.0523	1.0833	1.1213	1.1699	1.234	1.320	1.435	1.590	1.7

area. In addition, more of the prime area will be filled with active records than is the case in the separate overflow method. Coalesced chaining has an advantage over open addressing because an overflow record can be located almost immediately via the overflow list as opposed to the potentially time consuming process of examining a list of unrelated records.

The main disadvantage of the coalesced chaining technique when compared with separate chaining is the longer search time. This extra search time can arise because a coalesced list can be longer than a corresponding separate list for a given hashed address (i.e., primary bucket location). From the viewpoint of space requirements, coalesced chaining requires more memory than open addressing due to the pointer field that is associated with each bucket.

Certainly, further analysis of and experimentation with coalescing lists is required. It may be a particularly good technique for applications in which space is an important factor and yet a reasonably small ALOS is necessary.

4.4 Rehashing

The final technique we examine also involves the insertion of overflow records in the prime area (as was the case with open addressing and coalescing lists). In this instance, a sequence of address transformations as generated by unrelated hashing functions is used to locate a free location for an overflow record.

One of the phenomena present in open addressing is the problem of *primary clustering*. If we examine the linear probing method, for example, it becomes easy to visualize that, as records are inserted into the same area in a file, long searches for new record locations become more frequent. This phenomenon can be illustrated with an example. Referring to Figure 2, assume the set of keys {JONES, SMITH, ABRAHMS, WALKER} is transformed into the addresses {1, 1, 2, 7} respectively, of a small file of size eleven by a certain hashing function. Prior to the first insertion, the probability of a new record being inserted into a particular position is 1/11. In the second insertion, however, the probability that position 2 will become occupied is twice as great as any remaining available position, since the entry will be placed in position 2 if the key is mapped into either 1 or 2. Continuing in this manner, on the fourth insertion the probability that the new entry is placed in position 4 is four times as likely as its being placed in any remaining unoccupied position. Thus, the trend

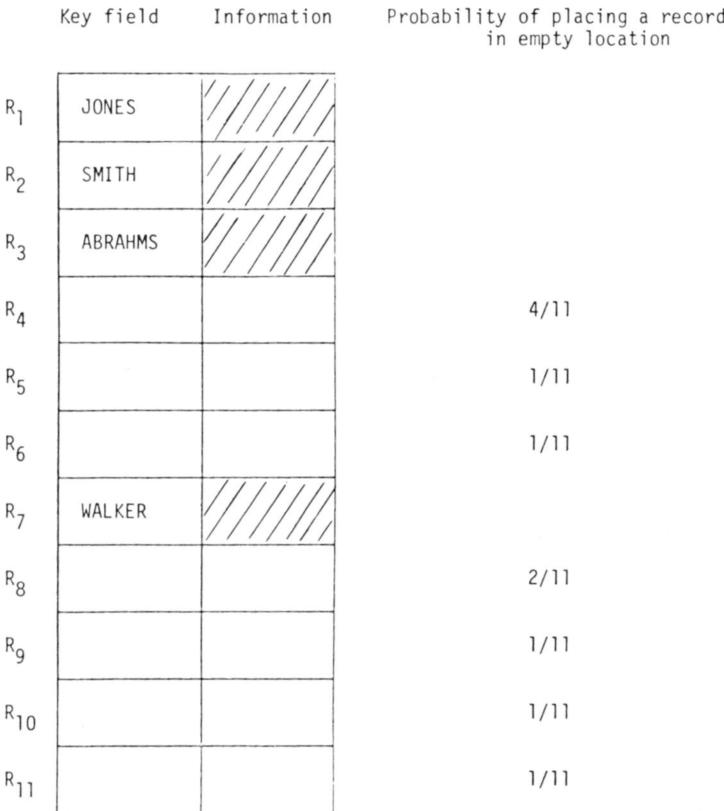

Key field
Information
Probability of placing a record in empty location
R1
JONES
R2
SMITH
R3
ABRAHMS
R4
4/11
R5
1/11
R6
1/11
R7
WALKER
R8
2/11
R9
1/11
R10
1/11
R11
1/11

FIGURE 2. An example illustrating unequal probabilities of record placement.

is for long sequences of occupied positions to become longer and a clustering effect takes place.

If consecutive keys $\{k, k + 1, k + 2, \ldots\}$ appear frequently in the key set, then the primary clustering problem can be relieved to some degree by using an open addressing technique in which the constant increment is some value c that is greater than 1 and relatively prime to m, the file size. This variation of the open addressing technique was discussed earlier in Section 4.1. However, even if this technique is used, some *secondary clustering* can occur as discussed in Knuth.[7]

The clustering phenomenon can be alleviated by rehashing, a method first described by de Balbine.[24] In this technique, the increment value c is computed by using a second hashing function. This second function is independent of the initial hashing function and it generates a value which is relatively prime to the file size. (If the probability that a key is mapped to the same address is in the order of $1/m^2$ when applied to two hashing functions, then these functions are said to be independent.) Knuth[7] suggests selecting m to be prime (when using the division method), and setting $H_1(k) = k \bmod m$ and $H_2(k) = 1 + (k \bmod (m - 2))$, where k is the key and m is the file size. This works particularly well if m and $m - 2$ are "twin primes" such as 1021 and 1019. A key of 125 generates the following sequence of probes for H_1 and H_2 as just given and assuming m is 11 (H_1 and H_2 will have values of 4 and 8, respectively):

$$\{4, 1, 9, 6, 3, 0, 8, 5, 2, 10, 7\}.$$

The algorithms for inserting and retrieving records using the rehashing technique are identical with those described earlier for open addressing, except that the increment c will be calculated using a second hashing function (i.e., $H_2(x)$) for a given key x.

Knuth[7] has shown by empirical tests that the expected number of probes in a random successful search is approximately $-\frac{1}{2}\log(1 - \alpha)$ when a bucket capacity of 1 is considered.

No empirical tests have been conducted to arrive at an approximation for the E[ALOS] for bucket capacities greater than 1. Conducting a series of tests for a variety of capacities would be very expensive; however, a main reason that such formulae have not been developed is that for most file applications (applications involving a bucket capacity of greater than 1), rehashing is impractical. In Section 6, we shall elaborate on the reasons for this.

Table 5 gives E[ALOS] using the same load factors present in the previous tables in this section. Notice that in general the E[ALOS] values are less than those obtained for open addressing.

We conclude our review of collision resolution techniques by stating that the best technique is very much dependent upon the type of application in which it is applied. In Section 6, we shall examine two important application areas and suggest which techniques are best for each application.

5 A COMPARATIVE ANALYSIS OF HASHING FUNCTIONS

A number of significant analyses of hashing functions have been performed, and in this section the basic approaches that have been used in studying hashing functions and the conclusions of these studies are described.

Buchholz[2] presents results from one of the first experimental analyses of hashing functions when applied to different key sets. While these experiments

TABLE 5. E[ALOS] for Rehashing in a Successful Search

Bucket capacity of 1	Load factor, α									
	.10	.20	.30	.40	.50	.60	.70	.80	.90	.95
	1.0536	1.1157	1.1889	1.2771	1.3862	1.5272	1.720	2.012	2.558	3.2

are quite limited in scope, his discussion of properties exhibited by key sets and the use of hashing functions taking these properties into consideration is quite significant. He suggests that there are two important distributions to consider: the distribution in the key space of keys for a key set, and the distribution of addresses in the address space when a hashing function is applied to that key set. A completely uniform set of keys is ideal, and direct addressing can be used in this case. A random distribution of keys in the key space allows at best a random distribution of addresses when a hashing function is applied. All key sets possess both elements of uniformity and randomness. Clusters give nonuniformity to a key set, but the irregular size and separation of these clusters does add a certain degree of randomness.

Buchholz states that hashing functions such as radix transformation, which try to randomize the key set, only destroy uniformity that could be used to advantage. He concludes that a good hashing function should reflect both the uniformity and randomness of the key set in the addresses it generates. His opinion is that the division method using a prime divisor is the best function for transforming unique numerical keys to addresses in a smaller range.

The analysis by Lum, Yuen, and Dodd[4] provides a major experimental, comparative evaluation of several hashing functions. They determine the ALOS and percentage of colliding records for many combinations of load factors, bucket capacities, hashing functions, and collision resolution techniques for a number of key sets. Eight different key sets that contain from 500 to 33,575 elements are used, but only two sets have more than 5000 elements and three sets have less than 1000 elements. Load factors vary from .5 to .95 inclusive by steps of .05. Bucket capacities of 1, 2, 5, 10, 20, and 50 are used. The hashing functions that are evaluated include the division method, digit analysis, the midsquare method, folding, radix transformation, and algebraic coding. The basic collision resolution techniques, open addressing and chaining with separate lists, are used.

The statistics which Lum et al. obtain are presented in tables rather than as graphs, which they state would be too difficult to interpret. The ALOS for each combination of factors mentioned above is not given, but it is averaged over the eight different key sets and the standard deviation is also provided. The same approach is used for presenting the percentage of colliding records. It is found that the two statistics are dependent on each other, the ALOS increasing when the percentage of colliding records in a file increases.

Lum et al. find that no hashing function performs consistently better than others, but the division method gives the best overall performance. In nearly all cases, it outperformed the theoretical randomization statistics as presented in Section 4.2 when separate overflow was used. Other functions may sometimes perform better, but they present a higher risk of obtaining inferior results more often. In particular, the algebraic coding method was just inferior to the division method and superior to the theoretical results when separate chaining overflow was employed. If open addressing is used, however, the algebraic coding performed poorly while the division and midsquare methods produced the best results. (For load factors below .75, the midsquare method consistently yielded particularly good results.) The results that are obtained confirm the conclusions of Buchholz. A random distribution of keys over addresses should not be a goal and an efficient hashing function should preserve the uniformity that exists in a key set.

For the hashing functions tested, Lum et al. state that open addressing should not be used with a bucket capacity of less than 10 records. For larger bucket capacities and with the division method, open addressing performs comparably to and sometimes better than chaining. The differences in ALOS between the two collision resolution techniques, however, is very small in these cases.

Lum[25] extends the analysis of Lum et al. by performing an analytical study of the hashing functions they tested. His approach is set-theoretic and allows the prediction and comparison of hashing function performance for all possible key sets from a key space. He identifies key distributions to which certain hashing functions are most applicable. Given a hashing function, keys are then selected that result in optimum performance. Lum's theory can be used to verify the experimental results of Lum et al.

It is questionable whether the selection of keys to suit a hashing function is a practical approach to indirect addressing as key sets may be defined with other factors in mind. Lum's analysis is complicated and since it is a relatively recent development, no evaluation of his work is available.

A recent paper by Severance and Duhne[6] entitled "A practitioner's guide to addressing algorithms" attempts to consolidate a number of commonly accepted rules used in address translation, particularly as they apply to distribution-independent hashing functions. They review a number of previously derived results for the different collision resolution techniques. Some new analysis is performed assuming a certain record loading order. An ordering of overflow records is prescribed, based on an assumption of unequal probability of record access as suggested by Heising[23] (in particular, Heising proposed that in many commercial applications, 80% of the retrievals affect only the most active 20% of a file's records). Empirical results are obtained for specific auxiliary memory devices and a number of "rules of thumb" are asserted. They include:

1. A good transformation is one which randomizes the assignment of identifiers (i.e., keys) over the entire memory space.
2. Faced with an arbitrary set of keys, the selection of a transformation technique is obvious: the division method is preferred.
3. Because of its random probing of secondary memory, the rehashing technique of collision resolution is likely to exhibit a relatively poor retrieval time for load factors in excess of .5.
4. Simplicity is the single most important advantage of the open addressing overflow method. This advantage is in no sense trivial since it is a domi-

nant concern of analysts involved with the rapid design of reliable and maintainable systems.

5. When the maximum utilization of available storage space is a primary design consideration, a chained technique of collision resolution is likely to be the best alternative.
6. When the use of an independent overflow area is desirable, total space requirements may be reduced by either increasing the primary area bucket size or by increasing the primary area loading factor.
7. Since comparatively few records will overflow a bucket in the primary memory area, there is no advantage to buckets of size greater than one in the overflow area.
8. If data records are retrieved with unequal probability, it is most advantageous to load them in the order of decreasing frequency of access. (Note that this holds if the file is relatively stable and most file activity is of a retrieval nature).
9. A good primary area loading factor should lie between .80 and .85
10. An analyst's primary responsibility is, simply, to assure that poor designs are avoided.

The first study to compare distribution-dependent and distribution-independent hashing functions was performed by Deutscher, Tremblay, and Sorenson.[17] This initial study compared the division method (the method which yields the best performance for distribution-independent functions), and the four distribution-dependent functions: the piece-wise linear function, Fourier hashing function, multiple frequency distribution function and the piece-wise linear function with interval splitting. Two different key sets were used in the experimentation; namely, a set of 3250 Library of Congress Catalog Card Numbers and 840 town names, and these were tested on five different load factors. It was found that the Fourier hashing function gave the highest average length of search for all load factors. For the set of town names, the piece-wise linear function out-performed the division method when open addressing collision resolution was used. These results, however, did not hold for the Library of Congress set and for both key sets the division method produced superior results when separate chaining was adopted.

The piece-wise linear function with interval splitting gave better results than the division method in almost all instances, but did not perform as well as the multiple frequency distribution function. The multiple frequency distribution function, however, required a larger amount of storage and more time to compute than the interval splitting technique since in the latter approach only those intervals which yielded poor performance were split to a significant degree.

For collision resolution with chaining, the multiple frequency distribution function was only slightly better than the division method. For collision resolution with open addressing, the multiple frequency distribution function outperformed the division method significantly (by factors ranging from 1.4 to 13.7). All the tests were performed assuming a bucket capacity of one.

In a second paper, Deutscher et al.[18] reconfirmed the analysis of the first paper with bucket capacities of greater than one. It must be noted that the multiple frequency distribution function did not perform significantly better than the division method with higher bucket capacities. Test results were reported on two of four theoretically derived distributions as well as the Library of Congress key set used in the initial experiments. The theoretically derived distributions each consisted of 800 integer keys. The keys were generated assuming (i) uniform distribution, (ii) skewed distribution, (iii) normal distribution, and (iv) clustered distribution. The results from (ii) and (iii) did not vary significantly from those of (i) and hence were not reported. In all cases, the multiple frequency distribution function showed its superiority when open addressing is employed.

The performance of the multiple frequency distribution function and the division method were compared when the requirement to reorganize a direct file and to redefine a hashing function was present. Reorganization was forced by continuing to add records to a file until a certain average length of search was violated. Once this happened, the file was reorganized and the load factor brought down to the original load factor before new additions were made. This process was continued as often as necessary to accommodate an insertion key set. In most cases, it was found that the multiple frequency distribution function required fewer reorganizations than the division method. For higher bucket capacities, however, the division method outperformed the multiple frequency distribution function. The multiple frequency distribution function was more consistent than the division method in the sense that after each reorganization the average length of search for this function returns to its approximate initial value.

The major conclusion derivable from these two experiments is that distribution-dependent functions (in particular, the multiple frequency distribution function) can give very good results when used in conjunction with open addressing. Insertion and deletion activity is possible with the multiple frequency distribution function, but one must be aware of the distribution of keys to which this function is applied.

The use of a distribution-dependent hashing function is often contingent on the number of operations and the amount of space required in computing function values. Deutscher[19] derived the results shown in Tables 6 and 7. To understand these entries, it is necessary to review the algorithms presented in Section 3.2. It becomes obvious from reviewing these tables that the use of distribution-dependent hashing functions becomes feasible if the average length of search that the functions provide justifies their computational complexity and storage requirements.

These final results, in conjunction with those expressed earlier (especially by Severance and Duhne[6], should give the analyst charged with the responsibility of designing direct files an overview of the expected performances for each of the address transformation methods described. Let us now turn our attention to a discussion of the application of address transformation techniques.

TABLE 6. Storage Requirements for Hashing Functions

	Parameters	Storage (in words)
Piece-wise linear function	m, n, a, L, j $N_i, G_i,\ 1 \leqslant i \leqslant j$	$j + 5$
Fourier hashing function	$m, a, d, \pi, t, \bar{x},$ $c_i, s_i,\ 1 \leqslant i \leqslant t$	$2t + 6$
Multiple frequency distribution function	$m, n, a, d, L, j, q,$ $N_{ik}, G_{ik},\ 1 \leqslant i \leqslant j,\ 1 \leqslant k \leqslant q$	$jq + 7$
Piece-wise linear function with interval splitting	$m, n, a, L, j, p,$ $N_i, G_i,\ 1 \leqslant i \leqslant s$	$s + 6$
Division method	m	1

TABLE 7. Arithmetic Operations for the Hashing Functions

	Addition/ subtraction	Multiplication/ division	Exponentiation	Trigonometric function evaluation
Piece-wise linear function	7	5		
Fourier hashing function	$5t + 5$	$5t + 8$		$2t$
Multiple frequency distribution function	$10q$	$7q + 1$		
Piece-wise linear function with interval splitting	$7v^{a} + 1$	$3v + 3$		
Division method	1	1		

[a] v is the average number of times that k is incremented in step 2 of algorithm Interval Splitting.

6 THE APPLICATION OF KEY-TO-ADDRESS TRANSFORMATION TECHNIQUES

In this section a discussion of some of the areas in which address transformation techniques have been applied is undertaken and some specific recommendations are made as to which address transformation strategy it is best to apply in a given situation. In particular, address transformations as applied to table handling and direct file access are considered. Problems encountered when using tables with large records and tables in a virtual storage environment are outlined. Finally, the applicability of address transformation algorithms to ordered files is described.

6.1 Table Handling

While our discussion has concentrated on files, it is obvious that many of the key-to-address transformation techniques are applicable to table handling—an activity which arises commonly in compilers, interpreters, assemblers, and in editing programs in many data processing applications. Because tables reside entirely in main memory, there are two siginficant properties which affect the decision of which key-to-address transformation technique should be applied in a particular situation.

Property 1.

The time to access a record, given its address, is approximately equal to (and in fact is generally less than) the time to perform an arithmetic operation, a logical comparison, or any other basic machine-level instruction.

Property 2.

Given the address of a record location, the time to access that location is the same for all locations in the table.

As an obvious and direct consequence of Property 1, we should avoid using hashing functions which require an extended amount of time to compute an initial address transformation. Therefore, hashing functions such as radix transformation, algebraic coding, and the more elaborate distribution-dependent methods should not be adopted. A list of hashing function candidates include the division, midsquare, folding, digit analysis, and piece-wise linear methods. This list is ordered approximately from most applicable to least applicable. And, unless the key (i.e., identifier) space is unusually distributed based on a lexical ordering of the keys, it is best to use the division method.

The second property, the property of equal access time, affects the decision as to what type of collision resolution technique should be adopted when a hashing algorithm is applied to table handling. Based on Property 2, a decision can be made immediately concerning the capacity of a bucket in a table. Since the time to access each record location is equal, there is no advantage in grouping a number of locations to form a bucket. That is, the fact that the next location to be accessed is physically adjacent to the current location is of no particular advantage in a table. Therefore, a bucket capacity of one should always be used in a table.

Tables 2–5 of Section 4 were all constructed assuming Property 2 and all show results for a bucket capacity of one. As a result, the following observations can be made. Rehashing is a better collision resolution technique than open addressing if the expense of a very little extra processing time to compute a rehash value is ignored. Chaining (coalesced or separate) is more attractive than rehashing if a small penalty in space for link fields is accepted. In addition, the searching of long chains of colliding records, some of which were marked previously as deleted, can be avoided in a chaining technique. This fact is not accounted for in Tables 2–5. Finally, separate chaining is superior to coalesced chaining mainly because records from more than one overflow chain are not coalesced to form even larger chains when using separate chaining. It should be noted, however, that if space is at a premium and record insertion and deletion are minimal, then coalesced chaining may be an attractive compromise because very little time would have to be spent maintaining coalescing lists and all record locations would reside in a primary area. In conclusion, we can say that using the division method with the separate chaining collision resolution technique is a good general key-to-address transformation strategy for tables; however, the special circumstances of a particular application may dictate that other techniques should be used.

6.2 File Searching

Just as we outlined two important properties when characterizing key-to-address transformation schemes for tables, we can propose two complementary properties for file searching.

Property 1A.

The time to access a record in a file, given its address, is significantly longer (in fact, in the order of 1,000 to 10,000 times longer) than the time to perform an arithmetic operation, a logical comparison, or any other basic machine-level instruction.

Property 2A.

Given the address of a record location, the time to access that location is not the same for all locations in the file. (In fact, it may take 10 to 100 times longer to access some record locations than others.)

Property 1A tells us that expending some processor time to compute a hashing function value is relatively insignificant when compared to the time to access a particular record of a file. If this extra processing time can yield a better set of hash values (i.e., a set of values with few collisions), then it would be time well spent. As a consequence of Property 1A, some of the more computationally expensive hashing functions such as the radix transformation, algebraic coding, multiple frequency, and piece-wise linear with interval splitting methods can realistically be considered in direct file processing. The results obtained by Lum et al.[4] and presented in Section 5 indicate, however, that the algebraic methods (i.e., radix transformation and algebraic coding) do not, in general, perform as well as the computationally simpler methods such as the division and midsquare methods. On the other hand, the results of Deutscher et al.[17] do tell us that the multiple frequency and interval splitting distribution-dependent methods can perform better than the division method assuming that (i) a fairly significant amount of space can be allocated for the hashing function tables, (ii) the keys used in an application are distributed in a manner similar to the sample set used to calculate the distribution-dependent function, (iii) the file must be relatively stable (i.e., only a small percentage of the transactions posted against the file should be insertions and deletions, otherwise, the distribution-dependency of the hashing function is lost), and (iv) open addressing is used.

Property 2A, the property of unequal access time, again affects the type of collision resolution technique to be adopted, as was the case for table handling. The primary reasons for unequal access times are the capability of a direct access device to bring in blocks of records at one time and the significant delays that are encountered with movable head direct access devices when a seek (i.e., arm movement) must take place. Whenever possible, it is advantageous to store a number of records together in a uniquely addressable block (i.e., a bucket) such that all records in the block can be transferred to or from a buffer area of main memory in one access (i.e., using a single I/O statement). The time to access a particular record location within a bucket is then minimized since a search for a record can be done in main memory. Therefore, bucket capacities should be made as large as possible subject to constraints on the size of buffer space available in main memory and the amount of time it takes to locate a record in a bucket, including data transfer time.

Even if large buckets are used, bucket overflow can still take place and a collision resolution technique must be adopted to locate overflow records. It is advisable to keep an overflow record as close as possible to its home location to avoid disk arm movements which can take a considerable amount of time. Therefore, open addressing and coalesced chaining, both using a linear probing strategy to locate an open location, appear to be good collision resolution techniques. Note that algorithm CHAINCOL in Section 4.3 should be altered so as not to search for open locations at the end of the file space and thus avoid unnecessary seeks. Separate chaining into the same seek area as a home location is a good strategy also, providing the creation of separate overflow areas for each seek area does not disrupt a contiguous auxiliary memory address space. Another disadvantage with separate overflow areas is that they are generally not blocked and a separate I/O request must be made for each record on an overflow chain. Rehashing should be avoided since an overflow location can be anywhere in the address space of the file. In conclusion, the division method using an open addressing linear probe collision resolution technique with a large bucket capacity appears to be the best overall strategy when directly accessing files. Again, special conditions may suggest the use of other techniques such as distribution-dependent hashing functions.

6.3 Other Considerations

There are some additional considerations that must be taken into account when considering key-to-address transformation techniques. One such consideration is the size of the record. Morris[3] suggested that large records all be placed in an overflow area and that the primary area, which he refers to as a *scatter table*, contain only pointer entries to the overflow area. In the event that the primary area contains only a few active entries, this technique can significantly save on storage since an empty pointer entry is substantially smaller than a larger record location. The scatter table technique is probably of little benefit in a direct file organization since the extra access via the scatter table incurs too much overhead.

A second consideration which we have neglected and which is discussed by Morris[3] deals with the storage of tables in virtual memory systems. In such a system a record access may inadvertently cause a page (or segment) fault. If this happens, then a time delay occurs because the required record is not residing in main memory and therefore it must be brought in to be accessed. In such cases, it is most efficient to select a means of access which ensures that consecutive references are, as often as possible, on the same page or segment. A linear probing scheme obviously becomes the most attractive technique.

As a final consideration when applying key-to-address transformation techniques let us look at the problem of directly accessing ordered files.

6.4 Direct access of ordered files

Held[26] presented three conditions which he felt are desirable for key-to-address transformation functions. (i) The function should not introduce additional secondary storage accesses in order to compute an address. (ii) The function should map the given sample key space uniformly across the address space. (iii) The function should be an order preserving function (i.e., if $K_1 < K_2$ then $H(K_1) \leqslant H(K_2)$ for any keys K_1 and K_2).

The first two conditions have been satisfied to some degree by all of the functions we have discussed. The third condition, however, has not been satisfied by all of the hashing functions—only some of the distribution-dependent functions, when combined with an appropriate collision resolution technique, satisfies this condition. We will elaborate on this point later in the section.

Held states that the order preserving condition is important whenever an attempt is made to handle queries involving qualifications specifying ranges on the primary key of a file (e.g., list all employees with employee numbers less than 60,000). Because the order preserving property is so difficult to satisfy, techniques other than key-to-address transformations are generally used to access records both directly and sequentially by order of primary key. Techniques involving the indexing (e.g., indexed sequential files and ordered index directories) or balanced trees have been used to obtain both relatively quick direct access and sequential access. (A detailed discussion of these techniques is outside the range of this survey. Knuth[7] and Tremblay and Sorenson [27] provide good references for these techniques.) Held combined the notions from hashing algorithms and directories to create a limited form of directory which he called a *generalized directory*. Basically, a generalized directory contains elements which map ranges of the key space into ranges of the address space in an order preserving manner. While Held was able to reduce the average length of search from that of a normal directory or balanced tree structure, the average number of accesses to locate a record is still of order $\log_c n$ for a file of size n with n/c directory items. What is desirable is an order preserving key-to-address transformation algorithm in which the average number of accesses is of order k where k is a constant, hopefully between 1 and 2.

Recall from Section 2 that the piece-wise linear function, multiple frequency function, and piece-wise linear function with interval splitting all had the semiorder preserving property: if $K_1 < K_2$, then $H(K_1) \leq H(K_2)$ for any keys K_1 and K_2. Note that it is sometimes impractical to use the whole key in the hashing function calculation. Instead the leftmost j bits of the key's representation can be chosen in such a way as to give a key space of 2^j values (see Rivest[28]) which remains order preserving. The distribution-dependent functions used in conjunction with a linear probe open addressing resolution technique can be made to be strictly order preserving if collisions are resolved in the following way. If $H(K_1) = H(K_2)$, for some K_1 and K_2, where $K_1 < K_2$, then K_1 is assigned to a lower address than K_2. Note that this assignment can be and should be done in such a way that if $K_1 < K_2$, $H(K_1) > H(K_2)$. An obvious way of ensuring an ordering of the file is to insert the records via, say, the multiple frequency function using linear probing, in an order identical with the ordering of the keys (i.e., sorting the records by key first and then inserting them). The net result is a file that can be accessed both directly and sequentially.

To exemplify this process, consider the result of hashing and inserting the sample numerical key set

46, 23, 18, 11, 65, 57, 94, 36, 13, 87, 70, 85, 61, 30, 49,

using a nondecreasing hashing function in which all the keys in the ranges 1–20, 21–40, 41–60, 61–80, and 81–100 are each hashed into a distinct bucket. This process is shown as sorting proceeds in Figure 3. The m (in our example

	3 records entered	6 records entered	9 records entered	12 records entered	15 records entered
bucket 1 (1-20)	18	11, 18	11, 13, 18	11, 13, 18	11, 13, 18
bucket 2 (21-40)	23	23	23, 36	23, 36	23, 30, 36
bucket 3 (41-60)	42	42, 57	42, 57	42, 57	42, 49, 57
bucket 4 (61-80)		65	65	65, 70	61, 65, 70
bucket 5 (81-100)			94	81, 87, 94	81, 87, 94

FIGURE 3. Trace of an address calculation sort.

5) buckets obtained during the hash and insert phase can now be trivially merged to yield the desired sorted file. Knuth[7] has shown that the average number of comparisons for this method is proportional to n. This result, however, holds only if the probability of hashing any key to any number between 1 and m is $1/m$. That is, the keys are uniformly distributed over the address space. The worst case occurs when all keys are mapped into the same bucket. In this case the performance of the method degenerates to order n^2.

The basic ordering process we have described was first discussed by Isaac and Singleton[15] when they described *address calculation* sorting. The notion of address calculation sorting was extended by Tarter and Kronmal.[16] Using a piece-wise linear hashing function, they calculated the expected number of comparisons required for key sets which were not uniformly distributed. With this hashing function, the expected number of comparisons was also found to be proportional to n.

The four distribution-dependent hashing functions discussed in Section 2 are all nondecreasing functions. When the file is initially constructed, the records in each bucket need only be kept in order to yield a sorted file. If the initial file is sorted before hashing, however, then the hashed file will also be completely ordered.

We are presently investigating the properties of the multiple frequency function and the piece-wise linear function with interval splitting with respect to the sorting process. In particular, the performance of these functions with and without preloading is being examined. Also, the performance of these functions with respect to volatile files is being evaluated. Indications are that these distribution-dependent hashing functions will yield a sorted file at very little cost—an important by-product in many applications involving the use of large files. These results will be reported in a later paper.

ACKNOWLEDGMENTS

This research was sponsored in part by the National Research Council of Canada, Grant Nos. A9290 and A9294. We should like to thank Janet Morck for her able assistance in typing the manuscript.

REFERENCES

1. William W. Peterson, "Addressing for random-access storage," IBM J. Res. Develop., Vol. 1, 130–146 April 1957.
2. Werner Buchholz, "File organization and addressing," IBM Systems J., Vol. 2, 86–110 June 1963.
3. R. Morris, "Scatter storage techniques," Communications of the ACM, Vol. 11, No. 1, 38–43, 1968.
4. V. Y. Lum, P.S.T. Yuen, and M. Dodd, "Key-to-address transform techniques: a fundamental performance study on large existing formatted files," Communications of the ACM, Vol. 14, No. 4, 228–239, 1978.
5. W. D. Maurer and T.G. Lewis, "Hash table methods," ACM Computing Surveys, Vol. 7, No. 1, 5–19, March 1975.
6. D. Severance and R. Duhne, "A practitioner's guide to addressing algorithms." Communications of the ACM, Vol. 19, No. 6, 314–326, 1976.
7. D.E. Knuth, Sorting and searching, the art of computer programming, Vol. 3. Reading: Addison-Wesley, 506–549, 1973.
8. Arnold I. Dumey, "Indexing for rapid random access memory systems," Computers and Automation, Vol. 5, No. 12, 16–9, 1956.
9. Andrew D. Lin, "Key addresing of random access memories by radix transformation," Proc. AFIPS Spring Joint Computer Conference, Vol. 23, 355–366, 1963.
10. G. Schay and N. Raver, "A method for key-to-address transformation," IBM J. Res. Develop., Vol. 7, 121–126, April 1963.
11. M. Hanan and F.P. Palermo, "An application of coding theory to a file address problem," IBM J. Res. Develop., Vol. 7, 127–129, April 1963.
12. Gary D. Knott, "Hashing functions," Computer J., Vol. 18, 265–278, August 1975.
13. Keith R. London, Techniques for direct access. Philadelphia: Auerbach Publishers, 1973.
14. Gary D. Knott, "Expandable open addressing hash table storage and retrieval, Proc. SIGEIDET Workshop on Data Description, Access, and Control, ACM, 187–206, 1971.
15. E.J. Isaac and R.C. Singleton, "Sorting by address calculation," J. ACM Vol. 3, 169–174, July 1956.
16. R.A. Kronmal and M.E. Tarter, "Cumulative polygon address calculation sorting," Proc. 20th Nat. Conf. ACM, 376–385, 1965.
17. R.F. Deutscher, J.P. Tremblay, and P.G. Sorenson, "A comparative study of distribution-dependent and distribution-independent hashing functions," Proc. ACM Pacific 75, San Francisco, 56–61, 17 and 18 April 1975.
18. R.F. Deutscher, P.G. Sorenson, and J.P. Tremblay, "Distribution-dependent hashing functions and their characteristics," Proc. Internat. Conf. on the Management of Data, ACM/SIGMOD, San Jose, 14–15, May 1975.

19. R.F. Deutscher, An analysis of distribution-dependent hashing functions M.SC. thesis, University of Saskatchewan, March 1975.
20. M.E. Tarter and R.A. Kronmal, ''Non-uniform key distribution and address calculation sorting,'' Proc. 21st Nat. Conf. ACM, 331–337, 1966.
21. M.E. Tarter and R.A. Kronmal, ''Estimation of the cumulative by Fourier series methods and application to the insertion problem,'' Proc. 23rd Nat. Conf. ACM 491–497, 1968.
22. Charles A. Olson ''Random access file organization for indirectly addressed records,'' Proc. 24th Nat. Conf. ACM, 539–549, 1969.
23. W.P. Heising, ''Note on random addressing techniques,'' IBM System J., Vol 2, 112–116, June 1963.
24. Guy, de Balbine, Ph.D. thesis, California Institute of Technology, 149–150, 1968.
25. V.Y. Lum, ''General performance analysis of key-to-address transformation methods using an abstract file concept,'' Communications of the ACM, Vol. 16, No. 10 603–612, 1973.
26. G.M. Held, ''Storage structures for relational data base management systems,'' Mem. No. ERL-M533, Electronics Research Laboratory Report, University of California, Berkeley 1975.
27. J.P. Tremblay and P.G. Sorenson, An introduction to data structures with applications. New York: McGraw-Hill, 1976.
28. R.L. Rivest, ''Analysis of associative retrieval algorithms,'' IRIA Rept. No. 54, Feb. 1974.

PART V

AUSTRALIAN COMPUTER SOCIETY

Paper selected by ACS as
the best paper submitted during
1977.

"The Implementation of a Database
Management System"
H.G. Mackenzie and J.L. Smith

The Australian Computer Society was founded in 1966 by the merger of five local computer societies to extend the knowledge and appreciation of digital and analog computers, automatic data processing systems, and computer-based automatic control systems and related theory; and to further the study and application of computer science and technology and related subjects in all branches of learning and enterprise. The ACS represents the Australian computing profession internationally, provides a forum for the discussion of computer matters, and advises on computer methods as they relate to the public interest.

More than 6,000 members hold membership in the ACS through its six branches in Australia. The society is a member of the International Federation for Information Processing (IFIP) and is affiliated with the Australian and New Zealand Association for the Advancement of Science.

Its publications include *The Australian Computer Journal*, published quarterly and the monthly *Australian Computer Bulletin*.

The ACS mailing address is P.O. Box 650, Crows Nest, N.S.W. 2065 Australia.

The Implementation of a Database Management System

H.G. Mackenzie and J.L. Smith

Division of Computing Research, CSIRO, Canberra.

This paper briefly traces the history of FORDATA, an implementation on CDC Cyber computers of the Codasyl Database Task Group's 1971 recommendations. It describes the characteristics and implementation of the various components of the system, and gives reasons for particular design decisions, and suggests possible system extensions.

KEYWORDS AND PHRASES: Computing Reviews Categories: 3.70, 3.73, 4.22, 4.33

INTRODUCTION

The Codasyl Database Task Group, known as DBTG, published reports in 1969 and 1971 (Codasyl, 1969, 1971), which specified a set of proposals for Database Management Systems. These proposals have produced a great deal of discussion on the most desirable architecture for Database systems, and have also been implemented by a number of manufacturers and other groups. We shall assume a basic familiarity with the Codasyl DBTG architecture; (Taylor and Frank, 1976) provides a good introduction.

The FORDATA system began with an implementation on a CDC 3600 computer by one of the present authors (J.L. Smith). It was originally based on the Codasyl DBTG's 1969 report, and was described at the fifth Australian Computer Conference (Smith, Chmura, and Johnson, 1972). The present paper docu-

---

EDITOR'S NOTE: *From The Australian Computer Journal, Vol. 9, No. 4, November 1977. Reprinted by permission of the publisher, Australian Computer Society, Inc.*

ments the changes that have taken place in the system over the last five years, during which the system has been primarily available on the Cyber76 computer system.

The present FORDATA system is based on the Codasyl DBTG 1971 Report (Codasyl, 1971). It consists of two Data Description Languages, two Data Manipulation Languages, and a Utility Package. There is one Data Description language, or DDL for schema, and one for subschema definition. There is one Data Manipulation Language, known as DML which provides the data manipulation commands defined in (Codasyl, 1971). This DML uses FORTRAN as its host language. A preprocessor converts FORTRAN augmented with DML commands to an equivalent FORTRAN program with calls to library routines in place of DML commands. It also inserts common blocks containing the user working area and the system communication locations, and other necessary FORTRAN declarations into each routine. As the listing produced by the DML translator includes line numbers which refer to the generated FORTRAN code, it is unusual in practice for listings of the generated code to be requested.

The second Data Manipulation language, known as QML, is designed for high level query only. No update commands are provided. It is implemented as a preprocessor which generates FORTRAN augmented with DML commands, and this must then be processed with the DML translator. Thus a query expressed in QML must pass through three translation stages, QML, DML and FORTRAN before it can be executed to produce output. This does not produce any practical complications as far as use is concerned, and the implementation was made much easier by using this cascaded preprocessor approach.

The system falls short of being a complete implementation in a number of areas.

1. It does not provide a COBOL host language interface. This is not as serious as it might appear, as an overwhelming proportion of the programming in CSIRO is done in FORTRAN.
2. There is no comprehensive multiaccess control system (discussed later). Thus the KEEP and FREE verbs are not implemented.
3. The MANDATORY/OPTIONAL property of set members is not implemented, a legacy of (Codasyl, 1969). The effective default is OPTIONAL.
4. The PRIVACY and CHECK clauses in the DDL are not available. Procedural data items, specified by a RESULT clause, may be used instead in many cases.
5. There is no Data Dictionary/Directory system. Although this may not be a component part of many present day Database Management Systems, it is often used in conjunction with them.
6. The ORDER verb is not implemented.
7. The available interactive system does not allow the full potential of database usage to be realized, although we expect this to be improved shortly.

2. ADDITIONAL FEATURES

In addition to the QML, several other improvements to the specifications have been implemented.

An extra DML command, (CHANGE), to augment the location mode specification, and exercise better control over record placement at run time has been implemented. This command also allows the user to inform FORDATA if he is presenting the records to be stored in a sorted set in sortkey order, allowing the time spent in searching the set or the index to be saved.

The currency suppression clauses in the STORE and FIND commands have been extended to allow the user to specify those sets whose currency updates are not to be suppressed. This has also proved very useful in practice.

An extension to format 6 of the FIND statement, to allow sets to be searched for a record containing keys equal to or greater than the key values supplied in the user working area, instead of matching on equality only, has been implemented. This enables efficient searches for records with data items within a range of values to be programmed in DML, without the programmer having to search through all members of the set. Any indexes defined on the set will be exploited.

An additional set mode called INDEX mode in which the major storage structure is a B-tree index (see Section 3.3). If the set is owned by SYSTEM there is no other storage structure, otherwise each member must be LINKED TO OWNER. This is the most efficient method of providing secondary indexing to a collection of records of one type which are not at the root level of a hierarchy.

A COBOL like definition for variable occurrence data items, with an upper bound being declared for the number of occurrences. The number of occurrences in any instance is controlled by a separate integer data item.

An extension of the MOVE verb to support the implementation of high level query languages. A list of database keys (a pointer-array) corresponding to a key value for a particular SEARCH or SORT key can be retrieved in a user working area array. Alternatively a count of the number of duplicates can be returned. The whole pointer-array structure of the index or pointer-array set can be traversed in key sort order using this command.

3. IMPLEMENTATION

There are a number of crucial design decisions which have to be made when implementing a Database Management System based on the Codasyl architecture. These decisions are interdependent, and determine the way in which other facilities may be added to the system. Some of the most important facilities involve the following:

1. I/O.
2. The interfaces between Database Management System, application programs and operating system.
3. Storage structure, and the access methods to be supported.
4. The representation of the object schema or subschema.
5. The binding time of the data structure to storage structure.

The considerations and tradeoffs involved in these decisions will be discussed, together with the alternatives, and the course of action adopted in implementing FORDATA.

3.1 I/O

The I/O system was implemented to take advantage of the architecture of the CYBER 76, and the features of that machine which influenced the design of the I/O system will be described. The CYBER 76 provides a hierarchy of two primary memories, one of 64K 60 bit words, called Small Core Memory, or SCM, and one of 512 thousand 60 bit words, called Large Core Memory, or LCM. SCM is used for the storage of executable instructions and data which is to be accessed in a random way, whilst LCM is used primarily for large block transfers to and from SCM. It is used by the operating system as a program swapping device. Single words of data can also be addressed, although this capability is not used in FORDATA. In its fast block transfer capability, LCM is similar to the Extended Core Storage, or ECS, available with the lower models of the CYBER range.

The database is divided into a number of areas, each of which is a separate random access file, resident on disk. Space on the disks on the CYBER 76 is allocated in multiples of a number of 512 word sectors. Each database area is divided into a number of "blocks," which must be a multiple of 512 words, matching the disc space allocation. Each block contains a number of "pages." System buffers in SCM and LCM are allocated to hold blocks and pages. I/O operations are done between the area files and the LCM block buffers.

There are relatively large, relatively slow, transfers of blocks to and from area files and LCM buffers, and smaller, much faster transfers between LCM block buffers and SCM page buffers. By having a two level system consisting essentially of pages of two different sizes, it was hoped to effectively use the transfer characteristics of the mass storage devices and the primary memories, and to reduce the amount of SCM necessary.

Due to several requests from overseas installations, FORDATA was modified to run on lower CYBER machines at the beginning of 1976. This necessitated altering the I/O significantly. At the same time a version was developed which used a single level paging system, for installations where Extended Core Storage was not available.

3.2 Application Program/DMBS/Operating System Interfaces

The application program makes requests to the database management system at run time. These requests are obeyed by routines which must access a translated version of the schema or subschema, the database and the user working area and the system locations of the application program.

The database management routines may either (1) reside in a supervisory program which communicates with a number of application programs accessing the database, or (2) may be part of the operating system, or (3) may be loaded with each running application program. The first alternative allows control over concurrent update of database areas at either the record or the page level. The supervisory program acts as a monitor for the database accessing programs. If, in addition, the database routines were reentrant, they could service multiple databases as well as multiple programs. The second alternative is similar to the first, but is less flexible, as in effect the supervisory program is absorbed by the operating system.

FORDATA is implemented using the third alternative. At the time that FORDATA was transferred to the CYBER 76 there was no efficient means of passing messages between running programs, although this has now been implemented (Ryan, 1976) and used in an experimental way.

Thus concurrent update in FORDATA is controlled in a gross way, at the area level, by allowing the operating system to prevent simultaneous access to a file which is being updated. This is less important in a batch than an interactive environment, and less important in the CSIRO context of databases with only a few users than in the context of an organization-wide database with many users.

Each application program must have access to a "user working area" which contains space for each data item defined in the subschema being used. It must also be able to access a set of system locations which are used by the database management system to notify the application program of the status of the last command executed. The user working area and the system locations must be private to the application program in the sense of being independent of any other program which is also accessing the database. They can therefore conveniently reside as part of the application program.

Current mass storage technology is best utilized if data are transferred to and from the database files in large blocks. This is done via buffers maintained by the database management system. In FORDATA there is one set of buffers for each running application program. If the database management system existed as an independent process, communicating with each running application program, then the system buffers could be associated with that process and isolated from the application program. In FORDATA, the system buffers are appended at INVOKE time to the end of the program's address space, and although they are not symbolically available to the program, they could be corrupted, (for example, by an array bounds error), in a way that would be difficult to detect. As far as we are aware, this has not yet occurred in practice.

3.3 Storage Structure and Access Methods

Fixed length records are allocated within pages. The size of any record must not exceed the page size. Each record has a 30-bit header, consisting of the record's size, its type and the number of the record within the page, called its line number. Each record is identified by its database key, a 30-bit quantity allocated when the record is created. It consists of the area number, the page number within the area, and the line number. The database key constitutes a virtual address, which must be mapped into a real address in the system buffers in SCM before the record can be assessed. This operation, together with any associated I/O operations, is performed extremely frequently and hence must be as fast as possible. The routines which implement this mapping are written in assembly code, and are the only parts of FORDATA not written in FORTRAN. To speed up the address mapping, the offset of each record within a page is kept in an array at the end of the page.

Each page has a three word page header, comprising housekeeping information such as the page type, the amount of space left in the page, a pointer to the next available word, an identification for the last run unit to update that page, etc.

When space is to be allocated for a record in an area, it would be possible to read pages from the area to the SCM system buffers and to compare the number of words available in the page with the number of words required until a page in which the space request could be satisfied was found. This would, however, be very inefficient, as many pages might be read in, only to be rejected. To avoid this, pages called map pages are allocated at regular intervals throughout an area. Each map page is associated with a large number of data pages, and contains the amounts of storage available in each of the associated data pages.

Thus to allocate space it is necessary only to scan the map page entries for a page with enough space to satisfy the request. In addition to making the search for a page with enough space to satisfy an allocation request more efficient, map page entries indicate whether a page has ever been referended previously. If not, no attempt is made to read the page's block to LCM. Instead, a slot in LCM is created for the block and initialized with empty pages, one of which is then copied to SCM. Thus an area need only have the map pages initialized before use.

Each record contains a 30-bit header containing the record size, type, and line number. It also contains space for all the data items declared in the schema. Records are grouped into sets either by embedded pointers (mode CHAIN), or by arrays of pointers kept in special auxilliary records (mode POINTER-ARRAY). All pointers between records are database keys.

The access methods are determined by the location mode property defined for each record type in the schema, and by the indexing properties defined on each set type. Location modes DIRECT, CALC and VIA SET as defined in (Codasyl, 1971) are supported.

The hashing algorithm provided by FORDATA starts with a quantity containing alternate one and zero bits, and does a bitwise exclusive or of all the CALC keys into this quantity. This is folded, and the result taken modulo the number of pages in the area. There is provision for the user to specify his own algorithm for any CALC record type. This would be done if the FORDATA supplied algorithm gave a highly skewed distribution for those keys actually present in the user's data.

Records with location mode VIA SET are placed in areas as close as possible to the point within the set where they are to be logically inserted. This facilitates sequential searching of a particular set occurrence. This sequential searching may be improved by declaring that an index is to be maintained for a data item or combination of items in the member records of the set. The indexing is specified in the schema either in conjunction with the declarations for sort keys, or by declaring that data items are to be search keys. The indexing technique currently implemented in FORDATA is a variant of the B-tree technique described in (Bayer and McCreight, 1972), and in (Knuth, 1973). This variant, in which records, or pages containing records, constitute the leaves of the index tree, and nonleaf nodes contain only pointers and keys, has been analyzed in (Wedekind, 1974). An important characteristic of this indexing technique is that the tree is guaranteed to be height balanced, that is any path from the root of the index to a leaf record is the same length as any other path. This remains true independently of the order in which the records are stored.

There are two types of indexing supported. For ordinary indexing, specified with sorted sets or with search keys, the records may not occur in the area in the order implied by the index, especially if they were not presented in that order. The second type of indexing, called page indexing, is specified in conjunction with sorted sets whose owner is SYSTEM, and maintains the records in the same area order as the sort order of the set. This occurs even if records are presented out of order, although it is more efficient to present them in sort key order. The area ordering is maintained by moving records if necessary, thus changing the record's database key, and violating the rule that database keys are constant over the life of the record. A sequential scan of the set can be done in a minimum number of disk accesses. Sets which are pages indexed must have only one member record type, and that member may not be a member of any other sets.

The index in a page indexed set is sparse, in that not all key values are present in the index. The lowest level of the index points to a page which contains member records, rather than to an individual record. This page is sequentially scanned for a match between keys in the record and keys in the user working area when a record retrieval based on the key values is done. Thus if there are n

records in a page, the index size will be reduced by a factor of n. A typical range of values for n would be 20 to 50. This type of indexing is equivalent to IBM's VSAM access method, (Wagner, 1973), and to Control Data's Indexed Sequential, (Control Data 1973).

3.4 Binding Storage Structure to Data Structure

The stage at which the data structure, represented by what the user defines in his schema and DML commands, is bound to the storage structure, that is the pointers, records, packed data items, indexes, calc chains, etc. on physical devices, is a factor affecting both performance and ease of implementation. It would be possible for the DML translator to generate code particularized to each database, which would allocate and delete storage, pack and unpack data items and pointers from records, follow chains and manipulate indexes, and perform other necessary operations. In this compilation approach, record, set and area names would not explicitly occur at the user's object code level. The time taken in interpreting the operation at run time would be minimized. However, this early binding of data structure to storage structure is difficult to implement and change. It also results in some loss of flexibility. In that the user could not write procedures containing DML commands in which record, set and area names are supplied as parameters.

In FORDATA, the DML translator uses the schema or subschema only to check the legality of the CML commands, and generates calls to subroutines which interpret the commands at run time in conjunction with the schema/subschema. This late binding approach offers greater versatility to the implementor. The interpretation time has not proved to be excessive, although it is possible that further extensions to FORDATA would involve generating code at DML translation time in cases where parameter values were explicitly known.

3.5 Representation of Object Schema and Subschema

The way in which the schema is represented at run time must facilitate efficient execution of DML commands. The object schema is represented as a collection of records stored in area zero. It is stored in the same way as the rest of the database, and a number of routines used to manipulate the database are also used to manipulate the schema. One can obtain the general flavor of the object schema structure by referring to Figures 1, 2, and 3 in which the object schema is itself represented as a Codasyl like database using Bachman diagrams (Bachman, 1969). A certain amount of licence has been used in deriving these diagrams, which are for expository purposes only and do not correspond exactly to the way that the object schema is represented. The sets in the dia-

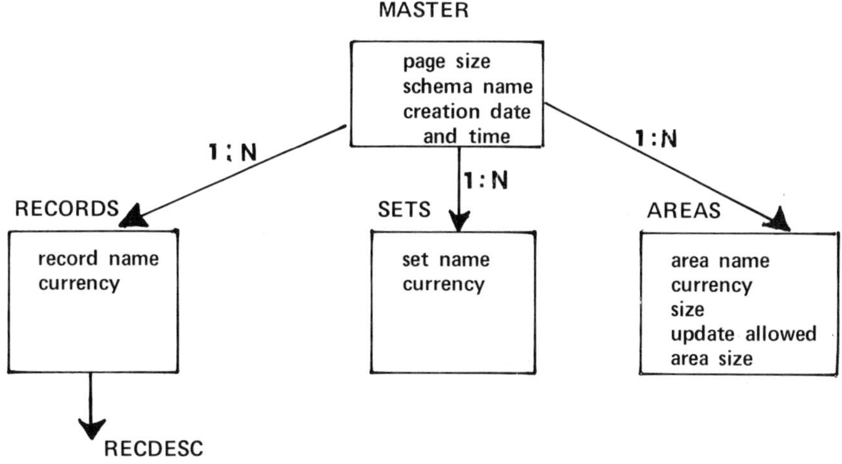

FIGURE 1

grams are marked 1:N or 1:1 depending on whether there may be more than one member record or not.

A root record, MASTER, is the owner of three sets containing members for each record, set and area defined in the schema. The currency information for each record, set and area is kept in these records, which must be accessed on each DML command to update the information. This is shown in Figure 1.

In order to make these records as small as possible, most of the record's properties are kept in a RECDESC record, and in sets which have RECDESC as owner. This is shown in Figure 2.

Each data item in the record has its name, type, size, user working area location and information for packing it into the stored record encoded within an ITEMINFO record. If the item has a source item in the owner record of a set for which the record is a member, then the SOURCEINFO record, containing the name of the source item in the owner record, and a pointer to the owner's RECDESC record, is present.

If the item is a procedure data item then a RESULTINFO record, containing the information specified in the RESULT clause of the DDL, will be present. The procedures which generate these data items are written in FORTRAN and DML, and may themselves cause other procedure data items to be generated. The RESULTINFO record is available to the procedure mainly for cases where the procedure is parameterised to be used in generating more than one data item.

If the record has location mode CALC, there will be a CALCINFO record for each of the CALC items defined in the DDL. Each CALCINFO contains a pointer to the ITEMINFO record for that item.

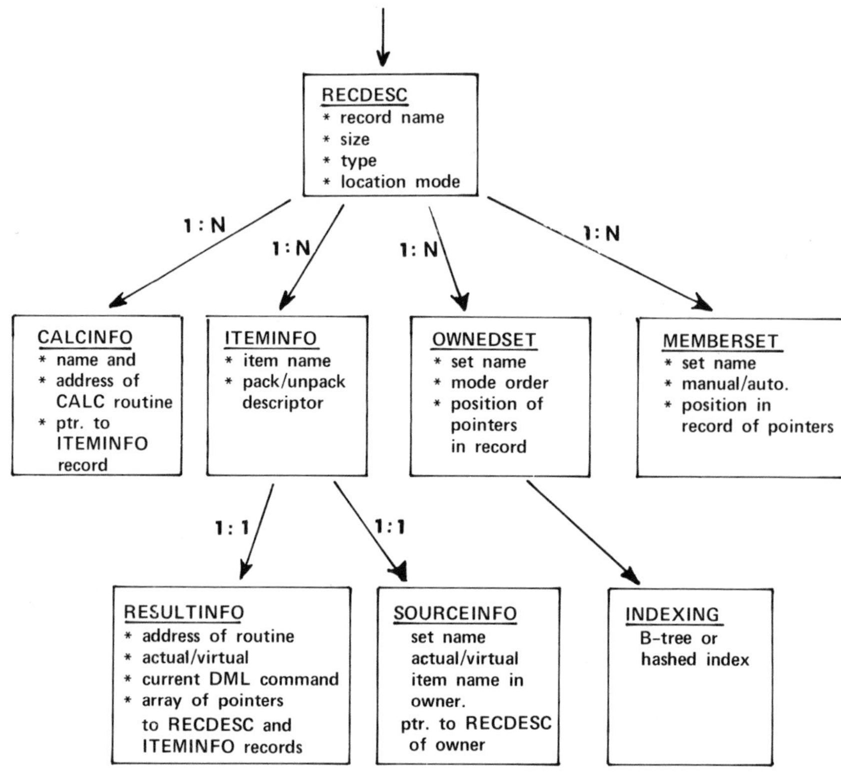

FIGURE 2

Sets of records are present for each set owned by the RECDESC in question, and for each set for which the RECDESC is a member. These OWNEDSET and MEMBERSET records contain the information necessary to manipulate the sets. Additional records are associated with the OWNEDSET and MEMBERSET records (Figure 3), and provide information on indexing, set occurrence selection, sort keys, search keys and alias data items.

Many records in this structure may be accessed during the interpretation of a single DML command. To make this accessing more efficient, many of the object schema records contain pointers or arrays of pointers to RECDESC or ITEMINFO records.

Representation of the object schema in this way has been very convenient as far as implementation is concerned. One disadvantage is that, as the schema is itself a collection of records in an area, it competes for space with the user's database pages in the system buffers and parts of it may be swapped to backing store. It also incurs overhead in that some pointers in the schema are database keys which have to pass repeatedly through the storage mapping process.

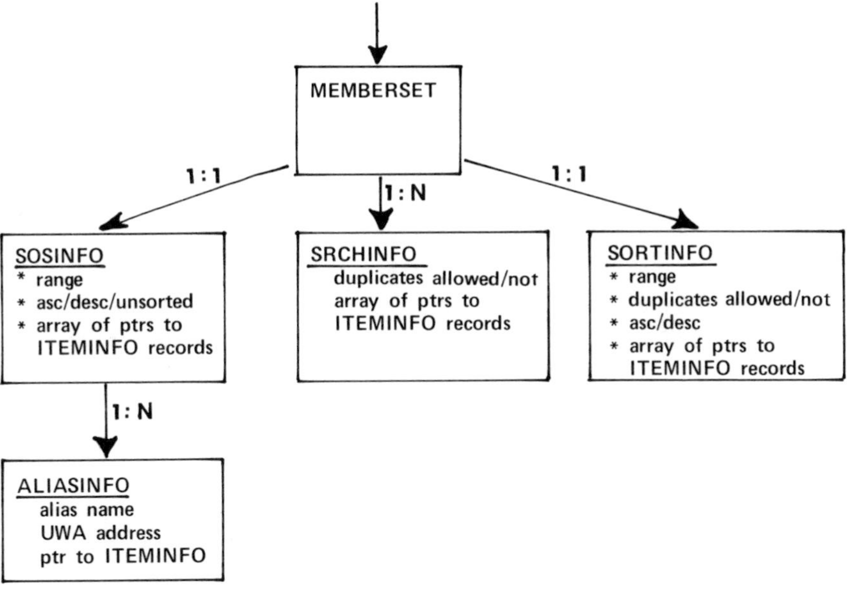

FIGURE 3

3.6 Translators

The input languages for the schema and subschema DDL, and the DML, QML and Utility packages are all defined using regular grammars. The languages were each specified as a set of nodes, (representing states), and arcs, (representing transitions between states). Each arc is labelled with an input symbol and an action to be performed, (for example consistency checking or code generation). Each translator has a starting state. If one of the arcs leading from that node was labelled with the current input symbol, then the action specified on that arc would be executed and the arc traversed to obtain a new current state. A package, SSTRAN, which enabled recognizers of this sort to be specified extremely easily is described in the Appendix.

After a certain amount of user experience had accumulated, it became evident that the DML as defined by the DBTG was at too low a level for quick production of programs. A higher level query language, called QML, was implemented to overcome this. The QML gets away from the very procedural, single record at a time logic of the DML. The user specifies a path through the schema diagram by naming records, data items or sets, and can specify constraints to be satisfied at any point in the path. Canned loops containing DML statements are generated to retrieve the data items specified explicitly or implicitly along the path. Each instance of the path is retrieved, as if the data items were stored in a tabular form. The path may be in the form of a tree. The data items are either returned to the user working area, or are printed, or are output to a user specified file for further processing. The QML package includes verbs to sort a generated file on specified items, to merge files, and to generate reports. Although it is still necessary to know the schema structure (in terms of its Bachman diagram), the production time of retrieval programs is greatly reduced. Of course the user may also write a program containing a mixture of QML, DML, and FORTRAN.

The subschema translator allows the user to select a subset of the areas, records, data items and sets defined in the schema. Areas may be specified as being useable for retrieval only, and in this case subsequent attempts to open them with update permission will be rejected. If the subschema specification does not include structural items that are essential for update, then the area containing those items will not be allowed to be opened for update under that subschema. For instance, for update to be possible, if a record is included in the subschema, then all sets for which that record is an automatic member must also be included.

3.7 Utilities

A utility package which allows the user to perform such functions as selective printing, dumping, auditing, increasing the length of an area, and recovery from database corruption, is available.

At INVOKE time, it is possible to specify that journal files of pages before or after modification be maintained. Each page on a journal file contains a number identifying the run in which it was written, and a journal file containing a history of runs may be kept. The Roll Back utility takes a journal file of pages before modification and restores a possibly corrupted database to a state at which it was known to be correct. This would be used in the event of a program or system abort, or a program logical error. The Roll Forward utility uses a dump of the whole database or area and, using a journal file of pages after modification, moves the state of the database forward to the last state at which it was known to be correct. As well as being used in the previously mentioned situations, this recovery method would be used where total loss of disk files had occurred.

4 CONCLUSION

In Section 1 a number of significant features of the CODASYL specifications which were not implemented were listed. The provision of FORTRAN host system instead of the specified COBOL host system was a decision based on predicted applications. FORTRAN is the most frequently used programming language amongst CSIRONET users (a situation reinforced by the Cyber installation), and the majority of applications of FORDATA have dealt with scientific databases. In these cases a requirement for privacy control beyond that provided by the SCOPE operating systems did not exist. The system could easily be extended to provide a COBOL host interface, but some difficulties would undoubtedly arise at the subschema level with the present choice of DDL.

Except for demonstrations on a lower CYBER system our experience and total development effort has been with the SCOPE 2 operating system on the Cyber 76. The characteristics of SCOPE 2 were a major influence on the design of FORDATA and forced a number of undesired limitations. In particular, in order to control a general multiaccess situation the FORDATA system would have to operate in a supervisory mode as described in Section 3.2. SCOPE 2 provides no efficient means for passing messages between executing processes (although this has now been implemented by Ryan (1976) and used for other local extensions to the operating system). Thus the KEEP and FREE verbs which form part of the CODASYL multiaccess control were not considered. Interactive database access has been limited for similar reasons.

Other CODASYL specified features were excluded as a compromise based on likely use and a desire to limit the workload in implementation and maintenance. For example the CHECK and ON clauses have an important role in database integrity, but it was thought that these controls were much more appropriate in situations where databases would be maintained by numerous application programmers. This has not been the case in CSIRO scientific databases. A number of facilities specified in the ORDER verb were more conveniently provided by a SORT command in the QML.

For similar reasons no effort was expended in producing translators which generated efficient code by a fairly complete binding at translation time. In a Cyber 76 environment the CPU had a bandwidth to main memory somewhat in excess of 200 million bits/sec. In contrast the common database storage medium of demountable disk packs has an average access time of 30 msec. and a transfer rate of 6.8 million bits/sec. In addition the SCOPE 2 scheduler does not accommodate I/O bound jobs well. Therefore from a global optimisation viewpoint there was much more to be gained by expending our effort in providing a range of access methods and secondary indexing, and multilevel paging, in order to reduce disk storage I/O. The exclusive use of execution time binding has proved advantageous in allowing continued evolution of the system without effecting existing databases and application programs. The most serious disruption has been to call for a retranslation of source schemas to coincide with a particular system update.

The performance of FORDATA is discussed in detail (Smith, 1976). We feel that it is fairly good at present, although there are areas of the implementation which could be improved significantly as indicated above. The additional features described in Section 2 provided some important enhancement, for our purposes. We believe that those changes reflected at the language level would be valuable provisions in any similar system. In the light of the more recent

ANSI-SPARC architecture some of these features would be properly contained at the internal schema level.

Several companion papers in this issue describe the experiences of some users with the system. The paper by Cook and Mayo (1977) describes a relatively small but quite complex database relating to a land use research project. The paper by Shortridge (1977) describes a large library retrospective search database, which at present occupies 400 Mc. and which when fully developed will occupy well over 1000 Mc. The paper by Mackenzie and Kelly (1977) describes a prototype abstract retrieval system, written to investigate ways of efficiently performing boolean operations on a DBTG structured database.

APPENDIX: SSTRAN, A Translator Writing Aid for Regular Grammars

The languages in the CODASYL DBTG proposals have each been defined using a regular grammar. A syntax analyser for such languages can be based on symbol state tables (Day, 1970). During syntax analysis the current state is determined by some number of ordered symbols occurring immediately prior in the input program stream. The legality of the next input symbol is completely determined by the current state. In processing this symbol the analyser moves to a new current state. Such a finite state machine is conveniently represented by a transition network (Conway, 1963), the nodes representing the possible states and the labels on the directed arcs representing the symbol which causes the corresponding state transition. By incorporating an appropriate action with each state transition of the analyser, a translated form of the input program can be generated as an output stream.

SSTRAN is a compiler-compiler for generating such translators, implemented for the Cyber range of computers. It requires two input files, one being a table of reserved symbols, and the other specifying the required finite state analyzer in a simple tabular format. The latter has a label field and a branching notation so that identical pieces of a state transition network need only be specified once. When using the branching facility a return label can also be specified, thus providing a subroutine or recursive facility. The user of SSTRAN must also provide a routine to read the input program stream, all error and other message generation routines, and the action routines.

SSTRAN was written by D.M. Ryan specifically for use in the FORDATA project. It has been used in a number of other language implementation projects.

REFERENCES

1. Bachman, C.W. ''Data structure diagrams.'' Database 1, 2, 1969.
2. Bayer, R. and McCreight, E. ''The creation and maintenance of large ordered indexes.'' Acta Informatica 173–189, 1972.

3. Codasyl. ''Database task group report, August 1969.'' Available from ACM, 1969.
4. Codasyl. ''Database task group report, April 1971.'' Available from ACM, 1971.
5. Control Data ''Record Manager Ref. Man.'' 1973.
6. Cook, B.G. and Mayo, K. ''A geographic database using FORDATA.'' Austral. Comput. J., Vol. 9, No. 4, Nov. 1977.
7. Klimbie, J.W. and Koffman, K.L. ''Data Base Management.'' North Holland, 1974.
8. Knuth, D.E. ''The Art of Computer Programming.'' Vol. 3. Sorting and Searching, 473–480. Addison Wesley, 1973.
9. Mackenzie, H.G. and Kelly, G. (1977) ''A query/update package for library or personal reference use.'' Austral. Comput. J., Vol. 9, No. 4, Nov. 1979.
10. Ryan, D.M. ''Communication between jobs on the Cyber 76.'' DAD p. 714. (Division of Computing Research Internal Publication), 1976.
11. Ryan, D.M. ''SSTRAN, A translator writing aid for regular grammars.'' DCR Internal Memorandum, 1977.
12. Shortridge, J.D. ''Development of a Bibliographic Search System using FORDATA.'' Austral. Comput. J., Vol. 9, No. 4, Nov. 1977.
13. Schenk, H. ''Implementation aspects of the codasyl DBTG proposals'' in (Klimbie and Koffman). pp. 399–412, 1974.
14. Smith, J.L., Chmura, J.T. and Johnson, B.V. ''A Database Management System modelled on the Codasyl Proposals.'' Proc. 6th Australian Computer Conference, pp. 360–365, 1972.
15. Smith, J.L. and Mackenzie, H.G. (1974) ''FORDATA Manual.'' CSIRO Division of Computing Research. August 1974. (Revised 1976).
16. Smith, J.L. ''Data Storage and Retrieval Facilities on CSIRONET.'' CSIRO Division of Computing Research. RCC/CMM/P25, 1976.
17. Taylor, R.W. and Frank, R.L. ''Codasyl Database Management Systems.'' Computing Surveys, 81 (March 1976) pp. 67–103.
18. Wagner, R.E. (1973) ''Indexing Design Considerations.'' IBM Systems Journal 124 1973 p. 351.
19. Wedekind, H. ''On the Selection of Access Paths in a Database System.'' In (Klimbie and Koffman), pp. 385–397, 1974.

PART VI

AUERBACH INFORMATION MANAGEMENT SERIES

Two significant papers selected
from the AUERBACH Information Management Series.

"Structured Programming"
Victor R. Basili

"Cryptography as a Control Feature"
Rein Turn

The AUERBACH Information Management Series created in 1973 is a managerially oriented resource of pragmatic papers organized to address specific functional areas of information management. Each of the papers is uniquely written to meet the perceived needs of the MIS manager.

The address is AUERBACH Publishers Inc., 6560 North Park Drive, Pennsauken, New Jersey 08109.

Structured Programming

Victor R. Basili

Dept. of Computer Science, University of Maryland

Part I

INTRODUCTION

Problem solution, leading to the development of executable programs, is a complex discipline. Because we must limit ourselves to programs that we can fully understand and manage intellectually, it is important that a methodology be developed for solving program development problems systematically.

Structured programming involves more than the simple task of coding; it goes to the heart of developing a solution to a programming problem. Statements appearing in industry literature shed some light on the goals and tenets of structured programming:

The purpose of structured programming is to control complexity through theory and discipline.

A major function of the structuring of a program is to keep a correctness proof feasible.

Structured programming allows verfication of the correctness of all steps in the design process and thus automatically leads to self-explicable and self-defensive programming style.

EDITOR'S NOTE: *From AUERBACH Computer Programming Management, 1978. Reprinted by permission from the publisher, AUERBACH Publishers Inc.*

The task of organizing one's thought in a way that leads, in a reasonable time, to an understandable expression of a computing task, has come to be called structured programming.

These statements indicate that a major objective of structured programming is simplification of the program development process. One way to harness complexity is to break a problem into small, easily understood pieces. In structured programming this is accomplished in two ways:

1. By using a few simple structures that aid in minimizing the number of interactions and interconnections of which the programmer must be aware; and
2. By keeping program segments small and therefore manageable.

The first goal can be accomplished by using a standard set of control structures like the ones shown in Figure 1. These structurers permit an algorithm to be organized and read from top-to-bottom; all control paths are clearly shown and easily followed.

The second goal can be accomplished by organizing the solution algorithm hierarchically. The first segment written is the solution algorithm representing the skeleton of the program. It is written using a set of abstractions that are natural to the problem area, in other words, using as notation, data, and operations that are at the level of the problem. These operations are considered algorithm primitives that may be decomposed into lower-level program segments. This decomposition process is continued until the program is completed.

To aid in applying the structured methodology, the language in which the algorithms are written should contain features. A notation should be available with statements that correspond to each of the control structures in figure 1. These can be defined by the normal sequential controls along with "if-then-else" and "while" statements. A second requirement is some mechanism for segmenting the algorithm so that a lower-level program segment can be substi-

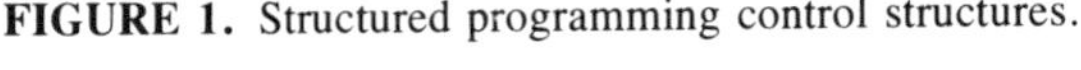
FIGURE 1. Structured programming control structures.

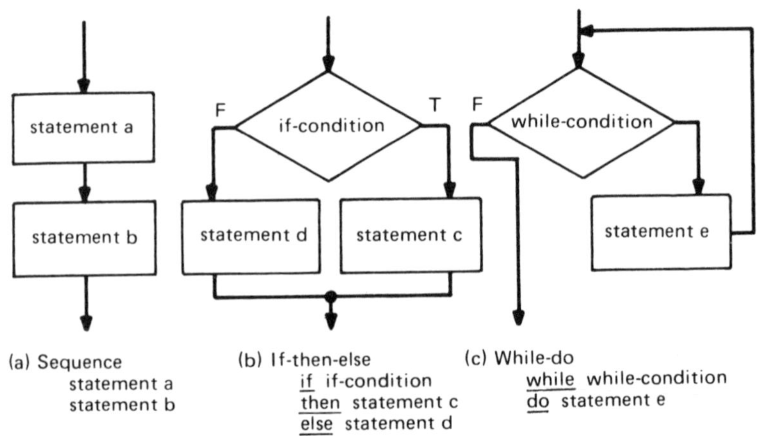

tuted for a higher- level constituent. This can be achieved with a form of macro substitution or a procedure call process that allows storing program subsegments under symbolic names.

Three successive expansions of a program using proper control structures are shown in figure 2. The segmenting mechanism used is macro substitution; keywords are used to indicate the control logic.

FOUNDATIONS OF STRUCTURED PROGRAMMING

Performing an algorithm decomposition in a well-structured way is not an easy task. Programmers need a way to view the algorithm that promotes understanding of the problem and the process of decomposition. One such way is to view the algorithm as a function. Note that this functional model of programs can be used to define a mathematical foundation for structured programming and also to demonstrate the correctness of structured programs.

FIGURE 2. Program expansion using control structures.

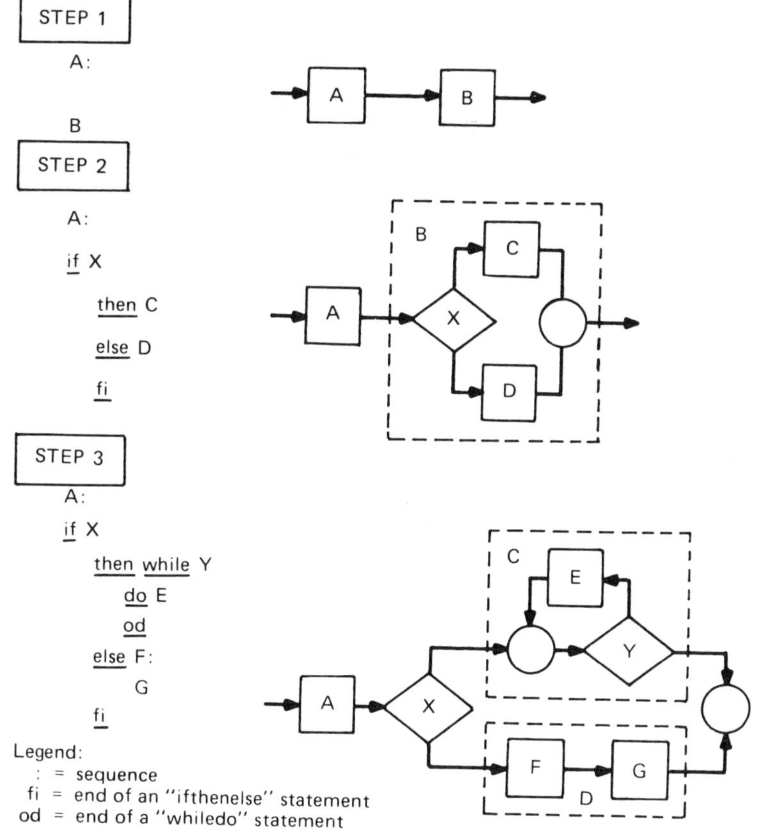

Function Definition

A function is a correspondence between members of a set R (the range) and a set D (the domain) such that each member of D corresponds to a unique member of R. A function can be characterized by one of the following:

Enumeration of a set of ordered pairs (d,r) where d is an element of D and r is an element of R, for example:

$$F = \{ (1,4),(2,5),(3,6),(4,7) \}$$

A rule which assigns to each d in D a unique r in R, for example:
$F = \{(x,y)$ such that x is an integer and $1 \leqslant x \leqslant 4$
and $y = x + 3\}$

An equation such as:
$y = f(x) = x + 3$ for integer x from 1 to 4

Flowchart Representation

We can represent a program in a specialized flowchart format. A flowchart is a graph that shows the flow of execution control of a program; let us limit our flowcharts to three types of boxes (nodes). Figure 3 shows the types of nodes we are using: the function node, predicate node, and collecting node.

A function node is used to show a function to be performed. A predicate node shows a decision in which the upper line leaving the node shows the path to take when the statement is true (or the decision is yes), and the lower line out is for false (or no). Collecting nodes are used where two arrows on a traditional flowchart would meet (i.e., as a joining point).

We can now define a *proper* program (see Figure 4) as a program in which:

There is precisely one input line and one output line.

For every node, there exists a path from the input line through the node to the output line.

Proper Programs and Functional Equivalency

A proper program truly represents a program function in that it has a single entry (defining the set of inputs) and a single exit (defining the set of outputs), and all the processing can be defined as a function from that input set to that

FIGURE 3. Types of flowchart nodes.

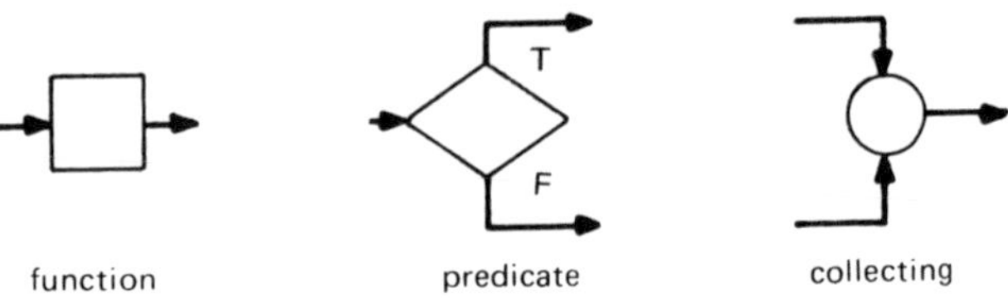

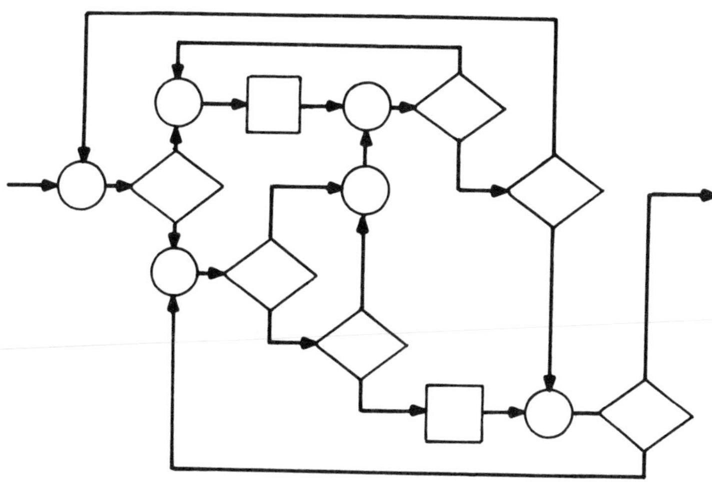

FIGURE 4. Flowchart of a proper program.

output set. In other words, the input is the domain of the set, and the output is the range; each input is the x of an ordered pair, each output is the y.

Two proper programs, then, are functionally equivalent if, for all inputs, each input is transformed into the same output (the unique y for the ordered pair with the input value x). This yields a way of examining the equivalence of two programs without concern over the specific algorithm used.

Composition and Decomposition

The basic operations for functions that we use in structured programming methodology are function *composition* and *decomposition*. A composition of two functions is a new function that represents the successive use of the values of one function as the argument of the other. This program graph (where x is the input to g, z is the output of g and the input of f, and y is the output of f).

$x \longrightarrow$ [g] $\longrightarrow z \longrightarrow$ [f] $\longrightarrow y$

can be represented by the composed function h where $h = f(g(x))$ or f^*g (read f composed with g) where

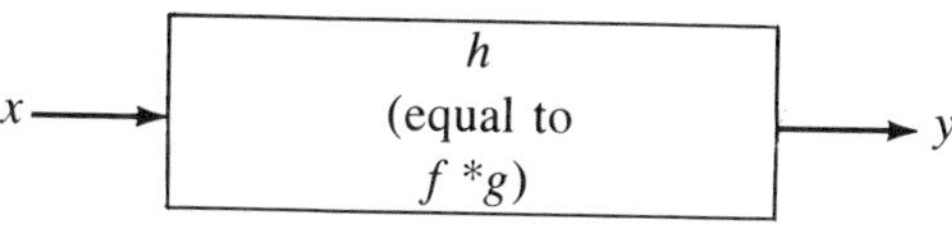

$f * g = (x,y)$ such that there is a $z = g(x)$ and $y = f(z)$

Another way of approaching this is to read these two equations as: the set of output z is the result of processing the set of input x through the function g, and the set of output y is the result of processing the set of input z through the function f; or the set of output y is the result of processing the set of input x through the function f and g (which together we refer to as h).

Clearly, for any function h there are many possible decompositions; but the concept of function decomposition is relevant in program development because it involves decomposing more general high-level abstraction solutions to more detailed specific subproblems. As such, in decomposition we are interested in a set of control structures that let us expand the control logic of a program in a simple, straightforward way so that the expanded functions are equivalent to the original function.

To find some set of proper program control graphs that cannot be further decomposed (and can, therefore, be used as the basis for any proper program structure), let us define a prime program. Let a subprogram of a program (flowchart) be a subset of connected nodes on a flowchart. A *prime program* is a proper program that has no *proper* subprogram of more than one node. The program in Figure 5 is a proper program, because it has no subprogram (connected set of nodes) of more than one node that is itself a proper program (i.e., where there is precisely one input line and one output line and, for every node, there exists a path from the input line through the node to the output line). Note that this concept is similar to that of prime numbers: any number can be decomposed into a canonical set of numbers that cannot be further decomposed.

Because an infinite number of prime program graphs (flowcharts) are possible, we must have criteria for choosing a particular set on which to base our program development. Some reasonable criteria are:

1. They should be sufficient for solving the problem.
2. There should be a small number of nodes (or individual concepts) to deal with.
3. They should abstract well to mathematical functions.
4. They should be useful to the particular application.

Figure 1 gives a set that satisfies the first three criteria. Other prime programs could be added to this set if they prove useful to the application environment.

Just as any nonprime number can be factored into a unique set of prime numbers, so any nonprime proper program can be decomposed into a unique

FIGURE 5. Prime program.

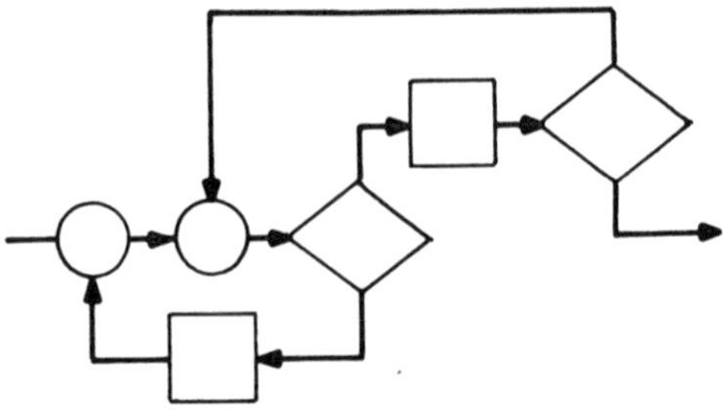

hierarchical structure of prime programs if any sequence of n nodes is reduced in a single step (see Figure 6). In other words, given any proper program, we can isolate all the prime programs and replace them by an equivalent function node generating a new, smaller proper program. In the smaller program, we can again isolate all the prime programs, replace them by their equivalent single function nodes and so on, until we are left with a single function node representing the entire program. In this way, we can expose the hierarchical structure of a program in terms of its prime programs knowing that the hierarchical structure was uniquely determined. Anyone applying the algorithm correctly would discover the same structure, because there is only one way to read and understand a program based on its prime programs. Thus, the writer of a program can be sure how readers will interpret what he has written.

PROCESS DESIGN LANGUAGE

One cannot produce effective software designs without good communication between users and designers as well as among the designers. It is important that the designer understand exactly what the user wants; otherwise, the user can end up with an interesting system that does not solve his problems. Communication requires a language or notation for specifying design that:

Is precise and unambiguous in the specification of a design

Helps the designer arrive at the design (i.e., can be geared to the level and application of the problem at hand)

Is usable for communication purposes (i.e., is readable and easily understood)

Secondary requirements are (1) that it be easy to translate from the design

FIGURE 6. Decomposition of a proper structured program into hierarchical structure.

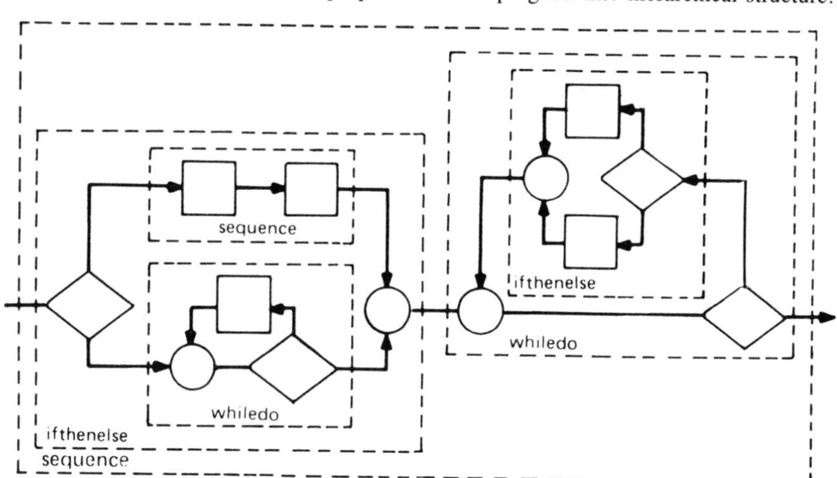

notation to a working algorithm in a procedural programming language, and (2) that the notation be usable for user guides and other forms of program documentation. A process (or program) design langugage (PDL) that is an open-ended specialization of natural language is recommended because it satisfies these criteria.

A PDL consists of an outer syntax—a set of fixed notational forms (the logical control and data structures)—and an inner syntax—a set of variable notational forms that involve the specific set of data items (e.g., integers) and operations (e.g., addition or multiplication) required for the problem area and the level of program development. At one level, PDL views design from a logical point of view without involving the physical storage and operations of any computer system. At another level, it gives us the ability to transform that design into an implemented program within the logical framework of the environment (i.e., programming language, operating system, and so forth).

The outer syntax of PDL describes how operations are to be sequenced and controlled as well as how data are to be organized and accessed. The data structures of the outer syntax should be standardized for the entire software development shop (i.e., should be independent of application). They constitute the notation primitives to be used in building the larger logical functions.

The inner syntax of data operations and tests (the variable notational form) are drawn from natural language, mathematics, programming practice, and the like and correspond to the inner syntax of formal languages. They are not, however, formalized in PDL. This is because they *should* vary with the particular application and level of detail needed to express the problem solution. A small number of control structures are used in this portfolio for the outer syntax; however, others may be added based on the needs of the particular shop.

Figure 7 lists four control structures. Note the use of indentation and separate lines for such key words as IF, WHILE, and so on. This leaves room in the design for comments. These key words act as separators or punctuation (spelled backward, they act as end delimiters), to set off the basic functions that are expressed in the language of the inner syntax. Note that the functions contained in the problem are at various levels of detail; the level of detail depends on the level of the PDL in the expanding PDL design of problem solution.

In addition to choosing an appropriate set of control structures for the PDL, a set of data structures for organizing the data should be chosen. Such structures as sets, queues, stacks, sequences, arrays, records, and scalars could be included. The logical organization of data is as important as, if not more important than the organization of control. In fact, the two organizations usually go hand in hand; that is, after the data have been logically organized, they define the way in which the processing should take place.

A PDL program can be defined by a data declaration enclosed by the key words data and atad and a procedure declaration enclosed by the key words proc and corp. Figure 8 gives an example of a whole PDL program. (Note that: = should be read as "is assigned the value of.") INPUT and OUTPUT in this

```
SEQUENCE
  DO
    SORT TRANSACTION FILE;
    UPDATE INVENTORY FILE WITH TRANSACTION FILE;
    PRINT INVENTORY REPORT
  OD

IFTHENELSE
  IF
    SS_TAX_GROSS ≥ CURRENT_SS_MAX
  THEN
    SET SS_TAX TO 0
  ELSE
    CALCULATE SS_TAX BASED UPON
    CURRENT_SALARY AND CURRENT_SS_MAX
  FI

IFTHEN
  IF
    SUM = NUMBER
  THEN
    OUTPUT NUMBER
  FI

WHILE
  WHILE
    INPUT ≠ EMPTY
  DO
    SAVE INPUT_RECORD IN PAYROLL_TABLE
  OD
```

FIGURE 7. List of control structures.

```
data
   sequence INPUT integer,
   sequence OUTPUT integer,
   integer MAX, A
atad
proc print maximum
   [next (OUTPUT) : = maximum (INPUT)]
   MAX : = 0
   [MAX : = maximum (MAX_in, INPUT)]
   while
      INPUT ≠ EOF
   do
   [MAX : = maximum (MAX, next (INPUT))]
      A : = next (INPUT)
      [MAX : = maximum (MAX, A)]
      if
         A > MAX
      then
         MAX : = A
      fi
od
next (OUTPUT) : = MAX
corp
```

FIGURE 8. A program PDL.

example are defined as sequences that are representations of file-like structures. The predicate INPUT ≠ EOF checks if the INPUT sequence has not encountered an end-of-file condition, and, if it has not, proceeds to execute the body of the loop. The square brackets [] are used to enclose comments; the comments are descriptions of the functions to be expanded, and the function expansions are indented on the lines below. Thus, the program can be read from top to bottom and from outside in, defining the various levels of function expansion in the program development.

PDL imposes no special restrictions or conventions on the inner syntax. The language or notations used should be as precise as necessary to communicate unambiguously what a particular function does. The amount of detail used varies with the level of expansion of the design; the closer we are to the level of the machine, the more detail is required. (It is logical that more detail would be required for Assembler program than for a COBOL program.) The choice of primitives used varies not only with the application and level but also with the audience. Note that primitives for a particular application and level tend to become standard in a shop, and acceptable shorthands will evolve; the full set of definitions and explanations of the shorthand notations should be maintained in a reference book.

Using a set of primitive control and data structures and a well-defined, unambiguous inner syntax of functions embedded in a standard notation allows designers to communicate design better. Users, designers, and maintenance programmers can then read them and understand, evaluate, and modify them as needed. Note that this type of program design lends itself to being archived in a program design library for reuse.

READING STRUCTURED PROGRAMS

The literature of program design is largely composed of existing programs. Programmers should use this literature to help create good solutions to problems similar to those already solved. This requires a collection of program designs in an archive available to programmers. It also requires that program designs and programs be readable and understandable.

Readability and understandability are fundamental properties of structured programs. They must be able to be read systematically—from the top to the bottom for sequence parts and from the outside to the inside for nested parts. Because each prime control structure is an indivisible building block of a structured program (in which execution control always enters the top and leaves the bottom), the control structure can be read and its functional effect on data understood without any concern for side effects in the flow of control. A structured program can therefore be viewed as a generalized assignment statement that creates new data from old.

One way to understand the effect of a program is to trace and mentally execute its statements a number of times, inventing data values as they are needed to follow a particular logic path for each execution. Although this seems like a reasonable approach, the number and complexity of logic paths can quickly become unmanageable. Consider the following six-line program:

f *p* then *a* else *b* fi
if *q* then *c* else *d* fi
if *r* then *e* else *f* fi
if *s* then *g* else *h* fi
if *t* then *i* else *j* fi
if *u* then *k* else *l*fi

where the number of possible execution paths is $2^6 = 64$. It would be very difficult to keep track of the effect of each path and summarize the resulting effect to understand what the program does.

Fortunately, there is another way to read a structured program and understand its effect—by recording the effect of each statement once for each program rather than for each execution path. This process is called *reading by stepwise abstraction*. The object is to transform each prime control construct into an abstraction that summarizes the possible outcome of the program segment under consideration, independent of the internal control structure and data operations. The goal here is to produce a hierarchy of loop-free, branch-free, sequence-free descriptions of the effect of program segments on data. This permits an immediate recognition of what the program segment does. For example, the program segment

$$\text{if } x > y \text{ then } z := x \text{ else } z := y \text{ fi}$$

is a branching program that abstracts to (composes to)

$$z := \text{maximum } (x,y).$$

The effect of reading by stepwise abstraction is to reduce systematically the number of paths that need to be considered. Reading and recording an abstraction creates stepwise shorter programs that are equivalent to the original program. Note, however, that abstraction does not mean vagueness, but rather another way of saying the same thing. The abstraction must be logically equivalent to the original program.

Because of the dynamic nature of program variables, it is convenient when writing an abstraction to distinguish the inputs of a generalized assignment statement from the outputs. For example, consider the abstraction

$$y := x,\ x := y$$

representing an exchange program. It is not clear that this generalized assignment sets y and x to the values of x and y on input, respectively. We can clarify the generalized assignment by appending the subscript ''in'' to all input variables to emphasize the separation of the input variables from the output variables. From the point of view of a programming language assignment statement, it is as though there is a distinct copy of the input values. Thus the abstraction

$$y := x_{\text{in}},\ x := y_{\text{in}}$$

is a clearer expression of the exchange function, showing that y has the value that x had on input, and x has the value that y had on input.

Thus, starting with a large structured program, each of the prime programs can be reduced to a generalized assignment statement that can further be reduced until the entire program has been reformulated as a single generalized assignment statement. Clearly this is not always easy to do. Even small programs can have complicated effects that are hard to summarize. But the search for expressions that abstract execution dynamics is crucial for program understanding. Effort exerted in formulating precise, clear abstractions of the effects of program segments on data leaves a programmer with a better understanding of what he is doing. It also leaves an understandable description of the program for anyone working on the project, maintaining the completed system, or attempting to learn how to design clear and effective program segments.

When this is done, programs can be read in a systematic way by associating a set of reading rules with the set of control structures used in the PDL. Examples of reading rules are:

SEQUENCE: Read the successive parts and summarize their sequential effect in the final outcome.

IFTHENELSE: Read the iftest true and the thenpart, then read the iftest false and the elsepart; summarize the two outcomes into a single outcome.

WHILEDO: Read the whiletest true and the dopart (be sure to verify that the whiletest eventually evaluates to false); then read the whiletest false (no operation) and summarize the outcome on exit.

These rules may seem simple because they are based on a simple set of prime control structures each of which has a minimal number of execution paths. More complicated prime control structures would yield more complicated reading rules (consider the reading rule for the prime program in Figure 5).

CORRECTNESS DEMONSTRATIONS

When developing a program design, we are interested in creating a program that is free of errors. There is, unfortunately, no absolute way to convince ourselves that the program we have developed is error free; the best we can do is gain confidence in the program as time goes on and no errors are found.

We can gain this confidence in several ways. One way is by inspecting the program and not uncovering any errors. This inspection can include everything from "desk checking" our own program to peer review of the design and code; it can also include correctness demonstrations. Clearly, inspection is a powerful way to detect errors, but it is not infallible; errors can be made in proofs just as easily as in programs. Second, we can gain confidence by testing the program and not uncovering any errors. Unfortunately, testing is not as thorough an error detection method as inspection, because it involves generating a finite number of test cases to verify the correctness of a program (or function) that has a potentially infinite number of inputs. The third approach to confidence building is using the system. If a program has been in the field for a year or two without bugs being reported, we can be fairly confident that it is error free.

But how do we get a program to be error free in the first place? The only way is to write it that way. The methodology proposed here for developing correct programs works as follows: start with the intended function of the program (i.e., the generalized assignment or abstraction of what the program is to do); proceed by function expansion of the specification. (This yields new lower-level functions equivalent to the original function.) A correctness demonstration is then possible to verify the equivalence of the high-level abstraction and the lower-level expanded function. That is, at each step in the program development process, we can evaluate the correctness of the current expansion before proceeding to the next expansion step. Thus, when the expansion of the whole program is complete, the resulting program is equivalent to its top-level specification.

Correctness demonstrations are simply demonstrations that a program meets its specifications. They may be made at several levels. Simply reading a program and being convinced that it does what the specifications say is an informal demonstration of correctness. In this section, a more formal kind of correctness is presented. Clearly, correctness demonstrations are never absolute; it is always possible to have made an error in the proof no matter how rigorous we are in carrying out the details. They do, however, provide the most effective approach to correct program development.

The ease with which we can read and evaluate a program's correctness is greatly influenced by the program structure. Using the primitive control structures, we can develop more formal correctness demonstrations for each individual construct by performing abstractions and expansions. This can be done by refining and systematizing the reading rules and including more careful means of validating the equivalence of an abstraction and its expansion. This validation process takes the form of a generic procedure defined for each prime program in the form of a correctness question. The correctness questions for the ifthenelse sequence and whiledo control constructs are given in the following subsections.

In the examples, a comma specifies that the set of statements can be performed in any order (i.e., in the example below, whether $x := y_{in}$ precedes $y := x_{in}$ or vice versa is immaterial). A semicolon specifies sequential execution of the statements separated by it (i.e., in the example below, $t := x$ must precede $x := y$ must precede $y := t$ in order of execution for the program to be correct).

Sequence Correctness

Consider the problem specification:

$$x := y_{in},\ y := x_{in}$$

and a program to carry out that specification:

$$t := x;\ x := y;\ y := t.$$

Does the program correctly carry out the specification? The correctness can be verified by a trace table (which shows the values of each variable after each step is executed):

	x	y	t
initial status	x_{in}	y_{in}	t_{in}
after $t := x$	x_{in}	y_{in}	x_{in}
after $x := y$	y_{in}	y_{in}	x_{in}
after $y := t$	y_{in}	x_{in}	x_{in}

Examining the resulting values of x and y we see that the program does carry out the intended function. The resulting assignments of a sequence of assignments can be described in terms of functional substitution.

> **Sequence Correctness Question:**
> Does the first part followed by the second part . . . followed by the nth part do the sequence (i.e., do the same things as the specification for the sequence)?

Ifthenelse Correctness

Consider the problem specification:

$$z := \max\,(x_{in}, y_{in})$$

and a program to carry out the specification:

f $x > y$ then $z := x$ else $z := y$

Are the program and functional specifications equivalent? The equivalence can be verified by the following questions:

Whenever $x > y$,
does $z := x$ do the same thing as $z := \max\,(x_{in}, y_{in})$, and
whenever $x > y$,
does $z := y$ do the same thing as $z := \max\,(x_{in}, y_{in})$?

Because the answer to the question is yes, we see that the program and specification are equivalent (i.e., the program is a correct expansion of the abstract specification).

> **Ifthenelse Correctness Question:**
> Whenever the iftest is true, does the thenpart do the ifthenelse specification, and whenever the iftest is false does the elsepart do the ifthenelse specification?

Whiledo Correctness

Consider the problem specification:

$$x := x_{in} + y_{in},\ x_{in} \geqslant 0\ ,\ y_{in} \geqslant 0$$

and a program to carry out that specification:

while $y > 0$ do $x := x+1$; $y := y-1$ od.

Is the program a valid expansion of the intended function? Before verifying the equivalence of the program and the specification, reading "is identical to" for $\equiv$ note that

f $\equiv$ while p do g od $\equiv$ if p then $g; f$ fi

In other words, there is a nonloop equivalent form for writing the while loop in terms of a sequence and an ifthenelse statement. The validity of the above statement is beyond the scope of this paper, but the graph in Figure 9 gives some feeling for why this is true.

Thus the correctness question for the whiledo can be stated:

Whiledo Correctness Question:
Does the loop always terminate,
and
whenever the whiletest is true, does the dopart followed by the whiledo do the whiledo specification
and
whenever the while test is false, does doing nothing do the whiledo specification?
Returning to the example, let us apply the correctness questions.
Does the loop terminate?
Yes, because y starts out greater than or equal to zero and is reduced by 1 each cycle and eventually becomes zero.
When $y \not> 0$ does $x := x + 1; y := y - 1; x := x + y$ do $x := x_{in} + y_{in}$?

Yes, by directly calculating the result of the sequence in a trace table:

	x	y
initial status	x_{in}	y_{in}
after $x := x + 1$	$x_{in} + 1$	y_{in}
after $y := y - 1$	$x_{in} + 1$	$y_{in} - 1$
after $x := x + y$	$x_{in} + y_{in}$	

yielding the intended function.
When $y \not> 0$ does doing nothing do $x := x_{in} - y_{in}$?
Yes, since when $y = 0$, doing nothing does $x := x_{in} + y_{in}$.

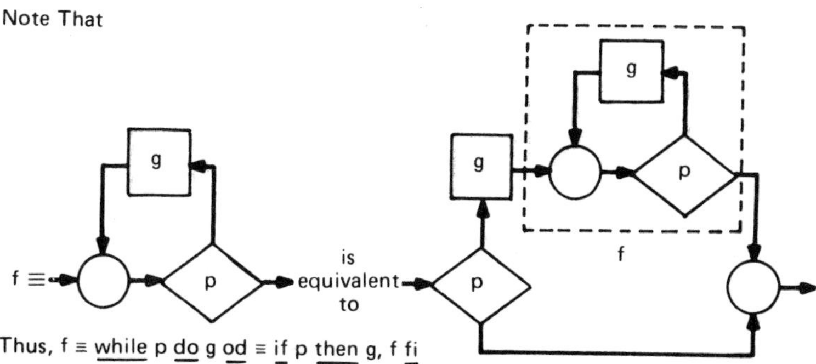

FIGURE 9. Correctness question for the whiledo expansion.

Having examined correctness for a set of small program segments, let us examine correctness for the first few steps of the small program defined in Figure 8 that prints the maximum value of an input sequence of positive integers. The intended function of the entire program was given by:

$$\text{next(OUTPUT)} := \text{maximum(INPUT)}$$

which was expanded to the three-function sequence:

$$\begin{aligned} \text{MAX} &:= 0 \\ \text{MAX} &:= \text{maximum}(\text{MAX}_{\text{in}},\text{INPUT}) \\ \text{next(OUTPUT)} &:= \text{MAX} \end{aligned}$$

We can demonstrate the correctness of this expansion by direct functional substitution. Combining the last two statements yields:

$$\text{next(OUTPUT)} := \text{maximum(MAX,INPUT)}$$

and combining this with the first statement yields:

$$\begin{aligned} \text{next(OUTPUT)} &:= \text{(O,INPUT)} \\ &:= \text{maximum(INPUT) if all inputs are positive.} \end{aligned}$$

We can demonstrate the correctness of the expansion from:

$$\text{MAX} := \text{maximum}(\text{MAX}_{\text{in}},\text{INPUT})$$

into the while loop by asking the three correctness questions associated with the while loop.

1. Does the loop terminate?

Yes, because the INPUT file is finite and each call on next advances the file on value and there is an end-of-file marker after the last element, the loop will terminate. (Note that this might suggest we verify that there is an end-of-file marker after the last record if we are not sure there is one.)

2. Whenever the whiletest is true, does the dopart followed by the whiledo do the whiledo specification?

Yes, as seen by the following trace table for MAX:

	MAX
initial status	MAX_{in}
dopart	MAX := minimum (MAX, next (INPUT)
whiledo specification	MAX := minimum (maximum (MAX, next (INPUT)), INPUT := maximum (MAX, next (INPUT), INPUT) := maximum (MAX, INPUT) since next (INPUT) is an element of INPUT

3. Whenever the whiletest is false, does doing nothing do the whiledo specification?

Yes, because the whiletest being false means we are at end-of-file and, therefore, the sequence is empty, so MAX := MAX_{in}= 0.

This type of correctness demonstration is important because correctness is such an important aspect of program production. Structured programming permits correctness proofs of programs. The extent to which a programmer can actually perform correctness proofs depends on how sure he is of the logic as written and/or the importance of the correctness of that section of code as well as his ability to work through a proof. Note that proofs become easier to do as the process becomes more familiar.

Part II

PROGRAM DESIGN AND FUNCTION EXPANSION

Program design begins with an intended function to be computed. The task is to design a program that is correct, understandable, and suitably efficient, and carries out the intended function. The intended function can be specified in terms of its input and output as well as by rules for computation and data handling. For a complex problem, for which specifications are often ill-posed and ambiguous and fail to cover all conditions, the first requirement is to specify the problem properly and then design an effective solution. This is not always easy to do, however, because the process of designing the solution often uncovers questions about the problem itself. Thus the process is often iterative: the problem is specified, a solution is attempted that exposes questions about the problem statement, the problem statement is further specified to answer those

questions, a solution to the modified problem specifi
so forth.

Structured program design is a problem-solving pro
structures for programs and provides a rationale for
stages in the process —better communication and conce
activity itself. The principal operation of designing structu
tion expansion—the replacement of a function by an equ
ture. This facilitates building correct programs of any size,

It is important to understand what is meant by top-down
expansion into prime control structures. Part I details the pro

It is also important to understand that to design the top le
or any refinement for that matter, requires fully understan
function and having a strategy in mind to realize it. It does no
coding before the strategy has been thought out. A superficia
(i.e., knowing most of the details) is not enough. It is the abi
from the details, organize them, and discuss the function at severa
tail that is real understanding of an intended function. Only with
understanding is it possible to program by function expansion, pl
stractions in an evolving structure and judiciously postponing deta
refinement.

Let us consider an example in which some intended function F
updated records, for example) is to be expanded into the program

$$G;\ \text{while } P \text{ do } H \text{ od}$$

at some level of refinement. In this example, G would print the account level headings and the *whiledo* would put out transaction information as long as the account number stayed the same. Now consider the following intermediate development paths:

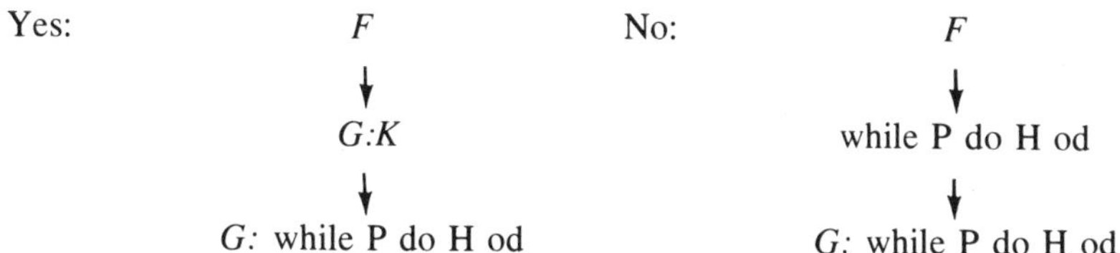

The **yes** path shows the function expansion of the design, which provides for the same functions to be represented at each intermediate step. G and K specify the intended functions of the two program subpieces (print account level headings and print transaction information, respectively) that comprise F. In this expansion, K specifies the function for the program's *while* loop. Note that each intermediate function plays a dual role—as a specification for further expansion and as an operation in the basic control structure created with it. K, for example, can be thought of as both a piece of the problem solution and a specification for a subproblem at the next level.

two problems. First, it is not a function expansion because es sight of G, which is part of the intended function F. This ent can happen easily when one subproblem takes care of the, of a program's intended function. Losing that "insignificant" rcent will of course result in a program that does not properly do needs to have done. Second, there is no specification of the in- ion of the *while* loop (i.e., K is missing). This invites the designer into a sea of details before showing what the details are supposed to

orrectness of each step of a function expansion can be verified: that is, uence $G;K$ can be checked for its equivalence to the function F, and the tness of the *whiledo* can be checked by testing its equivalence to the ion K, using the correctness questions given in Part I. This process is strated in the DEMONSTRATING CORRECTNESS section.

Note that functions for expansion in the development process define actions at subsequent expansions must carry out. They should describe only actions of the program part to which they are attached. They should reference only those data objects known at the point in the program at which they appear. They should be abstract without being vague, precise without being detailed.

THE PROBLEM-SOLVING ENVIRONMENT

Before discussing a particular problem, let us examine the various stages of program development. As stated earlier, the development process should aid in producing correct programs. The key to this is keeping each stage as simple and easy to understand as possible.

The problem-solving process can be divided into three parts:

Problem specification (requirements definition)

Solution specification

Solution development or design

Problem specification (requirements definition) consists of understanding a problem and specifying it with all associated constraints. Solution specification is designing a solution algorithm for a problem specification at a very high level. Solution development is specifying the details of that high-level solution algorithm in a step-by-step process by choosing the relevant data and control structures until an efficient executable algorithm has been written in a programming language. It is primarily for this last stage of development that structured programming and top-down development are to be used. It is important, however, to discuss these tools within the context of the entire problem-solving process in order to place them in proper perspective.

Problem Specification

Problem specification is the most important aspect of proble
ten the most difficult because requirements are not always kn
pressed. Mathematical functional concepts offer some assistan
a problem in terms of its input and output relationships. Even e
which are often a poorly treated ad hoc aspect of the problem-so
can be better defined using the mathematical functional approach.

Sample Problem Specification

A simple example has been chosen to show the use of the structured programming methodology, in order to demonstrate the technique with a reasonable amount of detail. Consider the problem of an accounting department that must update its official accounts file and produce a record of the transactions for a specific accounting period. A set of transactions (charges and credits) that occurred during the period must be applied to the account file and a report produced showing the old and new balances for each account in the file. We can assume that all input files are in account number order and ready to be read.

A more formal specification of the problem can be given as a function from the set of inputs to the set of outputs. The inputs consist of two files—an ACCOUNT_FILE and a TRANSACTION_FILE. ACCOUNT_FILE consists of a set of *acct* records whose format is

(account, balance)

Where ''account'' is the account number field, and ''balance'' contains the balance owed in the account. TRANSACTION_FILE consists of a set of *trans* records of the form

(account, type, amount)

where ''account'' is the account number for the transaction, ''type'' is a ''+'' or ''−'' showing whether the transaction is a credit or debit respectively, and ''amount'' is the amount of the transaction.

The outputs are to be a file of updated account balances, NEW_ACCOUNT_FILE, and a printed report of the activity change, OUTPUT. NEW_ACCOUNT_FILE is to consist of a set of *nacct* records of the form

(account, newbalance)

where ''newbalance'' contains the updated balance. OUTPUT consists of a series of print lines, called *outline*, of the form

(account, balance, newbalance).

unction from the inputs to the outputs can be defined as:

V__ACCOUNT__FILE, OUTPUT__REPORT:=
Update (ACCOUNT__FILE, TRANSACTION__FILE)

here := is read "is assigned the value of" and for each *acct* in ACCOUNT__FILE there is an *nacct* in NEW ACCOUNT__FILE such that:

account (*nacct*)= account *(acct)*,

newbalance (*nacct*)=balance *(acct)* + positive__trans–negative__trans, trans,
where for each *trans* in TRANSACTION__FILE with account *(trans)* = account *(acct)* #### and positive-trans=SUM all amount *(trans)* where type *(trans)*= '+' and negative-trans=SUM all amount *(trans)* where type *(trans)*=' –'

In addition, for each *acct* in ACCOUNT__FILE there is an *outline* in OUTPUT__REPORT such that:

account *(outline)*=account,*(acct)*,
balance*(outline)*= balance*(acct)* ,
newbalance*(outline)*=balance*(acct)* + positive.__trans–negative__trans

The above formulation is an expression of the problem in terms of a clear set of input/output variables and the functions to be performed (calculated). It represents a first step in the full specification of the problem. Constraints on the input variables (e.g., the acceptable ranges of account numbers and balances) are yet to be specified, as is error handling. In a full problem specification, all variable ranges are specified and all actions to be taken on erroneous data (e.g., a negative account balance or an unmatched account number) are defined. Note that error conditions are part of problem specification because functions are defined for all inputs, not just correct input data.

We will stop our problem specification here in order to keep the problem a reasonable size. It should be noted, however, that given this first step in the specification, error conditions, new problems, or details that arise as the project develops can be added. This type of functional definition can easily be added to or changed.

SAMPLE SOLUTION SPECIFICATION AND DEVELOPMENT

Generally, the second stage of project development, the solution specification, requires the greatest creative effort. Note that in the first pass at a solution algorithm one should not concentrate on the computer or specific programming language to be used or even the efficiency of the algorithm. The only concern should be development of a solution algorithm in terms of some appropriate set of high-level *primitives* (this term is defined in Part I). These primitives can be defined functionally and later turned into subroutines as refinement of the algorithm proceeds. Once a solution algorithm has been developed, further analysis can be devoted to increasing its efficiency. It should be understood, however, that the greatest degree of efficiency is introduced into a properly developed algorithm in the first pass of solution development.

It is worth nothing that this high-level algorithm provides an excellent form of documentation for the final product. Not only does it show the concise high-level view of the product design, but the actual statements of the algorithm can be used as comments in the final program. This provides specifications for the various subsegments of code and makes code reading and validation much easier.

Let us return to the problem of updating accounts. The functional specification of the problem is defined by the function "Update," which creates a new account file and output report. We shall now begin the decomposition of that function using the *stepwise refinement* (see Part I) process, continuing to use mathematical function notation.

We must first propose a solution strategy. We can use a standard technique for merging the information from two files; that is, attempting to read from each file, setting up read keys (acctkey and transkey) that have the value "true" if the READ was successful and "false" if the file is at end-of-file. If there is a record on the file, we store it in a local variable in order to manipulate it. We can then merge the ACCOUNT_FILE and TRANSACTION_FILE by letting the account records in the ACCOUNT_FILE drive the program, summing the TRANSACTION_FILE amounts for each account number.

For this example we shall assume that there is no account number on the TRANSACTION_FILE that is not on the ACCOUNT_FILE. We should record this assumption and the others mentioned earlier in the solution specification as follows:

ASSUME:

ACCOUNT_FILE, TRANSACTION_FILE sorted according to account number,

accounts on TRANSACTION_FILE are a subset of the accounts on ACCOUNT_FILE,

ACCOUNT_FILE and TRANSACTION_FILE have beeen rewound to start position

1. NEW_ACCOUNT_FILE, OUTPUT_REPORT:= Update (ACCOUNT_FILE, TRANSACTION_FILE)

(Note that the Dewey decimal numbering system is used to help show the nesting levels of the various expansions.

The first refinement of the Update function would be

1.1 *acct,* acctkey, ACCOUNT_FILE:=Read(ACCOUNT_FILE$_{in}$);

1.2 *trans,* transkey,TRANSACTION_FILE: =
Read(TRANSACTION_FILE$_{in}$);

1.3 NEW_ACCOUNT_FILE, OUTPUT_REPORT:= Update1 (*acct*, acctkey, ACCOUNT_FILE, *trans*, transkey, TRANSACTION_FILE)

Note that the statements are in the form output =Function (input) where commas separate multiple elements of the inputs and outputs. All elements that must be accessed by the function are listed.

The Read function sets acctkey to false if end-of-file has been encountered. If acctkey is true, the next record on the transaction file appears in *acct* and the account file is advanced to the next available record. An expansion of the Read function would be:

```
1.1.1     if
1.1.2        not end-of-file (ACCOUNT_FILE
1.1.3     then
1.1.4.1      acctkey:=true;
1.1.4.2      acct:=next (ACCOUNT_FILE)
1.1.5     else
1.1.6        acctkey:=false
1.1.7     fi
```

This expansion assumes a predicate that can check for an end-of-file condition and a routine following this one that reads the next record from the ACCOUNT_FILE and advances the ACCOUNT_FILE to the next available record. A similar routine would be written for the TRANSACTION_FILE.

The function Update 1 is a refinement of ''Update'' that assumes that the first record has been read from each file and the appropriate keys have been set for checking. Continuing the expansion process, Update 1 can become a *while* loop, letting the ACCOUNT_FILE drive the update process. This yields:

```
1.3.1  while
1.3.2     acctkey=true
1.3.3  do
1.3.4     OUTPUT_REPORT, NEW_ACCOUNT_FILE,
```

TRANSACTION_FILE, *acct,* acctkey,
ACCOUNT_FILE:=
Calculate-and-Output($acct_{in}$,
ACCOUNT_FILE$_{in}$, *trans,* transkey,
TRANSACTION_FILE$_{in}$)

1.3.5 od

The *do* part of the *while* loop specifies the function Calculate-and-Output, which in turn specifies each of the input parameters it requires to do its calculation and each of the output variables that it changes. Note that the function defined by Calculate-and-Output still resembles the functions defined by Update and Update 1.

The expansion of Calculate-and-Output would be:

1.3.4.1 newbalance, TRANSACTION_FILE :=
Calculate (balance($acct_{in}$), account($acct_{in}$),
$trans_{in}$,TRANSACTION_FILE$_{in}$):

1.3.4.2 NEW_ACCOUNT_FILE:=Write($acct_{in}$, newbalance),
OUTPUT_REPORT:=Print ($acct_{in}$, newbalance,
balance ($acct_{in}$)), *acct,* acctkey,
ACCOUNT_FILE:=Read(ACCOUNT_FILE$_{in}$)

where Calculate is defined such that newbalance is equal to balance ($acct_{in}$) plus the set of transaction amounts with the correct account number, transkey is true or false depending on whether end-of-file has been encountered on the transaction file, *trans* is the next record in TRANSACTION_FILE with an account number greater than the account number of $acct_{in}$, and TRANSACTION_FILE has been advanced to the next record.

The function Calculate can be decomposed into a sequence that represents a loop initialization art and a loop part.

1.3.4.1.1 newbalance := (*acct* in);

1.3.4.1.2 newbalance, TRANSACTION_FILE :=
Calculate (newbalance$_{in}$, account $acct_{in}$),
$trans_{in}$, TRANSACTION_FILE$_{in}$)

This second statement can then be expanded into the loop:

1.3.4.1.2.1 while

1.3.4.1.2.2. transkey= true *and* account (*acct*)=
account (*trans*)

1.3.4.1.2.3 do

1.3.4.1.2.4. new balance :=

newbalance$_{in}$\{ ± \} amount($trans_{in}$)
__add if type (*trans)* ='cf3a' \}
subtract if type (*trans* ='−'\},
trans, transkey, TRANSACTION__FILE:=
Read (TRANSACTION__FILE$_{in}$)

1.3.4.1.2.5 od

DEMONSTRATING CORRECTNESS

Let us stop the expansion at this point in order to demonstrate the correctness of this last loop expansion. To see if we have made a correct expansion, we must ask the three questions associated with *Whiledo correctness*.

Does the loop terminate?

Yes because the TRANSACTION__FILE has a finite number of records and only a finite number of transactions will have an account number equal to the account number of $acct_{in}$, the loop will terminate.

If the *whiletest* is true, will the *do* part followed by the intended function of the *wiledo*perform the same function as the *whiledo?*

Yes, because setting the newbalance equal to newbalance$_{in}$ updated the next valid set of transaction amounts is the same as setting the newbalance equal to newbalance$_{in}$ updated by the first $trans_{in}$, (because the *whiletest* is true [i.e., transkey is true because there is another record on the TRANSACTION__FILE, so $trans_{in}$ is defined, and the account number of $trans_{in}$ is equal to the account number of $account_{in}$]) updated by the rest of the valid set of transaction amounts (see Figure 10).

	newbalance	***trans***	**TRANSACTION_FILE**
initially	newbalance$_{in}$	$trans_{in}$	TRANSACTION_FILE$_{in}$
dopart	newbalance$_{in}$ ± amount ($trans_{in}$)	next(TRANSACTION FILE$_{in}$) if transkey = true, undefined otherwise	TRANSACTION_FILE advanced one record
whiledo function	newbalance$_{in}$ ± amount ($trans_{in}$) plus the next set of transaction amounts with the correct account number	the first transaction record in TRANSACTION FILE$_{in}$ with account number greater than account number of $acct_{in}$ if transkey = true, undefined otherwise	TRANSACTION_FILE$_{in}$ advanced past the current value of trans if transkey true, at end-of-file otherwise

FIGURE 10. Trace table showing Part 2 of the whiledo correctness demonstration.

If the *whiletest* is false, does doing nothing do the intended function of the whiledo?

Yes, because if $trans_{in}$ is undefined or the account number of $trans_{in}$ is not equal to the account number of $acct_{in}$ there are no updates to $newbalance_{in}$ and newbalance :=$newbalance_{in}$.

Although the proof carried out in this example was relatively informal, it demonstrates the capability of proving the correctness of program expansion. In this case, reading alone was probably sufficient to demonstrate correctness. In many circumstances, however, where the programmer or reader is unsure of an expansion, the correctness demonstration technique can be used informally to help gain confidence in the program's validity. In some cases, where the expansion is especially difficult or the penalty for error is sufficient to warrant the extra work (for instance, with the algorithm for controlling microwave oven output), the programmer may very well want to do a formal mathematical proof.

At this point, we will terminate the expansion of the update program, assuming that we have developed each of the subfunctions to a point where it is clear how further expansion should take place. Figure 11 gives the program design with the function Calculate expanded.

From Design Expansion to Programming Language

One problem that has not yet been addressed is how one carries this type of design expansion into a particular programming language, especially with respect to the control and data structures. Actually, many programming languages, especially the newer ones like PL/1 and Pascal, have capabilities that support structured programming. For environments where FORTRAN and COBOL are the required languages, preprocessors offer support. In those instances where neither is available, the structured programming structures can be simulated. Figure 12 shows a set of appropriate control structure simulations for FORTRAN and COBOL.

RECOMMENDED COURSE OF ACTION

Structured programming methods yield programs with fewer errors. This increases the cost-effectiveness of program development. The most important gain, however, is in the discipline of the methodology, because it provides an organized approach to problem solving. In addition, the tools of structured programming, stepwise refinement, and function specification aid in the development of products that are easy to maintain and lend themselves to modification.

```
data

    sequence  ACCOUNT_FILE record (account:integer,balance:integer)
    sequence  TRANSACTION_FILE record (account:integer,type:character,amount:integer)
    sequence  NEW_ACCOUNT_FILE record (account:integer, newbalance:integer)
    sequence  OUTPUT_REPORT record (account:integer, balance:integer, newbalance:integer)
    scalar  acctkey, transkey logical
    scalar  acct record (account:integer, balance:integer)
    scalar  trans record (account:integer, type:character, amount:integer)

atad

proc  update
    ASSUME:   ACCOUNT_FILE, TRANSACTION_FILE sorted according to account number,
              accounts on TRANSACTION_FILE are a subset of the accounts on ACCOUNT_FILE,
              ACCOUNT_FILE and TRANSACTION_FILE have been rewound to start position
1.    [NEW_ACCOUNT_FILE, OUTPUT_REPORT := Update(ACCOUNT_FILE, TRANSACTION_FILE)]
1.1.    acct, acctkey, ACCOUNT_FILE := Read(ACCOUNT_FILE_in);
1.2.    trans, transkey, TRANSACTION_FILE := Read(TRANSACTION_FILE_in);
1.3.    [NEW_ACCOUNT_FILE, OUTPUT_REPORT := Update1(acct,acctkey, ACCOUNT_FILE, trans, transkey, TRANSACTION_FILE)]
1.3.1.    while
1.3.2.          acctkey = true
1.3.3.    do
```

FIGURE 11(a). Sample program functional expansion.

```
1.3.4.          [OUTPUT_REPORT, NEW_ACCOUNT_FILE, TRANSACTION_FILE, acct, acctkey, ACCOUNT_FILE := Calculate-and-Output(acct_in,
                      ACCOUNT_FILE_in, trans_in, transkey_in, TRANSACTION_FILE_in)]
1.3.4.1.   [newbalance, TRANSACTION_FILE := Calculate(balance (acct_in), account(acct_in), TRANSACTION_FILE_in)
1.3.4.1.1.   newbalance: = balance(acct)
1.3.4.1.2.   [newbalance, TRANSACTION_FILE := Calculate(newbalance_in, account(acct_in), TRANSACTION_FILE_in]
1.3.4.1.2.1.   while
1.3.4.1.2.2.      transkey = true and account (acct) = account (trans)
1.3.4.1.2.3.   do
                                              {+}                                            {'+'}
1.3.4.1.2.4.1.   [newbalance :=newbalance_in  {-}  amount (trans_in) if type (trans_in) =  {'-'}
1.3.4.1.2.4.1.1.   if
1.3.4.1.2.4.1.2.      type (trans) = '+'
1.3.4.1.2.4.1.3.   then
1.3.4.1.2.4.1.4      newbalance := newbalance + amount (trans)
1.3.4.1.2.4.1.5.   else
1.3.4.1.2.4.1.6.      newbalance := newbalance — amount (trans)
1.3.4.1.2.4.1.7.   fi
1.3.4.1.2.4.2.   trans, transkey, TRANSACTION_FILE := Read (TRANSACTION_FILE_in)
1.3.4.1.2.5.   od
1.3.4.2.   NEW_ACCOUNT_FILE := Write (acct_in, newbalance),
                      OUTPUT_REPORT := Print (acct_in, newbalance, balance (acct_in)),  acct, acctkey, ACCOUNT_FILE := Read
                      (ACCOUNT_FILE_in)
               1.3.5.   od
                 corp
```

FIGURE 11(b). Sample program functional expansion (continued).

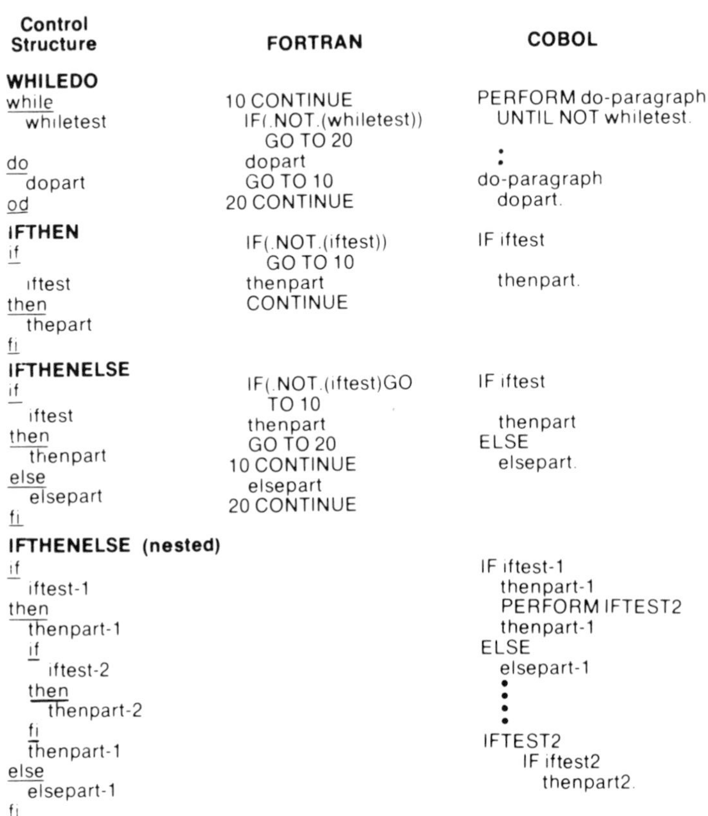

Control Structure	FORTRAN	COBOL
WHILEDO while whiletest do dopart od	10 CONTINUE IF(.NOT.(whiletest)) GO TO 20 dopart GO TO 10 20 CONTINUE	PERFORM do-paragraph UNTIL NOT whiletest. : do-paragraph dopart.
IFTHEN if iftest then thepart fi	IF(.NOT.(iftest)) GO TO 10 thenpart CONTINUE	IF iftest thenpart.
IFTHENELSE if iftest then thenpart else elsepart fi	IF(.NOT.(iftest)GO TO 10 thenpart GO TO 20 10 CONTINUE elsepart 20 CONTINUE	IF iftest thenpart ELSE elsepart.
IFTHENELSE (nested) if iftest-1 then thenpart-1 if iftest-2 then thenpart-2 fi thenpart-1 else elsepart-1 fi		IF iftest-1 thenpart-1 PERFORM IFTEST2 thenpart-1 ELSE elsepart-1 ⋮ IFTEST2 IF iftest2 thenpart2.

FIGURE 12. Control structure simulations for FORTRAN and COBOL.

REFERENCES

1. Basili, V.R. and A.J. Turner, "Iterative enhancement: A Practical Technique for Software Development," ACPM portfolio (14-01-05).
2. Conway, R. and D. Gries, An Introduction to Programming: A Structured Approach, Cambridge Massachusetts: Winthrop, 1973.
3. Linger, R.C. and H.D. Mills, "Definitional Text in Structured Programming," Proceedings of the Fourteenth Annual Technical Symposium: Computing the Mid-70's: An Assessment, Gaithersburg Maryland 1975.
4. Linger R.C., H.D. Mills, and B.I. Witt, Structured Programming Theory and Practice. Reading Massachusetts: Addison-Wesley, 1979.
5. Mills, H.D., "Mathematical Foundations of Structured Programming, IBM Technical Report, 1972.
6. Mills, H.D., "The New Math of Computer Programming," CACM 18, Vol. 1 (January 1975).

7. Mills, H.D., "How to Write Correct Programs and Know It." Proceedings of the International Conference on Reliable Software. Los Angeles California 1975 (SIGPLAN Notices No. 10, 6, June 1975).
8. Wirth, Niklaus, "On the Composition of Well-Structured Programs." Computer Surveys, Vol. 6, No. 4 (December 1974).

Cryptography as a Control Feature

Rein Turn
California State University

INTRODUCTION

An important responsibility of the DP manager is maintaining control over the use of the corporate DP system and its data. To achieve this, it is necessary to implement accountability systems, establish internal auditing groups, and employ a variety of computer and data security safeguards. A major goal is to prevent occurrences of computer crime; that is, the use of the corporate DP system by employees for perpetrating white-collar crimes or the penetration of the system by outsiders.[1] For example, computer systems have been used to maintain fictitious employees on payroll, order fictitious deliveries of products, and manipulate corporate assets and finances.[2]

The problem of detecting computer-aided crime is compounded by the nature of information processing and storage in computer systems. For example:

Data is stored in media not directly readable by people

Data can be erased or modified without leaving evidence

Computerized records do not have seals or signatures to verify authenticity or distinguish copies from originals

Data can be accessed and manipulated from remote terminals

Transactions are performed at high speeds without human monitoring or control

Programs specifying the processing rules are stored in the same media as data and thus can also be easily manipulated.

EDITOR'S NOTE: *From AUERBACH Data Processing Management, 1978. Reprinted by permission from the publisher, AUERBACH Publishers Inc.*

Although these examples also represent some of the reasons why computers are used in the first place, they do make management control difficult.

In addition to controlling use of the computer system by authorized employees, DP managers should address the problems associated with employees who may have access to the computer but are not authorized to use programs or access data files and with individuals who are outside the organization. They may attempt to bypass system safeguards in order to browse in files, capture control of the operating system,[3] or eavesdrop on communications links. The latter is relatively simple for anyone with some technical skill and resources, even in microwave transmission links.[4] The emergence of low-cost portable intelligent terminals makes sophisticated wiretapping possible, by inserting a terminal into the communications link for intercepting, modifying, and retransmitting data communications. Experiments have shown that such piggyback penetration of computer systems is feasible.[5]

Another problem is the lack of signatures or other authenticating material in digital messages. When two parties enter into a legally binding relationship by exchanging digital messages, each should require assurance that the messages are authentic and cannot be altered. At the present time, such assurances cannot be provided.

Whether a given DP system is a probable target for computer crime committed by internal or external people depends on several factors:

The nature of the corporation and its operations

Types of applications and data bases in the DP system

Opportunities for economic gain for the perpetrators

The size of the system's user population

The type of system and the capabilities available to users

For example, a remote time-shared system permitting users to submit assembly language programs offers more opportunities for computer crime than a system limiting its users to a fixed set of predefined transactions.

Determining both the potential threats against a DP system and the losses that may result are the reasons for security risk assessment.[6,7] Unfortunately, effective methodologies and techniques have not been developed.[8] It is important, therefore, that security safeguards be incorporated during the system design phase rather than added on later. The DP manager must recognize that security measures have become equally important design criteria as other functional capabilities.

The trend toward distributed computer systems with remote terminals, processors, and data bases, and the use of such systems for transmitting electronic mail, accentuates the need for securing associated data commmunications links and developing message authentication techniques. The use of cryptographic techniques for these purposes and the implications for the DP manager are topics of this paper.

BASIC CONCEPTS

There has always been a need to protect sensitive information in messages outside the physical control of the communicators in some communication channel.[9] Basically, there are two methods for providing protection:

1. Concealing the existence of the message by such techniques as including it with unrelated communications
2. Making the information in the message unintelligible by cryptographic techniques without attempting to conceal the existence of the message

The latter approach is far more practical in computer/communications systems.

As illustrated in Figure 1, a cryptographic system (cryptosystem) for secure communication between a sender (S) and a receiver (R) consists of the following elements:

A plaintext message (M) to be transmitted and protected

A very large family of invertible cryptographic transformations (ciphers) (T) applied to M to produce cipher text (E) and later to recover M by applying the inverse T^{-1} to E

A parameter (K, the key of the cryptosystem) that selects one specific transformation (T_K) from the family of transformations

A cryptosystem can be effective only if the communicators keep the key secret and the family T is large enough so that the correct K could not be guessed or determined by trial-and-error search techniques.

Such a system is used in the following manner. Prior to proceeding with communication, both S and R have agreed upon the family of transformations to be used and have established K (e.g., one communicator has selected K and communicated it to the other over a secure communication channel). Now S generates M and encrypts it by applying T_K: $E = T_K(M)$. The sender then transmits E. Upon receiving E, R applies the inverse transformation and recovers M: $M = T_K^{-1}(E)$. In the channel, E may be intercepted and subjected to

FIGURE 1. Application of cryptographic transformations.

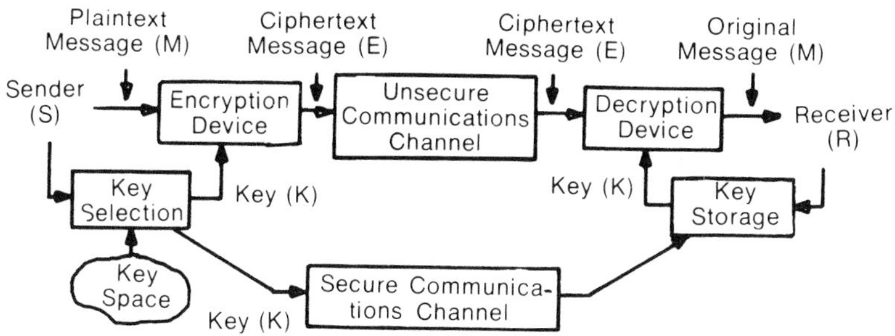

various cryptanalytic attacks aimed at M, K, or both. Since it must be assumed that the interceptor knows in detail the transformation being used, the security of the message rests entirely upon the interceptor not knowing which key was used.

More than 70 years ago, a set of effectiveness criteria for cryptosystems was stated by Kerkhoffs (as described by Shannon[10]):

The transformation used should be unbreakable (if not in theory then in practice).

The interceptor's knowledge of the family of transformations being used and of the cryptosystem equipment should not compromise the protection provided.

The key should be capable of providing all protection and should be easy to generate, store, transmit, and change.

The transformation used should be simple, requiring no complicated rules or mental strain.

Kerkhoffs' criteria were derived for manually operated communications systems, but they can be applied to computer/communications systems. Some changes, however, have occurred. For example, computers permit more complex transformations, and the keys can be changed more readily and frequently. On the other hand, computers have become important tools for cryptanalysis. Their use has greatly reduced the effectiveness of classical cryptographic transformations.[11]

In classical cryptography, all transformations are substitutions, transpositions, or product ciphers (combinations of substitutions and transpositions). If M is regarded as a string of characters from an alphabet (A), such as the English alphabet, a *monoalphabetic substitution* transformation replaces every character of A by either a character from a cipher alphabet (B) or a group of characters from B. These two cases are called monographic and polygraphic substitutions. Alphabet B is usually a permutation of A. A very simple form of a monoalphabetic substitution is the Caesar cipher, in which the cipher B is obtained by rotating the original alphabet A by a fixed number of character positions. This number is the key. Figure 2 illustrates a Caesar cipher in which K = 3 and A is rotated to the left. Because there are only 25 possible rotations for the English alphabet, this system is very easy to solve by trial-and-error methods.

FIGURE 2. Caesar cipher (K = 3).

Plaintext
alphabet A: a b c d e f g h i j k l m n o p q r s t u v w x y z

Ciphertext
alphabet B: d e f g h i j k l m n o p q r s t u v w x y z a b c

Plaintext message: sell all shares
Ciphertext: vhoo doo vkduhv

Polyalphabetic substitution transformations use several cipher alphabets (B_1, B_2, . . . , B_m), each of which is usually a Caesar cipher. They are used cyclically to determine what substitution is to be made. The key may be numeric (showing the amount of rotation for each alphabet used) or alphabetic (showing what character of each of the alphabets corresponds to the plaintext letter "a"). For example, when the key is "domino," the plaintext message "sell all shares" is encrypted as "vsxt nzo gtiesy." The longer the key (the more alphabets used), the more effective a polyalphabetic substitution is because it hides the original text more thoroughly. If K is at least as long as the message, the key is generated by a random process and is used only once. This cryptosystem is called a Vernam system and is, in theory and practice, unbreakable. Its use in computer/communications systems, however, is not practical because a very large K must be provided when the message volume is large.

Transpositions are rearrangements of characters in a message without changing the alphabet. Typically, a transposition operation is applied to a block of characters of the message. The key specifies which characters are to be interchanged. For example, in a block of six characters, with K specified as (136542), the word "profit" is changed to "optrfi." Character 3 replaces character 1, 6 replaces 3, and so forth as specified by the key until, finally, character 2 replaces 1. If the block is large, a transposition can be very effective.

Product transformations (repeated application of substitutions and transpositions) can be very effective "mixing transformations." One such transformation is the Data Encryption Standard (DES), recently approved by the National Bureau of Standards for nonmilitary agencies of the federal government.[12] DES is discussed in more detail in the next section. Other transformations based on complex mathematical formulas are being developed for application in computer/communications systems.[13] These are also examined.

Transformations based on substitutions only are called *stream ciphers*—each character of the message is encrypted independent of the others and can be transmitted as soon as it has been encrypted. Transformations that apply transpositions are called *block ciphers* because an entire block of characters must be encrypted before any can be transmitted. Furthermore, based on the structure of the communication and implementation of encryption, there are the following types:

End-to-end encryption, in which the sender encrypts the message and it remains encrypted while being transmitted through a network until it is received and decrypted by the receiver.

Link-by-link encryption, in which each communication link from switching center to switching center has its own encryption key. The communicators need only the key to the nearest switching center.

Super encryption, in which the communication system uses link-by-link encryption but the communicators use their own end-to-end encryption keys.

Link-by-link encryption increases key security by limiting each communicator to only one key to the nearest switching center and eliminating the need to make prior key transmissions. This means, however, that communicators are placing their trust in the communication system and its security. Messages must be decrypted at each switching center for reencryption for the next link. Thus, messages can be intercepted at the switching centers. Super encryption can avoid this problem.

DATA ENCRYPTION STANDARD (DES)

In 1977, the National Bureau of Standards approved DES as a federal standard. The Bureau decreed that DES is the only transformation to be used by civilian domestic agencies of the federal government.[12] DES has been published in full detail; its effectiveness derives from its complexity, number of possible keys (more than 10^{16}), and the security of keys used. DES is very resistant to cyptanalytic attacks even by large-scale use of computers, even though its absolute security has been questioned.[14] It has been claimed that one million special-purpose microprocessors, given the plaintext message and corresponding ciphertext, each microprocessor searching for the correct key at a rate of one million per second, could conceivably find the key within one day. The possibility of such a facility is not feasible in the near future.

Since DES will probably be used extensively both in government and private sector communications systems, it is described here in more detail. The DES transformation is an iterative nonlinear block product cipher that operates on 64-bit data blocks. It is very complex and suitable only for application by computer. Special-purpose integrated circuit chips have been developed for DES and are commercially available.[16] The DES algorithm, when used in reverse, is used for decrypting the ciphertext (using the same key, of course). The key is also a 64-bit word, but 8 bits are parity bits; thus, the effective key length is 56 bits. The DES transformation is applied as follows (see Figures 3, 4, and 5):

1. Given the 64-bit data block M, it is first divided into left- and right-hand parts of 32 bits each, L_0 and R_0. The 56-bit key (K) is similarly decomposed into two 28-bit parts, C_0 and D_0.
2. The following operations are now performed 16 times; the first pass is described here:
   a. The key to be used, K_1, is produced by generating C_1 and D_1 from C_0 and D_0 by shifting these a specified number of places to the left. Then the 48-bit K_1 is derived by selecting 24 specified bits from D_1 and C_1, as shown in Figure 5.
   b. L_1 is produced by replacing L_0 by R_0.
   c. R_1 is produced by computing a function, $f(R_0,K_1)$, and then adding it on a bit-by-bit basis with L_0. In computing $f(R_0 ,K_1)$, as shown in Figure 4, R_0 is first expanded to a 48-bit word and then added to K_1; 32 bits are chosen from the sum, and a transposition (permutation) is then applied,

$R_1 = L_0 + f(R_0,K_1)$. The strength of the entire DES transformation depends on the nonlinear operations in computing $f(R_0,K_1)$, that is, expansion of R_0 to 48-bit size and selection of the 32-bit word from the sum with K_1.

3. The last operation is combining L_{16} and R_{16} and applying a permutation that is inverse to the initial permutation performed on M before it was split into R_0 and L_0. The result is the 64-bit ciphertext E of M.

None of the operations are secret—the permutations used, the method of selecting key bits, and the method of expanding to a 48-bit length are published in full detail.[12] The protection accorded M derives from the complexity of the transformation and the number of possible keys. The theory of the operation of DES is not available, however; thus, there are no guidelines for modifying DES such as, for example, permit encrypting a larger block of data at a time or using

FIGURE 3. Enciphering compulation with DES.

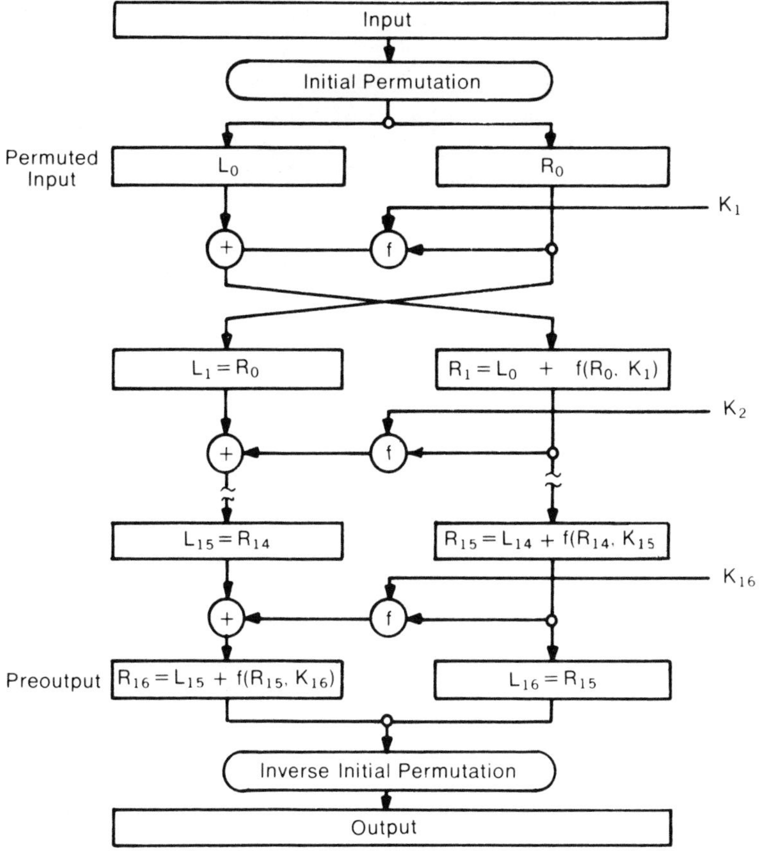

fewer iterations and still having an effective transformation. Clearly, programming DES operations in software would result in very slow operation of the encryption device and, consequently, the communication channel. In microcircuit versions of DES, however, device data rates of up to 1.6 megabits per second can be supported. The cost of DES devices ranges from $1000 to $5000 when implemented as standalone units.[16] The DES chip costs about $500.

There are three basic methods (Figure 6) for using DES in a communication system.[17] The first is in the form of an *electronic codebook*, in which, as described earlier, the 64-bit data block M is transformed to produce E. When the same key is used, the same E is obtained each time M is encrypted, much like using a codebook. The second method is *cipher feedback*, in which E_0 is produced from an initializing block, I_0, and then G_1 is produced by applying the transformation to E_0. E_1, corresponding to M_1 (the first data block to be encrypted), is produced by adding G_1 and M_1. Thus, the data blocks do not go through the DES transformation. The third method is *block chaining* in which the data block M_2 is first added to the ciphertext E_1 from transforming data block M_1; the sum is then transformed in the DES device. In general, this method provides greater protection than the other two.

Both the block chaining and cipher feed-back methods are useful when encrypting serial data for storage or stream-mode communication of character-oriented data; they are not useful for encrypting data to be randomly accessed in storage, or encrypting across packets in a packet communication system where the packets may arrive out of sequence. The electronic code book mode is suitable for these applications.

FIGURE 4. Generation of f(R,K) in DES.

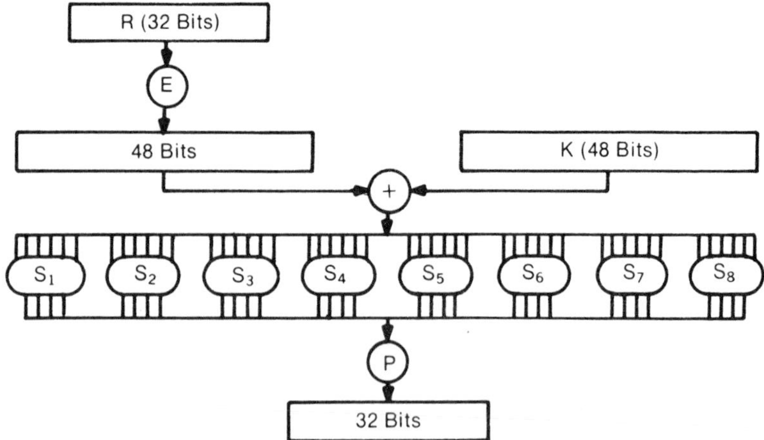

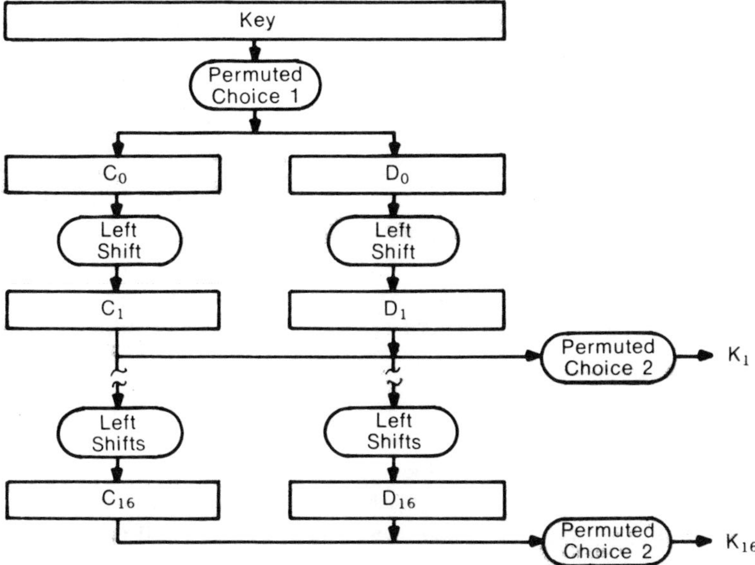

FIGURE 5. Key generation in DES.

FIGURE 6. Principal modes for using the DES.

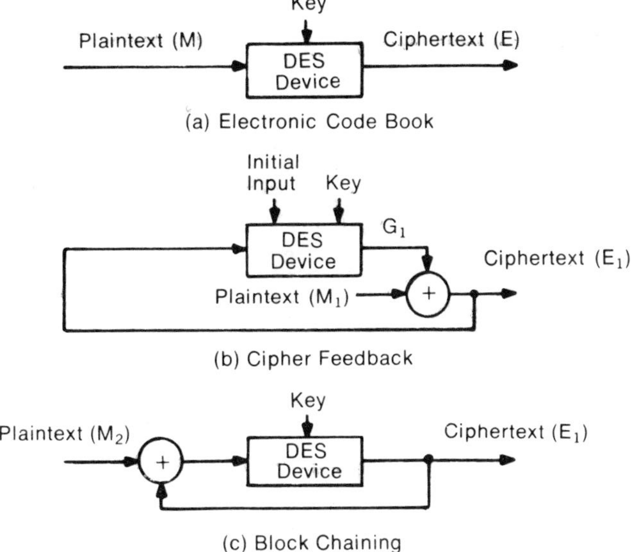

SUITABILITY CRITERIA

The suitability of a class of encryption transformations for application in a computer/communication or file system depends on the relevant characteristics of the particular application, inherent characteristics of the various classes of the selected transformations, and technical apsects of the system. Although the purpose of encryption is to make data secure when in transit or storage, the effects of its use on the utility of the application or system are equally important. A system might be designed to provide excellent security but at such a loss in performance or ability to use that it becomes practically useless.

Application characteristics that affect the choice of encryption transformations include:

The value of the information to be protected—assessing certain types of data (e.g., personal information) might be difficult, but risk analysis methods can provide assistance.[6,7] Time-dependence of the value is important—if the encryption transformation used can resist cryptanalytic attacks for T hours, but the value of the information decreases below a critical threshold within this time, the selected transformation may provide adequate protection.

The type of language used—information in a message (or computer record) is expressed in a language characterized by a vocabulary, grammar, syntax, and certain statistical characteristics (e.g., the relative frequency of occurrence of different characters of the alphabet). If a natural language (one that has evolved over a long period of time) is used, its characteristics tend to be useful for cryptanalysis.[9,10,17,18] When designing artificial languages (e.g., programming languages), the need for providing crytographic protection can be taken into account. Language characteristics can be designed so that their usefulness for statistical analysis is minimized.

Dimensions and dynamics of the application—these characteristics include the volume of messages or records that must be transmitted or stored, required rates and response times, nature of processing to be performed, and tolerances for errors. These establish a set of criteria that must be met by the cryptosystem used.

The most important characteristic of an encryption transformation is its ability to resist cryptanalytic attacks or attempts to test all keys by force. The following types of attacks are usually considered:

Statistical analyses of ciphertext, using language characteristics and testing hypotheses about possible keys or message content.

Attempts to determine the key used when the plaintext and corresponding ciphertext are available (the "known plaintext attack").

Mathematical analyses of the transformation used and formulation of sets of equations that could produce the key on the basis of intercepted ciphertext.

Correspondingly, the important intrinsic characteristics of cryptographic transformations are:

Size of the key space—it must be very large in order to make trial-and-error attempts to find the key impractical.

Effect of the transformation on language statistics—ideally, such language characteristics as relative frequencies of single letters, pairs of letters (diagraphs), and word structure should be completely masked and altered.

Complexity—the transformation should be complex enough to prevent mathematical analysis and multiply the time required for brute-force search. On the other hand, complexity affects the cost of application, in terms of both time and equipment used.

Effect on dimensions—such transformations as polygraphic substitutions of a character by a group of characters expand the length of ciphertext message over that of its plain text. This affects transmission time and storage requirements.

Error susceptibility—simple substitutions are applied independently for each character; thus, no error propagation can occur. Errors in block product transformations and in cipher feedback mode operation propagate throughout the block or subsequent ciphertext.

Length of the key—keys shorter than the message must be applied several times cyclically in the encryption process. This provides assistance in cryptanalysis. Long keys generated by a pseudorandom process based on a few short parameters (such as for random number generators) are also weak because the parameters (not the sequence) must be regarded as the true key. Systems that use randomly selected keys that are longer than the message and used only once are theoretically as well as practically unbreakable.[10] Large amounts of key must be available in active systems, and key generation, management, and security become serious problems.

Synchronization—such transformations as stream ciphers work only when the encryption/decryption devices are synchronized in time; both are in correct initial states when transmission begins and will remain so throughout the transmission. Loss of synchronization resulting from some error condition in the channel can prevent correct decryption. Block ciphers that do not use cipher feedback usually do not require time synchronization, but the beginning of the block must be clearly identified. The DES transformation has a self-synchronizing property even though an entire block may be lost when synchronization is lost. In general, the need for synchronization exposes the system to jamming attacks through deliberate insertion of noise into the communication link.

Simple monoalphabetic substitutions and transpositions do not hide language characteristics.[20] Polyalphabetic substitutions alter the single-character or digraph frequencies as a function of the length of the key (number of alphabets used). If the message is about 20 times as long as the key, computer-aided analysis can detect the language characteristics.[11] When higher-order statistics are also used, the difficulty of a statistical analysis attack is greatly reduced.[21] In messages or records expressed in such artificial languages as programming or query languages, language statistics can be designed to be less revealing (e.g., all characters could have an equal frequency of use, all words could be the same length, and all possible words could be used). Numerical data is also secure against statistical analyses, especially when long sequences of leading zeros are removed prior to encryption. On the other hand, artificial languages tend to have more rigid formats and syntax and thus assist cryptanalysts.

Technical considerations in the application of cryptographic techniques include:

Processing capability—this involves the availability of sufficiently high-speed processors to perform the encryption/decryption operations within the time constraints of the application and without unduly degrading the channel transmission capability.

Error environment—error characteristics of the communication channel are important in choosing the encryption system. For example, in a highly error-prone channel, using transformations that propagate errors or require continuous synchronization can lead to much wasted transmission resulting from the need either to retransmit messages that could not be decrypted or to resynchronize the system.

Operational environment—this consideration includes the type of system and its control as well as the training of system users and operators.

Key distribution and management—consideration should be devoted to the techniques used for key generation, distribution, and control. These techniques are most crucial in determining the success of a cryptosystem but are often overlooked in the beginning.

These factors must all be taken into account by the DP manager when considering encryption, particularly operator/user training. Experience has shown[9] that much of the success of cryptanalysts in breaking complex military and diplomatic cryptosystems can be directly associated with the improper security practices of system users. For example:

Using the same key many times to transmit different messages when such practice was contrary to system requirements, thus permitting the cryptanalyst to simultaneously hypothesize solutions and test them on several ciphertexts

Sending plaintext after failing several times to transmit the ciphertext without error

Using highly formatted repetitive text in encrypted messages that can be easily guessed in relation to the context of the language or application used and, therefore providing a source of plaintext for the cryptanalyst

Publishing a message verbatim that was earlier transmitted in encrypted form

Using the same key for longer periods of time than specified for the given cryptosystem, thus providing additional material for cryptanalysis beyond what is considered acceptable by system designers

Using an old key to send the new key, thus compromising the security of the new key.

In general, despite rigid operational restrictions, a great many ciphertext and corresponding plain text fragments might become available to interceptors/cryptanalysts. It is important, therefore, to use a cryptosystem that is as effective as possible in view of the application, system, performance, and cost. For example, if English text is to be transmitted, using the DES transformation would be superior to using stream ciphers based on polyalphabetic substitutions with relatively short keys. The latter, however, can be very effective in protecting numerical data.

There are practical requirements to consider when introducing encryption into a system in a commercial environment:[23]

Security in the system should depend on a minimum number of manual operations personnel, thus limiting the number of people who must be cleared to handle encryption keys.

Daily data terminal users and system operators should not handle keys or require special training to transmit encrypted messages.

Data link control procedures and protocols as well as network control programs should not require major modifications when encryption is introduced.

Data link throughput should not be reduced noticeably in the encrypted transmission mode, particularly in the case of artificially added redundancy (such as padding plaintext messages with random characters or using polygraphic substitutions).

The encryption transformations should not produce and transmit character groups that are also used by the communication system to control data links, switches, and so on. Means must be implemented to filter out such forbidden characters groups or, as a minimum precaution clearly identifying the ciphertext portions of a transmission so that these character groups are ignored by the network control programs.

There are numerous considerations and requirements that may be affected in varying degrees by introducing security requirements (encryption in particular) or that affect the choice of encryption transformations. Approximately 35 such requirements are examined in a recent publication.[24]

KEY MANAGEMENT

It is apparent from the preceding discussion that the security provided by those using a cryptosystem depends on security measures for the keys used. This is especially true for such systems as those using DES, in which all details of the transformations used are public knowledge. Thus, the problem is to generate, distribute, store, and apply keys in a secure manner. Some general principles have already been mentioned, such as minimizing the number of employees who are permitted to handle the keys. In addition, key management requirements for file systems differ from those used for communications systems:

In computer communications systems, encryption and decryption are performed at remote locations; thus, two copies of the key are required. In a file system, both operations are performed at the same location.

A computer communication system usually involves two individuals, but a file system involves many users who may require access and thus will share the key.

In a computer communication system, the message remains encrypted for a short period of time and is subject to interception only for this period of time. In a file system, encrypted records are at risk indefinitely.

Changing keys is a simple process in a computer/communications/system, but changing a key in a file system requires all records be reprocessed with the new key.

These differences affect the handling of keys and the selection and use of cryptosystems in file as opposed to communication systems. In file systems, it is necessary to store keys in the system for long periods of time and utilize them frequently, which tend to weaken key security.

In systems where keys are handled automatically, increased emphasis must be placed on reliable identification and authentication of users and systems involved in the communication process. Networks of computers are an especially demanding environment for key management when many users wish to engage in end-to-end encrypted communication with each other or require secure communications when interacting with a variety of systems in the network.

In link-by-link encryption systems, each link has a separate key that can be changed automatically each time a message is transmitted (or less frequently). The keys can be stored in the (tamperproof) encryption device in a read-only memory that can be physically distributed to switching centers at required intervals. Key management in this system is relatively simple and secure. If headers of messages are not encrypted, switching centers do not require access to the decrypted message and decryption and encryption for the next link can be processed within the device. At the receiving terminal, authentication of receiver identity must be required before the receiver is permitted access to the message. Standard identification/authentication techniques include using passwords or some individual characteristics (e.g., signature or fingerprint).

In end-to-end encryption, it is impractical for every subscriber to possess a separate key for every possible individual or system he may wish to communicate at some time. Storing many keys securely is as difficult as keeping them up to date. Instead, it has been suggested that a network security center should be established for both identifying/authenticating users and systems and distributing keys for the desired communication sessions.[25,26] For this purpose, a hierarchy of keys can be established: session keys, submaster keys, and master keys. Keys on the lowest level would be used to protect the data; keys on the higher level would be used to protect lower-level keys.[27,28] There must also be a master key that is kept secure without encrypting. This key can be in the possession of the network security officer. This approach is based on the premise that the best way to provide key security is to encrypt the keys.

The network security system concept works as follows:[25]

1. A user (X) who wants to communicate over an encrypted channel with another user (Y) by using end-to-end encryption identifies and authenticates his terminal and himself to the network security center (NSC) and then requests a key for communicating with Y.
2. NSC verifies from its data base the authority of X to communicate with Y and then contacts Y and identifies/authenticates the terminal and individual using it.
3. NSC now uses its submaster key (which is not available to X or Y) to communicate with the two terminals to deliver a key for the communication session between X and Y.
4. At the end of the communication, the session key is discarded.

This approach is quite promising for implementation in networks with a large user community. In smaller networks, more conventional key distribution approaches are appropriate, such as physical delivery of the keys to communicators who require end-to-end encryption. The key could be selected by referring to an identification number or code associated with each key. A nonsecure channel could then be used if there is confidence that the list of keys and their identification system have not been compromised.

MESSAGE AUTHENTICATION

Authentication of the veracity and source of digitally transmitted and stored messages is an important problem in applications where legally binding agreements are made or funds are disbursed through the use of communication systems. Electronic funds transfer systems (EFTS) and various interbank clearinghouse activities are examples. Recent advances in developing "one-way" and "trap-door" functions have brought the achievement of such message authentication capability much closer to reality.[13, 29–33]

In one-way functions, it is easy to apply the function to some variables but very difficult to apply the inverse of the function to the result in order to recover the original variables or find the inverse function. For example, it is easy to compute the sum of a given set of integers, but given the sum it is impossible to determine what the original numbers were because there are so many numbers that add up to the given value. Finding the roots of a very high-order polynomial is another example. The first suggestions for the use of one-way functions were for secure storage of passwords in computer memory.[29] Instead of passwords themselves, the results of transforming the password by a function (F) were stored. Each time a password was submitted, F was evaluated and compared with the stored value. If they agreed, a correct password was used. Because the inverse F^{-1} is very difficult to compute, it did not matter if anyone gained access to the list of transformed passwords in the computer memory.

Functions in which both F and F^{-1} are easy to apply but F^{-1} is very difficult to find even if F is known have additional applications. An individual (X) can generate such a pair, F_K and $F_X{}^{-1}$, and make F_X public while keeping sole possession of its inverse $F_X{}^{-1}$. Then, anyone can send X a message by using F for encryption, but only X can decrypt it. A digital signature feature can now be implemented as follows. When X sends a message to party Y and wants to verify that it came from no one else, X first applies to message M_X the inverse transformation $F_X{}^{-1}$: $E_X = F_X{}^{-1} (M_X)$. The receiver Y now applies the publicly available transformation F_X to recover M_X: $F_X(F_X{}^{-1}[M_X]) = M_X$. This message must be authentic because only X could have applied the first transformation, that is, $F_X{}^{-1}$. For added security, X could also use Y's transformation F_Y to encrypt E_X.

One class of such functions utilizes the difficulty level in factoring very large numbers (100 digits or more) into prime factors.[31] Its generation, however, is too complex for discussion in this portfolio. Its primary disadvantage is that many multiplications are required because it involves representing M as an integer and raising it to a power which is at least a 100-digit number.

A new function based on the so-called "knapsack packing" algorithm was recently developed. Because only addition and multiplication are involved in its use, the signature generation process is greatly accelerated. Like many ideas that are just beginning to emerge, no proof of the security or insecurity of the proposed signature functions has been produced. It is probable that, along with the interest in developing such functions, there will be an equal interest in finding ways to break them. Caution should be exercised in adopting any proposed signature function at the present time without a thorough independent evaluation.

REFERENCES

1. Parker, D. B. Crime by Computer. New York: Charles Scribner's Sons, 1976.
2. Allen, B. "Embezzler's Guide to the Computer." Harvard Business Review, 79–89, July–August 1975.
3. Linde, R. R. "Operating System Penetration." Proc. 1975 Nat'l. Computer Conf. 1975.
4. "Taps to Steal Data." Security World, 45–46, December 1972.
5. Carroll, J. M., and Reeves, P. "Security and Data Communications: A Realization of Piggy-Back Infiltration." Infor, 226–231, October 1973.
6. Courtney, R. H., Jr. "Security Risk Assessment in Electronic Data Processing Systems." Proc. 1977 NCC. 1977.

7. Reed, S. K. Automatic Data Processing Risk Assessment. Washington DC: National Bureau of Standards, NBSIR 77-1228, March 1977.
8. Glaseman, S., Turn, R., and Gaines, R. S. ''Problem Areas in Computer Security Assessment.'' Proc. 1977 NCC. 1977.
9. Kahn, D. The Codebreakers. New York: Macmillian, 1967.
10. Shannon, C. ''Communications Theory of Secrecy Systems.'' Bell System Technical Journal, 654–715, October 1949.
11. Tuckerman, B. A Study of Vigenere-Vernam Single and Multiple Loop Enciphering Systems. Yorktown Heights NY. IBM Thomas Watson Research Center, RC 2879, 1970.
12. Data Encryption Standard. Washington DC. National Bureau of Standards, FIPS PUB 46, January 1977.
13. Diffie, W., and Hellman, M. E. ''New Directions in Cryptography.'' IEEE Transactions on Information Theory, 644–654, November 1976.
14. Diffie, W., and Hellman, M. E. ''Cryptanalysis of the NBS Data Encryption Standard.'' Computer, 74–84, June 1977.
15. Branstad, D., Gait, J., and Katzke, S. Report of the Workshop on Cryptography in Support of Computer Security. Washington DC: National Bureau of Standards, NBSIR 77-1291, September 1977.
16. Computer Security and the Data Encryption Standard. Edited by D. Branstad. Washington DC: National Bureau of Standards, SP 500-27, February 1978.
17. Kent, S. T. ''Network Security: A Topdown View Shows Problem.'' Data Communications, 57–75, June 1978.
18. Gaines, H. F. Cryptanalysis. New York: Dover Publications Inc, 1956.
19. Sinkov, A. Elementary Cryptanalysis—A Mathematical Approach. New York: Random House, 1968.
20. Turn, R. ''Privacy Transformations for Databank Systems.'' Proc. 1973 NCC. 1973.
21. Tuchman, W. L., and Meyer, C. H. ''Efficacy of the Data Encryption Standard in Data Processing.'' Proc. 1978 Fall COMPCON. 1978.
22. Burris, H. R. ''Computer Network Cryptography Engineering.'' Proc. 1976 NCC. 1976.
23. Schmid, P. E. ''Review of Ciphering Methods to Achieve Communication Security in Data Transmission Networks.'' Proc. 1976 ICC, 1976.
24. Shankar, K. S., and Chandersekaran, C. S. ''The Impact of Security on Network Requirements.'' Symp. Proc.: Trends and Applications 1977 Computer Security and Integrity. IEEE, 1977.
25. Branstad, D. ''Encryption Protection in Computer Data Communications.'' Proc. Fourth Data Communications Symp. Quebec, Canada, 1975.
26. Heinrich, F. The Network Security Center: A System Level Approach to Computer Network Security. Washington DC: National Bureau of Standards, SP 500-21, Vol. 2, February 1978.
27. Cryptography. IBM Systems Journal, No. 2, 1978.
28. Everton, J. K. ''A Hierarchical Basis for Encryption Key Management in Computer Communication Network.'' Proc. 1978 International Communications Conf. Toronto, Canada, 1978.
29. Purdy, G. B. ''A High-Security Log-In Procedure.'' Communications of the ACM, (August 1974), 442–445.

30. Rivest, R. L., Shamir, A., and Adleman, L. ''A Method for Obtaining Digital Signatures and Public Key Cryptosystems.'' Communications of the ACM, 120–126, February 1978.
31. Merkle, R. C. ''Secure Communications in Insecure Channels.'' Communications of the ACM, 294–299, April 1978.
32. Merkle, R. C., and Hellman, M. E. ''Hiding Information and Signatures in Trapdoor Knapsacks.'' IEEE Transactions on Information Theory, 525–530, September 1978.
33. Shamir, A. A Fast Signature Scheme. Cambridge MA: Department of Mathematics, Massachusetts Institute of Technology, May 1978.

PART VII

DATA PROCESSING MANAGEMENT ASSOCIATION

Submitted by DPMA.

"The Emerging Philosophy of Data Processing Management"
Malcolm J. Heimendinger

Data Processing Management Association (DPMA) serves the information processing and computer management community. Among its principal objectives:

Education and research activities focused on the development of effective management programs for the self-improvement of the membership.

Encouragement of high standards of competence and conduct, and promotion of a professional attitude among the membership.

Fostering of a better understanding of the vital business role of data processing society, and the proper relationship of data processing to management.

Increasing member and public awareness of the impact of information processing and the computer on society and stressing members' responsibility to employers and society.

Advance the interest of members and society-at-large concerning computer-related legislation.

DPMA is located at 505 Busse Highway, Park Ridge, Illinois 66068.

The Emerging Philosophy of Data Processing Management*

Malcolm J. Heimendinger
Manager, Administration System and Computing Division
Cities Service Company

The promise inherent in this title is that by generalization, all data processing managers have a single philosophy and this bright new world of ours is bringing us a specific new identifiable change in that philosophy. Unfortunately, the world isn't that simple. Each of us is a unique, complex individual; we think differently, we react differently, we have different backgrounds, we have had different experiences, and our plans for the future also differ. The environment in which we operate varies from shop to shop, from area to area, from company to company.

Let it suffice to say that the portraits I present are reasonably general in character and not all inclusive. If you don't recognize yourself or your immediate superior, or even if you do, no one is harmed; there is no implication that you are anything but what you actually are.

With that background, let's take a look at the past, the conditions which permitted the old philosophy to exist, the extent to which it was acceptable, the new philosophy which is emerging and why, and generally the direction in which we are headed.

At this point, I would like to interject a thought. I feel that "data processing" is actually a misnomer. While the function of the equipment we utilize

* A Presentation To The Data Processing Management Association "New Orleans '78" International Conference, Hilton Hotel, New Orleans, Louisiana, November 1, 1978.

From "New Orleans '78" International Conference, November, 1978. Reprinted by permission of the publisher, Data Processing Management Association.

EDITOR'S NOTE: *From "New Orleans '78," International Conference, November 1978. Reprinted by permission of the publisher, Data Processing Management Association.*

is processing data, our jobs are "data providing." You may call it data management, but that is only one specific function of our work, and I think "data providing" is a more logical, much better definition than "data processing." That won't be an easy idea to sell, and I am not here to recommend it, but you might take it back with you.

However, do not be deluded into thinking that since you are your company's information processor, you possess inherent power. You are really the data provider, the computer does the processing. The importance is in the information and not in the process. The hand that carries the sword is never the sword.

About the only thing in our business that doesn't change is the fact that it's constantly changing. Managers who cannot cope with change will not be effective.

What is a DP manager? A guy who always has his resume up-to-date. That may be funny, but it is pretty damn tragic. In 1973, I read an article which stated, in part: "Several years ago, I made the unfortunate observation that if half of the people involved in systems and software in the United States suddenly lost their jobs, not a single project would be delayed. I believe that statement still holds true."

When we go far enough back, to a time before many of you had any concerns about anything, the beginning of data processing for most major organizations was unit record equipment. It was simply another set of tools, another group of machines not too dissimilar in usage from bookkeeping machines, hand-driven calculators, adding machines. Actually, in those days, printers were called accounting machines. They had selectors and accumulators that enabled them to select certain conditions and perform simple arithmetic functions. It was, if you will, an extention of existing traditional office methodology.

Some of you may remember that this organization, the Data Processing Management Association, for many years bore the name "National Machine Accountants Association." Most of us then in data processing came from the more traditional office operations: payroll, accounting, inventory control, payables, receivables, the generally recognized functions. And, most generally, this new data processing operation was placed in the controller's division—a logical and likely choice given the circumstances that prevailed.

We had a knowledge, an in-depth knowledge if you will, of the problems of the business we were trying to solve: payroll, inventory, receivables, payables. And we set about learning the technical requirements of these newfangled accounting machines. Frankly, we were a bit overwhelmed. We became so engrossed in how selectors worked and how critical timing was, that we began to adopt the "lingo" of the equipment. Partially, this resulted from our total absorption in and love of what we had learned. And, I would guess that although we would never admit it, it was partly to show outsiders just how sophisticated and how knowledgeable we were; a sort of "We know and you don't" attitude. We began to use the jargon that, unfortunately, still sets us aside.

At any rate, there we were, possessing an in-depth knowledge of the problems we were involved in, since we had worked in payroll, accounts payable, etc. Through hard work and too many late hours, we had also learned to make these machines work. It became quite evident that we were in a unique position, and we loved it. Our attitude was, "we know more about how to solve these problems than anyone else." That was probably true, at that time, due to this marriage of knowledge in two areas. As technology advanced, as new, larger, more sophisticated equipment emerged, as handling of purely accounting and clerical functions became less important to the total data processing area, we still maintained this air of superior knowledge.

For years DP managers were obsessed with the idea, carefully nurtured by the media, that they were on the shortcut path to executive management. After all, who knew more about the business than those involved in data processing? Most of us know better now, although a few have made it—not because they were DP managers, perhaps in spite of it, but because they were damn good managers.

One of those who has succeeded is Don Kelly. In 1977, he became Chief Executive Officer of Bismark Incorporated, a giant holding company which registered sales of $5.3 billion in 1976, with profits of $82.5 million. In an interview in "Data Management" published September, 1977, he was quoted as saying: "A good data processing manager is really no different than the manager of any other major segment of a company. Technical skills, while important, are secondary to having superior managerial skills. Any data processing manager who wants to play a more important role within his company has the responsibility to strengthen his general management skills, learn how to deal with people and organizational problems, in addition to those technical skills required to fill his managerial role."

Let's look at some of the characteristics a successful individual should have. Motivated, and a motivator. Ambitious and assertive. Neutralizes negative thinking. Aware of individual needs. Gives 100% always. Energetic. Responsible and realistic. Put them all together in perspective and they spell—*MANAGER!*

Of course, management itself is a function about which thousands of books have been written; untold millions of speeches have been made and an awful lot of garbage published. Yet, the number of absolute truths that have been promulgated about management are relatively few in number. There are opinions, there are ideas, there are concepts, some of which become fashionable, rise to a peak and, having attained a level of acceptance, tend to dwindle. Insofar as exact statements of fact which are true today, were true yesterday, and will still be true tomorrow, there are not too many. I promise you that I do not plan today to add to this very minimal number!

We must get away from the "I know it all, if you have a problem, see me" concept; and, I think by and large, we are beginning to. We seem to possess total absorption in technical expertise in the internals of systems development, in the internals of programming and all the new things that come along; data base, structured—name it. This tends to ignore the objectives of our employer corporation, and will destroy us unless we change.

Back in the olden days mentioned earlier, our not being knowledgeable of or not being involved in the real business of the company, not necessarily possessing a definite understanding of our business processes, was tolerated simply because the total dollars involved were not significant. No one was too concerned; Data Processing was a play toy, the "in" thing or status symbol. Management read all the business publications about the wonders of the computer and assumed the movement toward them was a logical step. *They* were expecting miracles. An "awe" gap existed between us and them. *That is no longer true. Today, they demand performance.*

In company after company, the share of the budget borne by the data processing function, both direct and related expense, is becoming more significant. These costs have to be justified. Initially, we justified the addition of equipment by job elimination in affected functions. As we moved from the simple problems to the more complicated, it became evident that that is not the real payoff. On the contrary, we found in many cases, the number of jobs increased. The real value is providing management the information needed to manage.

Obviously, there are no simple answers, but we are beginning to recognize there are questions to be resolved, and, at some point, we must come to grips with the problem. We must set standards and then see that the standards are adhered to. We must ensure that the level of output is acceptable in total, not just for a day or an hour and that the productive time available for individuals is within standards. Time available means total hours scheduled less nonproductive hours. Professional development, vacation, sickness, holidays, outside consulting do not get projects completed. Neither does answering the phone, goofing off, going to the rest room, etc. All of these things take time, we know they do, and they will continue to occur. How do you get your arm around it? With all of this "nonproductive" stuff, how do we schedule and manage our work?

For years, progress reports coming to us or to upper management might indicate a program was 80% coded. Sounds fine—but what is the basis for the 80%? Has 80% of the logic been coded, or is 80% of the time allocated for coding been consumed? It could well be that the remaining 20% may take as much time as the 80%, or it may take only 5% more. It's somewhat meaningless. We have seen reports that a program is 75% or 90% debugged. Does this mean that 90% of the instructions have been tested? Tested how? Desk checked, by running data through them, by running parallel data, or running properly generated test data? Has 90% of the time required for testing been utilized? Is the testing procedure proper, is it adequate, is it comprehensible?

Users place a great deal of credence in parallel runs. Parallel runs indicate that when successfully completed, the data that ran through the old program will also run through the new, and produce, hopefully, the same results. When the results vary, very careful analysis is required. While the problem may be in the new program, it is possible that the answers from the old one were wrong.

But, all that is known is that the specific situations covered by the data used gave an explainable result. Nothing indicates whether a combination of circumstances not encountered in that parallel test will come up during production status and bring everything to a screeching halt. This is why there is a move to utilize a good data set generator which generates test conditions involving virtually all logic combinations and is far superior to only historical data. Is there enough volume in the test data to determine what happens as increased volumes occur? Can you exceed the length of field? Will the alloted storage area be sufficient to take care of all probabilities?

All too often, we hear about efficiency: an efficient program, an efficient operation, an efficient system. Usually this refers to efficiency in equipment use. Is this really our objective? Should we not rather be looking for an effective system? One which meets the objectives of the problem? Which meets the objectives of the user? Which coincides with the operational and control requirements of the DP organization itself? Which can be done in an economical, cost-justified manner? Too much emphasis on efficiency often leads to ineffective results. Too many times by far, we have produced systems and programs that were efficient computer solutions, which maximized the computer's efficiency, yet placed unnecessary and unwarranted restrictions on the user's business operation. This is not acceptable! After all, any good system must be designed to service the business' functions and not change the business to serve the system's functions.

Here is where you must be practical. Some top flight programmers love to tinker with the code so as to reduce computer time to an absolute minimum. Commendable as that might be, there is a cost/benefit analysis required. If the program as currently coded requires only 2–4 minutes of CPU time each week, just how much programmer effort can be justified to get some amount of improved "efficiency?"

On the other hand, if it is a technical program with many iterations and requires 45 or more CPU minutes and is run daily, a significant improvement may be realized. In the old 360/65 days we had one such program which required almost four CPU hours. After rewriting two rather small routines, the run time was reduced to 40 minutes.

Last year it was reported that in the preceding three years, more than one-half of all data processing managers had been replaced. And, over 50% of those were replaced by people with no data processing experience. Disturbing? It should be! Corporate management has accepted for years the fact that management requires its own special expertise. A competent manager could be and frequently is, moved from one area of the business to a different, totally unrelated one, and still function adequately. He relies upon and fully utilizes his assigned staff. Oh, he needs to learn rather quickly about the technical aspect of what he is doing in order to understand what is going on, but he doesn't have to worry about the "nitty gritty." He doesn't have to involve himself in every minor day-to-day decision. He knows how to delegate, not only the responsibility for getting a job done, but also commensurate authority. The trick is, he holds his subordinate fully accountable for the delegated work.

That brings us to a fundamental principle of management-accountability. Are you held accountable for what you and your subordinates are doing? And, in turn, do you hold your subordinates responsible? Are you discharging your responsibility toward your superiors, toward your company, toward your peers?

A study conducted by The Diebold Research Program compared opinions of Corporate Chief Executive Officers against those of the top data processing executives in the same firms and produced several interesting points. For example, while both groups note Managerial Competence as the prime requisite for a Data Processing Executive, the Data Processing executives selected it by less than a 3:2 margin over other traits. On the other hand, the Chief Executives selected it by more than 2:1. To quote from the published report: ''The data suggest that most DP Managers would do well to sharpen their management skills and understanding of the organization in which they are embedded while deemphasizing any tendency to free lance within the organization.''

Let's get away from generalities and be a little more specific as to what changes are in process. Then we will assess their impact on both the individual manager and his operation.

What are the basic elements of Data Processing Management? Really, no different than any other management area in concept; variances are only in specifics. Here are three of the basics:

1. Managing the assigned resources.
2. Producing an acceptable, cost effective product.
3. Maintaining an image of credibility and reliability; in other words, customer satisfaction.

Specifically, what does ''managing the assigned resources'' mean? Well, in our business, there are two types of resources—people and equipment. And, of these two, managing people presents the greater problem.

The first thoughts that occur to many people in this regard, are ''leading,'' ''directing,'' or ''motivating'' employees. Actually, none of these really fits the bill. I submit that the principal role, the most challenging role, the most rewarding role of a good manager is *developing* people.

The initial step is establishment of identities. Your employees want and need to feel a part of the organization. To feel an integral part and not a nameless, unrecognized programmer, or analyst, or operator. To feel management's interest and concern in them and their progress. To feel a demonstrated awareness of their progress, their successes, their failures.

The most prevalent complaint I have heard from dissatisfied employees over the years has been this particular item. As long as they feel that way, motivation is impossible.

How gratifying to have your manager, or even better, his manager, call you by name—your own name and not someone else's—and say ''that was a fine job!'' Not quite as gratifying, but still an experience completely acceptable is to have him say ''Well, you had some problems, but you did learn something useful, didn't you?'' In both cases, the effective element was recognition.

Regular performance evaluations on a one-to-one basis between a manager and each subordinate are essential to maintaining good morale. These need to be planned, well-handled, constructive and positive in tone, and attainable objectives agreed upon. In addition, they need to be held often enough so that neither party loses sight of the objectives.

Managers at all levels need love! Some try to avoid the unpleasant aspects of management. They try to get love by being wishy-washy. They exercise little or no control over their people. Permissiveness, proved to have not worked successfully in child rearing, abounds in the work environment, and with the same lack of success. So, rather than gaining the ''love'' or admiration they anticipated by not requiring each employee to perform to capacity, they earn only con tempt.

This does not suggest a domineering, autocratic approach. Since our people are professionals, work with them as professionals. Set high, reasonable yet attainable standards, and expect them to live up to them. A very positive response will be realized.

Challenging an employee's ability by assigning more difficult tasks produces growth and maturity. No competent professional wants to be in a rut. So, rotate the more difficult assignments and projects and watch for unexpected dividends.

Let's now look at the second element: ''producing an acceptable, cost effective product.'' Do you recognize that our end product can be compared to a manufactured product such as a television, a car, a stereo, a boat? It can! For the programmer/analyst, it consists of systems and programs. For operations, it is the output—the reports, checks, etc.

To be acceptable, the system, the programs, the computer output must satisfy the user's needs. It must give him exactly what he wants in a manner and format approved by him.

However, in addition to its acceptability, it must be cost effective. So, it behooves the manager to produce the product within budgeted cost.

A moment ago I compared our product to a manufactured one. To carry along this analogy, the product acceptability and cost effectivness requirements can be approached with the same methodologies the manufacturing establishment uses—cost control and quality control.

Have any of you ever thought of quality control in the systems and programming areas? How do you determine an acceptable measure of quality? How do you exercise sufficient control so as to validate the quality?

The objectives of a Quality Assurance program are focused on those issues which affect the delivery of services to the user.

More specifically, a Quality Assurance program is aimed at four basic objectives for computer applications.

1. Reliability of performance.
2. Ease of operation in the Computer facility.
3. Effective use of hardware and software.
4. Ease of making modification and enhancements.

RELIABILITY OF PERFORMANCE

This concerns the operation and design of the system to insure that the data being processed by the system are accurate and that erroneous data are properly detected and remedied.

It includes adequate data controls, validation procedures, audit trails, and correctness of reports, as well as the quality of the data entry, processing, and report distribution procedures that insure the availability of the required information to the user on a timely basis.

EASE OF OPERATION IN THE COMPUTER FACILITY

This objective concerns whether the program or system is easily operated from the initial entry of the data through the distribution of output.

EFFECTIVE USE OF HARDWARE AND SOFTWARE

This objective is aimed at insuring that the capabilities of the hardware, operating systems software, and system utilities are used in an efficient manner.

EASE OF MAKING MODIFICATIONS AND ENHANCEMENTS

This objective addresses the ease with which modifications to a system can be made and is primarily concerned with the flexibility and open-ended construction of applications software and data.

After establishment of the Quality Assurance function comes the formulation of Standards. If you've never been involved, it is I can assure you, quite traumatic. But essential!

A *standard* is a rule which must be adhered to unless there are sound reasons for departure. In that event, prior management approval must be obtained. Items classified as standards have the following characteristics:

There is some practical means for assuring compliance.

It is explained in sufficient detail to leave no question as to whether or not it is being followed.

On the other hand, a *guideline* is defined as a normal way of doing things. While guidelines should generally be followed in the absence of overriding considerations, their application must be tempered by common sense and good technical judgment. Some standards currently in use in our shop are:

A maximum of 400K bytes of main storage shall be allocated per OS job.

The assignment of all system and subsystem codes is to be coordinated through Systems Planning.

Guidelines include:

Consider the consolidation of various types of error messages onto a single report for user convenience.

TP should be used for the transmission of reports to remote locations.

Of course, a simple, straighforward procedure needs to be put in place to handle changes as the need arises. We work from grass roots to handle this. A section of our Standards and Guidelines Manual explains how anyone may propose a change, the evaluation procedure involved, together with a supply of forms for proposing a change. In this section we state: "The responsibility for the *content and quality* of the standards and guidelines is shared by all members of the Division."

The last of our basics is *maintaining an image of credibility and reliability; in other words, customer satisfaction*. No matter how well we perform, no matter how well we produce, the way we are perceived is the way we are within our company. Once your image is tarnished, it's difficult to change.

As Managers, we must meet our objectives in such a way as to command respect. Respect for our actions, for our ability, for our public relations effort.

The modern D.P. manager has learned to accept change as normal. He has learned to be more realistic in estimating time requirements and costs involved in developing and implementing a system whether it be a new one or just an enhancement. As a result, fewer promises are made which cannot be attained.

Incidentally, we address this problem specifically in the quarterly performance reports which measure each manager's accomplishments against standards. One item indicates the number of jobs completed on time and the number late. Similarly, it shows how many were completed within the budget and the number with overruns. Obviously, acceptable variations are built in.

Thus, we are getting a handle on how well we are doing in this area. As you well know, a great deal of user complaints could be alleviated by better controlling such items. We need to develop an acceptable level of credibility in the user's eyes.

Of course we are going to have overruns! The important thing is first to improve our estimating capability, then maintain sufficient control on the job's progress to minimize overruns. However, when they do occur, we need to spot them sufficiently in advance of target date and cost so that we can advise the user. The reason needs to be pinpointed so corrective action can be taken where required.

Let me digress a minute, backing up a bit at the same time. I have been discussing the Performance Reports used by our Systems and Computing Division. Perhaps we should take a look at the reason we use them, what factors are being measured, and discuss their use and importance.

Any manager responsible for the performance of an activity needs to ask three basic questions periodically:

1. Are we performing adequately?
2. Are we getting better or worse?
3. To what, specifically, do I next need to pay attention?

The answer to the first question depends on a comparison of performance results against a norm of some kind. For Systems and Computing, a wide variety of norms may be used for comparison against performance, including operational plans, standards (both internal and external), policies and objectives. While each performance indicator has been chosen with comparability (to a norm) partly in mind, the focus of the actual performance report layouts is on the latter two questions. The underlying assumption is that norms will be developed and used over a period of time.

We utilize performance reports as management tools. Let's take a quick look at them:

Human Resource Utilization: This quarterly report measures the amount of development manpower devoted to each major user group, by kind of work performed. The report shows both planned and actual man-days in each category.

Project Activity: This report lists the projects under way for each major user group, indicating the current status of each.

Backlog: This report lists the pending Systems and Computing Requests for each major user group, the priority, the estimated size, benefit, range and status of each.

Key Factor Quarterly Graphs: A series of 16 graphs, on nine pages portrays the actual values for the previous year, current year to date, the plan for the remainder of the current year, plus those for the following year. These key factors are as follows:

1. Available man-days
2. Backlog (estimated man-days)
3. Projects completed with 10% of time (% of total projects)
4. Projects completed within 10% of budget (% of total projects)
5. Percent of indirect time (nonuser related) utilized
6. System availability (% of scheduled hours)
7. Production jobs carried over (days)

8. Number timesharing (TSO) sessions
9. TSO—maximum response time in seconds for 90% of all commands.
10. Database—maximum response time in seconds for 90% of all commands.
11. Unsuccessful production job completion—user problems (% of total)
12. Unsuccessful production job completion—Systems and Computing problems (% of total)
13. Equipment rental and depreciation expense $MM
14. Salary, burden and contract labor expense $MM
15. Total Systems & computing expense $MM
16. Costs not directly billed to user $M

For each graph, we define the variable, show the basis for the plan, the reason for variance, and its impact.

Controlling projects is addressed in another manual titled "Management Tools and Techniques." Included are the following areas:

Human Resource Management: It describes a process for measuring the utilization of developmental human resources, addressed to all Development Managers, Supervisors, and Analysts.

Work to be done is split into two categories—user work and internal work. User work is defined as being directly beneficial to a user organization, and consists of:

Consultation

Evaluation

System support

Enhancements

Planned projects

Unidentified projects

Internal work is that deemed necessary to maintain efficient and effective service to the user community, but not requested by any user. It consists of:

Performance enhancements

Internal support

Priorities and Scheduling: They describe a process for the prioritization and scheduling of development work, and addresses both users in operating and staff groups and our development Managers.

We utilize four levels of priority to classify development work. They are:

Mandated

High

Normal

Low

Mandated, high, and low priority work have adverse cost implications. Mandated and high priorities cause overstaffing, overtime, and excessive machine usage, while low priorities result in continually pulling people from the job. This forces significant retraining. Therefore, assignment of these priorities should be done only when there is a valid business reason. Criteria normally used to set priorities are:

Total estimated development cost

Profitability (cost/benefit)

Degree of risk

Age of request

Status of project

Due date

Project Management: It presents practices, guidelines, and reporting systems to be used by Project Managers, addressed to anyone who might act as a Project Manager. Project Management covers:

Project planning

Project control

User liaison

Reporting requirements

Under "User liaison," certain generalizations can be made about users, although there is no such thing as a "typical"user. For instance:

Users tend to be impatient

Users are busy people

Users understand time and money quite well

Users don't understand systems quality as well

Therefore, we must take a posture towards the user that:

Treats him as a valued business client

Is demanding of his time and involvement yet efficient in employing it.

Does not compromise with minimum internal standards

Performance Measurement: This describes the measures of performance that are germane to our activities, including both development and operation of systems, particularly addressed to all levels of our management and professional staff.

To gauge performance, we must collect data on what's going on and determine a trend rating. Normally, trends can be categorized as:

Highly favorable

Favorable

No change, or not applicable

Unfavorable

Highly unfavorable

Today's Data Processing Manager must recognize his two prime objectives:

Satisfy the needs of his clients in an effective and acceptable manner.

Develop his subordinates and himself.

In accomplishing this, he must institute effective controls while monitoring the work in progress. Delegation of responsibility, hand-in-hand with a commensurate level of authority, is essential. As a final step in this area, a high level of accountability must be utilized.

During the next few years, Executive Management will require adequate and acceptable levels of performance from Data Processing Management. This will necessitate change where necessary, conformity to the new requirements, and performance that is productive and cost effective. Those who can and do this well, survive—those who don't, won't.

We must get away completely from the bit and byte thinking. This new environment in which we must exist and survive can be summed up in three words:

Accountability

Credibility

Acceptability

PART VIII

SOCIETY FOR INDUSTRIAL AND APPLIED MATHEMATICS

These papers have been selected from the 1978 issues of SIAM Review and SIAM Journal on Computing to be representative of the kinds of papers published in these journals.

"Nineteen Dubious Ways to Compute the Exponential of a Matrix"
Cleve Moler and Charles Van Loan

"An Application of Bin-packing to Multiprocessor Scheduling"
E.G. Coffman, Jr., M.R. Garey, and D.S. Johnson

The Society for Industrial and Applied Mathematics (SIAM) is a professional membership association in the United States established in 1952 to

Further the application of mathematics to industry and science

Promote basic research in mathematics leading to new methods and techniques useful to industry and science

Provide media for the exchange of information and ideas between mathematicians and other technical and scientific personnel.

To support these objectives, SIAM holds two national meetings annually, and with the support of various government agencies, conducts research conferences which may offer international specialists as participants. Its approximately 3700 members are active in local section meetings. The society publishes numerous periodicals and monographs containing research and expository papers. It also sponsors the SIAM Institute for Mathematics and Society to promote the application of mathematics to the social sciences. SIAM is a member of American Federation of Information Processing Societies.

SIAM address is 33 South 17 Street, Philadelphia, Pennsylvania 19103.

Nineteen Dubious Ways to Compute the Exponential of a Matrix

Cleve Moler

Department of Mathematics, University of New Mexico, Albuquerque, New Mexico

Charles Van Loan

Department of Computer Science, Cornell University, Ithaca, New York

In principle, the exponential of a matrix could be computed in many ways. Methods involving approximation theory, differential equations, the matrix eigenvalues, and the matrix characteristic polynomial have been proposed. In practice, consideration of computational stability and efficiency indicates that some of the methods are preferable to others, but that none are completely satisfactory.

1. INTRODUCTION

Mathematical models of many physical, biological, and economic processes involve systems of linear, constant coefficient ordinary differential equations

$$\dot{x}(t) = Ax(t).$$

Here A is a given, fixed, real or complex n-by-n matrix. A solution vector $x(t)$ is sought which satisfies an initial condition

$$x(0) = x_0.$$

In control theory, A is known as the state companion matrix and $x(t)$ is the system response.

EDITOR'S NOTE: *From SIAM Review, Vol. 20, No. 4, October 1978. Reprinted by permission of the publisher, Society for Industrial and Applied Mathematics.*

In principle, the solution is given by $x(t) = e^{tA}x_0$ where e^{tA} can be formally defined by the convergent power series

$$e^{tA} = I + tA + \frac{t^2A^2}{2!} + \cdots .$$

The effective computation of this matrix function is the main topic of this survey.

We will primarily be concerned with matrices whose order n is less than a few hundred, so that all the elements can be stored in the main memory of a contemporary computer. Our discussion will be less germane to the type of large, sparse matrices which occur in the method of lines for partial differential equations.

Dozens of methods for computing e^{tA} can be obtained from more or less classical results in analysis, approximation theory, and matrix theory. Some of the methods have been proposed as specific algorithms, while others are based on less constructive characterizations. Our bibliography concentrates on recent papers with strong algorithmic content, although we have included a fair number of references which possess historical or theoretical interest.

In this survey we try to describe all the methods that appear to be practical, classify them into five broad categories, and assess their relative effectiveness. Actually, each of the "methods" when completely implemented might lead to many different computer programs which differ in various details. Moreover, these details might have more influence on the actual performance than our gross assessment indicates. Thus, our comments may not directly apply to particular subroutines.

In assessing the effectiveness of various algorithms we will be concerned with the following attributes, listed in decreasing order of importance: generality, reliability, stability, accuracy, efficiency, storage requirements, ease of use, and simplicity. We would consider an algorithm completely satisfactory if it could be used as the basis for a general purpose subroutine which meets the standards of quality software now available for linear algebraic equations, matrix eigenvalues, and initial value problems for nonlinear ordinary differential equations. By these standards, none of the algorithms we know of are completely satisfactory, although some are much better than others.

Generality means that the method is applicable to wide classes of matrices. For example, a method which works only on matrices with distinct eigenvalues will not be highly regarded.

When defining terms like reliability, stability, and accuracy, it is important to distinguish between the inherent sensitivity of the underlying problem and the error properties of a particular algorithm for solving that problem. Trying to find the inverse of a nearly singular matrix, for example, is an inherently sensitive problem. Such problems are said to be poorly posed or badly conditioned. No algorithm working with finite precision arithmetic can be expected to obtain a computed inverse that is not contaminated by large errors.

An algorithm is said to be reliable if it gives some warning whenever it introduces excessive errors. For example, Gaussian elimination without some form of pivoting is an unreliable algorithm for inverting a matrix. Roundoff errors can be magnified by large multipliers to the point where they can make the computed result completely erroneous, but there is no indication of the difficulty.

An algorithm is stable if it does not introduce any more sensitivity to perturbation than is inherent in the underlying problem. A stable algorithm produces an answer which is exact for a problem close to the given one. A method can be stable and still not produce accurate results if small changes in the data cause large changes in the answer. A method can be unstable and still be reliable if the instability can be detected. For example, Gaussian elimination with either partial or complete pivoting must be regarded as a mildly unstable algorithm because there is a possibility that the matrix elements will grow during the elimination and the resulting roundoff errors will not be small when compared with the original data. In practice, however, such growth is rare and can be detected.

The accuracy of an algorithm refers primarily to the error introduced by truncating infinite series or terminating iterations. It is one component, but not the only component, of the accuracy of the computed answer. Often, using more computer time will increase accuracy provided the method is stable. For example, the accuracy of an iterative method for solving a system of equations can be controlled by changing the number of iterations.

Efficiency is measured by the amount of computer time required to solve a particular problem. There are several problems to distinguish. For example, computing only e^A is different from computing e^{tA} for several values of t. Methods which use some decomposition of A (independent of t) might be more efficient for the second problem. Other methods may be more efficient for computing $e^{tA}x_0$ for one or several values of t. We are primarily concerned with the order of magnitude of the work involved. In matrix eigenvalue computation, for example, a method which required $O(n^4)$ time would be considered grossly inefficient because the usual methods require only $O(n^3)$.

In estimating the time required by matrix computations it is traditional to estimate the number of multiplications and then employ some factor to account for the other operations. We suggest making this slightly more precise by defining a basic floating point operation, or "flop," to be the time required for a particular computer system to execute the FORTRAN statement

$$A(I, J) = A\ (I, J) + T^*\ A\ (I, K).$$

This involves one floating point multiplication, one floating point addition, a few subscript and index calculations, and a few storage references. We can then say, for example, that Gaussian elimination requires $n^3/3$ flops to solve an n-by-n linear system $Ax = b$.

The eigenvalues of A play a fundamental role in the study of e^{tA} even though they may not be involved in a specific algorithm. For example, if all the eigenvalues lie in the open left half plane, then $e^{tA} \to 0$ as $t \to \infty$. This property is often called "stability" but we will reserve the use of this term for describing numerical properties of algorithms.

Several particular classes of matrices lead to special algorithms. If A is symmetric, then methods based on eigenvalue decompositions are particularly effective. If the original problem involves a single, nth order differential equation which has been rewritten as a system of first order equations in the standard way, then A is a companion matrix and other special algorithms are appropriate.

The inherent difficulty of finding effective algorithms for the matrix exponential is based in part on the following dilemma. Attempts to exploit the special properties of the differential equation lead naturally to the eigenvalues λ_i and eigenvectors v_i of A and to the representation

$$x(t) = \sum_{i=1}^{n} \alpha_i e^{\lambda_i t} v_i .$$

However, it is not always possible to express $x(t)$ in this way. If there are confluent eigenvalues, then the coefficients α_i in the linear combination may have to be polynomials in t. In practical computation with inexact data and inexact arithmetic, the gray area where the eigenvalues are nearly confluent leads to loss of accuracy. On the other hand, algorithms which avoid use of the eigenvalues tend to require considerably more computer time for any particular problem. They may also be adversely effected by roundoff error in problems where the matrix tA has large elements.

These difficulties can be illustrated by a simple 2-by-2 example,

$$A = \begin{bmatrix} \lambda & \alpha \\ 0 & \mu \end{bmatrix}.$$

The exponential of this matrix is

$$e^{tA} = \begin{bmatrix} e^{\lambda t} & \alpha \dfrac{e^{\lambda t} - e^{\mu t}}{\lambda - \mu} \\ 0 & e^{\mu t} \end{bmatrix}.$$

Of course, when $\lambda = \mu$, this representation must be replaced by

$$e^{tA} = \begin{bmatrix} e^{\lambda t} & \alpha t e^{\lambda t} \\ 0 & e^{\lambda t} \end{bmatrix}.$$

There is no serious difficulty when λ and μ are exactly equal, or even when their difference can be considered negligible. The degeneracy can be detected and the resulting special form of the solution invoked. The difficulty comes when $\lambda - \mu$ is small but not negligible. Then, if the divided difference

$$\frac{e^{\lambda t} - e^{\mu t}}{\lambda - \mu}$$

is computed in the most obvious way, a result with a large relative error is produced. When multiplied by α, the final computed answer may be very inaccurate. Of course, for this example, the formula for the off-diagonal element can be written in other ways which are more stable. However, when the same type of difficulty occurs in nontriangular problems, or in problems that are larger than 2-by-2, its detection and cure is by no means easy.

The example also illustrates another property of e^{tA} which must be faced by any successful algorithm. As t increases, the elements of e^{tA} may grow before they decay. If λ and μ are both negative and α is fairly large, the graph in Figure 1 is typical.

Several algorithms make direct or indirect use of the identity

$$e^{sA} = (e^{sA/m})^m.$$

The difficulty occurs when s/m is under the hump but s is beyond it, for then

$$\|e^{sA}\| \ll \|e^{sA/m}\|^m.$$

Unfortunately, the roundoff errors in the mth power of a matrix, say B^m, are usually small relative to $\|B\|^m$ rather than $\|B^m\|$. Consequently, any algorithm which tries to pass over the hump by repeated multiplications is in difficulty.

Finally, the example illustrates the special nature of symmetric matrices. A is symmetric if and only if $\alpha = 0$, and then the difficulties with multiple eigenvalues and the hump both disappear. We will find later that multiple eigenvalue and hump problems do not exist when A is a normal matrix.

It is convenient to review some conventions and definitions at this time. Unless otherwise stated, all matrices are n-by-n. If $A = (a_{ij})$ we have the notions

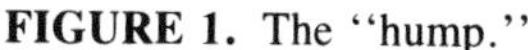

FIGURE 1. The "hump."

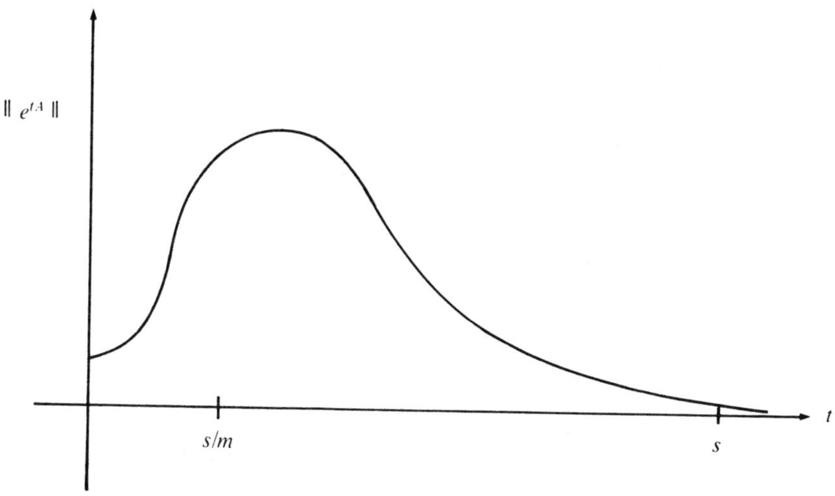

of transpose, $A^T = (a_{ji})$, and conjugate transpose, $A^* = (\overline{a_{ji}})$. The following types of matrices have an important role to play:

$$
\begin{aligned}
&A \text{ symmetric} \leftrightarrow A^T = A,\\
&A \text{ Hermitian} \leftrightarrow A^* = A,\\
&A \text{ normal} \leftrightarrow A^*A = A\,A^*,\\
&Q \text{ orthogonal} \leftrightarrow Q^TQ = I,\\
&Q \text{ unitary} \leftrightarrow Q^*Q = I\ ,\\
&T \text{ triangular} \leftrightarrow t_{ij} = 0, \qquad i > j,\\
&D \text{ diagonal} \leftrightarrow d_{ij} = 0, \qquad i \neq j.
\end{aligned}
$$

Because of the convenience of unitary invariance, we shall work exclusively with the 2-norm:

$$\|x\| = \left[\sum_{i=1}^{n} |x_i|^2\right]^{1/2}, \quad \|A\| = \max_{\|x\|=1} \|Ax\|.$$

However, all our results apply with minor modification when other norms are used.

The condition of an invertible matrix A is denoted by cond (A) where

$$\text{cond}\,(A) = \|A\|\,\|A^{-1}\|\,.$$

Should A be singular, we adopt the convention that it has infinite condition. The commutator of two matrices B and C is $[B, C] = BC - CB$.

Two matrix decompositions are of importance. The Schur decomposition states that for any matrix A, there exists a unitary Q and a triangular T, such that

$$Q^*AQ = T.$$

If $T = (t_{ij})$, then the eigenvalues of A are $t_{11}, \ldots, t_{nn}$.

The Jordan canonical form decomposition states that there exists an invertible P such that

$$P^{-1}AP = J,$$

where J is a direct sum, $J = J_1 \oplus \cdots \oplus J_k$, of Jordan blocks

$$J_i = \begin{bmatrix} \lambda_i & 1 & 0 & \cdots & 0 \\ 0 & \lambda_i & 1 & \cdots & 0 \\ \vdots & \vdots & & & \vdots \\ & & & & 1 \\ 0 & 0 & 0 & \cdots & \lambda_i \end{bmatrix} \qquad (m_i\text{-by-}m_i).$$

The λ_i are eigenvalues of A. If any of the m_i are greater than 1, A is said to be defective. This means that A does not have a full set of n linearly independent eigenvectors. A is derogatory if there is more than one Jordan block associated with a given eigenvalue.

2. THE SENSITIVITY OF THE PROBLEM

It is important to know how sensitive a quantity is before its computation is attempted. For the problem under consideration we are interested in the relative perturbation

$$\phi(t)=\frac{\|e^{t(A+E)}-e^{tA}\|}{\|e^{tA}\|}.$$

In the following three theorems we summarize some upper bounds for $\phi(t)$ which are derived in Van Loan.[32]

Theorem 1. *If* $\alpha(A) = \max\{\text{Re}(\lambda)|\lambda$ *an eigenvalue of* $A\}$ *and* $\mu(A) = \max\{\mu \mid \mu$ *an eigenvalue of* $(A^* + A)/2\}$, *then*

$$\phi(t) \leqq t\,\|E\|\,\exp\,[\mu(A) - \alpha(A) + \|E\|]t \qquad (t \leqq 0).$$

The scalar $\mu(A)$ is the "log norm" of A (associated with the 2-norm) and has many interesting properties.[35–42] In particular, $\mu(A) \geqq \alpha(A)$.

Theorem 2. *If* $A = PJP^{-1}$ *is the Jordan decomposition of* A *and* m *is the dimension of the largest Jordan block in* J, *then*

$$\phi(t) \leqq t\|E\|M_J(t)^2 e^{M_J(t)\|E\|t} \quad (t \geqq 0),$$

where

$$M_J(t)=m\,\text{cond}(P)\max_{0\leqq j\leqq m-1} t^j/j!.$$

Theorem 3. *If* $A = Q(D + N)Q^*$ *is the Schur decomposition of* A *with* D *diagonal and* N *strictly upper triangular* ($n_{ij} = 0$, $i \geqq j$), *then*

$$\phi(t) \leqq t\|E\|M_S(t)^2 e^{M_S(t)\|E\|t} \quad (t \geqq 0),$$

where

$$M_S(t)=\sum_{k=0}^{n-1}(\|N\|t)^k/k!.$$

As a corollary to any of these theorems one can show that if A is normal, then

$$\phi(t) \leqq t\|E\|e^{\|E\|t}.$$

This shows that the perturbation bounds on $\phi(t)$ for normal matrices are as small as can be expected. Furthermore, when A is normal, $\|e^{sA}\| = \|e^{sA/m}\|^m$ for all positive integers m implying that the "hump" phenomenon does not exist. These observations lead us to conclude that the e^A problem is "well conditioned" when A is normal.

It is rather more difficult to characterize those A for which e^{tA} is very sensitive to changes in A. The bound in Theorem 2 suggests that this might be the case when A has a poorly conditioned eigensystem as measured by cond (P). This is related to a large $M_S(t)$ in Theorem 3 or a positive $\mu(A) - \alpha(A)$ in Theorem 1. It is unclear that what the precise connectiion is between these situations and the hump phenomena we described in the Introduction.

Some progress can be made in understanding the sensitivity of e^{tA} by defining the "matrix exponential condition number" $\nu(A,t)$:

$$\nu(A,t) = \max_{\|E\|=1} \left\| \int_0^t e^{(t-s)A} E e^{sA} ds \right\| \frac{\|A\|}{\|e^{tA}\|}.$$

A discussion of $\nu(A, t)$ can be found.[32] One can show that there exists a perturbation E such that

$$\phi(t) \cong \frac{\|E\|}{\|A\|} \nu(A,t).$$

This indicates that if $\nu(A, t)$ is large, small changes in A can induce relatively large changes in e^{tA}. It is easy to verify that

$$\nu(A,t) \geqq t\|A\|,$$

with equality if and only if A is normal. When A is not normal, $\nu(A, t)$ can grow like a high degree polynomial in t.

3. SERIES METHODS

The common theme of what we call series methods is the direct application to matrices of standard approximation techniques for the scalar function e^t. In these methods, neither the order of the matrix nor its eigenvalues play a direct role in the actual computations.

METHOD 1. TAYLOR SERIES. The definition

$$e^A = I + A + A^2/2! + \cdots$$

is, of course, the basis for an algorithm. If we momentarily ignore efficiency, we can simply sum the series until adding another term does not alter the numbers stored in the computer. That is, if

$$T_k(A) = \sum_{j=0}^{k} A^j/j!$$

and fl $[T_k(A)]$ is the matrix of floating point numbers obtained by computing $T_k(A)$ in floating point arithmetic, then we find K so that fl $[T_K(A)] =$ fl $[T_{K+l}(A)]$. We then take $T_K(A)$ as our approximation to e^A.

Such an algorithm is known to be unsatisfactory even in the scalar case[4] and our main reason for mentioning it is to set a clear lower bound on possible performance. To illustrate the most serious shortcoming, we implemented this algorithm on the IBM 370 using ''short'' arithmetic, which corresponds to a relative accuracy of $16^{-5} \cong 0.95 \cdot 10^{-6}$. We input

$$A = \begin{bmatrix} -49 & 24 \\ -64 & 31 \end{bmatrix}$$

and obtained the output

$$e^A \simeq \begin{bmatrix} -22.25880 & -1.432766 \\ -61.49931 & -3.474280 \end{bmatrix}.$$

A total of $K = 59$ terms were required to obtain convergence. There are several ways of obtaining the correct e^A for this example. The simplest is to be told how the example was constructed in the first place. We have

$$A = \begin{bmatrix} 1 & 3 \\ 2 & 4 \end{bmatrix} \begin{bmatrix} -1 & 0 \\ 0 & -17 \end{bmatrix} \begin{bmatrix} 1 & 3 \\ 2 & 4 \end{bmatrix}^{-1},$$

and so

$$e^A = \begin{bmatrix} 1 & 3 \\ 2 & 4 \end{bmatrix} \begin{bmatrix} e^{-1} & 0 \\ 0 & e^{-17} \end{bmatrix} \begin{bmatrix} 1 & 3 \\ 2 & 4 \end{bmatrix}^{-1},$$

which, to six decimal places is,

$$e^A \simeq \begin{bmatrix} -0.735759 & 0.551819 \\ -1.471518 & 1.103638 \end{bmatrix}.$$

The computed approximation even has the wrong sign in two components.

Of course, this example was constructed to make the method look bad. But it is important to understand the source of the error. By looking at intermediate results in the calculation we find that the two matrices $A^{16}/16!$ and $A^{17}/17!$ have elements between 10^6 and 10^7 in magnitude but of opposite signs. Because we are using a relative accuracy of only 10^{-5}, the elements of these intermediate results have absolute errors larger than the final result. So, we have an extreme example of ''catastrophic cancellation'' in floating point arithmetic. It should be emphasized that the difficulty is not the truncation of the series, but the truncation of the arithmetic. If we had used ''long'' arithmetic which does not require significantly more time but which involves 16 digits of accuracy, then we would have obtained a result accurate to about nine decimal places.

Concern over where to truncate the series is important if efficiency is being considered. The example above required 59 terms giving Method 1 low marks in this connection. Among several papers concerning the truncation error of

Taylor series, the paper by Liou[52] is frequently cited. If δ is some prescribed error tolerance, Liou suggests choosing K large enough so that

$$\| T_K(A) - e^A \| \leqq \left(\frac{\|A\|^{K+1}}{(K+1)!} \right) \left(\frac{1}{1 - \|A\|/(K+2)} \right) \leqq \delta.$$

Moreover, when e^{tA} is desired for several different values of t, say $t = 1, \ldots, m$, he suggests an error checking procedure which involves choosing L from the same inequality with A replaced by mA and then comparing $[T_K(A)]^m x_0$ with $T_L(mA)x_0$. In related papers Everling[50] has sharpened the truncation error bound implemented by Liou, and Bickhart [46] has considered relative instead of absolute error. Unfortunately, all these approaches ignore the effects of roundoff error and so must fail in actual computation with certain matrices.

METHOD 2. PADÉ APPROXIMATION. The (p, q) Padé approximation to e_A is defined by

$$R_{pq}(A) = \left[D_{pq}(A) \right]^{-1} N_{pq}(A),$$

where

$$N_{pq}(A) = \sum_{j=0}^{p} \frac{(p+q-j)!p!}{(p+q)!j!(p-j)!} A^j$$

and

$$D_{pq}(A) = \sum_{j=0}^{q} \frac{(p+q-j)!q!}{(p+q)!j!(q-j)!} (-A)^j.$$

Nonsingularity of $D_{pq}(A)$ is assured if p and q are large enough or if the eigenvalues of A are negative. Zakian [76] and Wragg and Davies[75] consider the advantages of various representations of these rational approximations (e.g., partial fraction, continued fraction) as well as the choice of p and q to obtain prescribed accuracy.

Again, roundoff error makes Padé approximations unreliable. For large q, $D_{qq}(A)$ approaches the series for $e^{-A/2}$ whereas $N_{qq}(A)$ tends to the series for $e^{A/2}$. Hence, cancellation error can prevent the accurate determination of these matrices. Similar comments apply to general (p, q) approximants. In addition to the cancellation problem, the denominator matrix $D_{pq}(A)$ may be very poorly conditioned with respect to inversion. This is particularly true when A has widely spread eigenvalues. To see this again consider the (q,q) Padé approximants. It is not hard to show that for large enough q, we have

$$\operatorname{cond}\left[D_{qq}(A) \right] \simeq \operatorname{cond}(e^{-A/2}) \geqq e^{(\alpha_1 - \alpha_n)/2}$$

where $\alpha_1 \geqq \cdots \geqq \alpha_n$ are the real parts of the eigenvalues of A.

When the diagonal Padé approximants $R_{qq}(A)$ were computed for the same example used with the Taylor series and with the same single precision arithmetic, it was found that the most accurate was good to only three decimal places. This occurred with $q = 10$ and cond $[D_{qq}(A)]$ was greater than 10^4. All other values of q gave less accurate results.

Padé approximants can be used if $\|A\|$ is not too large. In this case, there are several reasons why the diagonal approximants ($p = q$) are preferred over the off diagonal approximants ($p \neq q$). Suppose $p < q$. About qn^3 flops are required to evaluate $R_{pq}(A)$, an approximation which has order $p + q$. However, the same amount of work is needed to compute $R_{qq}(A)$ and this approximation has order $2q > p + q$. A similar argument can be applied to the superdiagonal approximants ($p > q$).

There are other reasons for favoring the diagonal Padé approximants. If all the eigenvalues of A are in the left half plane, then the computed approximants with $p > q$ tend to have larger rounding errors due to cancellation while the computed approximants with $p < q$ tend to have larger rounding errors due to badly conditioned denominator matrices $D_{pq}(A)$.

There are certain applications where the determination of p and q is based on the behavior of

$$\lim_{t \to \infty} R_{pq}(tA).$$

If all the eigenvalues of A are in the open left half plane, then $e^{tA} \to 0$ as $t \to \infty$ and the same is true for $R_{pq}(tA)$ when $q > p$. On the other hand, the Padé approximants with $q < p$, including $q = 0$, which is the Taylor series, are unbounded for large t. The diagonal approximants are bounded as $t \to \infty$. □

METHOD 3. SCALING AND SQUARING. The roundoff error difficulties and the computing costs of the Taylor and Padé approximants increases as $t\|A\|$ increases, or as the spread of the eigenvalues of A increases. Both of these difficulties can be controlled by exploiting a fundamental property unique to the exponential function:

$$e^A = (e^{A/m})^m.$$

The idea is to choose m to be a power of two for which $e^{A/m}$ can be reliably and efficiently computed, and then to form the matrix $(e^{A/m})^m$ by repeated squaring. One commonly used criterion for choosing m is to make it the smallest power of two for which $\|A\|/m \leqslant 1$. With this restriction, $e^{A/m}$ can be satisfactorily computed by either Taylor or Padé approximants. When properly implemented, the resulting algorithm is one of the most effective we know.

This approach has been suggested by many authors and we will not try to attribute it to any one of them. Among those who have provided some error analysis or suggested some refinements are Ward,[72] Kammler,[97] Kallstrom,[116] Scraton,[67] and Shah.[56,57]

If the exponential of the scaled matrix $e^{A/2^j}$ is to be approximated by $R_{qq}(A/2^j)$, then we have two parameters, q and j, to choose. In Appendix 1 we show that if $\|A\| \leqq 2^{j-1}$ then

$$\left[R_{qq}(A/2^j)\right]^{2^j} = e^{A+E},$$

where

$$\frac{\|E\|}{\|A\|} \leqq 8\left[\frac{\|A\|}{2^j}\right]^{2q}\left(\frac{(q!)^2}{(2q)!(2q+1)!}\right).$$

This "inverse error analysis" can be used to determine q and j in a number of ways. For example, if ε is any error tolerance, we can choose among the many (q, j) pairs for which the above inequality implies

$$\frac{\|E\|}{\|A\|} \leqq \varepsilon.$$

Since $[R_{qq}(A/2^j)]^{2^j}$ requires about $(q + j + 1/3)n^3$ flops to evaluate, it is sensible to choose the pair for which $q + j$ is minimum. The table below specifies these "optimum" pairs for various values of ε and $\|A\|$. By way of comparison, we have included the corresponding optimum (k, j) pairs associated with the approximant $[T_k(A/2^j)]^{2^j}$. These pairs were determined from Corollary 1 in

TABLE 1. Optimum Scaling and Squaring Parameters with Diagonal Padé and Taylor Series Approximation

$\|A\|$ \ ε	10^{-3}	10^{-6}	10^{-9}	10^{-12}	10^{-15}
10^{-2}	(1,0) (1,0)	(1,0) (2,1)	(2,0) (3,1)	(3,0) (4,1)	(3,0) (5,1)
10^{-1}	(1,0) (3,0)	(2,0) (4,0)	(3,0) (4,2)	(4,0) (4,4)	(4,0) (5,4)
10^{0}	(2,1) (5,1)	(3,1) (7,1)	(4,1) (6,3)	(5,1) (8,3)	(6,1) (7,5)
10^{1}	(2,5) (4,5)	(3,5) (6,5)	(4,5) (8,5)	(5,5) (7,7)	(6,5) (9,7)
10^{2}	(2,8) (4,8)	(3,8) (5,9)	(4,8) (7,9)	(5,8) (9,9)	(6,8) (10,10)
10^{3}	(2,11) (5,11)	(3,11) (7,11)	(4,11) (6,13)	(5,11) (8,13)	(6,11) (8,14)

Appendix 1, and from the fact that about $(k + j - 1)n^3$ flops are required to evaluate $[T_k(A/2^j)]^{2^j}$

To read Table 1, for a given ε and $\| A \|$ the top ordered pair gives the optimum (q, j) associated with $[R_{qq}(A/2^j)]^{2^j}$ while the bottom ordered pair specifies the most efficient choice of (k,j) associated with $[T_k(A/2^j)]^{2^j}$.

On the basis of the table we find that Padé approximants are generally more efficient than Taylor approximants. When $\| A \|$ is small, the Padé approximant requires about one half as much work for the same accuracy. As $\| A \|$ grows, this advantage decreases because of the larger amount of scaling needed.

Relative error bounds can be derived from the above results. Noting from Appendix 1 that $AE = EA$, we have

$$\frac{\| [R_{qq}(A/2^j)]^{2^j} - e^A \|}{\| e^A \|} = \frac{\| e^A(e^E - I) \|}{\| e^A \|} \leqq \| E \| e^{\| E \|} \leqq \varepsilon \| A \| e^{\varepsilon \| A \|}.$$

A similar bound can be derived for the Taylor approximants.

The analysis and our table does *not* take roundoff error into account, although this is the method's weakest point. In general, the computed square of a matrix R can be severely affected by arithmetic cancellation since the rounding errors are small when compared to $\| R \|^2$ but not necessarily small when compared to $\| R^2 \|$. Such cancellation can only happen when cond (R) is large because $R^{-1}R^{-2} = R$ implies

$$\text{cond}(R) \geqq \frac{\| R \|^2}{\| R^2 \|}.$$

The matrices which are repeatedly squared in this method can be badly conditioned. However, this does not necessarily imply that severe cancellation actually takes place. Moreover, it is possible that cancellation occurs only in problems which involve a large hump. We regard it as an open question to analyze the roundoff error of the repeated squaring of $e^{A/m}$ and to relate the analysis to a realistic assessment of the sensitivity of e^A.

In his implementation of scaling and squaring Ward[72] is aware of the possibility of cancellation. He computes an a posteriori bound for the error, including the effects of both truncation and roundoff. This is certainly preferable to no error estimate at all, but it is not completely satisfactory. A large error estimate could be the result of three distinct difficulties:

1. The error estimate is a severe overestimate of the true error, which is actually small. The algorithm is stable but the estimate is too pessimistic.
2. The true error is large because of cancellation in going over the hump, but the problem is not sensitive. The algorithm is unstable and another algorithm might produce a more accurate answer.
3. The underlying problem is inherently sensitive. No algorithm can be expected to produce a more accurate result.

Unfortunately, it is currently very difficult to distinguish among these three situations.

METHOD 4. CHEBYSHEV RATIONAL APPROXIMATION. Let $c_{qq}(x)$ be the ratio of two polynomials each of degree q and consider $\max_{0 \leqq x \leq \infty} |c_{qq}(x) - e^{-x}|$. For various values of q Cody, Meinardus, and Varga[62] have determined the coefficients of the particular c_{qq} which minimizes this maximum. Their results can be directly translated into bounds for $\|c_{qq}(A) - e^{A}\|$ when A is Hermitian with eigenvalues on the negative real axis. The authors are interested in such matrices because of an application to partial differential equations. Their approach is particularly effective for the sparse matrices which occur in such applications.

For non-Hermitian (nonnormal) A, it is hard to determine how well $c_{qq}(A)$ approximates e^{A}. If A has an eigenvalue λ off the negative real axis, it is possible for $c_{qq}(\lambda)$ to be a poor approximation to e^{λ}. This would imply that $c_{qq}(A)$ is a poor approximation to e^{A} since

$$\|e^{A} - c_{qq}(A)\| \geqq |e^{\lambda} - c_{qq}(\lambda)|.$$

These remarks prompt us to emphasize an important facet about approximation of the matrix exponential, namely, there is more to approximating e^{A} than just approximating e^{z} at the eigenvalues of A. It is easy to illustrate this with Padé approximation. Suppose

$$A = \begin{bmatrix} 0 & 6 & 0 & 0 \\ 0 & 0 & 6 & 0 \\ 0 & 0 & 0 & 6 \\ 0 & 0 & 0 & 0 \end{bmatrix}.$$

Since all of the eigenvalues of A are zero, $R_{11}(z)$ is a perfect approximation to e^{z} at the eigenvalues. However,

$$R_{11}(A) = \begin{bmatrix} 1 & 6 & 18 & 54 \\ 0 & 1 & 6 & 18 \\ 0 & 0 & 1 & 6 \\ 0 & 0 & 0 & 1 \end{bmatrix},$$

whereas

$$e^{A} = \begin{bmatrix} 1 & 6 & 18 & 36 \\ 0 & 1 & 6 & 18 \\ 0 & 0 & 1 & 6 \\ 0 & 0 & 0 & 1 \end{bmatrix}$$

and thus,

$$\|e^{A} - R_{11}(A)\| = 18.$$

These discrepancies arise from the fact that A is not normal. The example illustrates that nonormality exerts a subtle influence upon the methods of this section even though the eigensystem, per se, is not explicitly involved in any of the algorithms.

4. ORDINARY DIFFERENTIAL EQUATION METHODS

Since e^{tA} and $e^{tA}x_0$ are solutions to ordinary differential equations, it is natural to consider methods based on numerical integration. Very sophisticated and powerful methods for the numerical solution of general nonlinear differential equations have been developed in recent years. All worthwhile codes have automatic step size control and some of them automatically vary the order of approximation as well. Methods based on single step formulas, multistep formulas, and implicit multistep formulas each have certain advantages. When used to compute e^{tA} all these methods are easy to use and they require very little additional programming or other thought. The primary disadvantage is a relatively high cost in computer time.

The o.d.e. programs are designed to solve a single system

$$\dot{x}=f(x,t), \quad x(0)=x_0,$$

and to obtain the solution at many values of t. With $f(x,t) = Ax$ the kth column of e^{tA} can be obtained by setting x_0 to the kth column of the identity matrix. All the methods involve a sequence of values $0 = t_0, t_1, \ldots, t_j = t$ with either fixed or variable step size $h_i = t_{i+1}-t_i$. They all produce vectors x_i which approximate $x(t_i)$.

METHOD 5. GENERAL PURPOSE O.D.E. SOLVER. Most computer center libraries contain programs for solving initial value problems in ordinary differential equations. Very few libraries contain programs that compute e^{tA}. Until the latter programs are more readily available, undoubtedly the easiest and, from the programmer's point of view, the quickest way to compute a matrix exponential is to call upon a general purpose o.d.e. solver. This is obviously an expensive luxury since the o.d.e. routine does not take advantage of the linear, constant coefficient nature of our special problem.

We have run a very small experiment in which we have used three recently developed o.d.e. solvers to compute the exponentials of about a dozen matrices and have measured the amount of work required. The programs are:

1. RKF45. Written by Shampine and Watts,[108] this program uses the Fehlberg formulas of the Runge–Kutta type. Six function evaluations are required per step. The resulting formula is fifth order with automatic step size control. (See also Forsythe et al.[4])
2. DE/STEP. Written by Shampine and Gordon,[107] this program uses variable order, variable step Adams predictor-corrector formulas. Two function evaluations are required per step.

3. IMPSUB. Written by Starner,[109] this program is a modification of Gear's DIFSUB[106] and is based on implicit backward differentiation formulas intended for stiff differential equations. Starner's modifications add the ability to solve "infinitely stiff" problems in which the derivatives of some of the variables may be missing. Two function evaluations are usually required per step but three or four may occasionally be used.

For RKF45 the output points are primarily determined by the step size selection in the program. For the other two routines, the output is produced at user specified points by interpolation. For an n-by-n matrix A, the cost of one function evaluation is a matrix-vector multiplication or n^2 flops. The number of evaluations is determined by the length of the integration interval and the accuracy requested.

The relative performance of the three programs depends fairly strongly on the particular matrix. RKF45 often requires the most function evaluations, especially when high accuracy is sought, because its order is fixed. But it may well require the least actual computer time at modest accuracies because of its low overhead. DE/STEP indicates when it thinks a problem is stiff. If it doesn't give this indication, it usually requires the fewest function evaluations. If it does, IMPSUB may require fewer.

Table 2 gives the results for one particular matrix which we arbitrarily declare to be a "typical" nonstiff problem. The matrix is of order 3, with eigenvalues $\lambda = 3, 3, 6$; the matrix is defective. We used three different local error tolerances and integrated over [0, 1]. The average number of function evaluations for the three starting vectors is given in the table. These can be regarded as typical coefficients of n^2 for the single vector problem or of n^3 for the full matrix exponential; IBM 370 long arithmetic was used.

Although people concerned with the competition between various o.d.e. solvers might be interested in the details of Table 2 we caution that it is the result of only one experiment. Our main reason for presenting it is to support our contention that the use of any such routine must be regarded as very inefficient. The scaling and squaring method of § 3 and some of the matrix decomposition methods of § 6 require on the order of 10 to 20 n^3 flops and they obtain higher accuracies than those obtained with 200 n^3 or more flops for the o.d.e. solvers.

This excessive cost is due to the fact that the programs are not taking advan-

TABLE 2. Work as a Function of Subroutine and Local Error Tolerance

	10^{-6}	9^{-9}	10^{-12}
RKF45	217	832	3268
DE/STEP	118	160	211
IMPSUB	173	202	1510

tage of the linear, constant coefficient nature of the differential equation. They must repeatedly call for the multiplication of various vectors by the matrix A because, as far as they know, the matrix may have changed since the last multiplication.

We now consider the various methods which result from specializing general o.d.e. methods to handle our specific problem.

METHOD 6. SINGLE STEP O.D.E. METHODS. Two of the classical techniques for the solution of differential equations are the fourth order Taylor and Runge-Kutta methods with fixed step size. For our particular equation they become

$$x_{j+1}=\left(I+hA+\cdots+\frac{h^4}{4!}A^4\right)x_j=T_4(hA)x_j$$

and

$$x_{j+1}=x_j+\tfrac{1}{6}k_1+\tfrac{1}{3}k_2+\tfrac{1}{3}k_3+\tfrac{1}{6}k_4,$$

where $k_1=hAx_j$, $k_2=hA(x_j+\frac{1}{2}k_1)$, $k_3=hA(x_j+\frac{1}{2}k_2)$, and $k_4=hA(x_j+k_3)$. A little manipulation reveals that in this case, the two methods would produce identical results were it not for roundoff error. As long as the step size is fixed, the matrix $T_4(hA)$ need be computed just once and then x_{j+1} can be obtained from x_j with just one matrix-vector multiplication. The standard Runge–Kutta method would require four such multiplications per step.

Let us consider $x(t)$ for one particular value of t, say $t = 1$. If $h = 1/m$, then

$$x(1)=x(mh)\simeq x_m=\left[T_4(hA)\right]^m x_0.$$

Consequently, there is a close connection between this method and Method 3 which involved scaling and squaring.[54,60] The scaled matrix is hA and its exponential is approximated by $T_4(hA)$. However, even if m is a power of 2, $[T_4(hA)]^m$ is usually not obtained by repeated squaring. The methods have roughly the same roundoff error properties and so there seem to be no important advantages for Runge-Kutta with fixed step size.

Let us now consider the possibility of varying the step size. A simple algorithm might be based on a variable step Taylor method. In such a method, two approximations to x_{j+1} would be computed and their difference used to choose the step size. Specifically, let ε be some prescribed local relative error tolerance and define x_{j+1} and x_{j+1}^* by

$$x_{j+1}=T_5(h_jA)x_j,$$
$$x_{j+1}^*=T_4(h_jA)x_j.$$

One way of determining h_j is to require

$$\|x_{j+1}-x_{j+1}^*\|\simeq\varepsilon\|x_j\|.$$

Notice that we are using a 5th order formula to compute the approximation, and a 4th order formula to control step size.

At first glance, this method appears to be considerably less efficient than one with fixed step size because the matrices $T_4(h_jA)$ and $T_5(h_jA)$ cannot be precomputed. Each step requires $5\,n^2$ flops. However, in those problems which involve large "humps" as described in § 1, a smaller step is needed at the beginning of the computation than at the end. If the step size changes by a factor of more than 5, the variable step method will require less work.

The method does provide some insight into the costs of more sophisticated integrators. Since

$$x_{j+1} - x_{j+1}^{*} = \frac{h_j A^5}{5!}\, x_j,$$

we see that the required step size is given approximately by

$$h_j \simeq \left[\frac{5!\,\varepsilon}{\|A^5\|} \right]^{1/5}.$$

The work required to integrate over some fixed interval is proportional to the inverse of the average step size. So, if we decrease the tolerance ε from, say 10^{-6} to 10^{-9}, then the work is increased by a factor of $(10^3)^{1/5}$ which is about 4. This is typical of any 5th order error estimate—asking for 3 more figures roughly quadruples the work. □

METHOD 7. MULTISTEP O.D.E. SOLVER. As far as we know, the possibility of specializing multistep methods, such as those based on the Adams formulas, to linear, constant coefficient problems has not been explored in detail. Such a method would not be equivalent to scaling and squaring because the approximate solution at a given time is defined in terms of approximate solutions at several previous times. The actual algorithm would depend upon how the starting vectors are obtained, and how the step size and order are determined. It is conceivable that such an algorithm might be effective, particularly for problems which involve a single vector, output at many values of t, large n, and a hump.

The problems associated with roundoff error have not been of as much concern to designers of differential equation solvers as they have been to designers of matrix algebra algorithms since the accuracy requested of o.d.e. solvers is typically less than full machine precision. We do not know what effect rounding errors would have in a problem with a large hump.

5. POLYNOMIAL METHODS

Let the characteristic polynomial of A be

$$c(z) = \det(zI - A) = z^n - \sum_{k=0}^{n-1} c_k z^k.$$

From the Cayley–Hamilton theorem $c(A) = 0$ and hence

$$A^n = c_0 I + c_1 A + \cdots + c_{n-1} A^{n-1}.$$

It follows that any power of A can be expressed in terms of $I, A, \ldots, A^{n-1}$:

$$A^k = \sum_{j=0}^{n-1} \beta_{kj} A^j.$$

This implies that e^{tA} is a polynomial in A with analytic coefficients in t:

$$\begin{aligned} e^{tA} &= \sum_{k=0}^{\infty} \frac{t^k A^k}{k!} = \sum_{k=0}^{\infty} \frac{t^k}{k!} \left[\sum_{j=0}^{n-1} \beta_{kj} A^j \right] \\ &= \sum_{j=0}^{n-1} \left[\sum_{k=0}^{\infty} \beta_{kj} \frac{t^k}{k!} \right] A^j \\ &\equiv \sum_{j=0}^{n-1} \alpha_j(t) A^j. \end{aligned}$$

The methods in this section involve this kind of exploitation of the characteristic polynomial.

METHOD 8. CAYLEY–HAMILTON. Once the characteristic polynomial is known, the coefficientss β_{kj} which define the analytic functions $\alpha_j(t) = \Sigma\, \beta_{kj} t^k / k!$ can be generated as follows:

$$\beta_{kj} = \begin{cases} \delta_{kj} & (k<n) \\ c_j & (k=n) \\ c_0 \beta_{k-1,n-1} & (k>n, j=0) \\ c_j \beta_{k-1,n-1} + \beta_{k-1,j-1} & (k>n, j>0) \end{cases}$$

One difficulty is that these recursive formulas for the β_{kj} are very prone to roundoff error. This can be seen in the 1-by-1 case. If $A = (\alpha)$ then $\beta_{k0} = \alpha^k$ and $\alpha_0(t) = \Sigma(\alpha t)^k/k!$ is simply the Taylor series for $e^{\alpha t}$. Thus, our criticisms of Method 1 apply. In fact, if $\alpha t = -6$, no partial sum of the series for $e^{\alpha t}$ will have any significant digits when IBM 370 short arithmetic is used.

Another difficulty is the requirement that the characteristic polynomial must be known. If $\lambda_1, \ldots, \lambda_n$ are the eigenvalues of A, then $c(z)$ could be computed from $c(z) = \Pi_1^n(z-\lambda_i)$. Although the eigenvalues could be stably computed, it is unclear whether the resulting c_j would be acceptable. Other methods for computing $c(z)$ are discussed in Wilkinson.[14] It turns out that methods based upon repeated powers of A and methods based upon formulas for the c_j in terms of various symmetric functions are unstable in the presence of roundoff error and expensive to implement. Techniques based upon similarity transformations break down when A is nearly derogatory. We shall have more to say about these difficulties in connection with Methods 12 and 13.

In Method 8 we attempted to expand e^{tA} in terms of the matrices $I, A, \ldots, A^{n-1}$. If $\{A_0, \ldots, A_{n-1}\}$ is some other set of matrices which span the same subspace, then there exist analytic functions $\beta_j(t)$ such that

$$e^{tA} = \sum_{j=0}^{n-1} \beta_j(t) A_j.$$

The convenience of this formula depends upon how easily the A_j and $\beta_j(t)$ can be generated. If the eigenvalues $\lambda_1, \ldots, \lambda_n$ of A are known, we have the following three methods.

METHOD 9. LAGRANGE INTERPOLATION.

$$e^{tA} = \sum_{j=0}^{n-1} e^{\lambda_j t} \prod_{\substack{k=1 \\ k \neq j}}^{n} \frac{(A - \lambda_k I)}{(\lambda_j - \lambda_k)}.$$

METHOD 10. NEWTON INTERPOLATION.

$$e^{tA} = e^{\lambda_1 t} I + \sum_{j=2}^{n} [\lambda_1, \ldots, \lambda_j] \prod_{k=1}^{j-1} (A - \lambda_k I).$$

The divided differences $[\lambda_1, \ldots, \lambda_j]$ depend on t and are defined recursively by

$$[\lambda_1, \lambda_2] = (e^{\lambda_1 t} - e^{\lambda_2 t})/(\lambda_1 - \lambda_2),$$

$$[\lambda_1, \ldots, \lambda_{k+1}] = \frac{[\lambda_1, \ldots, \lambda_k] - [\lambda_2, \ldots, \lambda_{k+1}]}{\lambda_1 - \lambda_{k+1}} \qquad (k \geqq 2).$$

We refer to MacDuffee[9] for a discussion of these formulae in the confluent eigenvalue case.

METHOD 11. VANDERMONDE. There are other methods for computing the matrices

$$A_j = \prod_{\substack{k=1 \\ k \neq j}}^{n} \frac{(A - \lambda_k I)}{(\lambda_j - \lambda_k)}$$

which were required in Method 9. One of these involves the Vandermonde matrix

$$V = \begin{bmatrix} 1 & 1 & \cdots & 1 \\ \lambda_1 & \lambda_2 & \cdots & \lambda_n \\ \vdots & \vdots & & \vdots \\ \lambda_1^{n-1} & \lambda_2^{n-1} & \cdots & \lambda_n^{n-1} \end{bmatrix}.$$

If v_{jk} is the (j, k) entry of V^{-1}, then

$$A_j = \sum_{k=1}^{n} v_{jk} A^{k-1},$$

and

$$e^{tA} = \sum_{j=1}^{n} e^{\lambda_j t} A_j.$$

When A has repeated eigenvalues, the appropriate confluent Vandermonde matrix is involved. Closed expressions for the v_{jk} are available and Vidysager[92] has proposed their use.

Methods 9, 10, and 11 suffer on several accounts. They are $O(n^4)$ algorithms making them prohibitively expensive except for small n. If the spanning matrices $A_0, \ldots, A_{n-1}$ are saved, then storage is n^3 which is an order of magnitude greater than the amount of storage required by any "nonpolynomial" method. Furthermore, even though the formulas which define Methods 9, 10, and 11 have special form in the confluent case, we do not have a satisfactory situation. The "gray" area of near confluence poses difficult problems which are best discussed in the next section on decomposition techniques.

The next two methods of this section do not require the eigenvalues of A and thus appear to be free of the problems associated with confluence. However, equally formidable difficulties attend these algorithms.

METHOD 12. INVERSE LAPLACE TRANSFORMS. If $\mathcal{L}[e^{tA}]$ is the Laplace transform of the matrix exponential, then

$$\mathcal{L}[e^{tA}] = (sI - A)^{-1}.$$

The entries of this matrix are rational functions of s. In fact,

$$(sI - A)^{-1} = \sum_{k=0}^{n-1} \frac{s^{n-k-1}}{c(s)} A_k,$$

where $c(s) = \det(sI - A) = s^n - \sum_{k=0}^{n-1} c_k s^k$ and for $k = 1, \ldots, n$:

$$c_{n-k} = -\operatorname{trace}(A_{k-1}A)/k, \qquad A_k = A_{k-1}A - c_{n-k}I \qquad (A_0 = I).$$

These recursions were derived by Leverrier and Faddeeva [3] and can be used to evaluate e^{tA}:

$$e^{tA} = \sum_{k=0}^{n-1} \mathcal{L}^{-1}\left[s^{n-k-1}/c(s)\right] A_k.$$

The inverse transforms $\mathcal{L}^{-1}[s^{n-k-1}\, c(s)]$ can be expresssed as a power series in t. Liou[102] suggests evaluating these series using various recursions involving the c_k. We suppress the details of this procedure because of its similarity to Method 8. There are other ways Laplace transforms can be used to evaluate e^{tA} [78,80,88,89,93]. By and large, these techniques have the same drawbacks as Methods $8-11$. They are $O(n^4)$ for general matrices and may be seriously effected by roundoff error. □

METHOD 13. COMPANION MATRIX. We now discuss techniques which involve the computation of e^C where C is a companion matrix:

$$C=\begin{bmatrix} 0 & 1 & 0 & \cdots & 0 \\ 0 & 0 & 1 & \cdots & 0 \\ \vdots & \vdots & & \ddots & \vdots \\ & & & & 1 \\ c_0 & c_1 & c_2 & \cdots & c_{n-1} \end{bmatrix}$$

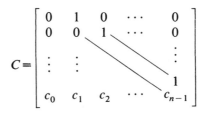

Companion matrices have some interesting properties which various authors have tried to exploit:

1. C is sparse.
2. The characteristic polynomial of C is $c(z)=z^n-\sum_{k=0}^{n-1}c_kz^k$.
3. If V is the Vandermonde matrix of eigenvalues of C (see Method 11), then $V^{-1}CV$ is in Jordan form. (Confluent Vandermonde matrices are involved in the multiple eigenvalue case.)
4. If A is not derogatory, then it is similar to a companion matrix; otherwise it is similar to a direct sum of companion matrices.

Because C is sparse, small powers of C cost considerably less than the usual n^3 flops. Consequently, one could implement Method 3 (scaling and squaring) with a reduced amount of work.

Since the characteristic polynomial of C is known, one can apply Method 8 or various other techniques which involve recursions with the c_k. However, this is not generally advisable in view of the catastrophic cancellation that can occur.

As we mentioned during our discussion of Method 11, the closed expression for V^{-1} is extremely sensitive. Because V^{-1} is so poorly conditioned, exploitation of property 3 will generally yield a poor estimate of e^A.

If $A=YCY^{-1}$, then from the series definition of the matrix exponential it is easy to verify that

$$e^A=Ye^CY^{-1}.$$

Hence, property (4) leads us to an algorithm for computing the exponential of a general matrix. Although the reduction of A to companion form is a rational process, the algorithms for accomplishing this are extremely unstable and should be avoided.[14]

We mention that if the original differential equation is actually a single nth order equation written as a system of first order equations, then the matrix is already in companion form. Consequently, the unstable reduction is not necessary. This is the only situation in which companion matrix methods should be considered.

We conclude this section with an interesting aside on computing e^H where $H=(h_{ij})$ is lower Hessenberg ($h_{ij}=0, j>i+1$). Notice that companion matrices are lower Hessenberg. Our interest in computing e^H stems from the fact that any real matrix A is orthogonally similar to a lower Hessenberg matrix. Hence, if

$$A=QHQ^T, \qquad Q^TQ=I,$$

then

$$e^A=Qe^HQ^T.$$

Unlike the reduction to companion form, this factorization can be stably computed using the EISPACK routine ORTHES.[113]

Now, let f_k denote the kth column of e^H. It is easy to verify that

$$Hf_k=\sum_{i=k-1}^{n} h_{ik}f_i \qquad (k\geqq 2),$$

by equating the kth columns in the matrix identity $He^H=e^HH$. If none of the superdiagonal entries h_{k-1} $h_{k-1,k}$ are zero, then once f_n is known, the other f_k follow immediately from

$$f_{k-1}=\frac{1}{h_{k-1,k}}\left[Hf_k-\sum_{i=k}^{n} h_{ik}f_i\right].$$

Similar recursive procedures have been suggested in connection with computing e^C.[104] Since f_n equals $x(1)$ where $x(t)$ solves $Hx=\dot{x}, x(0)=(0,\ldots,0,1)^T$, it could be found using one of the o.d.e. methods in the previous section.

There are ways to recover in the above algorithm should any of the $h_{k-1,k}$ be zero. However, numerically the problem is when we have a small, but non-negligible $h_{k-1,k}$. In this case rounding errors involving a factor of $1/h_{k-1,k}$ will occur precluding the possibility of an accurate computation of e^H.

In summary, methods for computing e^A which involve the reduction of A to companion or Hessenberg form are not attractive. However, there are other matrix factorizations which can be more satisfactorily exploited in the course of evaluating e^A and these will be discussed in the next section.

6. MATRIX DECOMPOSITION METHODS

The methods which are likely to be most efficient for problems involving large matrices and repeated evaluation of e^{tA} are those which are based on factorizations or decompositions of the matrix A. If A happens to be symmetric, then all these methods reduce to a simple very effective algorithm.

All the matrix decompositions are based on similarity transformations of the form

$$A = SBS^{-1}.$$

As we have mentioned, the power series definition of e^{tA} implies

$$e^{tA} = Se^{tB}S^{-1}.$$

The idea is to find an S for which e^{tB} is easy to compute. The difficulty is that S may be close to singular which means that cond (S) is large.

METHOD 14. EIGENVECTORS. The naive approach is to take S to be the matrix whose columns are eigenvectors of A, that is, $S = V$ where

$$V = [v_1|\ldots|v_n]$$

and

$$Av_j = \lambda_j v_j, \qquad j = 1, \ldots, n.$$

These n equations can be written

$$AV = VD,$$

where $D = \operatorname{diag}(\lambda_1, \ldots \lambda_n)$. The exponential of D is trivial to compute assuming we have a satisfactory method for computing the exponential of a scalar:

$$e^{tD} = \operatorname{diag}(e^{\lambda_1 t}, \ldots, e^{\lambda_n t}).$$

Since V is nonsingular we have $e^{tA} = V e^{tD} V^{-1}$.

In terms of the differential equation $\dot{x} = Ax$, the same eigenvector approach takes the following form. The initial condition is a combination of the eigenvectors,

$$x(0) = \sum_{j=1}^{n} \alpha_j v_j,$$

and the solution $x(t)$ is given by

$$x(t) = \sum_{j=0}^{n} \alpha_j e^{\lambda_j t} v_j.$$

Of course, the coefficients α_j are obtained by solving a set of linear equations $V\alpha = x(0)$.

The difficulty with this approach is not confluent eigenvalues per se. For example, the method works very well when A is the identity matrix, which has an eigenvalue of the highest possible multiplicity. It also works well for any other symmetric matrix because the eigenvectors can be chosen orthogonal. If reliable subroutines such as TRED2 and TQL2 in EISPACK[113] are used, then the computed v_j will be orthogonal to the full accuracy of the computer and the resulting algorithm for e^{tA} has all the attributes we desire— except that it is limited to symmetric matrices.

The theoretical difficulty occurs when A does not have a complete set of linearly independent eigenvectors and is thus defective. In this case there is no invertible matrix of eigenvectors V and the algorithm breaks down. An example of a defective matrix is

$$\begin{bmatrix} 1 & 1 \\ 0 & 1 \end{bmatrix}.$$

A defective matrix has confluent eigenvalues but a matrix which has confluent eigenvalues need not be defective.

In practice, difficulties occur when A is "nearly" defective. One way to make this precise is to use the condition number, $\operatorname{cond}(V) = \|V\| \, \|V^{-1}\|$, of the matrix of eigenvectors. If A is nearly (exactly) defective, then $\operatorname{cond}(V)$ is large (infinite). Any errors in A, including roundoff errors in its computation and roundoff errors from the eigenvalue computation, may be magnified in the final result by $\operatorname{cond}(V)$. Consequently, when $\operatorname{cond}(V)$ is large, the computed e^{tA} will most likely be inaccurate. For example, if

$$A = \begin{bmatrix} 1+\varepsilon & 1 \\ 0 & 1-\varepsilon \end{bmatrix},$$

then

$$V = \begin{bmatrix} 1 & -1 \\ 0 & 2\varepsilon \end{bmatrix},$$

$$D = \operatorname{diag}(1+\varepsilon, 1-\varepsilon),$$

and

$$\operatorname{cond}(V) = O\left(\frac{1}{\varepsilon}\right).$$

If $\varepsilon = 10^{-5}$ and IBM 370 short floating point arithmetic is used to compute the exponential from the formula $e^A = V e^D V^{-1}$, we obtain

$$\begin{bmatrix} 2.718307 & 2.750000 \\ 0 & 2.718254 \end{bmatrix}.$$

Since the exact exponential to six decimals is

$$\begin{bmatrix} 2.718309 & 2.718282 \\ 0 & 2.718255 \end{bmatrix},$$

we see that the computed exponential has errors of order 10^5 times the machine precision as conjectured.

One might feel that for this example e^A might be particularly sensitive to perturbations in A. However, when we apply Theorem 3 in § 2 to this example, we find

$$\frac{\|e^{(A+E)} - e^A\|}{\|e^A\|} \leqq 4\|E\|e^{2\|E\|},$$

independent of ε. Certainly, e^A is not overly sensitive to changes in A and so Method 14 must be regarded as unstable.

Before we proceed to the next method it is interesting to note the connection between the use of eigenvectors and Method 9, Lagrange interpolation. When the eigenvalues are distinct the eigenvector approach can be expressed

$$e^{tA} = V \operatorname{diag}(e^{\lambda_j t}) V^{-1} = \sum_{j=1}^{n} e^{\lambda_j t} v_j y_j^T,$$

where y_j^T is the jth row of V^{-1}. The Lagrange formula is

$$e^{tA} = \sum_{j=1}^{n} e^{\lambda_j t} A_j,$$

where

$$A_j = \prod_{\substack{k=1 \\ k \neq j}}^{n} \frac{(A - \lambda_k I)}{(\lambda_j - \lambda_k)}.$$

Because these two expressions hold for all t, the individual terms in the sum must be the same and so

$$A_j = v_j y_j^T.$$

This indicates that the A_j are, in fact, rank one matrices obtained from the eigenvectors. Thus, the $O(n^4)$ work involved in the computation of the A_j is totally unnecessary.

METHOD 15. TRIANGULAR SYSTEMS OF EIGENVECTORS. An improvement in both the efficiency and the reliability of the conventional eigenvector approach can be obtained when the eigenvectors are computed by the QR algorithm.[14] Assume temporarily that although A is not symmetric, all its eigenvalues happen to be real. The idea is to use EISPACK subroutines ORTHES and HQR2 to compute the eigenvalues and eigenvectors.[113] These subroutines produce an orthogonal matrix Q and a triangular matrix T so that

$$Q^T A Q = T.$$

Since $Q^{-1} = Q^T$, this is a similarity transformation and the desired eigenvalues occur on the diagonal of T. HQR2 next attempts to find the eigenvectors of T. This results in a matrix R and a diagonal matrix D, which is simply the diagonal part of T, so that

$$TR = RD.$$

Finally, the eigenvectors of A are obtained by a simple matrix multiplication $V = QR$.

The key observation is that R is upper triangular. In other words, the ORTHES/HQR2 path in EISPACK computes the matrix of eigenvectors by first computing its "QR" factorization. HQR2 can be easily modified to remove the final multiplication of Q and R. The availability of these two matrices has two advantages. First, the time required to find V^{-1} or to solve systems involving V is reduced. However, since this is a small fraction of the total time required, the improvement in efficiency is not very significant. A more important advantage is that cond (V) = cond (R) (in the 2-norm) and that the estimation of cond (R) can be done reliably and efficiently.

The effect of admitting complex eigenvalues is that R is not quite triangular, but has 2-by-2 blocks on its diagonal for each complex conjugate pair. Such a matrix is called quasitriangular and we avoid complex arithmetic with minor inconvenience.

In summary, we suspect the following algorithm to be reliable:

1. Given A, use ORTHES and a modified HQR2 to find orthogonal Q, diagonal D, and quasi-triangular R so that
$$AQR = QRD.$$
2. Given x_0, compute y_0 by solving
$$Ry_0 = Q^T x_0.$$
Also estimate cond (R) and hence the accuracy of y_0.
3. If cond (R) is too large, indicate that this algorithm cannot solve the problem and exit.
4. Given t, compute $x(t)$ by
$$x(t) = Ve^{tD} y_0.$$

(If we want to compute the full exponential, then in Step 2 we solve $RY = Q^T$ for Y and then use $e^{tA} = Ve^{tD}Y$ in Step 4). It is important to note that the first three steps are independent of t, and that the fourth step, which requires relatively little work, can be repeated for many values of t.

We know there are examples where the exit is taken in Step 3 even though the *underlying problem* is not poorly conditioned implying that the algorithm is unstable. Nevertheless, the algorithm is reliable insofar as cond (R) enables us to assess the errors in the computed solution when that solution is found. It would be interesting to code this algorithm and compare it with Ward's scaling and squaring program for Method 3. In addition to comparing timings, the crucial question would be how often the exit in Step 3 is taken and how often Ward's program returns an unacceptably large error bound.

METHOD 16. JORDAN CANONICAL FORM. In principle, the problem posed by defective eigensystems can be solved by resorting to the Jordan canonical form (JCF). If

$$A = P[J_1 \oplus \cdots \oplus J_k]P^{-1}$$

is the JCF of A, then

$$e^{tA} = P[e^{tJ_1} \oplus \cdots \oplus e^{tJ_k}]P^{-1}.$$

The exponentials of the Jordan blocks J_i can be given in closed form. For example, if

$$J_i = \begin{bmatrix} \lambda_i & 1 & 0 & 0 \\ 0 & \lambda_i & 1 & 0 \\ 0 & 0 & \lambda_i & 1 \\ 0 & 0 & 0 & \lambda_i \end{bmatrix},$$

then

$$e^{tJ_i} = e^{\lambda_i t} \begin{bmatrix} 1 & t & t^2/2! & t^3/3! \\ 0 & 1 & t & t^2/2! \\ 0 & 0 & 1 & t \\ 0 & 0 & 0 & 1 \end{bmatrix}.$$

The difficulty is that the JCF cannot be computed using floating point arithmetic. A single rounding error may cause some multiple eigenvalue to become distinct or vice versa altering the entire structure of J and P. A related fact is that there is no a priori bound on cond (P). For further discussion of the difficulties of computing the JCF, see the papers by Golub and Wilkinson[110] and Kågstrom and Ruhe.[111]

METHOD 17. SCHUR. The Schur decomposition

$$A = QTQ^T$$

with orthogonal Q and triangular T exists if A has real eigenvalues. If A has complex eigenvalues, then it is necessary to allow 2-by-2 blocks on the diagonal of T or to make Q and T complex (and replace Q^T with Q^*). The Schur decomposition can be computed reliably and quite efficiently by ORTHES and a short-ended version of HQR2. The required modifications are discussed in the EISPACK guide.[113]

Once the Schur decomposition is available,

$$e^{tA} = Qe^{tT}Q^T.$$

The only delicate part is the computation of e^{tT} where T is a triangular or quasitriangular matrix. Note that the eigenvectors of A are not required.

Computing functions or triangular matrices is the subject of a recent paper by Parlett.[112] If T is the upper triangular with diagonal elements $\lambda_1, \ldots, \lambda_n$, then it is clear that e^{tT} is upper triangular with diagonal elements $e^{\lambda_1 t}, \ldots, e^{\lambda_n t}$. Parlett shows how to compute the off-diagonal elements of e^{tT} recursively from divided differences of the $e^{\lambda_i t}$. The example in § 1 illustrates the 2-by-2 case.

Again, the difficulty is magnification of roundoff error caused by nearly confluent eigenvalues λ_i. As a step towards handling this problem, Parlett describes a generalization of his algorithm applicable to block upper triangular matrices. The diagonal blocks are determined by clusters of nearby eigenvalues. The confluence problems do not disappear, but they are confined to the diagonal blocks where special techniques can be applied.

METHOD 18. BLOCK DIAGONAL. All methods which involve decompositions of the form

$$A = SBS^{-1}$$

involve two conflicting objectives:

1. Make B close to diagonal so that e^{tB} is easy to compute.
2. Make S well conditioned so that errors are not magnified.

The Jordan canonical form places all the emphasis on the first objective, while the Schur decomposition places most of the emphasis on the second. (We would regard the decomposition with $S = I$ and $B = A$ as placing even more emphasis on the second objective.)

The block diagonal method is a compromise between these two extremes. The idea is to use a nonorthogonal, but well conditioned, S to produce a B which is triangular and block diagonal as illustrated in Figure 2.

Each block in B involves a cluster of nearly confluent eigenvalues. The number in each cluster (the size of each block) is to be made as small as possible while maintaining some prescribed upper bound for cond (S), such as cond (S) < 100. The choice of the bound 100 implies roughly that at most 2 significant decimal figures will be lost because of rounding errors when e^{tA} is obtained from e^{tB} via $e^{tA} = S\, e^{tB}S^{-1}$. A larger bound would mean the loss of more

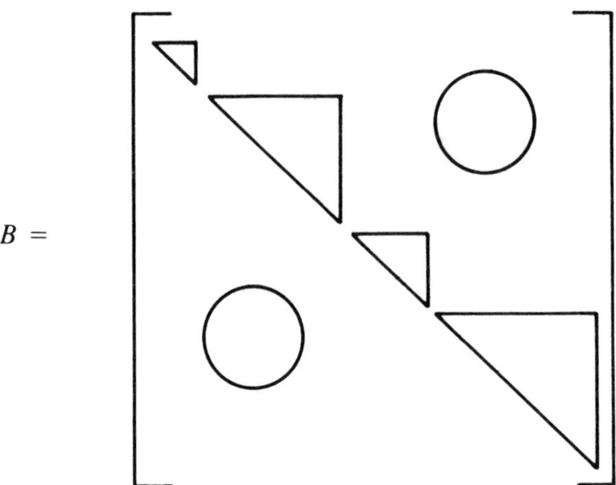

FIGURE 2. Triangular block diagonal form.

figures while a smaller bound would mean more computer time—both for the factorization itself and for the evaluation of e^{tB}.

In practice, we would expect almost all the blocks to be 1-by-1 or 2-by-2 and the resulting computation of e^{tB} to be very fast. The bound on cond (S) will mean that it is occasionally necessary to have larger blocks in B, but it will insure against excessive loss of accuracy from confluent eigenvalues.

G. W. Stewart has pointed out that the grouping of the eigenvalues into clusters and the resulting block structure of B is not merely for increased speed. There can be an important improvement in accuracy. Stewart suggests expressing each block B_j in the form

$$B_j = \gamma_j I + E_j$$

where γ_j is the average value of the eigenvalues in the jth cluster. If the grouping has been done properly, the matrices E_j should then be nearly nilpotent in the sense that E_j^k will rapidly approach zero as k increases. Since E_j is triangular, this will certainly be true if the diagonal part of E_j is small, that is, if all the eigenvalues in the cluster are close together. But it will also be true in another important case. If

$$E_j = \begin{bmatrix} \sqrt{\varepsilon} & 1 \\ 0 & -\sqrt{\varepsilon} \end{bmatrix},$$

where ε is the computer rounding unit, then

$$E_j^2 = \begin{bmatrix} \varepsilon & 0 \\ 0 & \varepsilon \end{bmatrix}$$

can be regarded as negligible. The $\pm\sqrt{\varepsilon}$ perturbations are typical when a double, defective eigenvalue is computed with, say, HQR2.

The fact that E_j is nearly nilpotent means that e^{tB_j} can be found rapidly and accurately from

$$e^{tB_j} = e^{\gamma_j t} e^{tE_j};$$

computing e^{tE_j} by a few terms of the Taylor series.

Several researchers, including Parlett, Ruhe, and Stewart, are currently developing computer programs based on some of these ideas. The most difficult detail is the proper choice of the eigenvalue clustering. It is also important for program efficiency to avoid complex arithmetic as much as possible. When fully developed, these programs will be fairly long and complicated but they may come close to meeting our other criteria for satisfactory methods.

Most of the computational cost lies in obtaining the basic Schur decomposition. Although this cost varies somewhat from matrix to matrix because of the iterative nature of the QR algorithm, a good average figure is 15 n^3 flops, including the further reduction to block diagonal form. Again we emphasize that the reduction is independent of t. Once the decomposition is obtained, the calculation of e^{tA} requires about 2 n^3 flops for each t. If we require only $x(t) = e^{tA}x_0$ for various t, the equation $Sy = x_0$ should be solved once at a cost of $n^3/3$ flops, and then each $x(t)$ can be obtained with n^2 flops.

These are rough estimates. There will be differences between programs based on the Schur decomposition and those which work with the block diagonal form, but the timings should be similar because Parlett's algorithm for the exponential is very fast.

7. SPLITTING METHODS

A most aggravating, yet interesting, property of the matrix exponential is that the familiar additive law fails unless we have commutivity:

$$e^{tB}e^{tC} = e^{t(B+C)} \Leftrightarrow BC = CB.$$

Nevertheless, the exponentials of B and C are related to that of $B + C$, for example, by the Trotter product formula:[30]

$$e^{B+C} = \dim_{m\to\infty} (e^{B/m}e^{C/m})^m.$$

METHOD 19. SPLITTING. Our colleagues M. Gunzburger and D. Gottleib suggested that the Trotter result be used to approximate e^A by splitting A into $B + C$ and then using the approximation

$$e^A \simeq (e^{B/m}e^{C/m})^m.$$

This approach to computing e^A is of potential interest when the exponentials of

B and C can be accurately and efficiently computed. For example, if $B = (A + A^T)/2$ and $C = (A - A^T)/2$ then e^B and e^C can be effectively computed by the methods of § 5. For this choice we show in Appendix 2 that

$$\|e^A - (e^{B/m}e^{C/m})^m\| \leqq \frac{\|[A^T, A]\|}{4m} e^{\mu(A)}, \tag{7.1}$$

where $\mu(A)$ is the log norm of A as defined in § 2. In the following algorithm, this inequality is used to determine the parameter m.

a. Set $B = (A + A^T)\,2$ and $C = (A - A^T)/2$. Compute the factorization $B = Q\ \mathrm{diag}\ (\mu_i)Q^T\ (Q^TQ = I)$ using TRED2 and TQL2.[113] Variations of these programs can be used to compute the factorization $C = UDU^T$ where $U^TU = I$ and D is the direct sum of zero matrices and real 2-by-2 blocks of the form

$$\begin{bmatrix} 0 & a \\ -a & 0 \end{bmatrix}$$

corresponding to eigenvalues $\pm\, ia$.

b. Determine $m = 2^j$ such that the upper bound in (7.1) is less than some prescribed tolerance. Recall that $\mu(A)$ is the most positive eigenvalue of B and that this quantity is known as a result of step (a).

c. Compute $X = Q\ \mathrm{diag}\ (e^{\mu_i/m})Q^T$ and $Y = Ue^{D/m}U^T$. In the latter computation, one uses the fact that

$$\exp\begin{bmatrix} 0 & a/m \\ -a/m & 0 \end{bmatrix} = \begin{bmatrix} \cos(a/m) & \sin(a/m) \\ -\sin(a/m) & \cos(a/m) \end{bmatrix}$$

d. Compute the approximation, $(XY)^{2^j}$, to e^A by repeated squaring.

If we assume $5\, n^3$ flops for each of the eigenvalue decompositions in (a), then the overall process outlined above requires about $(13 + j)\, n^3$ flops. It is difficult to assess the relative efficiency of this splitting method because it depends strongly on the scalars $\|[A^T, A]\|$ and $\mu(A)$ and these quantities have not arisen in connection with any of our previous eighteen methods. On the basis of truncation error bounds, however, it would seem that this technique would be much less efficient than Method 3 (scaling and squaring) unless $\mu(A)$ were negative and $\|[A^T, A]\|$ much less than $\|A\|$.

Accuracy depends on the rounding errors which arise in (d) as a result of the repeated squaring. The remarks about repeated squaring in Method 3 apply also here: there may be severe cancellation but whether or not this only occurs in sensitive e^A problems is unknown.

For a general splitting $A = B + C$, we can determine m from the inequality

$$\|e^A - (e^{B/m}e^{C/m})^m\| \leqq \frac{\|[B, C]\|}{2m} e^{\|B\| + \|C\|}, \tag{7.2}$$

which we establish in Appendix 2.

To illustrate, suppose A has companion form

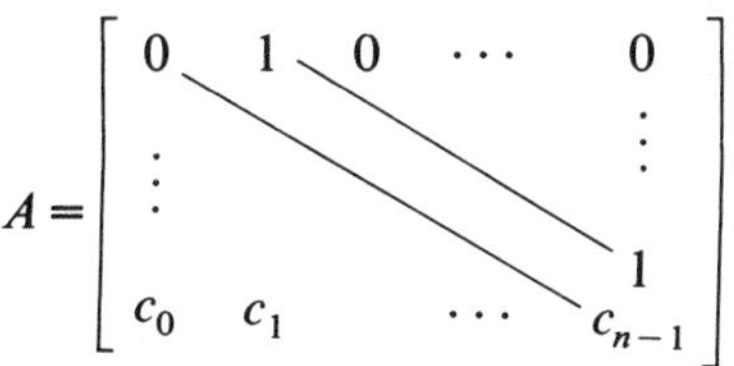

If

$$B=\begin{bmatrix} 0 & I_{n-1} \\ 0 & 0 \end{bmatrix}$$

and $C=e_n c^T$ where $c^T=(c_0,\ldots,c_{n-1})$ and $e_n^T=(0,0,\ldots,0,1)$, then

$$e^{B/m}=\sum_{k=0}^{n-1}\left[\frac{B}{m}\right]^k\frac{1}{k!}$$

and

$$e^{C/m}=I+\frac{e^{c_{n-1}/m}-1}{c_{n-1}}e_n c^T.$$

Notice that the computation of these scaled exponentials require only $O(n^2)$ flops. Since $\|B\|=1$, $\|C\|=\|c\|$, and $\|[B,C]\|\leqq 2\|c\|$, (7.2) becomes

$$\|e^A-(e^{B/m}e^{C/m})^m\|\leqq\frac{e^{1+\|c\|}\|c\|}{m}.$$

The parameter m can be determined from this inequality.

8. CONCLUSIONS

A section called "conclusions" must deal with the obvious question: Which method is best? Answering that question is very risky. We don't know enough about the sensitivity of the original problem, or about the detailed performance of careful implementations of various methods to make any firm conclusions. Furthermore, by the time this paper appears in the open literature, any given conclusion might well have to be modified.

We have considered five general classes of methods. What we have called polynomial methods are not really in the competition for "best." Some of them require the characteristic polynomial and so are appropriate only for certain special problems and others have the same stability difficulties as matrix decomposition methods but are much less efficient. The approaches we have outlined under splitting methods are largely speculative and untried and probably only of interest in special settings. This leaves three classes in the running.

The only generally competitive series method is Method 3, scaling and squaring. Ward's program implementing this method is certainly among the best currently available. The program may fail, but at least it tells you when it does. We don't know yet whether or not such failures usually result from the inherent sensitivity of the problem or from the instability of the algorithm. The method basically computes e^A for a single matrix A. To compute e^{tA} for p arbitrary values of t requires about p times as much work. The amount of work is $O(n^3)$, even for the vector problem $e^{tA}x_0$. The coefficient of n^3 increases as $\|A\|$ increases.

Specializations of o.d.e. methods for the e^A problem have not yet been implemented. The best method would appear to involve a variable order, variable step difference scheme. We suspect it would be stable and reliable but expensive. Its best showing on efficiency would be for the vector problem $e^{tA}x_0$ with many values of t since the amount of work is only $O(n^2)$. It would also work quite well for vector problems involving a large sparse A since no "nonsparse" approximation to the exponential would be explicitly required.

The best programs using matrix decomposition methods are just now being written. They start with the Schur decomposition and include some sort of eigenvalue clustering. There are variants which involve further reduction to a block form. In all cases the initial decomposition costs $O(n^3)$ steps and is independent of t and $\|A\|$. After that, the work involved in using the decomposition to compute $e^{tA}x_0$ for different t and x_0 is only a small multiple of n^2.

Thus, we see perhaps three or four candidates for "best" method. The choice will depend upon the details of implementation and upon the particular problem being solved.

APPENDIX 1. Inverse error analysis of Padé matrix approximation.

Lemma 1. *If* $\|H\|<1$, *then* $\log(I+H)$ *exists and*

$$\|\log(I+H)\| \leqq \frac{\|H\|}{1-\|H\|}.$$

PROOF. If $\|H\|<1$ then $\log(I+H)=\sum_{k=1}^{\infty}(-1)^{k+1}(H^k/k)$ and so

$$\|\log(I+H)\| \leqq \sum_{k=1}^{\infty}\frac{\|H\|^k}{k} \leqq \|H\|\sum_{k=0}^{\infty}\|H\|^k=\frac{\|H\|}{1-\|H\|}.$$

Lemma 2. *If* $\|A\| \leqq \frac{1}{2}$ *and* $p>0$, *then* $\|D_{pq}(A)^{-1}\| \leqq (q+p)/p$.

PROOF. From the definition of $D_{pq}(A)$ in § 3, $D_{pq}(A)=I+F$ where

$$F=\sum_{j=1}^{q}\frac{(p+q-j)!q!}{(p+q)!(q-j)!}\frac{(-A)^j}{j!}.$$

Using the fact that

$$\frac{(p+q-j)!q!}{(p+q)!(q-j)!}\leqq\left[\frac{q}{p+q}\right]^j$$

we find

$$\|F\|\leqq\sum_{j=1}^{q}\left[\frac{q}{p+q}\|A\|\right]^j\frac{1}{j!}\leqq\frac{q}{p+q}\|A\|(e-1)\leqq\frac{q}{p+q}$$

and so $\|D_{pq}(A)^{-1}\|=\|(I+F)^{-1}\|\leqq 1/(1-\|F\|)\leqq(q+p)/p$.

Lemma 3. *If* $\|A\|\leqq\frac{1}{2}$, $q\leqq p$, *and* $p\geqq 1$, *then* $R_{pq}(A)=e^{A+F}$ *where*

$$\|F\|\leqq 8\|A\|^{p+q+1}\frac{p!q!}{(p+q)!(p+q+1)!}.$$

PROOF. From the remainder theorem for Padé approximants,[71]

$$R_{pq}(A)=e^A-\frac{(-1)^q}{(p+q)!}A^{p+q+1}D_{pq}(A)^{-1}\int_0^1 e^{(1-u)A}u^p(1-u)^q du,$$

and so $e^{-A}R_{pq}(A)=I+H$ where

$$H=\frac{(-1)^{q+1}}{(p+q)!}A^{p+q+1}D_{pq}(A)^{-1}\int_0^1 e^{-uA}u^p(1-u)^q du.$$

By taking norms, using Lemma 2, and noting that $(p+q)/pe^{.5}\leqq 4$ we obtain

$$\|H\|\leqq\frac{1}{(p+q)!}\|A\|^{p+q+1}\frac{p+q}{p}\int_0^1 e^{.5}u^p(1-u)^q du$$

$$\leqq 4\|A\|^{p+q+1}\frac{p!q!}{(p+q)!(p+q+1)!}.$$

With the assumption $\|A\|\leqq\frac{1}{2}$ it is possible to show that for all admissible p and q, $\|H\|\leqq\frac{1}{2}$ and so from Lemma 1,

$$\|\log(I+H)\|\leqq\frac{\|H\|}{1-\|H\|}\leqq 8\|A\|^{p+q+1}\frac{p!q!}{(p+q)!(p+q+1)!}.$$

Setting $F=\log(I+H)$, we see that $e^{-A}R_{pq}(A)=I+H=e^F$. The lemma now follows because A and F commute implying $R_{pq}(A)=e^Ae^F=e^{A+F}$.

Lemma 4. *If* $\|A\| \leqq \frac{1}{2}$ *then* $R_{pq}(A)=e^{A+F}$ *where*

$$\|F\| \leqq 8\|A\|^{p+q+1}\frac{p!q!}{(p+q)!(p+q+1)!}.$$

PROOF. The case $p \geqq q$, $p \geqq 1$ is covered by Lemma 1. If $p+q=0$, then $F=-A$ and the above inequality holds. Finally, consider the case $q>p$, $q \geqq 1$. From Lemma 3, $R_{qp}(-A)=e^{-A+F}$ where F satisfies the above bound. The lemma now follows because $\|-F\|=\|F\|$ and $R_{pq}(A)=[R_{qp}(-A)]^{-1}=[e^{-A+F}]^{-1}=e^{A-F}$.

e^{A-F}.

Theorem A.1. *If* $\|A\|/2^j \leqq \frac{1}{2}$, *then* $[R_{pq}(A/2^j)]^{2^j}=e^{A+E}$ *where*

$$\frac{\|E\|}{\|A\|} \leqq 8\left(\frac{\|A\|}{2^j}\right)^{p+q}\frac{p!q!}{(p+q)!(p+q+1)!} \leqq \left(\frac{1}{2}\right)^{p+q-3}\frac{p!q!}{(p+q)!(p+q+1)!}.$$

PROOF. From Lemma 4, $R_{pq}(A/2^j)=e^{A+F}$ where

$$\|F\| \leqq 8\left[\frac{\|A\|}{2^j}\right]^{p+q+1}\frac{p!q!}{(p+q)!(p+q+1)!}.$$

The theorem follows by noting that if $E=2^jF$, then

$$\left[R_{pq}\left(\frac{A}{2^j}\right)\right]^{2^j}=[e^{A/2j+F}]^{2^j}=e^{A+E}.$$

Corollary 1. *If* $\|A\|/2^j \leqq \frac{1}{2}$, *then* $[T_k(A/2^j)]^{2^j}=e^{A+E}$ *where*

$$\frac{\|E\|}{\|A\|} \leqq 8\left(\frac{\|A\|}{2^j}\right)^{k}\cdot\frac{1}{k+1} \leqq \left(\frac{1}{2}\right)^{k-3}\frac{1}{k+1}.$$

Corollary 2. *If* $\|A\|/2^j \leqq \frac{1}{2}$, *then* $[R_{qq}(A/2^j)]^{2^j}=e^{A+E}$, *where*

$$\frac{\|E\|}{\|A\|} \leqq 8\left(\frac{\|A\|}{2^j}\right)^{2q}\cdot\frac{(q!)^2}{(2q)!(2q+1)!} \leqq \left(\frac{1}{2}\right)^{2q-3}\frac{(q!)^2}{(2q)!(2q+1)!}.$$

APPENDIX 2. Accuracy of splitting techniques

In this Appendix we derive the Inequalities (7.1) and (7.2). We assume throughout that A is an n-by-n matrix and that

$$A=B+C.$$

It is convenient to define the matrices

$$S_m=e^{A/m},$$

and

$$T_m = e^{B/m} e^{C/m},$$

where m is a positive integer. Our goal is to bound $\|S_m^m - T_m^m\|$. To this end we shall have to exploit the following properties of the log norm $\mu(A)$ defined in § 2:

$$\text{(i)}\ \|e^{tA}\| \leqq e^{\mu(A)t} \qquad (t \geqq 0)$$
$$\text{(ii)}\ \mu(A) \leqq \|A\|$$
$$\text{(iii)}\ \mu(B+C) \leqq \mu(B) + \|C\|.$$

These and other results concerning log norms are discussed in references [35]–[42].

Lemma 1. *If* $\Theta \geqq \max\{\mu(A), \mu(B)+\mu(C)\}$ *then*

$$\|S_m^m - T_m^m\| \leqq m e^{\Theta(m-1)/m} \|S_m - T_m\|.$$

PROOF. Following Reed and Simon [11] we have

$$S_m^m - T_m^m = \sum_{k=0}^{m-1} S_m^k (S_m - T_m) T_m^{m-1-k}.$$

Using log norm property 1 it is easy to show that both $\|S_m\|$ and $\|T_m\|$ are bounded above by $e^{\Theta/m}$ and thus

$$\|S_m^m - T_m^m\| \leqq \sum_{k=0}^{m-1} \|S_m\|^k \|S_m - T_m\| \, \|T_m\|^{m-1-k}$$

$$\leqq \|S_m - T_m\| \sum_{k=0}^{m-1} e^{\Theta k/m} e^{\Theta(m-1-k)/m},$$

from which the lemma immediately follows.

In Lemmas 2 and 3 we shall make use of the notation

$$F(t)\big|_{t=t_0}^{t=t_1} = F(t_1) - F(t_0),$$

where $F(t)$ is a matrix whose entries are functions of t.

Lemma 2.

$$T_m - S_m = \int_0^1 e^{tB/m} \left[e^{(1-t)A/m}, \frac{1}{m} C \right] e^{tC/m} dt.$$

PROOF. We have $T_m - S_m = e^{tB/m} e^{(1-t)A/m} e^{tC/m}\big|_{t=0}^{t=1}$ and thus

$$T_m - S_m = \int_0^1 \left\{ \frac{d}{dt}\left[e^{tB/m} e^{(1-t)A/m} e^{tC/m} \right] \right\} dt.$$

The lemma follows since

$$\frac{d}{dt}\left[e^{tB/m} e^{(1-t)A/m} e^{tC/m} \right] = e^{tB/m}\left[e^{(1-t)A/m}, \frac{1}{m} C \right] e^{tC/m}.$$

Lemma 3. *If X and Y are matrices then*

$$\|[e^X, Y]\| \leqq e^{\mu(X)} \|[X,Y]\|.$$

PROOF. We have $[e^X, Y] = e^{tX} Y e^{(1-t)X}|_{t=0}^{t=1}$ and thus

$$[e^X, Y] = \int_0^1 \left\{ \frac{d}{dt}\left[e^{tX} Y e^{(1-t)X} \right] \right\} dt.$$

Since $d/dt[e^{tX} Y e^{(1-t)X}] = e^{tX}[X,Y]e^{(1-t)X}$ we get

$$\begin{aligned} \|[e^X, Y]\| &\leqq \int_0^1 \|e^{tX}\| \, \|[X,Y]\| \, \|e^{(1-t)X}\| dt \\ &\leqq \|[X,Y]\| \int_0^1 e^{\mu(X)t} e^{\mu(X)(1-t)} dt \end{aligned}$$

from which the lemma immediately follows.

Theorem A.2. *If* $\Theta \geqq \max\{\mu(A), \mu(B)+\mu(C)\}$, *then*

$$\|S_m^m - T_m^m\| \leqq \frac{1}{2m} e^{\Theta} \|[B,C]\|.$$

PROOF. If $0 \leqq t \leqq 1$ then an application of Lemma 3 with $X \equiv (1-t)A/m$ and $Y \equiv C/m$ yields

$$\begin{aligned} \|[e^{(1-t)A/m}, C/m]\| &\leqq e^{\mu(A)(1-t)/m} \|[(1-t)A/m, C/m]\| \\ &\leqq e^{\Theta(1-t)/m} \frac{(1-t)}{m^2} \|[B,C]\|. \end{aligned}$$

By coupling this inequality with Lemma 2 we can bound $\|T_m - S_m\|$:

$$\begin{aligned} \|T_m - S_m\| &\leqq \int_0^1 \|e^{tB/m}\| \, \|[e^{(1-t)A/m}, C/m]\| \, \|e^{tC/m}\| dt \\ &\leqq \int_0^1 e^{\mu(B)t/m} e^{\Theta(1-t)/m} \frac{(1-t)}{m^2} \|[B,C]\| e^{\mu(C)t/m} dt \\ &\leqq \frac{1}{2} e^{\Theta/m} \frac{\|[B,C]\|}{m^2}. \end{aligned}$$

The theorem follows by combining this result with Lemma 1. □

Corollary 1. *If* $B=(A+A^*)/2$ *and* $C=(A-A^*)/2$ *then*

$$\|S_m^m - T_m^m\| \leqq \frac{1}{4m} e^{\mu(A)} \|[A^*,A]\|.$$

PROOF. Since $\mu(A)=\mu(B)$ and $\mu(C)=0$, we can set $\Theta=\mu(A)$. The corollary is established by noting that $[B,C]=\frac{1}{2}[A^*,A]$. □

Corollary 2.

$$\|S_m^m - T_m^m\| \leqq \frac{1}{2m} e^{\mu(B)+\|C\|} \|[B,C]\| \leqq \frac{1}{2m} e^{\|B\|+\|C\|} \|[B,C]\|.$$

PROOF. $\max\{\mu(A), \mu(B)+\mu(C)\} \leqq \mu(B)+\|C\| \leqq \|B\|+\|C\|.$

ACKNOWLEDGMENT

We have greatly profited from the comments and suggestions of so many people that it is impossible to mention them all. However, we are particularly obliged to B. N. Parlett and G. W. Stewart for their very perceptive remarks and to G. H. Golub for encouraging us to write this paper. We are obliged to Professor Paul Federbush of the University of Michigan for helping us with the analysis in Appendix 2. Finally, we would like to thank the referees for their numerous and most helpful comments.

REFERENCES

Background.

1. R. Bellman, Introduction to Matrix Analysis, New York: McGraw-Hill, 1969.
2. C. Davis, Explicit functional calculus, J. Linear Algebra Appl., 6 (1973), pp. 193–199.
3. V. N. Faddeeva, Computational Methods of Linear Algebra, New York: Dover Publications, 1959.
4. G. E. Forsythe, M. A. Malcolm, and C. B. Moler, Computer Methods for Mathematical Computations, Englewood Cliffs, New Jersey: Prentice-Hall, 1977.
5. J. S. Frame, Matrix functions and applications, part II: Functions of matrices, IEEE Spectrum, 1 (April, 1964), pp. 102–108.
6. ——————, Matrix functions and applications, part IV: Matrix functions and constituent matrices, Ibid., 1 (June, 1964), pp. 123–131.
7. ——————, Matrix functions and applications, part V: Similarity reductions by rational or orthogonal matrices, Ibid., 1 (July, 1964), pp. 103–116.
8. F. R. Gantmacher, The Theory of Matrices, Vols. I and II, New York: Chelsea Publishing Company, 1959.
9. C. C. MacDuffee, The Theory of Matrices, New York: Chelsea Publishing Company, 1956.

10. L. Mirsky, An Introduction to Linear Algebra, London: Oxford University Press, 1955.
11. M. Reed and B. Simon, Functional Analysis, New York: Academic Press, 1972.
12. R. F. Rinehart, The equivalence of definitions of a matrix function, Amer. Math. Monthly, 62 (1955), pp. 395–414.
13. P. C. Rosenbloom, Bounds on functions of matrices, Ibid., 74 (1967), pp. 920–926.
14. J. H. Wilkinson, The Algebraic Eigenvalue Problem, London: Oxford University Press, 1965.

Properties and representations.

15. T. M. Apostol, Some explicit formulas for the matrix exponential, Amer. Math. Monthly, 76 (1969), pp. 284–292.
16. R. W. Atherton and A. E. De Gance, On the evaluation of the derivative of the matrix exponential function, IEEE Trans. Automatic Control, AC-20 (1975), pp. 707–708.
17. A. Bradshaw, The eigenstructure of sample data systems with confluent eigenvalues, Internat. J. Systems Sci., 5 (1974), pp. 607–613.
18. R. Bellman, Perturbation Techniques in Mathematics, Physics, and Engineering, New York: Holt, Rinehart, and Winston, 1964.
19. J. C. Cavendish, On the norm of a matrix exponential, SIAM Review, 17 (1975), pp. 174–175.
20. C. G. Cullen, Remarks on computing e^{At}, IEEE Trans. Automatic Control, AC-16 (1971), pp. 94–95.
21. F. Fer, Resolution de l'equation matricelle $dU/dt = pU$ par produit infini d'exponentielles, Acad. Roy. Belg. Bull. Cl. Sci., 44 (1958), pp. 819–829.
22. E. P. Fulmer, Computation of the matrix exponential, Amer. Math. Monthly, 82 (1975), pp. 156–159.
23. B. Kågstrom, Bounds and perturbation bounds for the matrix exponential, BIT, 17 (1977), pp. 39–57.
24. T. Kato, Perturbation Theory for Linear Operators, Chap. 9, New York: Springer-Verlag, 1966.
25. R. B. Kirchner, An explicit formula for e^{At} , Amer. Math. Monthly, 74 (1967), pp. 1200–1204.
26. H. O. Kreiss, Über Matrizen die beschränkte Halbgruppen erzeuge, Math. Scand., 7 (1959), pp. 71–80.
27. D. L. Powers, On the eigenstructure of the matrix exponential, Internat. J. Systems Sci., 7 (1976), pp. 723–725.
28. E. J. Putzer, Avoiding the Jordan canonical form in the discussion of linear systems with constant coefficients, Amer. Math. Monthly, 73 (1966), pp. 2–7.
29. N. M. Rice, More explicit formulas for the exponential matrix, Queen's Mathematical Reprints no. 1970–21, Queen's University, Kingston, Ontario, 1970.
30. H. F. Trotter, Product of semigroups of operators, Proc. Amer. Math. Soc., 10 (1959), pp. 545–551.
31. C. F. Van Loan, A study of the matrix exponential, Numerical Analysis Report no. 7, Department of Mathematics, University of Manchester, Manchester, England, 1975.
32. ———, The sensitivity of the matrix exponential, SIAM J. Numer. Anal., 14 (1977), pp. 971–981.

33. G. H. Weiss and A. A. Maradudin, The Baker–Hausdorff formula and a problem in crystal physics, J. Math. and Phys., 3 (1962), pp. 771–777.
34. A. D. Ziebur, On determining the structure of A by analyzing e^{At}, SIAM Review, 12 (1970), pp. 98–102.

Log norms and stability.

35. W. A. Coppel, Stability and Asymptotic Behavior of Differential Equations, Boston: D. C. Heath, 1965.
36. G. Dahlquist, Stability and error bounds in the numerical integration of ordinary differential equations, Transactions of the Royal Institute of Technology, no. 130, Stockholm, Sweden, 1959.
37. C. A. Desoer and H. Haneda, The measure of a matrix as a tool to analyze computer algorithms for circuit analysis, IEEE Trans. Circuit Theory, CT-19 (1972), pp. 480–486.
38. E. Deutsch, On matrix norms and logarithmic norms, Numer. Math., 24 (1975), pp. 49–51.
39. C. V. Pao, Logarithmic derivatives of a square matrix, J. Linear Algebra Appl., 6 (1973), pp. 159–164.
40. ———, A further remark on the logarithmic derivatives of a square matrix, Ibid., 7 (1973), pp. 275–278.
41. T. Strom, Minimization of norms and logarithmic norms by diagonal similarities, Computing, 10 (1972), pp. 1–9.
42. ———, On logarithmic derivatives, SIAM J. Numer. Anal., 12 (1975), pp. 741–53.

Survey articles.

43. M. Healey, Study of methods of computing transition matrices, Proc. IEEE, 120 (1973), pp. 905–912.
44. C. B. Moler, Difficulties in computing the exponential of a matrix, Proceedings of the Second USA–Japan Computer Conference, A.F.I.P.S., Montvale, New Jersey, 1975, pp. 79–82.

Truncated Taylor series.

45. L. Y. Bahar and A. K. Sinha, Matrix exponential approach to dynamic response, Computers and Structures, 5 (1975), pp. 159–165.
46. T. A. Bickart, Matrix exponential: Approximation by truncated power series, Proc. IEEE, 56 (1968), pp. 372–373.
47. G. J. Bierman, Power series evaluation of transition and covariance matrices, IEEE Trans. Automatic Control, AC-17 (1972), pp. 228–231.
48. D. A. Calahan, Numerical solution of linear systems with widely separated time constants, Proc. IEEE, 55 (1967), pp. 2016–2017.
49. K. C. Daly, Evaluating the matrix exponential. Electron. Lett., 8 (1972), p. 390.
50. W. Everling, On the evaluation of e^{At} by power series, Proc. IEEE, 55 (1967), p. 413.
51. D. A. Gall, The solution of linear constant coefficient ordinary differential equations with APL, Comput. Methods Mechanics and Engrg., 1 (1972), pp. 189–196.
52. M. L. Liou, A novel method of evaluating transient response, Proc. IEEE, 54 (1966), pp. 20–23.
53. J. B. Mankin and J. C. Hung, On roundoff errors in computation of transition ma-

trices, Reprints of the Joint Automatic Control Conference, pp. 60–64, University of Colorado, Boulder, Colorado, 1969.

54. E. J. Mastascusa, A relation between Liou's method and fourth order Runge–Kutta method for evaluation of transient response, Proc. IEEE, 57 (1969), pp. 803–804.
55. J. B. Plant, On the computation of transient matrices for time invariant systems, Ibid., 56 (1968), pp. 1397–1398.
56. M. M. Shah, On the evaluation of e^{At}, Cambridge Report CUED/B-Control TR8, Cambridge, England, 1971.
57. ———, Analysis of roundoff and truncation errors in the computation of transition matrices, Cambridge Report CUED/B-Control TR12, Cambridge, England, 1971.
58. C. J. Standish, Truncated Taylor series approximation to the state transition matrix of a continuous parameter Markov chain, J. Linear Algebra Appl., 12 (1975), pp. 179–183.
59. D. E. Whitney, Propogated error bounds for numerical solution of transient response, Proc. IEEE, 54 (1966), pp. 1084–1085.
60. ———, More similarities between Runge-Kutta and matrix exponential methods for evaluating transient response, Ibid., 57 (1969), pp. 2053–2054.

Rational approximation

61. J. L. Blue and H. K. Gummel, Rational approximations to the matrix exponential for systems of stiff differential equations, J. Computational Phys., 5 (1970), pp. 70–83.
62. W. J. Cody, G. Meinardus, and R. S. Varga, Chebyshev rational approximation to exp (− x) in [0, + ∞] and applications to heat conduction problems, J. Approximation Theory, 2 (1969), pp. 50–65.
63. W. Fair and Y. Luke, Padé approximations to the operator exponential, Numer. Math., 14 (1970), pp. 379–382.
64. S. P. Norsett, C-polynomials for rational approximation to the exponential function, Ibid., 25 (1975), pp. 39–56.
65. E. B. Saff, On the degree of best rational approximation to the exponential function, J. Approximation Theory, 9 (1973), pp. 97–101.
66. E. B. Saff and R. S. Varga, On the zeros and poles of Padé approximants to exp (z), Numer. Math., 25 (1975), pp. 1–14.
67. R. E. Scraton, Comment on rational approximants to the matrix exponential, Electron. Lett., 7 (1971), pp. 260–261.
68. J. L. Siemieniuch, Properties of certain rational approximations to e^{-z}, BIT, 16 (1976), pp. 172–191.
69. G. Siemieniuch and I. Gladwell, On time discretizations for linear time dependent partial differential equations, Numerical Analysis Report no. 5, Department of Mathematics, University of Manchester, Manchester, England, 1974.
70. D. M. Trujillo, The direct numerical integration of linear matrix differential equations using Padé approximations, Internat. J. for Numer. Methods Engrg., 9 (1975), pp. 259–270.
71. R. S. Varga, On higher order stable implicit methods for solving parabolic partial differential equations, J. Math. Phys., 40 (1961), pp. 220–231.
72. R. C. Ward, Numerical computation of the matrix exponential with accuracy estimate, SIAM J. Numer. Anal., 14 (1977), pp. 600–610.

73. A. Wragg and C. Davies, Evaluation of the matrix exponential, Electron. Lett., 9 (1973), pp. 525–526.
74. ———, Computation of the exponential of a matrix I: Theoretical considerations, J. Inst. Math. Appl., 11 (1973), pp. 369–375.
75. ———, Computation of the exponential of a matrix II: Practical considerations, Ibid., 15 (1975), pp. 273–278.
76. V. Zakian, Rational approximants to the matrix exponential, Electron. Lett., 6 (1970), pp. 814–815.
77. V. Zakian and R. E. Scraton, Comments on rational approximations to the matrix exponential, Ibid., 7 (1971), pp. 260–262.

Polynomial methods.

78. G. J. Bierman, Finite series solutions for the transition matrix and covariance of a time-invariant system, IEEE Trans. Automatic Control, AC-16 (1971), pp. 173–175.
79. J. A. Boehm and J. A. Thurman, An algorithm for generating constituent matrices, IEEE Trans. Circuit Theory, CT-18 (1971), pp. 178–179.
80. C. F. Chen and R. R. Parker, Generalization of Heaviside's expansion technique to transition matrix evaluation, IEEE Trans. Educ. E-9 (1966), pp. 209–212.
81. W. C. Davidon, Exponential Function of a 2-by-2 Matrix, Hewlett-Packard HP65 Library Program.
82. S. Deards, On the evaluation of exp (tA), Matrix Tensor Quart., 23 (1973), pp. 141–142.
83. S. Ganapathy and R. S. Rao, Transient response evaluation from the state transition matrix, Proc. IEEE, 57 (1969), pp. 347–349.
84. I. C. Goknar, On the evaluation of constituent matrices, Internat. J. Systems Sci., 5 (1974), pp. 213–218.
85. I. I. Kolodner, On exp (tA) with A satisfying a polynomial, J. Math. Anal. Appl. 52 (1975), pp. 514–524.
86. Y. L. Kuo and M. L. Liou, Comments on "A novel method of evaluating e^{At} in closed form," IEEE Trans. Automatic Control, AC-16 (1971), p. 521.
87. E. J. Mastascusa, A method of calculating e^{At} based on the Cayley-Hamilton theorem, Proc. IEEE, 57 (1969), pp. 1328–1329.
88. K. R. Rao and N. Ahmed, Heaviside expansion of transition matrices, Ibid., 56 (1968), pp. 884–886.
89. ———, Evaluation of transition matrices, IEEE Trans. Automatic Control, AC-14 (1969), pp. 779–780.
90. B. Roy, A. K. Mandal, D. Roy Choudhury, A. K. Choudhury, On the evaluation of the state transition matrix, Proc. IEEE, 57 (1969), pp. 234–235.
91. M. N. S. Swamy, On a formula for evaluating e^{At} when the eigenvalues are not necessarily distinct, Matrix Tensor Quart., 23 (1972), pp. 67–72.
92. M. Vidysager, A novel method of evaluating e^{At} in closed form, IEEE Trans. Automatic Control, AC-15 (1970), pp. 600–601.
93. V. Zakian, Solution of homogeneous ordinary linear differential equations by numerical inversion of Laplace transforms, Electron. Lett., 7 (1971), pp. 546–548.

Companion matrix methods.

94. A. K. Choudhury et al., On the evaluation of e^{At}, Proc. IEEE, 56 (1968), pp. 1110–1111.

95. L. Falcidieno and A. Luvinson, A numerical approach to computing the companion matrix exponential, CSELT Rapporti technici, No. 4, 1975, pp. 69–71.
96. C. J. Harris, Evaluation of matrix polynomials in the state companion matrix of linear time invariant systems, Internat. J. Systems Sci., 4 (1973), pp. 301–307.
97. D. W. Kammler, Numerical evaluation of exp (At) when A is a companion matrix, unpublished manuscript, University of Southern Illinois, Carbondale, Illinois, 1976.
98. I. Kaufman, Evaluation of an analytical function of a companion matrix with distinct eigenvalues, Proc. IEEE, 57 (1969), pp. 1180–1181.
99. ———, A note on the "Evaluation of an analytical function of a companion matrix with distinct eigenvalues," Ibid., 57 (1969), pp. 2083–2084.
100. I. Kaufman and P. H. Roe, On systems described by a companion matrix, IEEE Trans. Automatic Control, AC-15 (1970), pp. 692–693.
101. I. Kaufman, H. Mann, and J. Vlach, A fast procedure for the analysis of linear time invariant networks, IEEE Trans. Circuit Theory, CT-18 (1971), pp. 739–741.
102. M. L. Liou, Evaluation of the transition matrix, Proc. IEEE, 55 (1967), pp. 228–229.
103. A. K. Mandal et al., Numerical computation method for the evaluation of the transition matrix, Ibid., 116 (1969), pp. 500–502.
104. W. E. Thomson, Evaluation of transient response, Ibid., 54 (1966), p. 1584.

Ordinary differential equations.

105. B. L. Ehle and J. D. Lawson, Generalized Runge–Kutta processes for stiff initial value problems, J. Inst. Math. Appl., 16 (1975), pp. 11–21.
106. C. W. Gear, Numerical Initial Value Problems in Ordinary Differential Equations, Prentice-Hall, Englewood Cliffs, New Jersey, 1971.
107. L. F. Shampine and M. K. Gordon, Computer Solution of Ordinary Differential Equations—The Initial Value Problem, W. H. Freeman and Company, San Francisco, 1975.
108. L. F. Shampine and H. A. Watts, Practical solution of ordinary differential equations by Runge–Kutta methods, Sandia Lab Report SAND 76-0585 Albuquerque, New Mexico, 1976.
109. J. Starner, Numerical solution of implicit differential-algebraic equations, Ph.D. Thesis, University of New Mexico, Albuquerque, New Mexico, 1976.

Matrix decomposition methods.

110. G. H. Golub and J. H. Wilkinson, Ill-conditioned eigensystems and the computation of the Jordan canonical form, SIAM Review, 18 (1976), pp. 578–619.
111. B. Kågstrom and A. Ruhe, An algorithm for numerical computation of the Jordan normal form of a complex matrix, Report UMINF 51.74, Department of Information Processing, University of Umea, Umea, Sweden, 1974. To appear in Trans. Math. Softwave.
112. B. N. Parlett, A recurrence among the elements of functions of triangular matrices, Linear Algebra Appl., 14 (1976), pp. 117–121.
113. B. T. Smith, J. M. Boyle, J. J. Dongarra, B. S. Garbow, Y. Ikebe, V. C. Klema, C. B. Moler, Matrix Eigensystem Routines: EISPACK Guide, 2nd ed., Lecture Notes in Computer Science, 6, Springer-Verlag, New York, 1976.

Integrals involving e^{At}.

114. E. S. Armstrong and A. K. Caglayan, An algorithm for the weighting matrices in the sampled-data optimal linear regulator problem, NASA Technical Note, TN D-8372, 1976.
115. J. Johnson and C. L. Phillips, An algorithm for the computation of the integral of the state transition matrix, IEEE Trans. Automatic Control, AC-16 (1971), pp. 204–205.
116. C. Kallstrom, Computing exp (A) and exp (As) ds, Report 7309, Division of Automatic Control, Lund Institute of Technology, Lund, Sweden, 1973.
117. A. H. Levis, Some computational aspects of the matrix exponential, IEEE Trans. Automatic Control, AC-14 (1969), pp. 410–411.
118. C. F. Van Loan, Computing integrals involving the matrix exponential, Cornell Computer Science Report TR 76-270, 1976.

Selected applications.

119. F. H. Branin, Computer methods of network analysis, Proc. IEEE, 55 (1967), pp. 1787–1801.
120. R. Brockett, Finite Dimensional Linear Systems, John Wiley, New York, 1970.
121. K. F. Hansen, B. V. Koen, and W. W. Little, Stable numerical solutions of the reactor kinetics equations, Nuclear Sci. Engrg., 22 (1965), pp. 51–59.
122. J. A. W. Da Nobrega, A new solution of the point kinetics equations, Ibid., 46 (1971), pp. 366–375.

An Application of Bin-packing to Multiprocessor Scheduling

E. G. Coffman

*Department of Computer Science,
Pennsylvania State University, University Park, Pennsylvania.*

M. R. Garey, D. S. Johnson

Bell Laboratories, Murray Hill, New Jersey

We consider one of the basic, well-studied problems of scheduling theory, that of nonpreemptively scheduling n independent tasks on m identical, parallel processors with the objective of minimizing the "makespan," i.e., the total timespan required to process all the given tasks. Because this problem is *NP*-complete and apparently intractable in general, much effort has been directed toward devising fast algorithms which find near-optimal schedules. The well-known LPT (Largest Processing Time first) algorithm always finds a schedule having makespan within $4/3 = 1.333 \cdots$ of the minimum possible makespan, and this is the best such bound satisfied by any previously published fast algorithm. We describe a comparably fast algorithm, based on techniques from "bin-packing," which we prove satisfies a bound of 1.220. On the basis of exact upper bounds determined for each $m \leqq 7$, we conjecture that the best possible general bound for our algorithm is actually $20/17 = 1.176 \cdots$.

Key words. bin packing, multiprocessor scheduling, approximation algorithms, worst-case analysis, performance bounds

1. INTRODUCTION

One of the fundamental problems of deterministic scheduling theory is that of scheduling independent tasks on a nonpreemptive multiprocessor system so as

EDITOR'S NOTE: *From SIAM Journal on Computing, Vol. 7, No. 1, February, 1978. Reprinted by permission of the publisher, Society for Industrial and Applied Mathematics.*

to minimize overall finishing time.[1,2,3] Formally, we are given a set $\mathcal{T} = \{T_1, T_2, \cdots, T_n\}$ of *tasks*, each task T_i having *length* $l(T_i)$, and a set of $m \geqq 2$ identical *processors*. A *schedule* in this case can be thought of as a partition $\mathcal{P} = \langle P_1, P_2, \cdots, P_m \rangle$ of $\mathcal{T}$ into m disjoint sets, one for each processor. The ith processor, $1 \leqq i \leqq m$, executes the tasks in P_i. (Since the tasks are assumed to be independent, we may restrict our attention to schedules in which no idle time is inserted between consecutively executed tasks. For the same reason, the particular sequence in which tasks are executed on a processor is unconstrained and irrelevant for this problem.) The *finishing time* for the schedule $\mathcal{P}$ is then given by

$$f(\mathcal{P}) = \max_{1 \leqq i \leqq m} l(P_i)$$

where for any $X \subseteq \mathcal{T}$, $l(X)$ is defined to be $\Sigma_{T \in X} l(T)$.

An *optimum m*-processor schedule $\mathcal{P}^*$ is one that satisfies $f(\mathcal{P}^*) \leqq f(\mathcal{P})$ for all partitions $\mathcal{P}$ of $\mathcal{T}$ into m subsets. Since there are only a finite number of possible partitions, such an optimum schedule must exist, and we let $\mathcal{T}_m^* = f(\mathcal{P}^*)$ denote its finishing time.

The problem of finding an optimum schedule appears to be quite difficult in general. All known algorithms require computation time that grows exponentially with the number of tasks. This is not surprising, however, in light of the fact that this problem is known to be "*NP*-complete" and hence computationally "equivalent" to a host of other notoriously intractable problems.[8] These computational difficulties force us to lower our sights somewhat and seek instead reasonably efficient algorithms that find "near-optimal" schedules.

Let A be an algorithm that, when given $\mathcal{T}$ and m, constructs a partition $\mathcal{P}_A[\mathcal{T}, m]$ of $\mathcal{T}$ into m subsets. We shall use $F_A[\mathcal{T}, m]$ to denote the finishing time of $\mathcal{P}_A[\mathcal{T}, m]$, i.e., $F_A[\mathcal{T}, m] = f(\mathcal{P}_A[\mathcal{T}, m])$. The *m-processor performance ratio* for A is then defined by

$$R_m(A) = \sup\left\{ \frac{F_A[\mathcal{T}, m]}{\mathcal{T}_m^*} : \text{all task sets } \mathcal{T} \right\}.$$

We would like to find an efficient algorithm A such that $R_m(A)$ is as close to 1 as possible, for all $m \geqq 2$ (the problem is trivial for $m = 1$).

R.L. Graham[2,3] describes a sequence $A_1, A_2, \cdots$ of algorithms such that $\lim_{i\to\infty} R_m(A_i) = 1$ for all $m \geqq 2$. Unfortunately these algorithms require computation time growing exponentially with m and become more and more like exhaustive search as the guaranteed accuracy improves. (Sahni[7] presents similarly behaved algorithms. The best of the previously published *polynomial-time* algorithms is the LPT algorithm,[2,3] which satisfies

$$R_m(\text{LPT}) = \frac{4}{3} - \frac{1}{3m}.$$

In this paper we present a simple iterative algorithm, based on ideas from bin packing,[5,6] which substantially improves on this worst-case performance and also seems to outperform LPT on the average.*

In the next section we discuss the bin-packing problem and the well known first fit decreasing algorithm for it. We then describe the new results about this algorithm which have motivated the design of our scheduling algorithm and helped us produce upper bounds on its worst case behavior. The scheduling algorithm itself, called MULTIFIT, is then presented in § 3, along with our results about it. The remainder of the paper, §§ 4 and 5, are devoted to the proofs of the new bin-packing results.

2. BIN-PACKING

Our scheduling algorithm is based on the bin-packing algorithm first fit decreasing (abbreviated FFD). The bin-packing problem is in a sense the dual problem to the scheduling problem defined above. Given $\mathcal{T}$ as before, and a bound C, a *packing* is a partition $\mathcal{P} = \langle P_1, P_2, \cdots, P_m \rangle$ of $\mathcal{T}$ such that $l(P_i) \leqq C$, $1 \leqq i \leqq m$. The tasks T_i are here thought of as *items* with *size* $l(T_i)$, which are placed in *bins* of *capacity* C. Our goal is to minimize the number m of bins used in the packing. We let $OPT[\mathcal{T}, C]$ denote this minimum possible value of m. As before, the problem of finding an optimum packing appears to be intractable. The algorithm FFD is an attempt to find a near-optimum packing quickly. It constructs a packing $\mathcal{P}_{FFD}[\mathcal{T}, C]$ as follows.

First, the items in $\mathcal{T}$ are put in "decreasing order," that is, they are re-indexed so that $l(T_1) \geqq l(T_2) \geqq \cdots \geqq l(T_n)$. Then a packing is built up by treating each item in succession, and adding it to the lowest indexed bin into which it will fit without violating the capacity constraint. More formally, we might describe the packing procedure as follows:

1. Set $P_i \leftarrow \varphi$, $1 \leqq i \leqq n$, and $j \leftarrow 1$.
2. Set $k \leftarrow \min \{i \geqq 1: l(P_i) + l(T_j) \leqq C\}$.
3. Set $P_k \leftarrow P_k \cup \{T_j\}, j \leftarrow j + 1$.
4. If $j \leqq n$, go to 2. Otherwise, halt.

Let us denote by $FFD[\mathcal{T}, C]$ the number m of nonempty bins in $\mathcal{P}_{FFD}[\mathcal{T}, C]$. It was proved[5,6] that for all $\mathcal{T}$ and C

$$FFD[\mathcal{T}, C] \leqq \frac{11}{9} OPT\, [\mathcal{T}, C] + 4.$$

In the following, however, we shall be interested in a different question about

* The algorithm described here is also an improvement, both in worst-case behavior and experimental case behavior, over the earlier version.[4]

FFD: namely, "given $\mathcal{T}$ and m, how large does C have to be so that $FFD[\mathcal{T}, C] \leqq m$?"

This question will of course have many different answers, depending on $\mathcal{T}$ and m. We are interested, however, in finding an answer that works for *all* $\mathcal{T}$ and m. To obtain such an answer, we shall ask "how large does C have to be, *in terms of* $\mathcal{T}_m^*$, so that, for all $\mathcal{T}$ and m, $FFD[\mathcal{T}, C]$ is guaranteed to be m or less?"

Recalling our definition of $\mathcal{T}_m^*$ from § 1, we note that, in terms of the bin packing problem,

$$\mathcal{T}_m^* = \min\{C: OPT[\mathcal{T}, C] \leqq m\}.$$

Thus $\mathcal{T}_m^*$ is the smallest bin capacity which allows $\mathcal{T}$ to be packed into m or fewer bins. We now define

$$r_m = \inf\{r: \text{for all } \mathcal{T}, FFD[\mathcal{T}, r\mathcal{T}_m^*] \leqq m\}.$$

The intent of this definition is that r_m be the least "expansion factor" by which the optimum bin capacity should be enlarged to guarantee that FFD will use no more than m bins. However, the definition allows for the possibility that, while expansion factors arbitrarily close to r_m will work, the limiting value r_m itself does not. That this cannot happen (and hence that "inf" could have been replaced by "min") is proved as part of the following "monotonicity lemma."

Lemma 2.1. *For every $\mathcal{T}$ and any $r \geqq r_m$, $FFD[\mathcal{T}, r\mathcal{T}_m^*] \leqq m$.*

PROOF. We first show that $FFD[\mathcal{T}, r_m\mathcal{T}_m^*] \leqq m$ for every $\mathcal{T}$. Suppose, to the contrary, that $\mathcal{T}$ is a set for which $FFD[\mathcal{T}, r_m\mathcal{T}_m^*] > m$. Consider the application of the FFD algorithm to $\mathcal{T}$ with capacity $C = r_m\mathcal{T}_m^*$. Each time the algorithm places a particular item in a bin other than the first bin, this is because the size of that item would have caused the total size in each lower-indexed bin to exceed C by some positive amount. Let δ be the least such excess over all items and all such "unsuccessful" attempted placements. Then, for every capacity C', $C \leqq C' < C + \delta$, exactly the same packing will be obtained with bin capacity C' as with C, and hence $FFD[\mathcal{T}, C'] > m$. However, by the definition of r_m, we know that there exist ratios r arbitrarily close to r_m for which $FFD[\mathcal{T}, r\mathcal{T}_m] \leqq m$. Choosing such an r with $r\mathcal{T}_m^* < C + \delta$, we obtain a contradiction to the assumed counter-example, proving that $FFD[\mathcal{T}, r_m \mathcal{T}_m^* \leqq m$.

Now suppose that, for some $\mathcal{T}$ and $\alpha > 1$, $FFD[\mathcal{T}, +\alpha r_m\mathcal{T}_m^*] > m$. We shall use $\mathcal{T}$ to construct a set $\bar{\mathcal{T}}$ for which $FFD[\bar{\mathcal{T}}, r_m\bar{\mathcal{T}}_m^*] > m$, contradicting what we have just proved. Consider any optimal packing of $\mathcal{T}$ into m bins of size $\mathcal{T}_m^*$. Enlarge the capacity of each optimal bin to $\alpha\mathcal{T}_m^*$ and augment $\mathcal{T}$ to form $\bar{\mathcal{T}}$ by adding new items, each smaller than the smallest item in $\mathcal{T}$, so that every enlarged bin becomes completely filled. Thus we have that $\bar{\mathcal{T}}_m^* =$

$\alpha \mathcal{T}_m^*$. Furthermore $FFD\ [\bar{\mathcal{T}},\ \alpha\ r_m \mathcal{T}_m^*] > m$ because the (m + 1)st bin will be started before any of the new items are placed. But then we have $FFD[\bar{\mathcal{T}}, r_m \bar{\mathcal{T}}_m^*] > m$, which is the desired contradiction. The lemma follows.

Thus r_m is indeed the desired minimum "expansion factor" and every capacity greater than $r_m \mathcal{T}_m^*$ will also work, so that we need not be concerned about possible anomalies. By determining the values of r_m, $m \geqq 2$, we will therefore be obtaining general answers to the question "how large does C have to be, in terms of $\mathcal{T}_m^*$?"

Table 1 gives the best upper and lower bounds we have discovered for r_m. As can be seen, we know the exact value of r_m for $2 \leqq m \leqq 7$, and our upper and lower bounds are quite close for $m \geqq 8$. Since $r_4 = r_5 = r_6 = r_7 = \frac{20}{17}$, and the best lower bound we have been able to find for $m \geqq 8$ is also $\frac{20}{17}$, we conjecture that in fact $r_m = \frac{20}{17}$ for all $m \geqq 4$.

The proofs of the lower bounds cited in Table 1 are straightforward, since all that is required is an example $\mathcal{T}$ such that $FFD(\mathcal{T}, C) > m$ whenever $C <$ (lower bound) $\cdot\ \mathcal{T}_m^*$. These lower bound examples for $m = 2$, $m = 3$, and $m \geqq 4$ are illustrated in Figures 1, 2, and 3. In each case the items are represented by rectangles which are labeled by their sizes, and the bins by stacks of items.

The proofs of the upper bounds for $m \leqq 7$ involve case analyses which grow more and more complicated as m increases. These proofs have been omitted at the suggestion of the referees, but a full version of this paper containing them is available from the authors. We shall limit ourselves here to proving the general 1.220 upper bound, which in fact holds for all $m \geqq 2$. The proof will be postponed until §§ 4 and 5, however, so that we may first see how we incorporate FFD into a scheduling algorithm, and how we use the values of r_m to bound the worst-case behavior of that algorithm.

3. THE ALGORITHM MULTIFIT

In the light of the results described in the preceding section, one might propose the following scheduling algorithm: Given $\mathcal{T}$ and m, set $C = r_m \cdot \mathcal{T}_m^*$ and run FFD on $\mathcal{T}$ and C. By definition of r_m, $\mathcal{P}_{FFD}[\mathcal{T}, C]$ will be made up of m or fewer sets, and hence will correspond to a valid schedule for $\mathcal{T}$ and m with finishing time $C = r_m \cdot \mathcal{T}_m^*$ or less, which would certainly be "near-optimal" in light of our bounds on r_m.

TABLE 1. Bounds on r_m

m	2	3	4, 5, 6, 7	8 or more
Upper bound on r_m	$\frac{8}{7}$	$\frac{15}{13}$	$\frac{20}{17}$	1.220
Lower bound on r_m	$\frac{8}{7}$	$\frac{15}{13}$	$\frac{20}{17}$	$\frac{20}{17} = 1.176\cdots$

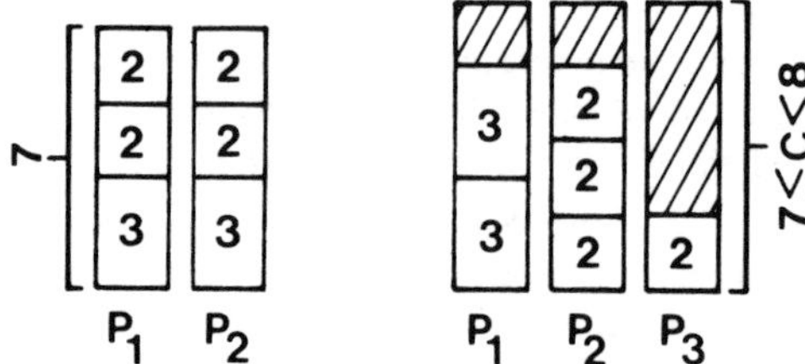

FIGURE 1. Example showing $r_2 \geqq 8/7$.

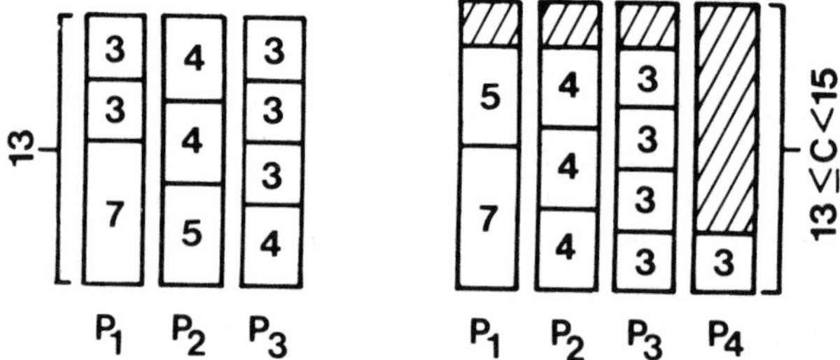

FIGURE 2. Example showing $r_3 \geqq 15/13$.

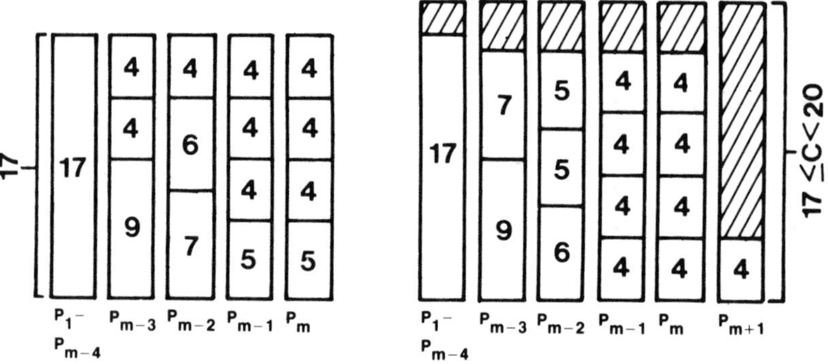

FIGURE 3. Example showing $r_m \geqq 20/17$, for all $m \geqq 4$.

Unfortunately this approach depends on knowing the value of $\mathcal{T}_m^*$ in advance, and it is just as difficult to determine $\mathcal{T}_m^*$ as to find an optimum schedule. A second idea would be to make repeated trials with FFD and different values of C until we find the least C for which $FFD[\mathcal{T}, C] \leqq m$, and take the schedule resulting from this bin capacity. If we assume that all tasks have integer lengths, there are two natural ways to attempt this. One would be to try each integer C in turn, starting from some obvious lower bound on $\mathcal{T}_m^*$, until we found one for which $FFC(\mathcal{T},C) \leqq m$; this would be the desired minimum value of C. Unfortunately, this procedure might require a large number of repeated trials of FFD and would be very costly in terms of running time. A common way of reducing the number of trials in such a search is to use *binary search*: Start with known upper and lower bounds on C, and at each step run FFD for a value of C midway between the current upper and lower bounds. If $FFD[\mathcal{T}, C] > m$, C becomes the new lower bound and we continue; if $FFD[\mathcal{T}, C] \leqq m$, C becomes the new upper bound. At each step we thus halve the potential range and so we should narrow in on the minimum value of C quite rapidly.

Unfortunately, binary search will only be guaranteed to do this if for every $C_1 < C_2$, $FFD[\mathcal{T}, C_1] \leqq m$ implies $FFD[\mathcal{T}, C_2] \leqq m$. Although this general monotonicity property does hold for $m = 2$, it fails for $m \geqq 3$. Figure 4 demonstrates that there exists a list $\mathcal{T}$ such that $FFD[\mathcal{T}, 60] = 3$ but $FFD[\mathcal{T}, 61] = 4$. Thus binary search is *not* guaranteed to find the least C such that $FFD[\mathcal{T}, C] \leqq m$. However, recall that Lemma 2.1 tells us that binary search *will* be guaranteed to narrow in on a capacity $C \leqq r_m \mathcal{T}_m^*$. Therefore, binary search can still be used to find a near-optimum schedule, and this is the approach taken in our algorithm MULTIFIT.

We begin our description of MULTIFIT by specifying the initial lower and upper bounds, C_L and C_U, used in the binary search. These are given in the following two lemmas.

Lemma 3.1 *Let* $C_L[\mathcal{T}, m] = \max\{(1/m)l(\mathcal{T}), \max_i\{l(T_i)\}\}$. *Then for all* $C < C_L[\mathcal{T}, m]$, $FFD[\mathcal{T}, C] > m$.

PROOF. This follows from the obvious fact that $\mathcal{T}_m^* \geqq C_L[\mathcal{T}, m]$.

FIGURE 4. $\mathcal{T}$ such that FFD$[\mathcal{T}, 61] >$ FFD $[\mathcal{T}, 60]$.

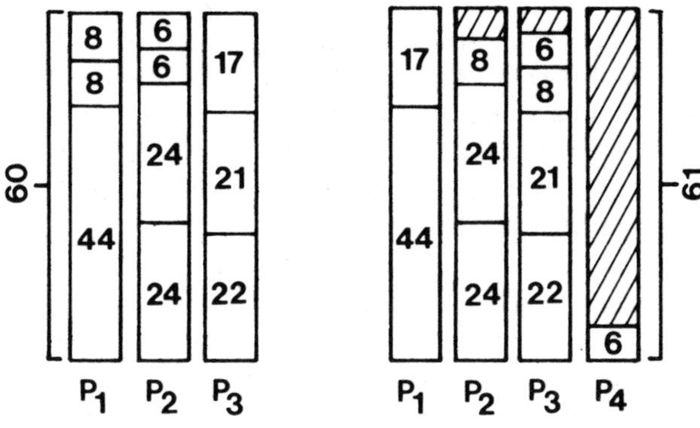

Lemma 3.2. *Let* $C_U[\mathcal{T}, m] = \max\{(2/m)l(\mathcal{T}), \max_i \{l(T_i)\}\}$. *Then for all* $C \geqq C_U\mathcal{T}, m]$, $FFD\ [\mathcal{T}, C] \leqq m$.

PROOF. Suppose $C \geqq C_U[\mathcal{T}, m]$ and $FFD[\mathcal{T}, C] > m$, and assume without loss of generality that $l(T_1) \geqq l(T_2) \geqq \cdots \geqq l(T_n)$, that is, $\mathcal{T}$ is indexed in nonincreasing order by item size. Let T_j be the first item to go in bin P_{m+1} under FFD. Clearly we must have $j \geqq m + 1$. If $l(T_j) > C/2$, then since $\mathcal{T}$ is indexed in nonincreasing order $l(T_i) > C/2$, $1 \leqq i \leqq m + 1$. This implies

$$l(\mathcal{T}) > \frac{mC}{2} \geqq \frac{mC_U[\mathcal{T}, m]}{2} \geqq l(\mathcal{T}),$$

a contradiction. If on the other hand $l(T_j) \leqq C/2$, then by the fact that T_j did not fit in any of the first m bins, each must have contained items whose total size exceeded $C/2$, and we again have $l(\mathcal{T}) > mC/2$ and a contradiction.

We are now prepared to give a precise description of MULTIFIT. MULTIFIT takes as input a task set $\mathcal{T}$, a number of processors m, and a bound k on the desired number of iterations. Its first step is to put $\mathcal{T}$ into nonincreasing order, so that all subsequent applications of FFD will not have to reorder $\mathcal{T}$ themselves. It then proceeds by binary search for the desired number of iterations as follows:

1. Set $CL(0) \leftarrow C_L[\mathcal{T}, m]$;
   $CU(0) \leftarrow C_U[\mathcal{T}, m]$;
   $I \leftarrow 1$.
2. If $I > k$, halt.
   Otherwise, set $C \leftarrow [CL(I-1) + CU(I-1)]/2$.
3. If $FFD[\mathcal{T}, C] \leqq m$, set $CU(I) \leftarrow C$;
   $CL(I) \leftarrow CL(I-1)$;
   $I \leftarrow I + 1$;
   and go to 2.
4. If $FFD[\mathcal{T}, C] > m$, set $CL(I) \leftarrow C$;
   $CU(I) \leftarrow CU(I-1)$;
   $I \leftarrow I + 1$;
   and go to 2.

The final value $CU(k)$ gives the smallest value of C found for which $FFD[\mathcal{T}, C] \leqq m$. Either the corresponding schedule has been generated along the way (and could have been saved, storage space permitting), or else it has not yet been generated because $CU(k) = C_U[\mathcal{T}, m]$. In either case, the schedule can now be generated by a single additional application of FFD, and this schedule is the output of MULTIFIT.

Before beginning our analysis of the worst case behavior of MULTIFIT, let us first examine how long it takes to run.

We first note that the application of FFD referred to in steps 3 and 4 need not be run to completion if $FFD[\mathcal{T}, C] > m$, but can be halted as soon as the first item enters bin P_{m+1}. This, plus the fact that $\mathcal{T}$ is already in decreasing order, means that each application of FFD need only take $O(nm)$ steps (and can actually be implemented to take $O(n \log m)$ steps using techniques described.[5] Thus the total time for MULTIFIT, including the initial sorting of $\mathcal{T}$ by size and the k iterations of FFD is $O((n \log n) + knm)$ or $O((n \log n) + (kn \log m))$, depending on implementation. This is to be compared to the time required to run the LPT algorithm.[2,3] LPT involves the same initial sorting step, followed by a packing procedure which is quite comparable to one execution of FFD's packing procedure, and also can be implemented to run in either $O(nm)$ or $O(n \log m)$ time. Thus LPT does have a slight advantage over MULTIFIT in timing when $k > 1$. However, as we shall see, there is apparently no reason to choose $k > 7$ in applying MULTIFIT, and thus for large values of n, both algorithms will have execution times dominated by the time for the initial sort, and hence will be comparable. Of course, for small values of n both algorithms are so fast as to make matters of relative timing purely academic.

We now turn to the question of how the two algorithms compare as to the quality of the schedules they produce. We have already presented in § 1 the main result about the worst-case behavior of LPT. For MULTIFIT, our main result is presented in Theorem 3.1, where $MF(k)$ stands for the version of MULTIFIT in which k is the specified number of iterations.

Theorem 3.1. *For all* $m \geqq 2$, $k \geqq 0$, $R_m(MF[k]) \leqq r_m + (1/2)^k$.

PROOF. Suppose m and k are such that $R_m(MF[k]) > r_m + (1/2)^k$. Recall from the definition of $R_m(A)$ in § 1 that this means there exists a $\mathcal{T}$ such that when $MF[k]$ is applied to $\mathcal{T}$ and m, the resulting schedule has finishing time exceeding $(r_m + (1/2)^k) \cdot \mathcal{T}^*_m$. Since this finishing time cannot exceed the final value $CU(k)$, we thus have

$$CU(k) \geqq (r_m + (1/2)^k) \cdot \mathcal{T}^*_m. \tag{3.1}$$

Consider the final value $CL(k)$. By the process of binary search, $CU(k) - CL(k) = (1/2)^k \cdot (C_U[\mathcal{T}, m] - C_L[\mathcal{T}, m]) \leqq (1/2)^k \cdot \mathcal{T}^*_m$, since $C_U[\mathcal{T}, m] \leqq 2\ C_L[\mathcal{T}, m]$ and $C_L[\mathcal{T}, m] \leqq \mathcal{T}^*_m$. Thus we must have

$$CL(k) \geqq r_m \cdot \mathcal{T}^*_m. \tag{3.2}$$

But then, since $r_m > 1$ for $m \geqq 2$, this means that $CL(k) > C_L[\mathcal{T}, m]$. This implies that FFD must have been performed with bin capacity $CL(k)$ at some point during the operation of the algorithm, and yielded $FFD[\mathcal{T}, CL(k)] > m$. However, this is impossible as, in light of (3.2), it violates Lemma 2.1.

Combining Theorem 3.1 with the bounds of r_m presented in Table 1, we present in Table 2 a comparison of the worst case behavior of $MF[k]$ and LPT for various values of m and k. The lower bound on $R_m(MF[k])$ for all k which is presented in the last row of the table follows from the same examples (Figures 1, 2, and 3) used to provide lower bounds on r_m.

TABLE 2. A Comparison of Worst Case Bounds

$m=$	2	3	4	5	10	50
$R_m(\text{LPT})=$	1.167	1.222	1.250	1.267	1.300	1.327
$R_m(MF[5])\leqq$	1.174	1.185	1.208	1.208	1.251	1.251
$R_m(MF[6])\leqq$	1.158	1.169	1.192	1.192	1.236	1.236
$R_m(MF[7])\leqq$	1.151	1.162	1.184	1.184	1.228	1.228
$R_m(MF[k])\leqq$	1.143	1.154	1.176	1.176	1.176	1.176

From Table 2 it can be seen that $MF[5]$ has better worst-case behavior than LPT for all $m \geqq 3$ and $MF[6]$ and $MF[7]$ are better for all $m \geqq 2$. Further improvement is possible by choosing larger values of k, but for $k = 7$ the bound is already quite close to the limiting value, except for the cases where $m \geqq 8$ and our bounds on r_m are not tight. If our conjecture that $r_m = \frac{20}{17}$ for all $m \geqq 8$ is true, then the upper bounds on $R_m(MF[k])$ for $m = 10$ and $m = 50$ would be the same as those for $m = 4$ and $m = 5$.

We remind the reader that the figures in Table 2, attractive as they are, are only *worst-case* bounds. In practice the algorithms can be expected to do much better. To get a feel for how much improvement might be expected, and how the algorithms might compare as to average-case behavior, three limited simulation tests were run, each covering 10 task sets with $m = 10$. In Test 1, each task set consisted of 30 tasks with sizes chosen independently according to a uniform distribution between 0 and 1. In Test 2 each task set again consisted of 30 tasks, this time with sizes being the sum of 10 independent choices from the uniform distribution, to simulate a normal distribution. For both these tests $C_L[\mathcal{T}, m]$ was taken as an estimate of $\mathcal{T}_m^*$, and since this could well have been an under-estimate, the values for $F_A[\mathcal{T}, m]/\mathcal{T}_m^*$ might be somewhat inflated. To circumvent this difficulty, in Test 3 we generated our task sets so that $\mathcal{T}_m^*$ was known in advance. We started with 10 tasks of size 1, divided each independently into 2, 3, or 4 subtasks, whose relative sizes were so randomly chosen. $\mathcal{T}$ consisted of the approximately 30 subtasks so constructed, and we automatically had $\mathcal{T}_{10}^* = 1$. (As a matter of curiosity, we might note that in no case did any of the algorithms reconstruct an optimum schedule, though all came close.)

Our results are summarized in Table 3, which for each test gives the average value of $F_A[\mathcal{T}, m]/\mathcal{T}_m^*$ (or our possibly inflated estimate of it) for LPT, $MF[7]$, and $MF[7]'$, where the last-named algorithm is the earlier and inferior version of MULTIFIT.[4]

TABLE 3. Average Values of $F_A[\mathcal{T}, m]/\mathcal{T}_m^*$

Test	1	2	3
LPT	1.074	1.023	1.051
$MF[7]$	1.024	1.023	1.016
$MF[7]'$	1.033	1.065	1.021

Due to the limited and somewhat arbitrary nature of these simulations, one should not be prepared to draw far-reaching conclusions from them. However, we might note that, although $MF[7]$ and LPT came out in a dead heat in Test 2, the improvement provided by $MF[7]$ over LPT is clear in the other two tests, where in fact $MF[7]$ found a better schedule in 19 out of the 20 cases, the remaining case being a tie. It also might be noted that $MF[7]$ always found its ultimate schedule by the 6th iteration, so that $MF[6]$ could just as well have been used, for a slight saving in running time.

4. UPPER BOUND PROOFS: PRELIMINARIES.

The problem of proving an upper bound on r_m is considerably simplified if we can focus our attention on a "normalized" situation. In this section we show how this can be done, and thus set up a framework for such proofs. We illustrate this framework by using it directly to prove an easy upper bound of $r_m \leqq 5/4 = 1.250$ for all $m \geqq 2$. In the next section we show how more sophisticated analysis can yield a 1.220 general bound. The same basic framework can also be used as a starting point when proving the exact upper bounds for $m \leqq 7$ summarized above in Table 1.

In what follows we shall be dealing primarily with sets $\mathcal{T}$ of items which are ordered by size. It is therefore convenient to define formally a *list* to be an ordered set $\mathcal{T} = \{T_1, T_2, \ldots, T_n\}$ such that $l(T_1) \geqq l(T_2) \geqq \cdots \geqq l(T_n)$. For any pair of integers $p \geqq q$, we define a *(p/q)-counterexample* to be a list $\mathcal{T}$ and number M of bins such that

$$FFD(\mathcal{T},p) > M \geqq OPT(\mathcal{T},q).$$

Thus, through it is possible to pack the items of $\mathcal{T}$ into M bins of capacity q, FFD is unable even to pack them into M bins of the larger capacity p. It is easy to see that $r_m > p/q$ implies the existence of a (p/q)-counterexample with $M = m$.

A *minimal (p/q)-counterexample* consists of a list $\mathcal{T}$ and number M of bins such that all of the following hold:

a. $\mathcal{T}$ and M form a (p/q)-counterexample;
b. For all lists $\mathcal{T}'$ satisfying (a), $|\mathcal{T}'| \geqq |\mathcal{T}|$;
c. For all m, $1 \leqq m < M$, $r_m \leqq p/q$.

Thus a (p/q)-counterexample is minimal if there exists neither a (p/q)-counterexample for the same number of bins having fewer items nor a (p/q)-counterexample for a smaller number of bins. It is not difficult to see that the existence of a (p/q)-counterexample implies the existence of a minimal (p/q)-counterexample. It follows that if $r_m > p/q$, there must exist a minimal (p/q)-counterexample having $M \leqq m$.

In a normalized proof of an upper bound r on r_m we assume the existence of a minimal (p/q)-counterexample, for a convenient p and q satisfying $r = p/q$, and derive a contradiction from that assumption. In such proofs we will be able to use many general properties which must be obeyed by such a minimal counterexample. We now turn to the task of deriving some of these properties.

We shall assume for the rest of this section that the list $\mathcal{T}$ and number m of processors provide a minimal (p/q)-counterexample. Our first observation is an immediate consequence of the definitions.

Lemma 4.1. *$\mathcal{T}$ and m must satisfy the following:*

a. *$FFD(\mathcal{T}, p) = m + 1$ and $OPT(\mathcal{T}, q) = m$;*

b. *All items on $\mathcal{T}$, except the last, are assigned to the first m bins by FFD.*

In all that follows, we shall let $\mathcal{P} = \langle P_1, P_2, \ldots, P_{m+1}\rangle$ be the FFD packing of $\mathcal{T}$ into bins of capacity p and $\mathcal{P}^* = \langle P_1^*, P_2^*, \ldots, P_m^*\rangle$ be the optimal packing of $\mathcal{T}$ into bins of capacity q. For subsets X and Y of $\mathcal{T}$, we shall say that X *dominates* Y if there is a $1-1$ mapping $f\colon Y \to X$ such that $l(y) \leqq l(f(y))$ for all $y \in Y$. Using this concept and the following lemma, we can draw some interesting conclusions about $\mathcal{P}$ and $\mathcal{P}^*$.

Lemma 4.2 (cancellation lemma). *Let $I, J \subseteq \{1, 2, \ldots, m+1\}$ be such that $|I| = |J| = k > 0$. Then the set $X = \bigcup_{i\in I} P_i$ cannot dominate the set $Y = \bigcup_{j\in J} P_j^*$.*

PROOF. Suppose X dominates Y, and let $f\colon Y \to X$ be the mapping involved. Consider the list $\mathcal{T}' = \mathcal{T} - X$ obtained by deleting the items of X from $\mathcal{T}$ while retaining the same relative ordering of the remaining items. Since we have deleted *exactly* those items which were contained in the bins P_i, $i \in I$, the FFD packing of $\mathcal{T}'$ will be identical to that for $\mathcal{T}$ except that those bins will be missing. Thus $FFD(\mathcal{T}', p) = m - k + 1$. Now consider the packing $\mathcal{P}^*$, and construct a new packing $\mathcal{P}'$ by interchanging each item $y \in Y$ with its image $f(y)$. Since $l(y) \leqq l(f(y))$, we thus must have $l(P_i') \leqq l(P_i^*)$ for all $i \notin J$, $1 \leqq i \leqq m$. Moreover, bins P_j', $j \in J$, contain only items of X (although they may have $l(\mathcal{P}_j') > q$). Thus by deleting all elements of X from $\mathcal{P}'$, we obtain a packing of $\mathcal{T}'$ into at most $m - k$ bins of capacity q. Hence $OPT(\mathcal{T}', q) \leqq m - k$, and since $m - k < m$, this contradicts the presumed minimality of $\mathcal{T}$ and m.

Lemma 4.3. $|\mathcal{P}_i^*| \geqq 3$, $1 \geqq i \geqq m$.

PROOF. Suppose first that $P_i^* = \{x\}$. Let j be such that $x \in P_j$. Then P_j dominates P_i^*, contrary to Lemma 4.2. Suppose next that $P_i^* = \{x, y\}$, where x precedes y in the (decreasing) ordering of $\mathcal{T}$. Suppose $x \in P_j$ and $y \in P_k$ in the FFD packing. If $j = k$, then P_j dominates P_i^*, a contradiction. Suppose $j < k$. Then the fact that y went to the right of the bin containing x, even though $l(x) + l(y) \leqq q < p$, means that P_j must have contained a second item z, in addition to x, when y was assigned. Thus z preceded y in $\mathcal{T}$ and so $l(z) \geqq l(y)$, and P_j

dominates P_i^*, again a contradiction. Finally, suppose $j > k$. Then, since y follows x in $\mathcal{T}$, it cannot be the first item to go in P_k; call that first item z. Since z is the first item in a bin to the left of the one containing x, z must have preceded x in $\mathcal{T}$ and hence $l(z) \geqq l(x)$. Therefore P_k dominates P_i^*, giving us our final contradiction.

Lemma 4.4 $|P_i| \geqq 2,\ 1 \leqq i \leqq m$.

PROOF. Suppose $P_i = \{x\}$, for some i, $1 \leqq i \leqq m$. Then we must have $l(x) + l(T_n) > p$, where T_n is the last, and hence smallest, item in $\mathcal{T}$. But this means that $l(x) + l(y) > q$ for all $y \in \mathcal{T}$, so if P_j is the optimal bin containing $|P_j^*| = 1$, contrary to Lemma 4.3.

The next lemmas obtain bounds on the item sizes. Let $\alpha = l(T_n)$ denote the size of the smallest item.

Lemma 4.5. $\alpha > (m/(m - 1))(p - q)$.

PROOF. For $1 \leqq i \leqq m$, since T_n did not fit in P_i, we have $l(P_i) + \alpha > p$. Hence

$$\sum_{i=1}^{m} l(P_i) + m\alpha > mp.$$

However, since all items are contained in m bins of capacity q in $\mathcal{P}^*$,

$$\sum_{i=1}^{m} l(P_i) + \alpha < mq.$$

The lemma follows.

Lemma 4.6. *For all* $T_i \in \mathcal{T}$, $l(T_i) \leqq q - 2\alpha$.

PROOF. This follows immediately from Lemma 4.3, which imples that T_i must be in a bin with at least two other items in $\mathcal{P}^*$.

At this point, we can already illustrate the use of these lemmas by proving an easy upper bound on r_m.

Theorem 4.1. *For all* $m \geqq 2$, $r_m \leqq 5/4$.

PROOF. Suppose $\mathcal{T}$ and m provide a minimal (5/4)-counterexample. By Lemma 4.5, $l(T_n) = \alpha > 1$. Thus no optimal bin can contain more than three items. By Lemma 4.3 this means that $|P_i^*| = 3,\ 1 \leqq i \leqq m$, and hence $|\mathcal{T}| = 3m$. By Lemmas 4.1 and 4.4, this means that there must be a P_i, $1 \leqq i \leqq m$, with $|P_i| = 2$. Let $P_i = \{x,y\}$. Since T_n did not go in P_i, we must have $l(x) + l(y) + \alpha > 5$. Thus by Lemma 4.3 we must have

$$5 < 2(q - 2\alpha) + \alpha = 8 - 3\alpha.$$

This imples $\alpha \leqslant 1$, a contradiction.

In order to prove stronger results, we will need to take a more detailed look at the FFD packing $\mathcal{P}$ of our minimal (p/q)-counterexample. Let us label the items of $\mathcal{T}$ according to their assigned locations in $\mathcal{P}$ as follows: If $|P_i| = k$, then the elements of P_i are denoted by $P_i[j]$, $1 \leqq j \leqq k$, in the order in which they were assigned to P_i. $P_i[j]$ is the first item assigned (the earliest in the ordering of $\mathcal{T}$) , and so on. A bin P_i, $1 \leqq i \leqq m$, is a *k-bin* if it contained exactly k items when first an item was assigned to a bin to its right (i.e., when $P_{i+1}[1]$ was assigned). This is in distinction to a *k-item bin*, which is merely a bin P_i, $1 \leqq i \leqq m$, with $|P_i| = k$. The *base level* $b(P_i)$ of a k-bin P_i, is defined as $\Sigma_{j=1}^{k} l(P_i[j])$, whereas the *final level*, or simply *level*, is just $l(P_i)$. If P_i is a k-bin, we call the items $P_i[j]$, $1 \leqq j \leqq k$, *regular items*, and all $P[j], j < k$, are called *fallback items*. A *fallback k-bin* is a k-bin P_i such that $|P_i| > k$, that is, one that contains fallback items. A *regular k-bin* is one which contains no fallback items. (Observe that none of these definitions applies to bin P_{m+1}, a bin which, being last, is atypical and will not enter very strongly into our arguments.)

The final lemma of this section gives a list of properties that follow from these definitions and the manner in which FFD operates.

Lemma 4.7. *In* $\mathcal{P} = \langle P_1, P_2, \ldots, P_{m+1} \rangle$,

a. *If* $P_i[j]$ *is a regular item, then it precedes in* $\mathcal{T}$ *all* $P_{i'} j'$ *with* $i < i' \leqq m + 1$ *and* $1 \leqq j' \leqq |P_{i'}|$, *and all* $P_i[j']$ *with* $j < j' \leqq |P_i|$.
b. *If* $1 \leqq k < k'$, *all k-bins are to the left of all k'-bins.*
c. *If* $\{P_i : s \leqq i \leqq t\}$ *is the set of k-bins, then* $b(P_s) \geqq b(P_{s+1}) \geqq \ldots \geqq b(P_t) > (k/(k+1)) \cdot p$.
d. *For each* $k > 1$, *all regular k-bins are to the left of all fallback k-bins.*

PROOF. Parts a, b, and c are all straightforward consequences of the fact that $\mathcal{T}$ is ordered by decreasing item size. We derive d from b and c by contradiction. Suppose P_i is a fallback k-bin, P_j is a regular k-bin, and $j > i$. Then, since T_n, the smallest item, went in a bin to the right of P_j, we have $b(P_j) + l(T_n) = l(P_j) + l(T_n) > p$. But we also have $l(P_i[k+1]) \geqq l(T_n)$ and, by (c), $b(P_i) \geqq b(P_j)$. Thus $l(P_i) \geqq b(P_i) + l(P_i[k+1]) \geqq b(P_j) + l(T_n) > p$, a contradiction.

We conclude from Lemma 4.1, Lemma 4.4, and Lemma 4.7, that if $\mathcal{P}$ is the FFD packing for a minimal (p/q)-counterexample, it consists of a (possibly vacuous) sequence of fallback 1-bins, followed by a (possibly vacuous) sequence of regular 2-bins, followed by a (possibly vacuous) sequence of fallback 2-bins, followed by a (possibly vacuous) sequence of regular 3-bins, and so on, with the last nonempty bin P_{m+1} containing the single item T_n, which is the last and hence smallest item on $\mathcal{T}$.

In § 5 we expand on this picture, using information derived from the particular values of $p = 122$ and $q = 100$ to derive a general bound $r_m \leqq 1.220$. More specific arguments, using values of m as well as those of p and q, are required when proving the exact upper bounds of Table 1.

5. THE GENERAL UPPER BOUND

Theorem 5.1 $R_M \leqq 1.22$ *for all* $m \geqq 2$.

PROOF. Suppose the theorem is false. Then there exists a minimal (122/100)-counterexample, provided say by $\mathcal{T} = \{T_1, T_2, \ldots, T_n\}$ and m. We first derive some constraints on the sizes of the items in $\mathcal{T}$.

By Lemma 4.5, we know that for some $\Delta > 0$,

$$l(T_n) = 22 + \Delta. \tag{5.1}$$

Since T_n is the smallest item, this means that all items are at least this large. Furthermore, by Lemma 4.6 we can conclude that

$$l(T_i) \leqq 56 - 2\,\Delta, \qquad 1 \leqq i \leqq n. \tag{5.2}$$

Our final observation gives us an upper bound on Δ. Suppose $\Delta > 4$. Then every item must have size exceeding 26, and so no bin in $\mathcal{P}^*$, with its capacity of 100, can contain more than 3 items. By Lemma 4.3, this means that all bins in $\mathcal{P}^*$ contain *exactly* 3 items, and $n = 3m$. On the other hand, if a bin P_i in $\mathcal{P}$, $1 \leqq i \leqq m$, contained two or fewer items, we would have $l(P_i) + l(T_n) \leqq 2(56 - 2\Delta) + (22 + \Delta) = 134 - 3\Delta < 122$, which would violate the FFD packing rule. Thus every one of the first m bins of $\mathcal{P}$ contains at least 3 items and so $n \geqq 3m + 1$, a contradiction. We thus conclude that

$$0 < \Delta \leqq 4. \tag{5.3}$$

The remainder of the proof consists of a weighting argument in which each item is assigned a ''weight'' based on its size and where it was placed in the FFD packing $\mathcal{P}$. This weighting will have the property that each P_i, $1 \leqq i \leqq m$, will contain items whose total weight is *at least* $100 - \Delta$. In addition, except for a very limited number of bins, in the optimal packing $\mathcal{P}^*$ each bin will contain weight *no more* than $100 - \Delta$. A conservation-of-total-weight argument will then allow us to contradict the assumption that we had a counterexample.

We group the items of $\mathcal{T}$ into seven classes based on the structure of $\mathcal{P}$ as it was described at the end of the previous section. Since all items have size less than 56 from (5.2), there are no fallback 1-bins in $\mathcal{P}$. Since all items exceed 22 in size from Equation 5.1, there are no bins in $\mathcal{P}$ which contain more than 5 items. We classify items as to which of the remaining possible bin types contain them, and as to size. The observations made concerning item sizes will follow from the fact that $\mathcal{P}$ is an FFD packing, and $l(P_i) > 122 - l(T_n) = 100 - \Delta$ for all i, $1 \leqq i \leqq m$.

The two items in each regular 2-bin, except the last (rightmost) such bin, both exceed $(100\text{-}\Delta)/2$ in size, and are *type-*X_2. If both items in the last regular 2-bin exceed $(100\text{-}\Delta)/2$ in size, they are also *type-*X_2; otherwise they are both *type-Z*.

TABLE 4. Item Weights $w(T_i)$

Item type	$0 < \Delta \leqq 12/5$	$12/5 < \Delta \leqq 4$
X_2	$50 - \frac{\Delta}{2}$	$50 - \frac{\Delta}{2}$
Y_2	$l - \Delta$	$l - \Delta$
X_3	$\frac{100}{3} - \frac{\Delta}{3}$	$\frac{100}{3} - \frac{\Delta}{3}$
Y_3	$l - \Delta$	$l - \Delta$
X_4	$25 - \Delta/4$	$25 - \Delta/4$
X_5	22	$25 - \Delta/4$
Z	l	l

The two regular items in each fallback 2-bin must total at least $2(122)/3$ in size, by Lemma 4.7(c), and are *type-*Y_2.

The three items in each regular 3-bin, except possibly the last one, all exceed $(100\text{-}\Delta)/3$ in size and are *type-*X_3. If all three items in the last regular 3-bin exceed $(100\text{-}\Delta)/3$ in size, they are also *type-*X_3; otherwise all three are *type-Z*.

The three regular items in each fallback 3-bin must total at least $3(122)/4$ in size, and are *type-*Y_3.

The four items in each regular 4-bin, except possibly the last one, all exceed $(100\text{-}\Delta)/4$ in size and are *type-*X_4. If all four items in the last regular 4-bin exceed $(100\text{-}\Delta)/4$ in size, they are also *type-*X_4; otherwise all four are again *type-Z*.

The remaining items are all of size at least $22 + \Delta$ and are *type-*X_5. These consist of T_n, all the fallback items in fallback 2- and 3-bins, and all the items in 5-item bins.

Now we are prepared to define our weighting function. The weight of an item depends on Δ, the item's type, and the item's size. These dependencies are described in Table 4, where l denotes the size of the item.
Observe from the table that

$$w(T_i) \leqq l(T_i), \quad \text{for all } T_i \in \mathcal{T}. \tag{5.4}$$

Moreover, for any fixed range of Δ, the weight of a *type-*X_{i+1} item never exceeds the weight of a *type-*X_i item, $2 \leqq i \leqq 4$, and all items have weight at least 22.

For any set S of items, let $w(S) = \Sigma_{T_i \in S}\, w(T_i)$. We first show that $w(P_i) \geqq 100 - \Delta$, $1 \leqq i \leqq m$. Clearly this holds for bins with two *type-*X_2 items, three *type-*X_3 items, or four *type-*X_4 items, and for all 5 item bins. Also, the (at most) three bins composed solely of *type-Z* items have this property since the sum of the item sizes in such a bin, as with all the other P_i, $1 \leqq i \leqq m$, must exceed $100\text{-}\Delta$, and each *type-Z* item has weight equal to its size.

This leaves just the fallback 2-bins and 3-bins to be accounted for. A fallback 3-bin contains three *type-*Y_3 items and one *type-*X_5 item, since the three *type-*Y_3 items total at least 3(122)/4 in size. Thus the total weight of such a bin is at least

$$\frac{3(122)}{4} - 3\Delta + 22 = 113.5 - 3\Delta > 100 - \Delta,$$

since $\Delta \leqq 4$ by (5.3).

A fallback 2-bin contains two *type-*Y_2 items whose total size is at least 2(122)/3 and hence one *type-*X_5 item. If $0 < \Delta \leqq 12/5$ the total weight of such a bin is at least

$$\frac{2(122)}{3} - 2\Delta + 22 = \frac{310}{3} - 2\Delta > 100 - \Delta.$$

On the other hand, if $12/5 < \Delta \leqq 4$, the total weight is at least

$$\frac{2(122)}{3} - 2\Delta + 25 - \frac{\Delta}{4} = \frac{319}{3} - \frac{9}{4}\Delta > 100 - \Delta.$$

Thus $w(P_i) \geqq 100 - \Delta$, $1 \leqq i \leqq m$, and in fact we can conclude that

$$w(\mathcal{T}) \geqq (100 - \Delta)m + w(T_n). \tag{5.5}$$

Next we consider the optimal packing $\mathcal{P}^*$. We first claim that no optimal bin containing a *type-*Y_2 or *type-*Y_3 item can exceed 100-Δ in total weight. This is clear since the weight of such an element is Δ less than its size, by (5.4) no other item weighs *more* than its size, and by definition $l(P_i^*) \leqq 100$, $1 \leqq i \leqq$ m.

Next we consider the possible optimal bins that contain only *type-*X_2, -X_3, -X_4, and -X_5 items. Recall that the sizes of such items are at least $(100 - \Delta)/2$, $(100 - \Delta)/3$, $(100 - \Delta)/4$, and $22 + \Delta$, respectively. Clearly no optimal bin can contain more than four of them and, by Lemma 4.3, each optimal bin must contain at least three items. Table 5 presents a partial enumeration of the conceivable configurations, for each stating whether it is permitted by the size constraints and, if so, the maximum possible weight for such a bin. A configuration is not listed if its total size clearly exceeds that for some listed con-

TABLE 5. Upper Bounds on $w(P_i^*)$ for Bins with All Type-X_i items

Configuration	$0 < \Delta \leqq 12/5$	$12/5 < \Delta \leqq 4$
$X_2 X_3$ —	Impossible	Impossible
$X_2 X_4 X_4$	$100 - \Delta$	$100 - \Delta$
$X_3 X_3 X_3$	$100 - \Delta$	$100 - \Delta$
X_2 — — —	Impossible	Impossible
$X_3 X_4$ — —	Impossible	Impossible
$X_3 X_5 X_5 X_5$	$100 - \dfrac{\Delta + 2}{3}$ $(0 < \Delta \leqq 1/4)$	Impossible
	Impossible $(1/4 < \Delta \leqq 12/5)$	
$X_4 X_4 X_4 X_4$	$100 - \Delta$	$100 - \Delta$

figuration which is "impossible," due to the size constraints, or if its total weight is trivially dominated by that for some permissible configuration already listed. In the table, a "—" in a configuration stands for *any type-*X_i item, $2 \leqq i \leqq 5$.

In no case does the maximum total weight for a permissible configuration exceed $100 - \Delta$. Thus any optimal bin whose total weight exceeds $100 - \Delta$ must contain at least one of the (at most) 9 *type-Z* items. From Equation 5.4 the total weight of any such optimal bin is at most 100, giving an "excess" weight of at most Δ. Since there are at most 9 such bins, we thus have

$$w(\mathcal{T}) \leqq (100-\Delta)m+9\Delta. \tag{5.6}$$

Combining (5.5) and (5.6), we obtain

$$w(T_n) \leqq 9\Delta. \tag{5.7}$$

For $0 < \Delta \leqq 12/5$, (5.7) implies that

$$w(T_n) \leqq 9\Delta \leqq 108/5 < 22,$$

a contradiction. When $12/5 < \Delta \leqq 4$, there can be only 5 *type-Z* items, as the four items in the last regular 4-bin must all exceed $22 + \Delta \geqq 25 - \Delta/4$ and hence are *type-*X_4 rather than *type-Z*. Thus in this case we must have

again a contradiction.

Having obtained contradictions in all cases, it follows that a minimal (122/100)-counterexample cannot exist, proving the theorem. □

The reader may have noted that there is a certain amount of slack left in the arguments of this proof, suggesting that better bounds could be proved using much the same methods. This is indeed the case, but all that seems possible is a very slight lowering of the bound—not enough to reduce it to 1.21, for instance. Since we conjecture that the right answer is $20/17 = 1.176 \cdots$, we have settled for the 1.22 bound, judging that the additional effort and complication that might be introduced by an attempt to obtain such a slight improvement would not be justified.

REFERENCES

1. K. R. Baker, Introduction to Sequencing and Scheduling, New York: John Wiley, 1974.
2. R. L. Graham, Bounds on multiprocessing timing anomalies, SIAM J. Appl. Math., 17, pp. 416–429, 1969.
3. ———, Bounds on the performance of scheduling algorithms, Computer and Job/Shop Scheduling Theory, E. G. Coffman, ed., New York: John Wiley, Chap. 5, 1976.
4. D. S. Johnson, Fast allocation algorithms, Proceedings. 13th Annual IEEE Symposium on Switching and Automata Theory, IEEE, New York, pp.144–154, 1972.

5. ———, Near-optimal bin-packing algorithms, Ph.D. thesis, Mathematics Department, Massachusetts Institute of Technology, Cambridge, 1974.
6. D. S. Johnson, A. Demers, J. D. Ullman, M. R. Garey, and R. L. Graham, Worst-case performance bounds for simple one-dimensional packing algorithms, SIAM J. Comput., pp. 299–326, 1974.
7. S. Sahni, Algorithms for scheduling indpendent tasks, J. Assoc. Comput. Mach., 23, pp. 116–127, 1976.
8. J. D. Ullman, Complexity of sequencing problems, Computer and Job/Shop Scheduling Theory, E. G. Coffman, ed., New York. John Wiley, Chap. 4, 1976.

PART IX

ASSOCIATION FOR EDUCATIONAL DATA SYSTEMS

Two papers selected
by AEDS from papers submitted during 1978.

"The Whens and Hows of Computer Based Instructional Simulation"
Robert S. Ellinger and Bobby R. Brown

"A Management Information System for Academic Administrators"
Michael J. Powers

The Association for Educational Data Systems (AEDS) is a private, non-profit educational organization founded in 1962 by a group of professional educators and technical specialists in educational applications. Its intention is to provide a forum for the exchange of ideas and information about the relationship of modern technology to modern education.

The members of the association include educators and technical experts representing public elementary and secondary schools, higher education, state and local departments of education, and other professional and technical groups interested in educational applications of data processing technology.

AEDS is the host for an annual conference which attracts international attendees and exhibitors. There are 25 chapters, including two in Canada, which conduct workshops throughout the year on topics related to educational data processing. AEDS is a member of American Federation of Information Processing Societies.

AEDS publishes three quarterly periodicals: the AEDS Bulletin, Monitor, and Journal; as well as proceedings of the annual convention.

AEDS is located at 1201 Sixteenth Street, N. W., Washington, D. C. 20036.

A Management Information System for Academic Administrators

Michael J. Powers

Associate Professor and Director of Applied Computer Science at Illinois State University

In times of decreasing financial support, declines and shifts in enrollment, and ever increasing demands for accountability the academic administrator has a critically important role to play as a manager of resources. In general the academic administrator, especially at the dean or department chair level, is not well prepared for this role; his appointment is more likely to be based on scholarly achievement than on management experience or skill. The problem is compounded by the general lack of information support systems tailored to the specific needs of the academic administrator. This paper examines the problem of providing such information support systems. It describes a pilot project for providing this support in phases which are coordinated with the academic administrator's increasing sophistication as a manager of resources.

THE ACADEMIC ADMINISTRATOR AS MANAGER

The term "academic administrator" refers here to the positions of provost, dean and department chairperson. This is distinguished from the term nonacademic administrator which includes the various business functions, admissions, registration, and so on. The nonacademic administrator at a university has long been recognized as a manager. Indeed, his duties and responsibilities are not significantly different from what one would expect to find in the commercial world.

EDITOR'S NOTE: *Presented at AEDS Annual Convention, May 1978. Reprinted by permission of the author.*
This paper won the Best Paper Award of the 1978 AEDS Annual Convention.

The academic administrator, on the other hand, has not been traditionally viewed as a manager. His appointment to and retention in his administrative position is more likely to be based on scholarly achievement than on management experience or skill. Whether good or bad, this is a reality based on a long tradition and hence is not likely to change appreciably in the near future. Unfortunately, however, life is changing for the academic administrator in ways he cannot control. He may have been chosen as a scholar and he may be evaluated as a scholar, but his financial support is decreasing and student enrollments are declining and shifting around him. His very survival and the survival of those under him will be critically influenced by his ability to manage the resources at his disposal.

The problem, then, is that the academic administrator will have thrust upon him a very definite management role; but because of background and interest, he may be ill prepared to accept that role. It is unrealistic to believe that the problem can be solved by an overnight change in the reward structure under which he operates. The only feasible approach is (1) to train the academic administrator in how to manage (an especially critical need at the department chairperson level) and (2) to provide the information tools required to support his management function. This paper concerns a pilot project to define and provide the key information tools which can be used by the academic administrator to support his efforts in the management and allocation of resources. But it must be viewed in context. Reports do not make decisions, people do. Reports can support the decision making process, but their level of sophistication must match the level of managerial sophistication of the academic administrator who is using them.

The following section discusses the nature of the information required by the academic administrator and the problems inherent in providing information support to academic managers. It is followed by sections which describe the multiphase approach used in the pilot project.

INFORMATION SUPPORT FOR THE ACADEMIC ADMINISTRATOR

The Nature of the Information Required by the Academic Administrator

There are certain roadblocks inherent in attempting to provide information support for academic administrators. An understanding of the nature of these roadblocks can help avoid many hours of frustration. But first it helps to have a general understanding of the functions within an organization which require information support. A nice overview of these ideas, together with additional references is given in a paper by Foster and Gamble of Cincom Systems. The point is to build a logical model of the organization based on *what* the organization does, *not how* it does it. The basic building blocks are *events* which are made up of tasks or activities. There are three types of events.

Operational events occur on a day to day basis as the organization provides its service. Universities register students, schedule classes, assign classes to classrooms, hire faculty, provide student financial aid, and so on. These events provide the basic data about the university.

Control events occur to monitor and regulate the operational events in order to optimize the performance of the organization within the context of objectives established by the organization. Data generated by operational events are used by control events. Control events in a university include monitoring class size and setting class enrollment levels, evaluation of faculty performance, budget control, and so on.

Planning events occur in order to define objectives and to establish strategies for accomplishing these objectives. Again data generated by operational events are used, together with certain data from outside the organization (e.g., national or regional college enrollment trends) to produce historical summaries and future trend information for use in the planning events.

The Provost and Deans are almost exclusively involved with planning events; department chairmen are involved with control events and *should be* involved with planning events. Note that the information to support the control and planning events is generated by the operational events—the basic business functions of the university.

Roadblocks to Providing Useful Information for the Academic Administrator

One significant roadblock is the academic administrator himself. As mentioned before, he has limited management experience. The reward structure in which he operates provides no real motivation for him to develop this management experience. And even when he does recognize his management role, he is usually unable to define the information support he requires. Some form of "gentle" management training is required.

The organization itself is a second major roadblock. First of all, information to support the *planning events* of academic administrators usually does not exist, at least in a format which is convenient and useable by a person who is likely to be a novice manager. Most moderate to large academic organizations have well defined computer based systems to support the operational events. Examples include systems for class scheduling, registration, financial aid, the usual accounting functions, and so on. Control events are usually supported reasonably well by these same systems. Ideally, of course, systems to support planning events should also be based on these operational support systems, but in most cases systems support for planning functions is grossly deficient. The support which does exist is often a poor adaptation of a system designed to support control functions. Even that is usually directed toward the nonacademic areas of the university, the governing board, and various external agencies rather than toward the academic administrator.

Worse yet, the organizational structure of the university can almost guarantee that information support for the academic administrator will not come easily. The placement of the computer and systems support function within the organizational structure of the typical university severely hampers the academic administrator who wishes to define the information systems necessary to support his planning activity. In the typical business organization there is a direct vertical relationship from the clerical or production level, which is involved with operational events, through middle management levels, involved with control events, to upper level management, involved with planning events (see Figure 1). Upper management's planning activity is a direct outgrowth of the control and operational activities below it. Planning systems can be defined as natural extensions of the more basic systems. Equally important, upper management is in a position, politically, to ensure support for these systems.

A similar vertical relationship exists in the academic institution, but it is based on the business/administrative side of the organization instead of the academic side. Academic administrators are not part of this vertical structure. Their planning support needs do not grow quite as naturally out of existing operational and control systems. But more importantly they are not in a position politically to ensure the support they require (see Figure 2).

Recognizing these problems helps the organization to deal with them. A significant amount of data concerning the operation of the university may well be available. But if it is not packaged as part of a system to support the planning activity of academic administrators, attempting to use it in that way will only produce frustration.

Dealing with the organizational problem involves the solution of certain political problems; this will likely be both difficult and time consuming. Ultimately a solution is necessary; short term it may not be. The pilot project de-

FIGURE 1.

BUSINESS ORGANIZATION

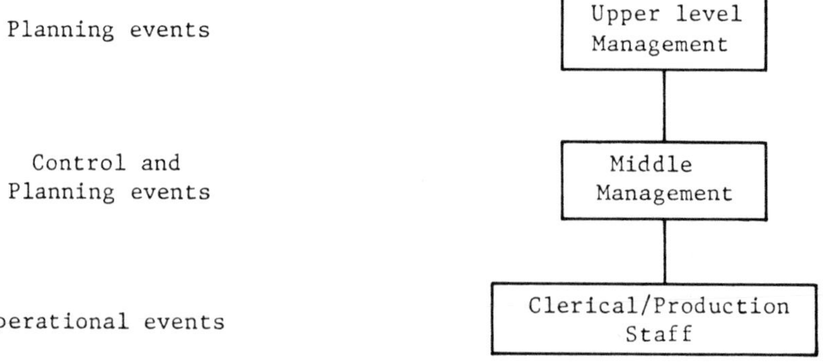

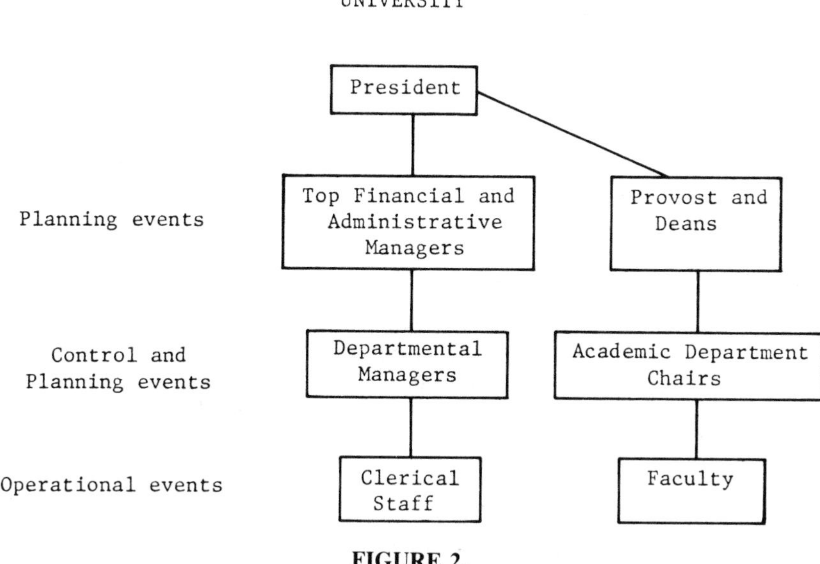

FIGURE 2.

scribed here is being carried on totally outside the Computer Services area using the resources of the Applied Computer Science faculty and students.

Management Training and its Impact on Information System Design

The overall objective of the pilot project described here was to provide a set of information tools to support academic administrators in their managerial decision making processes. These tools would be directed almost exclusively to planning activities as opposed to control activities. While the actual design and implementation of such a management information system can be a significant challenge, the definition of requirements which must precede it can be even more difficult. The users of the system must, in the final analysis, make these definitions. Recognizing that the administrators involved had differing levels of sophisticaction in the use of computer reports as management tools, a multiphase approach was taken. The basic idea was to implement a first approximation to a solution as quickly as possible. It was an accepted part of the overall plan that this initial implementation would be relatively short-lived. The initial implementation was in part a tool by which user sophistication could increase. Suggestions for refinements would be expected as the tools were used, thus laying a solid groundwork for a more sophisticated set of tools in the future.

The approach, then, contained the following elements:

involvement of key academic administrators with at least a moderate level of "managerial sophistication" in the initial definition of the information requirements,

provision of an initial set of tools to be used by a larger group of administrators within the context of "gently" training them in their roles as managers,

revision and extension of the initial set of tools based on experience gained from their use,

continued repetition of these last two steps.

This follows the fairly traditional approach to providing management information support (see Figure 3). The significant difference in this setting is that, given the relatively low level of management sophistication at the start, one expects fairly substantial gains each time through the cycle. This, of course, results in continuing *substantial* changes in the information system. This is costly, but well worth it. The approach serves as a catalyst: it captures the attention and interest of the academic administrator and helps him define his needs as his management ability evolves.

DEFINITION OF THE BASIC SYSTEM

Thus far the project has centered in the College of Arts and Sciences with fifteen academic departments and eighteen distinct cost centers. The principal driving force behind the initiation of the project was the dean of the college

FIGURE 3.

INFORMATION SYSTEM LIFECYCLE

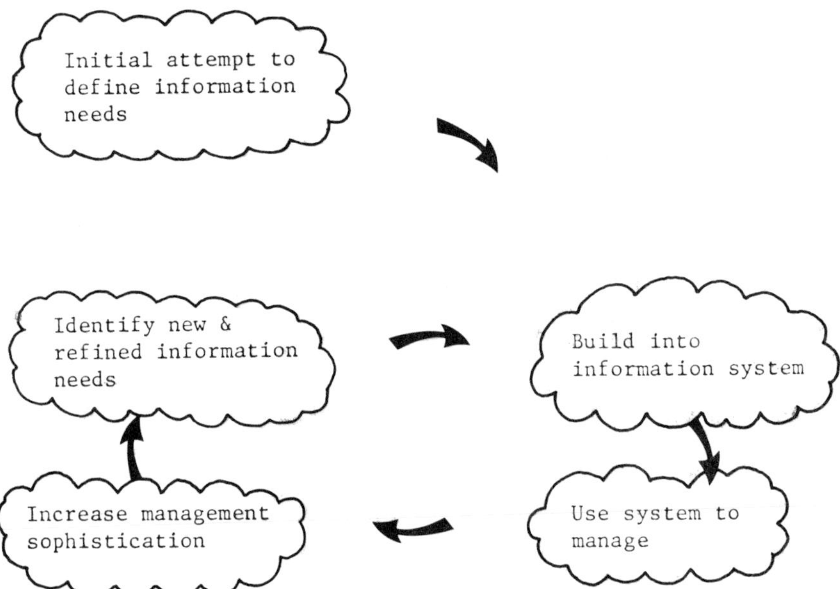

who felt a strong need for reasonably rapid access to information which could support a plan for continuous evaluation of programs in terms of quality, trends, and efficient utilization of resources.

The Basic Reports

The first phase of the project was primarily concerned with the analysis of historical data, with an elementary forecasting capability to be added in phase two. The first step was to define a set of reports which could serve as a good first approximation to an ultimate solution and which were feasible to implement using limited resources and drawing off data produced by existing systems supporting the basic operational events of the university.

It soon became apparent that, if anything, the academic administrator was bombarded with too much data. He received too much detail in some areas, not enough in others, and rarely was it packaged in a format which supported his planning activity. The primary objective, then, was to define a department based report which would contain, in compact form, the essential information required to support basic planning for resource utilization at the department and college level.

The result was a very compact and readable *Department Profile Report* which presents in highly summarized form the key information, from a performance and resource utilization perspective, concerning a department's operation. The report for each department is less than five pages long and has columns to display up to nine years of information. College and university level summaries are also available in the same format. The information is organized in six sections outlined below.

1. Student Data
   Average number of majors and minors per semester categorized by undergraduates and graduates both on-campus and extension.
   Number of degrees awarded in that major for the year categorized by degree type.
   Placement of graduates for the year categorized by degree type and type of placement (teaching, nonteaching, advanced education, other).
2. Department Course Data
   Average number of students enrolled in courses within the department per semester categorized by course level.
   Average number of credit hours produced by the department per semester categorized by course level.
3. Faculty Status Data
   Faculty FTE allocated to the department categorized by regular lines and temporary lines.
   Number of faculty holding rank in the department categorized by tenured, probationary, temporary and by percent of assignment within the department.

The tenure status of the faculty, showing the number tenured and probationary faculty by rank and the number of tenure decisions to be made that year.

4. Faculty Assignment Data

   The number of faculty FTE allocated and the number actually assigned in several categories: direct instruction, indirect instruction, administration, sabbatical, research, and other.

   The number of graduate and undergraduate assistants allocated.

   A teaching load ratio of credit hours produced to FTE assigned to direct instruction.

5. Faculty Activity Data

   The number of publications produced by faculty in the department in various categories.

   The number of research and service projects in progress.

   A measure of the external grants applied for and received.

6. Financial Data

   Dollars budgeted and actually spent for the fiscal year within each account category.

   A productivity ratio of total dollars spent to credit hours generated.

The tremendous power of this tool lies in its compactness and its completeness. The academic administrator has, contained within five pages, a complete profile of his operation for up to nine years. This report may well flag certain trouble spots which require a more detailed examination. With this in mind several slightly more detailed reports were designed. Two of these are briefly described below.

The *Department Majors* report shows, for each department, where its majors are generating credit hours. There is a two page report for each department, one for on-campus and one for off-campus majors. For each course level (100, 200, etc.) the number of hours generated by the department's majors is shown. These hours are broken into five groups. The top four departments in which the majors generated hours that term are listed separately, with all remaining hours placed in the fifth group. The format permits up to five columns for which the user may specify the semesters desired. Trends in credit hour generation by a given department's majors are easy to spot.

The *Course Enrollment Analysis* report reverses the view given by the Department Majors report. It analyzes each course offered by the department in terms of which majors are taking the course. For each course the number of enrollments are broken into five groups. The top four majors enrolled in that course are listed separately, with all remaining enrollments placed in the fifth group. The percentage of students successfully completing the course are also shown for each group. The format permits up to three columns for for which the user may specify the semesters desired. Trends in student enrollments and the effects of shifting distributions among majors at the university are highlighted nicely.

The data base designed to support this system permits several other detailed reports, but the reports presented above are representative of the key tools provided by the first phase of the project. While these reports cover only past history, they do provide the academic administrator with a helpful perspective on where his unit is coming from, together with any apparent trends. And this perspective is presented in a unified manner within the context of the entire operation of the unit, not as a random smattering of disjoint pieces of data. To be sure, the system is not sufficiently flexible and it lacks some highly desirable modeling capabilities. But it represents an effective first step. It is a useful tool in its own right. And it can be used to help academic administrators gain the necessary managerial sophistication to permit them to play an active role in the definition of a more flexible system.

An Overview of the Initial System Design

A detailed description of the system design is not appropriate here. The design is too dependent on local conditions, especially on the local systems used to support the various "operational events." There are, however, several ideas which are transportable and hence of general interest.

This first phase of the system contained two major subsystems: a file building and maintenance subsystem and a report writing subsystem. The file building activity was designed to draw on existing computer files whenever possible, using separate manual input only in those instances when the required data was not already captured in machine readable form. The subsystem maintains four *highly summarized* sequential files.

1. The "program-majors file" contains one record for each major in each year/term. Each record contains the number of majors and minors, the number of graduates and their placement, and the hours generated by those majors in various departments (at the same level of detail as that used in the Department Majors report).
2. The "department-course file" contains one record for each course in each department in each year/term. Each record contains enrollment data at the same level of detail as the course analysis report.
3. The "personnel file" contains one record for each department in each year/term. Each record contains the data to support the faculty status, assignment, and activity sections of the department profile report.
4. The "financial file" contains one record for each department in each fiscal year. Each record contains the budget and actual figures in each account category.

Typically each file is updated by summarizing several highly detailed files designed to support various existing operational event oriented systems. The procedure is clumsy, but need not be frequently performed. The clumsiness and inflexibility is unavoidable, due largely to the fact that existing "operational event" systems were not designed to accommodate "planning event" systems for academic administrators.

With respect to the report writing subsystem, note that the implementation of the Department Profile report is not at all a straightforward problem. For each department, up to nine years worth of data from each of the four files must be used to print a single section of the report. Good structured design techniques are essential here.

FUTURE DEVELOPMENT OF THE SYSTEM

A forecasting capability will be added during the second phase of the project. Just as in phase one, the real challenge will lie in defining the capabilities desired and the rules under which they will operate. During the next year while the phase one reports are used by the Dean of Arts and Sciences and his department chairpersons as part of a review-evaluation-planning activity, a small subset of these people will begin to define the forecasting requirements. The approach will be simple and straightforward, providing only those capabilities which current academic administrators will be able to effectively use as management tools. Implementation will probably consist of a new subsystem to generate "future records" based on a set of input parameters and the historical records in each of the four files of the data base. The input parameters will involve, among other things, assumptions about overall enrollment trends, shifting patterns of student interest, and financial support available. The report writing subsystem can then be used to display combinations of historical data and forecasted data in the familiar format of the reports from phase one.

The system, even at the end of phase two, will be far from ideal. It will be clumsy, only moderately responsive, and rather inflexible in terms of its ability to meet currently undefined needs. A real purpose will have been served; a set of tools will have been provided where none currently exist. Yet the more successful these tools are, the sooner they will become inadequate. As the users become more sophisticated in the use of these reports as management tools, they will demand more timeliness and flexibility. It seems, at this point, that the ultimate solution must involve a redefinition of certain key "operational event" systems and their implementation in a database environment. This will be a major undertaking. It involves far more than plunging ahead and purchasing a database management system and then converting existing systems to it. It means first modeling a significant part of the organization in terms of operational, control, and planning events. Both the academic and nonacademic arms of the organization must be involved. The fundamental thesis of this approach[1] is that the operational events of an organization remain fairly constant, while the planning events are the most volatile. To first model the organization and then establish the database design giving heaviest (but not exclusive) weight to the design implications imposed by the operational events will result in a more stable and flexible database design. Ideally, phase three will include this organizational modeling and database software support in the key operational areas. This will provide the necessary technical base to support planning oriented systems for academic administrators. As a result of the first two phases academic administrators will have grown in their ability to use information systems to manage their areas, and they will have a clear understanding of their information requirements.

REFERENCE

1. Foster, Cory and Ocie Gamble, "Information System Architecture," Cincon Systems, Inc., Cincinnati, 1976.

The Whens and Hows of Computer Based Instructional Simulation

Robert S. Ellinger

Department of Geography University of Iowa

Bobby R. Brown

Gerard P. Weeg Computing Center University of Iowa

Computer Assisted Instruction (CAI) and in particular that subgroup of CAI called Computer Based Instructional Simulation (CBIS) can be an effective tool for teaching certain types of concepts. This is particularly true for instructional simulation. This paper will address three questions. First, what makes a good CBIS? Second, for what types of learning is CBIS best suited, when is the CBIS doing its job? Third, how do you evaluate the job it's doing?

INTRODUCTION

Computer Assisted Instruction (CAI) and in particular that subgroup of CAI called Computer Based Instructional Simulation (CBIS) can be an effective tool for teaching certain types of concepts. To date, however, most studies comparing CBIS with other teaching methods have measured aspects of the student's performance for which the traditional teaching forms would be expected to perform at their best, e.g., factual recall and concept definition. This is due in large measure to the fact that current evaluation methods are best suited to evaluating the results of these types of learning. It has long been recognized that CBIS does have unique capabilities for teaching; often these capabilities have been referred to as desirable but unassessed benefits (Edwards).

EDITOR'S NOTE: *Presented at AEDS annual Convention, May 1978. Reprinted by permission of the authors.*

This paper will specify these benefits and test for them in a CBIS package. In order to assess the potential benefits of CBIS, we will address three questions. First, what makes a good CBIS? Second, for what types of learning is CBIS best suited? Third, how should you evaluate the effectiveness of CBIS? We will suggest testing methods and demonstrate their use on two CBIS packages.

GENERAL PROPERTIES OF CAI

Many properties of CAI have been touted as desirable features of an instructional system. Among these are student motivation, feedback, error detection and correction, reproducibility of teaching, the lack of perturbability of the computer, freedom of students to work at their own pace, the individualization of instruction, the ability to improve the way the material is taught, and the record-keeping ability of the computer (Inbar and Stoll). While we do feel that *all* of these attributes are important and are achievable on a fully developed CAI package, CAI packages to date have not made proper use of even these features because of the inexperience of program authors and lack of guidelines for them; this has led to much justified criticism of CAI.

One potential benefit of CAI was not mentioned in the list above; the potential for providing enhanced ''intuitive grasp'' of concepts and interrelationships. Alfred Bork (1977) notes that:

> ''A complaint often registered at doctoral examinations is that some graduate students can carry out the mathematical manipulations, even for very advanced problems, but have little physical intuition as to what is happening.''

He goes on to suggest that CBIS or ''controlled worlds'' will give the student the experience and insight necessary to gain the intuition to understand the problem.

WHEN: EFFECTIVE INSTRUCTIONAL DESIGN FOR CBIS

As has been suggested, CBIS is exceptionally effective for teaching certain types of concepts and quite unsuitable for teaching other types. CBIS is particularly well suited for teaching process concepts, the interrelationships between process concepts, and multifaceted/multistep problem solving.

Process Concepts

Process concepts are conceptualizations of processes. Normally, these processes take place through time and across space. Process concepts are at the highest level of cognitive learning and the student needs the maximum amount of assistance. This type of concept is difficult to teach using traditional methods because the processes cannot be shown in action—when they can, as in a movie, the student has no control over the independent variables nor the environment. In physics, chemistry, and biology the laboratory has been used to supplement the material taught in the classroom, so that the student gains a greater understanding of the process by experience—the experiment. Pedagogic experiments are performed with the student "controlling" the variables so that he can see the cause-effect relationship and the processes in action. Unfortunately many processes take too long, are too subtle to be noticed, or are too cosmic or too microscopic in nature to be brought into the laboratory. But, as Bork noted, the intuitive understanding of these concepts can be extremely important. Further, the social sciences face another problem; the objects of interest are the economy, the political and social systems, and the people of a region. And students cannot experiment with these processes—only politicians can. For these types of concepts CBIS can fill the laboratory-learning gap.

CBIS has many of the positive instructional attributes of well planned lab work, plus certain advantages over laboratory experiments. Depending on the type of terminal—teletype or teletype emulator CRT, semigraphics CRT, graphics CRT, or color graphics CRT—a CBIS can come extremely close to duplicating the feel of the laboratory situation for the student. The advantages of CBIS include: the enhancement of certain features of the experimental experience so that these features are perceived the first time through; the ability to speed up or slow down time; and the ability to enlarge or contract the space that the experiment requires, so that the patterns and processes can be easily perceived. Thus, CBIS can be used to great advantage for teaching process concepts because it can focus on and enhance the image of a process as it is simulated.

Interrelationships Between Concepts

The relationships between concepts are also difficult to teach, especially when the concepts involve processes. Relationships between concepts are difficult to teach using traditional methods because traditional teaching methods are static, so cause-effect relationships are difficult to demonstrate. While the demonstration of the general form of relationships is possible using audio-visual aids, the student will still have difficulty coming to an understanding of the magnitude of the relationship. This is the second type of concept for which CBIS is ideally suited. CBIS allows the student to guide or use the independent variables to predict variables. When the student creates the causes and sees the effects, the magnitude of the relationship should become apparent. And by understanding the magnitude of the relationship he should be able to predict the effect that the given values of an independent variable will have on the dependent variable and to choose values of independent variables that will produce a given effect on the dependent variables—two ways that a student can demonstrate a clear and accurate understanding of the relationship between the variables.

Multifaceted/Multistep Problem Solving

Multifaceted/multistep problem solving is the third type of learning that is properly taught using CBIS. Problem solving techniques, particularly when the problems have multiple variables, or use multiple step procedures, are among the most difficult types of procedures to teach because they involve both cognitive and behavioral learning processes. CBIS can provide the controlled environment in which the student can learn part or all of the problem solving techniques that he will need to know before he actually is faced with the problem.

Multifaceted/multistep problems are those that usually require repeated practice to learn to solve, or those techniques that students "learn by doing"; examples of such problems include learning to play in competitive sports, drive a car, fly an aircraft, handle complex machinery, diagnose and repair communications equipment, or design and construct lighting for plays. For several of these examples CBIS has long been used. Learning emergency procedures on aircraft is a prime example—it would be bad for business to lose several Boeing 747s while pilots were practicing in them. Other examples, while less dramatic, can be cited to illustrate the use of CBIS to help the "students" learn problem solving techniques. Diagnostic techniques are being taught to medical students in preparation for their practice on patients. Law students can practice preparing and presenting briefs and cases. Business students in accounting, management and marketing use CBIS to practice their decision making. In all cases multiple variables need to be accounted for, and there are multiple problems to be solved.

Since the early 1960's, many business schools have used noninteractive simulations, like the "Executive Game" to teach their MBA students management techniques in a competitive business situation. The students compete against one another with profit being the main criterion for deciding success or failure. Since many of these games have since been written or rewritten in interactive simulations, e.g., Market, they must be valuable to teaching management procedures. These management procedures that are being taught are of the multifaceted/multistep variety. In the management games, some variables are controlled by the student and others are not. Independent variables include the price of the goods, the fixed and variable costs associated with producing the goods, research and developments costs, and marketing costs, plus a sundry of other controllable costs depending on the simulation. Independent variables that are not controlled by the student include the prices and advertising investments of other firms (students) and "random" events like new labor costs and fires in warehouses. This forces the student to make decisions in a realistic manner or face business failure and a low grade in the course. Likewise, it gives him a chance to see how good his problem solving ability is when compared to his peers, so that he can decide whether he should attempt a career in management, and also where his strengths and weaknesses lie.

Simulations designed to help the student learn diagnostic, problem-solving, or decision making techniques must have output that is sufficiently realistic so that the student feels he is actually making the decisions or solving the problem while he is running the simulation—otherwise the simulation is at least a partial failure. So for simulation designed for this purpose in particular, the mode of output is extremely important.

HOW: PROPERTIES OF CBIS: THEIR USE AND EVALUATION

The Use of Special Properties of CBIS

When you decide to write a CBIS for teaching, there are several properties of CBIS that you should be aware of. First, CBIS should be used only when it is the best instructional method for the material. Second, good CBIS should use the maximum capabilities of the terminals and computer system. Third, as CBIS becomes complex it should have more documentation. Fourth, a good CBIS package should contain sufficient ancillary material and programming to make learning easy for the student.

Use CBIS Only When Needed

The best known, and by far the most realistic and sophisticated CBIS's, the simulations of every phase of the Apollo moon missions, were constructed for teaching process concepts, the relationships between concepts, and multifaceted problem solving abilities. Astronauts and ground personnel were given every conceivable type of problem to solve that might be encountered during a mission. They repeatedly practiced solving these problems, learning the relationships of the system hardware and software in the process, to the point that when a potential catastrophe occurred in Apollo 13 the CBIS system actually produced the solution to the problem. So first, good CBIS should concentrate on teaching processes or process concepts, their relationships, and multi-faceted-problem solving. Other less time-consuming teaching methods should be used when less complex concepts or techniques are taught.

Maximize Capabilities

Second, a good CBIS should make the best possible use of the computer system's and terminal's capabilities. There are two philosophies for attacking the presentation of a simulation: by using standard techniques, i.e., making the material "teletype-33" compatible; or by fully using the inherent capabilities of the computer complex on which you are working. The first philosophy is justified by the fact that "ALL terminals" can use the program, making the simulation transportable, or easily transferable from terminal to terminal. This is of great importance on campuses where there are five or six different types of terminals, and not one of sufficient number to serve a large class. The generally unrealized expense of this type of programming is complete underdevelopment of the visual illustrations and graphic demonstrations so important to good teaching. The importance of these visual illustrations is well documented (Lackmann) and well known to all teachers. For a long time the blackboard (and recently the overhead projector) was the most important teaching aid in the lecture classroom. So, too, the graphic capabilities of the computer complex should be of the highest value to CBIS when used appropriately. Unfortunately, the program complexity increases with the complexity of the visual effects, but this is no excuse for not utilizing the capability of the computer system, any more than lack of ability to draw is a good excuse for not using the blackboard. Nor is the excuse of incompatibility of terminals sufficient because there are simple ways to program so that terminals with similar capabilities but different instruction sets, can use the CBIS materials.

Documentation

Third, while documentation is important in all CBI, it is doubly so in CBIS due to its complexity. It is imperative to document the concepts and techniques and their underlying assumptions in detail. This documentation can be either in the form of computer tutorial material or manuals. If there is one problem that all CAI packages suffer from, it is the lack of adequate documentation. This is particularly true as the CAI packages increase in complexity, like CBIS. Generally what documentation there is, is in the form of a few notes from the author to himself that are undecipherable to any but those as thoroughly familiar with the package as the author. Or a ''user's'' manual that describes only how to start the program and a little about the concepts taught in a haphazard manner.

Actually there are three types of manuals and two modes for presentation of this material. First, there is the instructor's manual. It should include the objectives the package is designed to teach, the format and structuring of the presentation of the concepts, background information on the concepts, and suggestions for integrating the material into the course. The second manual is the user or student manual that should include any necessary information that the student needs to know before running the package, instructions on how to get the package into operation, instructions on how to get out of trouble, and supplementary information on the origin of the concepts of the package. The third manual is the technical manual. It should explain the purpose and structure of the various programs in the package, lists or legends of the variables, arrays, and pointers or indicators, so that a programmer can make the site-specific modifications required when a complex package is moved to a new computer complex. A detailed description of the organization of these manuals is beyond the scope of this paper but an excellent document of this organization is already available (CONDUIT).

There are two modes available to the author for presentation of the material contained in the manuals, particularly the user manual, printed or interactive. Normally, manuals on how to use something, be it a chainsaw or computer program, come in the form of a booklet, as this is the only economic way to transmit the information. However, the author of the computer program has another tool readily at his disposal, the computer. With it he can present appropriate material and instructions to the user in interactive form. But this brings up the question: what is appropriate material? We believe that appropriate material includes instructions or help units that let the user know what is coming next in the simulation; that explains the details of alternatives when the user is asked to make a choice; or that explains the details and bases of concepts used by the simulation, in tutorial format. Inappropriate material includes the rules of the simulation; supplementary references; long, detailed explanations of the concepts or of the workings of the simulation. While the distinction between appropriate and inappropriate material may be a bit fuzzy, the best rule of thumb would be, if there are more than 24 lines 80 characters long (one normal CRT screen full) of explanatory material without a user response, then the material belongs in a manual. Use interaction, don't write a textbook. And if there is ever a decision between a little more documentation or not, always write more. (It can always be ignored but may be important to someone at sometime for reasons that are not apparent to you.)

Ancillary Material

The fourth property of good CBIS is that it must have sufficient ancillary material, in the forms of both tutorials and manuals, to allow for effective and efficient use of the simulation. The one distinguishing characteristic of instructional simulations is that they are designed to teach complex processes and concepts. They can't do their job properly unless the user understands the simulation and its bases. There are several simulations that would be excellent instructional simulations, but for the fact that the authors failed to realize that the complete simulation would overwhelm the beginning user with too many multiple options.

Good CBIS material provides for these neophytes in one of two ways. First, the simulation can be constructed in several versions, simple to complex, so that the beginner can get a feel for using the simulation before graduating to the next more complex version. In actuality one simulation can be devised that accomplishes this task of creating multiple versions. It is done by asking the user what level he wishes to work at, then defaulting to standard options for the beginner while allowing the advanced user more options. If the user's decision time is an important variable in the simulation, this can be decreased as the level of expertise increases.

The second type of ancillary material CBIS can provide help to the neophyte is to construct a set of tutorial lessons to teach concepts and options to the student. These lessons can include traditional CAI tutorials (programmed instruction, games, and minisimulations) and sections of the actual simulation, grading to the complete use of the simulation. In practice, both of these teaching techniques can be used together.

Evaluation of CBIS

While CBIS can be an effective tool for teaching certain types of concepts and techniques—given a good understanding of its properties for teaching—the tool has been very difficult to evaluate. Often this difficulty is partly due to lack of understanding of what the simulation is supposed to be teaching and in part to lack of good methodology for evaluating student's performance.

Suppose that a teacher has some material that he thinks can be taught best using CAI. He should only use CBIS if he can demonstrate to himself, at least, that the material falls into one of the three categories described above; process concepts, relationships between concepts, or multifaceted/multistep problem solving. Otherwise he should opt for some other type of CAI. One major problem with CAI is that authors of material fit the material to the mode of instruction instead of the mode of instruction to the material, as should be the case. To insure that the author is not using an overkill method of instruction he should write a series of goals and objectives, then decide which would be taught using CBIS and which using other methods. This also will help to cut down on the immense amount of development time required. In writing down his goals and objectives, the author has begun the process of writing the evaluation, that is, he has something that he can test for. But, if the author's material is suitable for CBIS, the author faces the problem that there are few methods available for the evaluation.

Evaluation of CBIS Package: The Salesman on the Beach

This problem was encountered in tests of two CBIS packages written to teach spatial marketing principles to beginning undergraduate human geography students. The first, called the "The Salesman on the Beach" (Rushton et al.) was developed in the early 1970s to teach the principles of spatial competition in one spatial dimension. The student is told that there are two ice cream salesmen attempting to sell ice cream on a beach and both are attempting to maximize their profits. They can move their ice cream wagons anywhere along the beach—their location is initially the only variable that they can change. Two students represent the two ice cream salesmen who must decide where they should locate to make the most profit. Each student is faced with environmental considerations beyond his control—the location of the population that is nonuniform across space and the other student's location. In later units the students also control the price, which adds another controllable and uncontrolled variable to the problem for each student. This material fits the range of CBIS because the students are learning process concepts, and are learning to solve multifacets problems.

This package was among the first interactive CBIS's in geography and thus the first version was a bit rough because there were no clear principles or properties of CBIS. A second version was constructed attempting to more closely follow the properties described above. However, the hardware limited the attempt—only 300 baud hardcopy terminals were available at the time, so that while the terminals' and system's capabilities were maximized, these were little more than the standard ASCII teletype-33 capabilities. And while the documentation was extensive for the time, with a 13 page student manual and a 27 page instructor-programmer's manual (Rushton et al.) the manuals were somewhat deficient. This was due primarily to a lack of guidelines. Also, the program has no ancillary materials though the lesson units were constructed on a scale of graduated complexity. So, it is obvious, at the outset, that this package would be less than completely successful.

An experiment was run in 1973 to test the utility of this package. It was hypothesized that a group of students using the CBIS package would show a problem solving ability superior to that of a group of students using traditional methods, but that their ability to define concepts would be slightly poorer. The results of the experiment (Table 1) showed these tendencies, but not to a statistically significant degree (Ellinger and Frankland).

The conclusions reached after this experiment were indefinite. First, either instructional method worked equally well. Second, the costs were definitely all in favor of the traditional methodology, but it was recognized that the costs of all CAI would continue to decline so that the cost element would not be a factor (or would favor the CBIS material). Third, many of the students using the CBIS material felt that they learned more and that the material was presented in a more enjoyable fashion than by learning the same material in the traditional manner, but that the CBIS program still had some problems—the chief being the length of time the student had to wait while the program was printing out (this was more a function of the terminal speed than of any inherent programming problem). So, not surprisingly, the experiment was inconclusive.

Evaluation of the Spatial Marketing Simulation

A second experiment has just been completed on another geographic CBIS package. This package, called the "Spatial Marketing Simulation," was developed in 1976–77 to teach descriptive spatial location theory to beginning economic and human geography students. The theory deals with the reasons that firms will choose given locations within a region (the size of a state) to locate, or why firms that chose certain locations within the region were successful or unsuccessful. It is apparent that this theory is much more complex than the model previously described requiring a student to deal with many more eco-

TABLE 1. Student's Test of Difference Between Control and CAI Groups[a]

	Total	Definition Section	Problem Solving Section
Pretest	1.45	0.21	0.40
Posttest	0.46	0.33	0.65

[a] After Ellinger and Frankland.

nomic process concepts and the relationship between these concepts when they interact with the dependent variable. The theory is designed to teach the ability to solve the problems of "where the firm should locate to make the greatest profit or the least loss" and "why some firms are successful and some unsuccessful." This theory is an obvious candidate for a CBIS package, following the ideas suggested above.

The package fully develops the properties described above, making full use of a semigraphics terminal with cursor addressing, page, line, and element erasure, and many other terminal functions, as well as many software functions like disabling and sensing break. The package is well documented with a 17-page student manual, a 55-page instructor-programmer's guide, and a 15-page user's guide, plus a large number of interactive help units designed to give help at any query in the simulation part of the package. There are also seven lessons, taking approximately 12 hours to complete, designed to teach the students the concepts, relationships, and necessary problem-solving skills to properly use the simulation. This package has all the necessary properties described above to meet the requirements of a good CBIS package.

In the experiment one section of beginning human geography students received instruction via the CBIS package while two sections received instruction via the traditional lecture/discussion/paper and pencil exercises (Ellinger and Brown). A pretest revealed no significant differences between the groups. The results of the posttest are shown in Table 2.

The mean, S.D., t, and probability values are given for the total posttest scores and for three subscores of interest.

Although significant differences favoring the CBIS group were found on the posttest total score, the subscore results are more interesting. For the "definition" subscore results the group differences are very small, not significant, with the CBIS group mean slightly higher. The absence of significant differences in performance for simple factual recall was expected because this is a known capability of CBIS. Results similar to these are frequently observed in comparisons of instructional simulations with "traditional" instruction.

Without the two additional subscores which, along with the definition subscore constitute the total score, we would not have observed any superior performance attributable to the CBIS group. On the subscores reflecting CBIS's

TABLE 2. Evaluation of the Spatial Marketing Simulation

	Total Test		Definitions	
	CBIS[a]	Control+	CBIS	Control
Mean	11.76	8.19	2.96	2.84
S.D.	2.98	2.66	1.05	.97
t-value	3.68		.406	
Prob.	>.0001		n.s.d.	
	Relationships		**Problem Solving**	
	CBIS	**Control**	**CBIS**	**Control**
Mean	5.18	3.89	3.75	2.07
S.D.	1.44	1.44	1.58	1.57
t-value	2.84		3.41	
Prob.	>.005		>.001	

[a] $n = 14$; $+ = 37$

capability to teach, the ability to solve multifaceted/multistep problems, and the ability to properly relate two or more process concepts, the differences observed between the groups were in the predicted direction.

The contrast in the student performance outcomes of the two experiments above is so marked as to require no further comment. However, some comments on other differences may be worth noting. First, clearly stated instructional objectives were presented for the design, implementation, and evaluation of the "Spatial Marketing Simulation" while derived objectives were stated at the time of revision for "The Salesman on the Beach." Second, the careful development of an evaluation instrument (also based on the instructional objectives) that allowed observation of three types of performance permitted the observation of group differences. The relative lack of precision of the posttest for "The Salesman on the Beach" simulation did not permit the observation of differences in performance. At this time it is impossible to say whether any unassessed differences between the groups existed.

CONCLUSION

While they are not new or original, we feel that the "whens and hows" discussed here have served us well; we recommend them to you. First, make sure that the material and instructional design require CBIS; second, use the full capabilities of the terminal and computer system; third, document; fourth, use ancillary material when needed to the fullest extent. Then, in your formative evaluation, test for those process concepts, relationships, and problem-solving abilities that you have developed the simulation to teach. For the accomplishment of appropriate instructional tasks, a well designed CBIS package is a powerful tool. Such a CBIS package when properly evaluated should show clear cut observable instructional benefits.

NOTES

1. Teletype-33 programming also increases any deficiencies in the desired features of CAI mentioned above.

REFERENCES

Bork, Alfred, "Computers as an Aid to Increasing Physical Intuition," Physics Computer Development Project, p. 3, 1977.

CONDUIT, Documentation Guidelines, Trinka Dunnigan ed. CONDUIT C/O Computer Center, University of Iowa (1976).

Edwards, Judith et al., "How Effective is CAI? A Review of Research," Educational Leadership, pp. 147–153, 1975.

Ellinger, Robert S., and Bobby R. Brown, "So You Want to Simulate: Guidelines and Evaluation of Computer Based Instructional Simulation," submitted to Journal of Geography in Higher Education.

Ellinger, Robert S., and Phillip Frankland, "Computer-Assisted and Lecture Instruction: A Comparative Experiment," Journal of Geography, pp. 109–120, 1976.

Lackmann, "Treading the Troubled Waters of Training: Some Simple Guidelines for Improving Learning Efficiency," Journal of Educational Technology Systems, Vol. 5, pp. 284–287, 1976.

Rushton, G. et al., "Salesman and the Beach: a CAI Package," Department of Geography, University of Iowa, 27 pages, 1973. (Also) Ellinger, Robert S. et al., Student Manual for Computer Based Instruction Units in Central Place Theory, Department of Geography, University of Iowa, 13 pages, 1972.

Index